Family Size and Achievement

STUDIES IN DEMOGRAPHY

General Editors
Eugene A. Hammel
Ronald D. Lee
Kenneth W. Wachter

Family Size and Achievement

JUDITH BLAKE

UNIVERSITY OF CALIFORNIA PRESS
Berkeley   Los Angeles   London

University of California Press
Berkeley and Los Angeles, California

University of California Press, Ltd.
London, England

Copyright © 1989 by
The Regents of the University of California

Library of Congress Cataloging in Publication Data

Blake, Judith.
Family size and achievement / Judith Blake.
p. cm.
Bibliography: p.
Includes index.
ISBN 0-520-06296-5 (alk. paper)
1. Students—United States—Social conditions—Case studies.
2. Academic achievement—Case studies.   3. Family size—United
States—Case studies.   4. Birth order—United States—Case studies.
5. Cost and standard of living—United States—Case studies.
I. Title.
LC205.B57   1989
390.19′341—dc19
88-5741
CIP

Printed in the United States of America

1 2 3 4 5 6 7 8 9

To LeRoy and Laura

Contents

Preface

Research on the scale described in this volume is made possible by the support of an extensive system of resources. Only a part of this system is internal to my base university—UCLA. A major share lies outside the campus in funding agencies and, above all, in consortia and institutions that have made large-scale surveys available for secondary analysis.

To list the external debts first, I am happy to thank the Russell Sage Foundation, the National Science Foundation, and the Fred H. Bixby Foundation, all of which provided funding directly for this project. In addition, I have been fortunate in having a professorial chair at UCLA, endowed by the Fred H. Bixby Foundation, which has furnished basic research support over the years. My initial impetus for this project stemmed from a National Institute of Child Health and Human Development grant to study childlessness and the one-child family.

The second major external debt is to the suppliers of the surveys analyzed here—to the Social Sciences Data and Computation Center at the University of Wisconsin which was a source of "cleaned" tapes for the 1955 and 1960 Growth of American Families Studies, the 1970 National Fertility Study, and the 1962 and 1973 Occupational Changes in a Generation surveys; the National Center for Health Statistics, which made Cycles II and III of the Health Examination Survey available; the National Center for Education Statistics, which supplied the tapes of the survey High School and Beyond; the National Opinion Research Center, which contributed the General Social Surveys, 1972–1986; and the Inter-University Consortium for Political and Social Research at the University of Michigan which provided the tapes for the Youth in Transition study. Some of these contacts I made personally, others were made for me by Elizabeth Stephenson of the Data Archives Library at the Institute for Social Science Research, UCLA. Libbie Stephenson's tenacity and industry in tracking down data have been indispensible, and her persuasiveness has more than once made me the beneficiary of the kindness of strangers. Finally, work on this research was revolutionalized by a massive gift of personal computers from IBM to the UCLA campus. These "PCs" provided previously unheard of flexibility for making charts and tables.

On campus, my greatest appreciation goes to the research assistants who have worked on this project—all graduate students at the time and some long elevated to jobs elsewhere after having received their degrees. The project started with the expert help of Jorge Del Pinal and Sandra Rosenhouse. Its long-term support has been from Inas Elattar and Jennifer Frost Bhattacharya. Their technical skill, intelligence, and unfailing good spirits consistently advanced an enterprise that, on occasion, seemed endless. Excellent additional assistance was provided by Hannah Balter, Wendy Chang, and Jackie Peng.

The manuscript was expertly and cheerfully typed by the staff of the School of Public Health's Word Processing Center. Special thanks go to Mary Hunter, the Center's head, Gila Weinstein, and Rebecca Tehrani, who gave the manuscript their particular attention. I am also grateful for the computer time provided by the campus over the years. Given the size of the data sets being analyzed, this supplement to external grants was essential.

My colleagues in the Population and Family Health Division of the School of Public Health have contributed greatly to my pleasure in being located at an academically distinguished campus. Faculty members do not always get along so well, and I have never taken this aspect of my life for granted.

I wish also to thank the anonymous reviewers of the book whose excellent comments and criticisms were, in almost every case, taken seriously and acted upon in revisions.

Finally, my family has kept the spark alive. My husband, LeRoy Graymer, has been unstinting in his affection, support, and good fellowship, to say nothing of his role as a formidable intellectual fly-wheel. Laura Davis, herself in the thick of producing a doctoral dissertation in cell biology, has increasingly become a friend and colleague as well as a beloved daughter. Russell Graymer, my husband's son, in addition to being a most welcome companion, has provided insights into a young man's experience with graded schooling, college, and graduate school. But for my intimate association with these young people, I would have suffered in trying to understand the behavior of thousands of anonymous respondents.

1

NUMBER OF SIBLINGS AND OPPORTUNITY: RATIONALE, DATA, AND METHODS OF STUDY

Does being reared in either a large or a small family have significant consequences for people's life chances? This book focuses on that question, investigating the advantages and disadvantages of differential family size for educational attainment and cognitive ability. It also examines whether personal characteristics that are relevant to achievement differ by the number of siblings individuals have.

Our concentration on the cognitive and educational consequences of family size follows on a history in social science of examining the effect of family background on education, occupation, and income. A distinguished legacy of research has demonstrated that parents' social and economic characteristics are major predictors of men's educational attainment and that educational attainment is the single most important known determinant of men's occupational status (Blau and Duncan 1967; Featherman and Hauser 1978). The focus of this reseach was primarily on the meritocratic issue of whether education, occupation, and income were becoming more or less influenced by family background as the nation moved toward a so-called postindustrial society. The research on education concentrated particularly on the determinants of college-going, and whether this opportunity was increasingly or decreasingly class-bound over time.

The importance of education for occupation, and of family background for education, led naturally to investigators' curiosity about how differential family background is translated into young people's educational success or truncation. What are the intervening variables between a family's socioeconomic status and a child's educational attainment? This question, among others, was addressed by

William Sewell and a range of colleagues in the Wisconsin Study—a sample of high school seniors who were followed over time (for a summary, see Sewell and Hauser 1980). As is well known, Sewell's work suggested the importance of parental encouragement to continue to college as a major factor intervening between parental socioeconomic status and the educational attainment of offspring.

Sewell's work represented a significant change from the Blau and Duncan/Featherman and Hauser model in that Sewell was not concerned with trends in adult mobility specifically, but rather with the inner workings of the family as a socializing, motivating, and supporting structure in relation to youngsters' educations. However, the Wisconsin Study, like a number of others succeeding it (Alexander and Eckland 1974, 1975; Alexander, Eckland, and Griffin 1975; Eckland and Alexander 1980) was similar to the meritocratic studies in assuming that the chief educational issue was differential access to college schooling. This assumption led to a concentration on high school seniors as the relevant population for study. The emphasis on the chances of getting to college not only targeted research on those who were poised for the "next step" after high school, but also pinpointed the family's socioeconomic status as the principal family background variable. This socioeconomic emphasis is understandable because college-going, unlike graded schooling, involves substantial direct costs, as well as escalating indirect ones, since a young adult is being kept out of the full-time labor force to pursue an education. Although researchers have themselves noted that the studies of high school seniors begin "too late" in the educational process (Kerckhoff 1980), in the social sciences we are just beginning to take seriously the fact that much of the inhibition to educational attainment in this country has occurred, and continues to occur, early in life—in the grades and the first years of high school. At this point, we may consider briefly why the research focus became so fixated on the question of who goes to college.

Between 1900 and 1950, the nation experienced spectacular increases in high school completion (Folger and Nam 1967). As Suter has pointed out, a substantial share of this increase in high school graduation was due to improved progress through elementary school—a lessening tendency for students to be held back and enrolled in grades too low for their age (Suter 1980). In effect, the population at risk of having a high school education increased because more people made it through grade school. The great increase in high school graduation led naturally to a broadening public expectation that a college education was the next plausible goal for just about everyone (Trow 1961; Berg 1975), and this goal became a part of the symbolic politics of the country. It was logical, therefore, that social scientists would begin asking how realistic this goal was for young people of different social and economic backgrounds. Social research on educational opportunity became heavily loaded, and continues to be loaded, with studies of youngsters who are well along in high school.

During the years since many of these studies were begun, it has become clear that educational attainment was not to be ever upward and onward for a share of Americans. For males who turned 18 between 1964 and 1974 high school graduation rates leveled off at around 83 percent (Suter 1980). As Suter emphasizes, a good share of this failure to complete secondary school is a consequence of being held back earlier on, and dropping out when the age limitation allowed, rather than simply dropping out as a junior or senior in high school. By 1981, 86 percent of males age 25 to 29 had attained a high school degree or more (U.S. Bureau of the Census 1984*b*), but this percentage had remained essentially unchanged since 1976. As Kerckhoff has said (1980),

> it seems apparent that the significant processes which determine the ultimate distribution of educational attainments begin before high school; they certainly begin well before the senior year in high school.

The present study considers, as dependent variables, various levels of education among adults, as well as important antecedents of completed educational attainment among young people. Although the explanatory model is very similar to the one used by the classic status-attainment studies, this research focuses on the influence of a family structure variable whose independent effects have been largely ignored in research on educational opportunity to date—the number of siblings in the respondent's family of orientation. In virtually all of the studies mentioned so far, number of siblings (or sibsize) has been treated as a control variable solely rather than a separate focus for analysis.[1] In some cases, as in all but the most recent followups of the Wisconsin Study, the variable was not even included in the model (see, for example, Sewell and Shah 1967; and Alexander and Eckland 1980). The research reported on here will, by contrast, concentrate on the effects of sibsize at each level of education and the relative importance of the various family background variables (including sibsize) at each stage of educational attainment.

Why has sibsize been largely ignored in research on educational attainment? A number of reasons may be mentioned. First, if one's focus is on the meritocratic problem, then to consider in any detail the importance of number of siblings would be an unnecessary diversion. The same is true of Sewell's focus on interpersonal parental influence as a factor affecting senior's after-high-school educational goals.

Second, as we shall see, if one is sampling youngsters who have already reached the status of seniors in high school, the influence of sibsize on achievement variables will be greatly attenuated and distorted. Youngsters from large families have disproportionate school drop-out rates. Hence, seniors from large families have already been strongly selected *by* sibsize for intellectual ability, and drive and ambition.

Third, sibsize has been ignored as an explanatory variable because there has been a lack of clarity concerning how it operates, or even whether it may be considered to have independent effects on achievement variables. We shall discuss this issue shortly in this chapter, and throughout the book we shall bring as much evidence to bear on it as we can.

Finally, there is considerable disagreement and confusion concerning the interaction of sibsize and birth order. The need to deal with birth order if one is going to study the independent effects of sibsize makes it understandable that researchers whose foci lay with other major problems concerning educational attainment did not see fit to embark casually on the study of independent sibsize effects. In this book, we have attempted to look at birth order effects by first laying out a theoretical framework in chapter 5 and then controlling for background variables in a manner not previously attempted. Again, no magical solutions to knotty problems are claimed, but we believe we may have clarified some previously rampant confusion.

Why does the influence of number of siblings merit special attention? One reason is that all of the studies of educational attainment that have included sibsize as a control have found that its overall effect was as great as, or greater than a measure of the father's occupational position (see, for example, Blau and Duncan 1967; Hauser 1971; Featherman and Hauser 1978). Given that students of social mobility attach importance to father's occupational status as an influence on men's educational attainment (see, for example, Blau and Duncan 1967, chs. 1, 5, 9, and 12; and Duncan, Featherman, and Duncan 1972, chap. 3), the equal or greater effect of number of siblings deserves some attention.

Second, there is a major body of literature concerning the association between number of siblings and IQ, or some other measure of cognitive ability. Since intellectual ability is a significant predictor of educational attainment, it has seemed to us to be important to put together an analysis of sibsize effects on both intellectual ability and educational attainment. As will be seen in chapter 4, this effort has led to a critical distinction between components of ability and their relation to both sibsize and education.

Third, we have found it curious that the sociological and demographic concern with group size as an explanatory variable has ignored so conspicuously the influence of family size on educational attainment. If expectations, social controls, levels of intimacy and communication, and formality and informality vary so significantly by group size, why would we not believe that educational opportunity does not also vary by family size?

Fourth, the influences of family size on individuals are a subject of widespread public speculation. Everyone comes from a family of some size or other, and everyone who came from a family of more than one child has a "position" in the sequence of children. For most people, as they cast their thoughts back to their childhood, these factors were very important *at that time*. In the relatively limited world of childhood, position in the family may be the single most important source of power and authority, or lack of it. People have countless ad hoc reasons for believing in the advantages or disadvantages of being an oldest, middle, or youngest child. Most of these reasons are plausible. The same is true of public views of the only child, views that until very recently perhaps may be summed up in the dictum that "being an only child is a disease in itself." Indeed, the belief that being an only child is a significant handicap appears to be so generally accepted that research psychologists Thompson and Maltes suggest that it is a "cultural truism"— an unchallengeable given (Thompson 1974). Going beyond her own research Thompson has noted, in a 1974 review of the popular and scientific literature on the effects of birth order and family size, that only children are usually viewed as being selfish, lonely, and maladjusted (Thompson 1974). A 1977 survey of the literature on the only child by psychologist Toni Falbo stated that the presence of siblings is popularly assumed to have both positive and negative effects, but the lack of siblings is believed to have only negative consequences (Falbo 1977). My own research on national samples in the United States shows a preponderance of negative evaluations of only children, as well as an aversion to choosing the only child as a preferred family size (Blake 1981).

In this volume we shall bring together information on a variety of characteristics of only children and those from families of various sizes—small and large. We will also study birth order. Many of these data will challenge popular conceptions about the "advantages" and "disadvantages" of coming from a family of a given size. Perhaps the most surprising finding is that it has proven to be almost impossible, on average, to find advantages inhering in large sibsizes—at least by the measures we have used. We do not doubt that some advantages exist—at least for some families. Nor do we pretend to have measured everything "important." We will have occasion to reiterate this many times. Nonetheless, contrary to any romantic notions that may be entertained about life in large families, the outcome measures we have used do not recommend family groups of this size as childrearing units. We believe that a not inconsequential result of this study will be information of this sort.

Fifth, family size is a variable that most couples can control with a high degree of precision. Thus, information about its "effects" is more useful to people than information about other powerful predictors of their child's attainment over which parents can exert relatively little control—for example, their own past educational attainment, their occupation, their race, or their religion.

Sixth, we believe that studies showing the effects of differential sibsize on the individuals involved have an important message to convey in the debate about the relative disadvantages or advantages of rapid or slow population growth. Since the birth rate is the variable in the population growth equation that is usually believed to be amenable to manipulation by public policy (either to increase reproduction or to lower it), it seems to us to be of critical importance to evaluate the tangible advantages and disadvantages of high and low fertility for the children involved in such families—to measure items such as IQ and educational attainment. If, in the face of a substantial body of systematic information that large families are not advantageous to the children involved, one wishes to claim that rapid population growth has advantages for the society at large (Simon 1977, 1981, 1983; and Simon and Kahn 1984), one requires exceptionally compelling macroeconomic and macrosocietal arguments.

Finally, coming from a large, or relatively large family, has been the fate of most adults in our population. A relatively modest proportion of adults has been brought up in small families. As we shall emphasize a number of times in this volume, the revolution in sibsize is just beginning in this country, with the advent of the so-called baby-bust and the attendant decline in the variability, as well as the number, of children per woman. As social scientists become aware of this fact, it may be helpful also to be aware of the probable implications of moving from a society in which most people were reared in large families to one in which most are reared in small ones. We shall consider in the next section this issue of the disparity between the average family size of women and the average sibsize of their children.

THE VARIABILITY OF CHILDREN'S FAMILY SIZE

With family size per woman currently below replacement level in the United States, and relatively low average fertility a characteristic of American women at least since the turn of the century, many readers may wonder whether a study of differential sibsize effects is not an empty exercise. Have not most people been brought up in small families for generations? Is not coming from a large family—a family of five, six, or seven or more offspring—a very rare experience even for older adults in the samples being studied? These questions, surprisingly, must be answered in the negative. Although the United States does, in truth, have low average fertility

Table 1.1. Percentage Distribution by Sibsize, White Men and Women Age 20 and Over, and White Children Age 6 to 18, Various Surveys.

Survey	Sibsize							Total	(N)
	1	2	3	4	5	6	7+		
Adults									
GAF 1955									
Female Respondents	8	15	16	14	12	9	26	100	(2,643)
GAF 1960									
Female Respondents	10	19	18	15	10	9	19	100	(2,895)
OCG 1962									
Male Respondents	6	13	15	14	11	10	31	100	(18,485)
Wives	7	14	16	14	12	9	27	100	(15,181)
NFS 1970									
Female Respondents	7	19	20	16	11	8	19	100	(5,137)
Husbands	7	20	20	15	11	8	19	100	(4,891)
OCG 1973									
Male Respondents	7	16	18	15	11	9	24	100	(26,963)
Wives	7	17	18	15	11	9	23	100	(20,828)
GSS 1972–1986									
Males and Females	6	16	17	15	11	9	26	100	(16,798)

	Children								
HES, Cycle II 1963–1965 Boys and Girls Age 6–11	4	21	26	21	11	6	11	100	(4,511)
HES, Cycle III 1966–1970 Boys and Girls Age 12–17	7	22	26	16	10	6	13	100	(3,310)
YIT, Sophomores 1966 Boys	6	22	25	20	12	6	8	100	(1,911)
HSB, Sophomores 1980 Boys and Girls	5	22	27	20	11	7	9	100	(14,648)
HSB, Seniors 1980 Boys and Girls	6	22	26	20	12	6	8	100	(10,109)

per woman, the fact is that most living adults have come from relatively large families, and this is true even today. As table 1.1 demonstrates, those surveys that sample American adults of all ages or of a wide age range (the General Social Surveys, 1972–1986, and Occupational Changes in a Generation, 1962 and 1973) find that between 59 and 66 percent of white respondents come from families of four or more children. Indeed, between 33 and 41 percent come from families of six or more children. Even among youngsters, close to one-half come from families of four or more children.

Clearly, the concentration of family size per woman, or per couple, at the low end of the family size continuum is a conceptual model that does not apply to the family size continuum into which a sample of individuals was born. Although the number of women who have had large families has been shrinking, the number of people who have come from such families is still very large. This is because it takes some time for people from the larger families of the past to work their way out of the population but also, more importantly, because every society is disproportionately made up of the offspring of the more fertile women. As a consequence, even in an era of low fertility per woman, differential sibsize turns out to be a significant influence on individual's educational achievement. Readers who require further convincing on this point may turn immediately to chapter 8 where evidence is presented on the family size of women and children for the country as a whole (from census and vital statistics data), and where comparisons are made among the Depression, baby boom, and "baby bust" generations. This analysis will demonstrate that, although for many women the fertility transition has been in place for some time, the real revolution in the family size of children is just beginning. Our image of the socialization and upbringing of most children as taking place in small families has been highly inaccurate. Children in the United States are just starting, on a large scale, to be brought up in small families.

THE DILUTION HYPOTHESIS AND THE PROBLEM OF CAUSATION

Why is number of siblings assumed to have negative effects on child and adult achievement outcomes? Our main hypothesis is that this effect occurs because of a dilution of familial resources available to children in large families, and a concentration of such resources in small ones. What kinds of resources are diluted?

Paramount among the divisible resources are the parents' time, emotional and physical energy, attention, and ability to interact with children as individuals. These resources are not only diluted by the presence of many siblings, but by the fact that in larger families the mother is pregnant, or recovering from pregnancy, for some years (especially if we take into account that she may have some miscarriages in the process of producing a large family). The strains involved in the process of *producing* a large family are seldom, if ever, noted in the literature, but they cannot fail to have implications for the dilution of parental childrearing capabilities.

A second obvious type of dilution concerns that of the parents' material resources. This type of dilution involves not only the parents' treatment of individual children—the ability to provide personal living space, cultural advantages such as travel, specialized instruction such as music lessons, specialized medical or dental care, as well as continuous and advanced schooling—but, as well, to provide settings the advantages of which are *not* divisible: living in a desirable neighborhood, or having a wide range of excellent reading material or recorded music in the house (Douglas and Blomfield 1958; Espenshade 1976; Lazear and Michael 1980; Smith and Ward 1980; Espenshade, Kamenske, and Turchi 1983).

Related to this second type of dilution is the parents' ability to provide children with privacy and freedom from impingement by other siblings. Moreover, it appears that being brought up in a large family versus a small one dilutes youngsters' sense of urgency about playing and associating outside of the family group, thereby making youngsters from large families more parochial and limited in their understanding of a variety of social roles (Heise and Roberts 1970).

Additionally, as Zajonc (1976) has suggested, the overall intellectual level of the home may be more "childlike" in large families than in small ones. Children may saturate the environment in large families so that it may be rare for adult conversation, vocabulary, and interests to hold sway. This type of dilution may be more prevalent now than in the past when parents were more autocratic and less permissive of children being heard as well as seen.

Finally, children's claim to being part of the parental group, as distinct from the children's group, is almost inevitably diluted when there are numerous offspring. It is far easier, and more readily legitimated, to answer no to a question from a child such as "Are you going out to dinner without me?" (or to the movies, or on vacation) when there are numerous children than when there are only two, or even only one. Children in small families can far more readily define themselves as being part of "the gang" (namely parents) than can children from large ones. Children from small families can thus extract more individual attention and interaction from parents than the latter might have voluntarily provided given their druthers.

Objections can, of course, be raised to the dilution hypothesis and, indeed, to the whole idea that differential sibsize has genuine effects on child and adult outcomes. With regard to the dilution of parental time, attention, and interaction, it can be argued that siblings provide not only distraction but compensation. We shall bring some evidence to bear on this issue in chapter 5 when we discuss Zajonc's (1976) hypothesis of a "teaching deficit" among last-born children. In general, however, we would argue that the notion that older siblings typically, and on average, function *in loco parentis* assumes too much about sibling goodwill and maturity. Moreover, even if older siblings are helpful to younger ones, we must remember that youngsters are not adults and are seldom, if ever, the emotional and intellectual equivalent of parents (Feagans and Farran 1982).

We should mention as well that, insofar as number of children affects parents' socioeconomic status (or SES)—for example, Duncan, Featherman, and Duncan (1972) have found that number of children affects the occupational status of the father—then measures of the effects of parental SES on outcomes for their children reflect, in part, the indirect effect of sibsize on the children (via the sibsize effect on parents' SES and the parents' SES effect on the children). There is thus, in our research, an *un*measured sibsize effect on parental SES that may partially offset any tendency to overstate such sibsize influence as we have measured.

More serious are objections to assigning any causal importance to findings concerning sibsize effects on the ground that such effects are spurious. This argument takes a number of forms. One is the claim that even after controlling for parental education, socio-economic status, rural–urban background, and family intactness, one is simply measuring the effects of additional parental characteristics that have been omitted in the model (Lindert 1978). Principal among these are parental IQ, parental personality characteristics, and parental perceptions of desirable qualities in children ("child quality") that lead couples to have small or large families. With regard to IQ, parents of few children are said to be genotypically more "intelligent" than parents of many children (due to self-selection) and IQ is believed to be highly heritable (Eckland 1967, 1971; Jensen 1969; Spaeth 1976; Scarr and Weinberg 1977, 1978). Chapter 4 will deal with this argument in some detail by questioning the assumptions and presenting sibsize effects for both verbal and nonverbal cognitive ability. Moreover, our controls for parents' education and occupational status are, in part, controls for parents' IQ (Longstreth et al., 1981).

As for personality characteristics of the parents that might be associated with the number of children couples have, we may mention the major American fertility studies that have attempted to correlate personality characteristics with fertility behavior—the Indianapolis Study and Family Growth in Metropolitan America. In both cases, even at the bivariate level (only one independent variable related to the dependent variable), such characteristics as "drive to get ahead," manifest anxiety, ambiguity tolerance, and need for achievement bore no relation either to number of children desired or to fertility planning success. A major conclusion of these studies is that, even at the bivariate level, the kinds of personality characteristics that one might believe to be associated with family size desires and family planning success are, in fact, virtually worthless as predictors—independent variables (Kiser and Whelpton 1958; Westoff, Potter, Sagi, and Mishler 1961; Westoff, Potter, and Sagi 1963). As a consequence of these findings, more recent national fertility studies have not attempted to use personality variables as predictors of fertility. These results suggest that unmeasured personality and achievement drive variables, over and above what will have been captured by us through parents' background characteristics, are probably not of major importance in invalidating our causal interpretation. A second line of evidence is presented in chapter 7, where we bring current data to bear on parents' values concerning desirable qualities in children as well as the number of children parents actually have.

Finally, there is the argument that parental desires for "child quality" are what primarily determine the number of children parents want to have. Hence, sibsize is said not to influence child quality but, rather, is itself influenced by parents' desires for such quality. We discuss this argument in detail in chapters 6 and 7 from both a theoretical and empirical point of view. For example, we point out that the desire for child quality is not the only determinant of family size, and even where it is a salient feature, its effects cut both ways—there are parents who believe that large families produce higher-quality children, and most people think that having an only child is not a ticket to quality (Blake 1979). Further, we control for parental background variables that are themselves predictors of family size desires, and so, to that extent, we also obviate the claims that the relationship is spurious.

We do not pretend to satisfy completely a diligent critic with regard to these issues. We do believe, however, that our results will suggest that genuine sibsize effects exist and that their magnitude in many cases is substantial. It is incumbent upon those who doubt the existence of such effects to advance our knowledge further by bringing additional information to bear on this topic.

THE DATA SETS

This research has capitalized on numerous existing studies of adults and children. Indeed, to our knowledge we have used most of the largest, publicly available, national data sets based on modern sampling methods that included the variables needed on the respondents and respondents' parents, and that did not have (in our view) unacceptable nonresponse rates and other basic data problems. This approach has had multiple advantages and, as might be expected, some disadvantages as well. On the plus side, a major advantage has been replication of findings among many different studies while we used a relatively standardized model for analysis. A second advantage has been number of cases—in all almost 150,000. Additionally, the samples involved were, in all instances, drawn by scientifically valid methods and, in most cases, are highly representative of the national population of the ages involved. Exceptions here are the three fertility studies—the Growth of American Families Studies of 1955 and 1960 and the National Fertility Study of 1970—all of which are confined to women in the reproductive ages and somewhat skewed toward the higher end of the educational continuum. The research strategy has the further advantage of capturing cross-sectional data for individuals that span a time period from the 1950s to the present. We are thus able to look at sibsize effects over approximately a thirty-year time period. And, finally, we have been able to take advantage of millions of dollars worth of data collection, coding, and magnetic-tape "cleaning" by our social science colleagues who initiated the studies (for reasons and interests quite different from our own). Access to these basic data in computerized form is what has made this present study possible.

What are the disadvantages of our approach? A major disadvantage for this writer has been the scale of the undertaking. Handling this many disparate data sets—subsetting, recoding, checking, and learning their idiosyncrasies—is a formidable task. The originators of each of these studies, who know their every idiosyncrasy, will doubtless always be able to fault me for not being equally knowledgable. I can only hope that such inaccuracies and omissions as may exist are more than counterbalanced by the gains from reanalysis and replication on numerous data sets. A second problem is that one does not have "tailor-made" information or variables. This disadvantage is, however, more clear after the fact than it was prior to the analysis, because theories relating to the study of sibsize have been neither plentiful nor of signal excellence. On the basis of what has been done here, I believe that it will be more fruitful to initiate research directed to studying sibsize differences. In effect, future investigations can be directed quite readily to targeted data-gathering in a way that was far from obvious prior to the analyses presented here. A third limitation of the present research is that it relates to whites only. This limitation is based on a variety of constraints. A principal one is the small number of nonwhites in early samples prior to the practice of oversampling. Another constraint is the relative frequency of father-absent families among nonwhites, and the difficulty of ascertaining types of information on both parents comparable with the data for whites (which, of course, refer to periods of less divorce and nonmarital childbearing than is true for whites today). The amount of effort involved in coming to grips with the idosyncrasies of the nonwhite subsamples among many different studies seemed so overwhelming as to threaten the entire undertaking.

Additionally, like most students of sibsize differences, we are studying unrelated individuals. As a number of analysts have pointed out, if it were possible to generate large, random samples of families, a major methodological problem that bedevils research on unrelated individuals could be avoided—namely, the fact that there are apparently numerous *un*measured familial characteristics of importance for educational attainment. Samples of related individuals obviate the need to search for measures of such characteristics since, whatever the characteristics are, the study design controls for them (see, for example, Jencks and others 1972; Chamberlain and Griliches 1975; Corcoran, Jencks, and Olneck 1976; Behrman and Taubman 1976; Jencks and Brown 1977; Taubman 1976; Leibowitz 1977; Olneck 1977; Sewell and Hauser 1977; Hauser and Sewell 1986).

However, this advantage of sibling studies has been, in practice, offset by a number of major disadvantages. To date the existing samples relating to educational, occupational, and earnings outcomes (except the one used by Hauser and Sewell to be discussed below) have been exceptionally small—sometimes fewer than 100 pairs of siblings. Additionally, all of the samples have been not only opportunistic (originally gathered for other reasons) but highly selected as well. For example, the Hauser and Sewell study, which follows up an original sample of high school graduates in Wisconsin in 1957, and gathers data on their siblings, is too selected to capture much of the educational effects of sibsize. The original sample is of youngsters who have already made it through high school, whereas, as we shall see, many youngsters from large families have already dropped out prior to high school graduation—some having quit in the grades, some before entering high school, and some in high school. Finally, samples of siblings (regardless of size) have been shown by Griliches (1979) to have measurement problems that result in significant family biases in the data. This fact helps to account for the contradictory findings from such studies. In their analysis of the Wisconsin sibling data (1986), Hauser and Sewell have attempted by various strategems to overcome this problem, but their efforts have been criticized on statistical grounds (Chiswick 1986).

Another major reason for wanting to have data on siblings within the same family is to identify the determinants of intrafamilial variability among siblings. Clearly, this is an important research task in and of itself since, although on average siblings share half the same genes, this proportion does not hold for all individuals. Moreover, in addition to the fact of genetic/intrafamilial environmental interaction, no two siblings can have exactly the same "environment" because siblings are part of the environment for each other.

Studies of siblings within the same family become particularly critical if one believes that the cognitive differences *between* siblings are almost as great as the differences between unrelated individuals (Woodworth 1941; Jensen 1980; Rowe and Plomin 1981; Scarr and Grajek 1982; Plomin and Daniels 1987). We question, however, whether this extreme position is justified by the existing data. For example, the much-cited calculation by Jensen (1980) that 44 percent of IQ variability is due to variability among siblings within families does not rest on actual data relating to within-family versus between-family variability. Rather, Jensen splices together data from two studies that used two different IQ tests and assumes that all residual variance equals within-family variance. Specifically, he uses the Mercer data, for Riverside, California, school children who took the WISC (Wechsler Intelligence Scale for Children), to compute between-family variance due to race and socioeconomic status. This variance he underestimates.[2] He then uses an apparently unpublished study of his own (in which children were given the Lorge-Thorndike IQ test) to compute between-family variance within race and SES groups. The residual variance (except for 5 percent due to measurement error) is assumed to be within-family variance although it is actually (in unknown amounts) within-family variance and error variance (all other sources of variance). Jensen does not have independently measured data on within-family variance in IQ. In effect, the claims made for the importance of within-family variance in IQ (for example, Scarr and Grajek 1982) are based on the assumption that whatever variance is left over from actual data on between-family variance must be within-family variance. But, what is left over is all kinds of error in the model of between-family variance, as well as possible within-family variance.[3] In a more recent estimate of within-family and between-family variance in mental ability (Hauser and Sewell 1986), measures of mental ability among siblings are not based on the same test in the same year of schooling for all primary respondents and siblings respectively (see, for example, Sewell and Hauser 1977, 263–264), and no controls are introduced for differences in age at testing (or grade in school at testing) between the primary respondent and the sibling. Hence, again within-family variance is inflated.

We can argue also that even if much of the variance in cognition were not shared by siblings, and even if the shared amount is partly genetic, we are still rightfully interested in the environmental component of the shared variance (the environmental component of the between-families variance), because that may be the only component that can be controlled, or readily controlled.

Finally, our research does not measure educational outcomes and presumed antecedents (such as youthful IQ) for the same individuals. We can only hope that our work will stimulate financing for the type of longitudinal data gathering that would make it possible to study antecedent and outcome variables for the same individuals by number of siblings. It appears that data of this type may become available in the future through the National Longitudinal Surveys of Labor Market Behavior being conducted at Ohio State University.

Let us now turn to a brief description of the data sets upon which the analysis in this volume is based. For adults, the studies are Occupational Changes in a Generation, 1962 and 1973; the General Social Surveys, annual surveys for 1972–1986; and three of the major national fertility studies, Growth of American Families, 1955 and 1960, and the National Fertility Study, 1970. For young people, the studies are Cycles II and III of the Health Examination Survey; Youth in Transition; and High School and Beyond, sophomores and seniors.[4]

Occupational Changes in a Generation, 1962 and 1973

The 1962 version of the study Occupational Changes in a Generation (OCG 1962) was carried out in conjunction with the monthly Current Population Survey of the U.S. Bureau of the Census. The study directors, Peter M. Blau and Otis Dudley Duncan, were thus able to take advantage of the technical and sampling skills of the Census staff in implementing the gathering of additional information required for the study. The OCG 1962 survey (conducted in March of that year) was composed of men age 20 to 64 years old in the civilian, noninstitutional population. The stratified, multistage, cluster sample included over 35,000 occupied dwelling units that contained approximately 25,000 respondents eligible for the OCG questionnaire. Completed questionnaires or followup interviews were obtained from 20,700 of these men (83 percent) who represented about 45 million men in the eligible population. Data can be weighted to compensate for nonresponse.

The special OCG data were obtained from a "leave-behind" questionnaire that the eligible respondents were asked to fill out and mail back to the Bureau of the Census. Of necessity, this document had to be short and relatively simple to complete. The supplementary OCG data included the birthplaces of the respondent and of his mother and father; number of siblings and birth order; educational attainment of respondents' oldest brother (if any); size of community of residence at age 16; type of school attended up to age 16; age at entering first job and occupation, industry, and class of worker of this job; family living arrangements up to age 16; occupation of the father when the respondent was about 16 years old; educational attainment of the father; marital status; and for married men living with their spouses, the number of the wife's siblings and the father's occupation. The regular Current Population Survey interview (as distinct from the OCG supplement just discussed) obtained not only the usual labor-force information but age, sex, color, educational attainment, income, marital and household status, and number of children ever born. No data on religion could be gathered because of Census Bureau restrictions, nor was it possible to obtain any attitudinal data. The combination of CPS data and the OCG supplement allows one to analyze sibsize effects on the educational attainment of the respondents' wives, as well as of the respondents themselves.

The directors of the 1973 Occupational Changes in a Generation study, David Featherman and Robert M. Hauser, attempted insofar as possible to replicate the 1962 study (see, Featherman and Hauser 1978, 6–9). Complete replication was, of course, not possible, due in part to the fact that Current Population Survey (CPS)

procedures had changed somewhat over the 11-year period since
the 1962 study. As well, the cohorts interviewed in 1973 were, on
average, more educated than the 1962 men and hence, theoretically,
were better able to provide accurate information. The OCG 1973
supplement to the CPS monthly survey was obtained by means of
a mailout/mailback questionnaire rather than a leave-behind instrument as in the 1962 study. Combining this method with tele-
phone and personal followups by CPS interviewers produced an
increased response rate over 1962, 88 percent versus 83 percent.

Another change from the 1962 study resulted from the fact that
the CPS sample had increased in size to over 48,000 household
interviews, netting 33,600 completed OCG questionnaires (88 percent). This figure includes supplementary oversampling of blacks
and Hispanics. The 1973 OCG respondents differed slightly in age
from the 1962 cases. The 1973 respondents were age 20 to 65,
whereas those in 1962 were 20 to 64.

In the present analysis we have included only whites, making a
total of 18,966 men in 1962 and 27,549 men in 1973. Included as
well are derived data on 15,549 wives in 1962 and 21,491 wives in
1973.

The General Social Surveys, 1972–1986

The General Social Surveys, conducted by the National Opinion
Research Center of the University of Chicago, are under the direction of James A. Davis and Tom W. Smith. These national surveys
have been conducted annually since 1972 and, up through 1986, a
total of 20,056 interviews have been completed. Each survey is an
independently drawn sample of English-speaking persons 18 years
of age and over, living in noninstitutional arrangements in the
continental United States. The surveys thus contain independently
sampled men and women (that is, the women are not the wives of
the men as in the two OCG samples). Since we are only using
whites and no one under the age of 20, the number of respondents
analyzed here is 16,829.

The General Social Surveys, or GSS, were based on a modified
probability sampling technique for three years, 1972 through 1974.
A multistage probability sample was used to the block level, at
which point quota sampling was employed with quotas based on

age, sex, and employment status. After 1974, funding was provided to make a full-probability sample possible. The 1975 and 1976 surveys were conducted with a transitional sample design—one-half full probability and one-half block quota. After 1976 all surveys were based on a full-probability design. A detailed account of sampling procedures may be found in the appendices of the cumulative codebooks of the General Social Surveys.

As is well-known to survey researchers, the General Social Surveys contain hundreds of items ranging from extensive background information on respondents to a wide variety of attitudinal questions. In this analysis, we have used primarily major background information on the respondents and their parents. However, in chapter 8, we have also analyzed a variety of attitudinal responses as well. In all cases, we have pooled the annual data and treated them as, essentially, one survey.

The Fertility Surveys

Our desire to present data on the educational achievement of women by sibsize led us to include the results of the three major fertility surveys containing information on number of siblings as well as the requisite information on the respondents' parents.

The first of these surveys is the 1955 Growth of American Families study, or GAF study, a national sample of 2713 white married women living with their husbands or temporarily separated because their husbands were in the armed forces. These women constituted a scientific probability (a real probability) sample of the approximately 17 million wives in the U.S. population having the characteristics mentioned above. The sample restrictions mean that the 1955 GAF study's women represented, among women 18 to 39, about 67 percent of all women; 75 percent of all white women; about 91 percent of white, ever-married women; and almost 100 percent of those living with their husbands.

Ninety-one percent of the women chosen for the sample gave interviews. This is a high rate of response (compare the rates for the OCG samples, for example). The interviews took place in the respondents' homes and were conducted by the highly trained national field staff of the University of Michigan survey research center. The project directors were Ronald Freedman, Pascal K.

Whelpton, and Arthur A. Campbell. The interviews averaged about 75 minutes in length and were, of course, focused primarily on issues of the respondents' fertility and family planning behavior.

A detailed exposition of the sampling techniques and possible biases may be found in Freedman, Whelpton, and Campbell (1959), appendix C. We may mention here that, compared with the white women, married once with husband present, in the 1950 census, the GAF 1955 women were somewhat more educated at every level, and the educational discrepancy was particularly marked at the grade school level—16 percent grade-school educated in the sample and 21 percent in the census.

The 1960 Growth of American Families survey was a lineal descendant of the 1955 GAF survey. The 1960 design included 2985 white married women age 18 to 44. We have not used the small sample of nonwhite women. Conducted by the Survey Research Center of the University of Michigan under the direction of Pascal K. Whelpton, Arthur A. Campbell, and John E. Patterson, the study is based on a national, area probability sample. As with the 1955 study, the refusal rate was exceptionally low. Only 6 percent of the eligible respondents refused to be interviewed. In all, the interviewers were able to complete 88 percent of the interviews they sought.

A detailed account of the sampling techniques may be found in Whelpton, Campbell, and Patterson (1966), appendix A. As with the 1955 study, the sample is somewhat more educated than comparable women in the 1960 Census.

Finally, the 1970 National Fertility Study was also a descendant of the early GAF study and the last of the national fertility surveys performed in a university setting. The 1970 study was designed by Charles F. Westoff and Norman B. Ryder of Princeton University and the field work was carried out by the Institute of Social Research at Temple University. Ever-married women age 18 to 44 (instead of currently married women as in the earlier surveys) were sampled using a multistage area probability technique. For a detailed discussion of the sampling methods employed, the reader is referred to Westoff and Ryder (1977), appendix A. The study completion rate was 80 percent—lower than the prior fertility surveys. In all, completed interviews were obtained from 6752 respondents. We have analyzed selected results for 5442 white respondents.

Like the two prior surveys, the 1970 study somewhat overrepresents well-educated women and systematically underrepresents women who have grade school and incomplete high school educations. It is also true that the 1970 National Fertility Study has smaller proportions of central city residents than comparable 1970 census data, and this underrepresentation occurs in every comparison by race, age, and marital status.

The 1970 study obtained detailed background information about the respondents' husbands and, hence, in analyzing this survey we have been able to present some results for the women's husbands as well. The reader should bear in mind, however, that as with the wives in the 1962 and 1973 OCGs, the husbands were not independently sampled, nor were they interviewed.

Cycles II and III of the Health Examination Survey

Between 1960 and 1970, three cycles of the Health Examination Surveys were completed by the National Center for Health Statistics. Each focused on a different age grouping—Cycle I on the age group 18 to 79, Cycle II on ages 6 through 11, and Cycle III on ages 12 through 17. Cycle I was begun in 1960 and completed in 1962. Cycle II's survey spanned 1963 to 1965, and Cycle III's 1966 to 1970. Only Cycles II and III concern us here, since Cycle I did not contain information on the respondent's number of siblings. These cycles were based on probability samples of noninstitutionalized children and youths. Cycle II included 7119 children out of the 7417 originally sampled, and Cycle III included 6768 young people out of the 7514 originally sampled. Restriction to white non-Hispanics reduced the number in Cycle II still further to 4511, and in Cycle III, to 3310. A portion of this reduction is also due to the difficulty of ascertaining sibsize for some of the young people in the surveys (to be discussed in the forthcoming section on predictors).

The general format of both Cycle II and Cycle III was a physical examination by physicians and dentists in a mobile unit, and psychological and ability testing by trained psychologists. Additional information on health and behavior, as well as parental background information, was derived from a parent questionnaire, a youth questionnaire for 12 to 17 year olds, a questionnaire sent to the school, and data from the young person's birth certificate; these were combined with the examination and test results when the findings from all parts of the survey were processed. Descriptions of the surveys may be found in reports by the National Center for Health Statistics (1967*a*, 1974).

A major advantage of the Health Examination Surveys is that they are not keyed to school populations and, hence, do not select only those children who have remained in school. Since our data on adults show a direct relation of sibsize and the probability of dropping out of high school prior to graduation, it is important to avoid this bias by sibsize as much as possible. Nonetheless, because the population sampled consists of noninstitutionalized children, there is some (unknown) underrepresentation of children whose problems are extreme enough to require institutionalization, or who are in institutions for other reasons, such as orphanhood or parental desertion. There is also underrepresentation of youngsters who have dropped out of school *and* left home—a fact which, we believe, affects some of our findings concerning the young people in Cycle III. However, these data sets afford unique opportunities for controls, and avoid many of the more vexing problems of selection *by* sibsize that occur when special groups (such as particular high school classes, or particular test takers) are sampled. (The reader should note that by "selection" we mean the purposive or nonpurposive exclusion or inclusion of certain groups in a sample. Thus, a study of sibsize based on high school graduates, or even seniors in high school, has lost from consideration all those youngsters who dropped out of school previously—youngsters who are typically disproportionately from large families. The sample is thus—inadvertently, perhaps—selected by sibsize and *against* those from large families.)

Youth in Transition

The survey Youth in Transition was designed as a national longitudinal study of boys who were beginning the tenth grade in public high schools. The base year was 1966 and, for our analysis, we have confined ourselves to the 1966 data. These data were based on a multistage probability sample of 2200 boys. We are using 1912 white boys. (An exposition of the sampling methodology may be found in chapter 1, Bachman et al. [1969].) The sampling design provides a representative cross-section of virtually all tenth-grade boys in United States public schools, as well as a cross-section of the schools themselves. The field work was performed by the Survey Research Center of the University of Michigan under the general direction of Jerald G. Bachman.

Interviews with the boys were carried out during October and November of 1966. The interviewing took place in the schools during school hours. After the interviews were all completed, respondents spent half a day taking a battery of group tests, among them the Quick Test of verbal ability that we will use in this volume. The interview schedule obtained information on the boys' families and a wide range of academic and attitudinal issues relating to the boys' present and future schooling. As will be seen, we will make use of only a share of this information.

High School and Beyond

High School and Beyond is a study of almost 60,000 high school sophomores and seniors of both sexes, conducted for the National Center for Education Statistics by the National Opinion Research Center of the University of Chicago. The baseline project was under the general direction of James S. Coleman, Thomas Hoffer, and Sally Kilgore. The baseline data to be used here were collected in 1980. The whole sample included regular public schools, public schools with large numbers of Hispanics, non-Catholic private schools, Catholic private schools, public "alternative" schools, and private schools devoted to high-achieving students. In this analysis, we use respondents in the base year, 1980, and only white non-Hispanics in regular public schools. The cases were further reduced because of missing data on major variables in our analysis (to be discussed in the section on predictors). The total number of respondents in our analysis is 14,648 sophomores and 10,109 seniors.

The study design selected students through a two-stage probability sample, with schools as the first-stage units and students within schools as the second-stage units. For example, for seniors—with the exception of special strata such as Cuban Hispanic, Other Hispanic, or Alternative Schools which were oversampled—schools were selected with probability proportional to estimated enrollment, and within each school 36 seniors were randomly selected. The total number of schools in the sample, as designed, was 1122.

Although, because of refusals and absences (primarily the latter), the sample realized differed somewhat from the sample drawn, use of weights should lead to correct estimates (within sampling error) of the population of the twelfth-grade students in the United States in spring 1980, and correct estimates for subgroups within it. Preliminary comparisons have shown that the weights give estimates reasonably close to those from other data sources. Discussion of the sampling procedures may be found in National Opinion Research Center (1980); also in chapter 1 and appendix A of Coleman, Hoffer, and Kilgore (1982c).

The data were collected between February 1 and May 15, 1980. Sophomore and senior groups within each school met separately and completed the questionnaires and the tests in one session. The questionnaires were self-administered, but a member of the school staff administered the cognitive tests.

THE DEPENDENT VARIABLES

Our investigation of the influence of sibsize on educational attainment has involved a number of detailed questions carrying us beyond the simple influence on total years of schooling achieved. We have examined the effect of sibsize on different levels of education—years of graded schooling, high school graduation, chances of high school graduates going to college, and chances of college attendees receiving their diplomas. This analysis is presented in chapters 2 and 3. In considering this range of dependent variables, we not only followed an analytical strategy laid out by Featherman and Hauser (1978), but we suspected that the sibsize influence would be detected early in the educational process—that the major educational question for people from large families would not be, did they get to college?, but rather, did they graduate from high school? As the research progressed, it became clear that we had underestimated the precocity of the deleterious effects of large family size. Even after controls for family background factors other than sibsize, individuals from large families have been found to be especially prone to truncating their educations prior to finishing grade school or starting high school.

By now the reader will have noted that we are using years of schooling attained (grades completed) as a proxy for educational attainment in the qualitative sense. In this decision (dictated as much by data concerns as by theory), we are supported by past research showing that, on average, the most important variable for future status attainment is the amount of schooling attained, rather than the quality of school or the individual's performance (Hauser 1971; see, also Alwin 1974, 1976). Quite clearly, were one to be studying recruitment into rarified intellectual or professional elites, the assumptions involved here might be untenable.

We should mention, as well, that our interest in educational attainment is not confined to what economists would call "investment education"—namely, education that has occupational effects and that, as such, "pays for itself." Education has important political and social consequences in a democratic society. For this reason, we will consider sibsize as a predictor of social attitudes in chapter 8. In addition, educational attainment has "consumption value." By and large, educated people find the world a more satisfying and interesting place and, as a consequence, they enjoy life more.

Although this volume focuses on the schooling effects of sibsize, the marked educational differentials for adults by number of siblings that we found begged the question of how such variability came about. In trying to provide at least partial answers to this question, we have studied the influence of sibsize on variables that we know to bear important connections with schooling—cognitive ability (chapter 4), and educational goals as well as parental influences on these goals (chapter 6). Additionally, we have looked at sibsize effects on personality measures and school performance, plus achievement orientation and extracurricular activities among school children (chapter 7). For these analyses, we have used the samples of young people already discussed. In sum, we have employed the samples of adults to document educational attainment differences by sibsize, and the samples of youngsters to try to explain these differences.

A critical reader may ask why we have stopped the analysis with educational attainment when the ultimate social science concern is with inequality of final destination—occupation and income? The reasons for not going beyond education in this analysis are both practical and theoretical. Practically, as has just been discussed, we have attempted to find, in childhood, sibsize influences on variables that, in turn, affect education. We believe that this focus demands more concern than attention to occupation and income, which have been studied extensively. Theoretically, we know from prior research that family background is most influential on the immediately proximate determinant of the achievement process— education. Education absorbs family background effects and then, itself, affects occupation and income. Moreover, we know from the status-attainment studies that many other variables enter between education and occupational attainment, and between occupational attainment and income. Most of these variables have not been measured, as is evident by the model's relatively poor predictions on occupation and, especially, on income (Blau and Duncan 1967; Jencks et al. 1972; Olneck 1977; Featherman and Hauser 1978; Sewell and Hauser 1980). As will become evident, the task we have set for ourselves has proven to be challenging enough without further considering occupation and income.

We should mention as well that we believe it to be unrealistic to *expect* to find a strong linear relation between education and income, if only because education has "consumption" as well as "investment" effects on individuals. "Consumption" education may have negative effects on income-seeking behavior. Put simply, the more people become aware of the things that life holds over and above a given level of income, the more likely are they to see effort expended on additional income acquisition as involving major opportunity costs. Hence, many highly educated people may come to develop sophisticated preferences for leisure, and/or nonmarket work, over income. In effect, education helps to get people out of a squirrel cage, as well as making them better runners within one.

THE PREDICTORS

A major advantage of the present analysis is that we have been able to use comparable predictors throughout the basic modeling process for all of the surveys. Naturally, for specialized analyses we have augmented this model. But, we have been concerned, insofar as possible, to present comparable calculations in all of the studies. The basic model of educational attainment among adults has followed closely the status-attainment model of Blau and Duncan (1967), and Featherman and Hauser (1978). We have used, as parental background characteristics, the father's socioeconomic index (SEI), father's education, whether or not the father was a farmer, and whether the parents' marriage was intact while the respondent was growing up. As well, we have included the respondent's age as an indicator of the period during which he or she was reared, and, of course, the respondent's sibsize. Following Marjoribanks and Walberg (1975) and Marjoribanks (1976, 1977), we use the term "sibsize" for number of siblings in the respondent's family of birth, including the respondent him or herself. Thus, "sibsize one" is used for only children, and "sibsize seven-plus" for those from families of seven or more. In most cases, it has been possible in our regressions to use these variables in interval form. Farm background and broken family are dichotomies. For some of the analyses of attitudinal data using the General Social Surveys, 1972–1986, we have included religion as a predictor as well. For children, we have used, on occasion, the mother's education in addition to the father's (for reasons that will be obvious in the analysis), and for some analyses we have used measures of cognitive ability, grades in school, and parents' postsecondary expectations for the respondent. For the adults, appendix A, table A.1, presents a breakdown of these background variables by sibsize. Appendix A, table A.2, shows a breakdown of the predictors by sibsize for the samples of children.

These tables illustrate well the importance of controlling for family background and age if one wishes to examine the effects of sibsize. With regard to adults, as can be seen from appendix A, table A.1, in all of the surveys there is a marked negative relationship between number of siblings and parental socioeconomic status, or SES. Respondents with many siblings have less-educated fathers (OCG 1962 and 1973, males; GSS 1972–1986, both sexes) who have lower-status occupations (SEI). Indeed, it is striking what high proportions generally of adult respondents' fathers did not complete grade school—from 38 percent in OCG 1962 to 26 percent in GSS 1972–1986. For OCG 1962, 66 percent of fathers had a grade school education or less; for OCG 1973, this figure is 56 percent, and for GSS 1972–1986, it is 47 percent.

Even more striking is the sibsize difference on this variable. In the 1962 data, of respondents from sibsizes one and two, 21 percent of their fathers did not complete grade school, but 54 percent of the fathers of respondents from sibsizes seven-plus were so disadvantaged. For OCG 1973, comparable figures are 18 to 20 percent and 53 percent, and for GSS 1972–1986 they are 15 to 16 percent and 46 percent.

It is worth noting as well that, because of the marked tendency for only children to come from broken families (compared to youngsters from other small families), the SES of "singletons" is not the highest. It is, of course, typically much higher than that of children in large famiies.

Appendix A, table A.1, also calls our attention to how sharply farm versus nonfarm background distinguishes sibsizes. In OCG 1962, only 14 to 15 percent of respondents from sibsizes one and two had a farm background, but 43 percent of those from sibsizes seven-plus did so; for OCG 1973 these figures are 11 and 38 percent; and for GSS 1972–1986 they are 10 and 35 percent.

The tabulation by religion for GSS 1972–1986 is of some interest as well. We see that although there is a slight disproportion of Catholics in the larger sibsizes, the percentages differ little for Catholics and Protestants across sibsizes. In effect, the fact that we cannot control for religion in most of the surveys would not seem to be a major influence on our analysis.

These tables thus emphasize that most of the adults in our analysis have come from exceptionally limited backgrounds because of the strong negative association of number of siblings and parental SES characteristics.

For youngsters (appendix A, table A.2), the negative association of parental advantage and sibsize is strikingly evident as in the adult studies. Even among the selected group of high school sophomores and seniors, the relationship of large sibsize and parental disadvantage is maintained. In HSB (1980), 35 percent of those from sibsizes seven-plus have fathers who did not complete high school, whereas this is true of 16 percent of those in two-child families. The HSB data unfortunately do not disaggregate to the grade-school level for youngsters' parents. The fact that only children are not as advantaged as those from sibsizes two or three is evident for the youthful couples, as it is for adults.

In sum, these tables encompassing ten major national surveys of adults and children, and spanning a broad period of years, tell a strikingly similar story. Being from a large family has meant, on average, having relatively disadvantaged parents, while being from a small family has meant relatively advantaged ones. The exception to the regularity of this relationship has been the only child who, because it comes disproportionately from a broken family, has less advantage than children from other small sibsizes. As we shall see, this fact goes a long way toward explaining the slight deficits in the achievement of only children.

A detailed discussion of the predictors in each survey may be found in appendix A.

ANALYTICAL METHODOLOGY

Much of the analysis in this volume involves ordinary least squares regression (OLS). For readers unfamiliar with this methodology, we may mention that it allows us to examine the effect of one variable (like sibsize) on another (like educational attainment)—a bivariate relationship. The method also allows us to introduce additional variables (for example, father's education and father's SEI) along with sibsize—multivariate analysis. We are thus able to take account of the fact that less-advantaged parents tend to have larger numbers of children. If we did not introduce controls for parental background, our interpretation of sibsize effects would be confounded. That is, it would be unclear whether a negative relationship between sibsize and education was due to sibsize, or to the fact that less-advantaged parents have larger families.

Our theoretical interest in the effect of sibsize is expressed in terms of the regression coefficient (the unstandardized coefficient) or slope, which measures how much effect a change in sibsize has, for example, on total years of education attainment. The regression coefficient can be compared across samples and, unlike the coefficient of multiple determination (the amount of variance explained, R^2), it is not affected by differences in variability in the independent variables. Because sibsize is highly correlated with all of the other predictors in the model, we do not attempt to partition R^2 and account for a given amount of variance explained by sibsize, or any other variable (Morgan 1958; Goldberger and Jochem 1961).[5] When we wish to compare the *relative* importance of variables in the model, we use standardized regression coefficients and, as in chapter 6, path coefficients. Standardized coefficients express the value of variables on the same scale and thus allow us to examine the importance of sibsize relative to father's education, or father's SEI, as predictors of a given level of the respondent's education. For a technical discussion of the points in this paragraph the reader may consult Blalock (1967); Cain and Watts (1970); Tukey (1954); Achen (1982).

On occasion, when we have dichotomous dependent variables (such as attending or not attending college, given high school graduation), we have used logistic regression, a form of regression allowing dichotomous dependent variables. And, when we wish to present the reader with actual values of the dependent variable for different sibsizes (while controlling for other variables in the model), we have used multiple classification analysis, which is another form of multiple regression (Andrews et al. 1973). Unlike ordinary least squares regression, multiple classification analysis (MCA) allows us to use predictors as weak as the nominal level of measurement, and does not require that the relationships with the dependent variable be linear. Multiple classification analysis also does not necessitate the deletion of all cases having missing data on any variable, so that the use of MCA as well as ordinary least squares regression gives us an added "fix" on the analysis—in many cases we see how it looks with so-called "pairwise" deletion of missing cases (MCA) as well as "listwise" deletion necessitated by ordinary least squares regression. Finally, the use of multiple classification analysis allows us to see the actual position of the only child in relation to those from other small families. When presenting the results of multiple classification analysis, we typically use the unadjusted means, the adjusted means (what the mean would have been if the group had been exactly like the total sample with respect to its distribution over all other predictors), the eta (the ability of the predictor, using the categories given, to explain variability in the dependent variable), and the beta, which is analogous in inter-pretation to the standardized regression coefficient in ordinary least squares. We have also availed ourselves of the pattern variable option in multiple classification analysis, which has allowed us to form categorical interaction terms. This option has been used exten-sively in chapter 3 and will be explained further there.

We should emphasize again in this section that our focus of interest in this volume is on the achievement effects of sibsize, given certain reasonable and well-accepted controls for parental background variables. We are not concerned with the development of a complete explanatory model for the prediction of educational attainment, or the other dependent variables considered here. Our interest in additional explanatory variables lies in whether they would lessen or obliterate the sibsize effect, a problem that has already been discussed in a prior section.

This very general statement about statistical methodology is supplemented in individual chapters by discussions of particular methodological problems of relevance to those chapters.

2

EDUCATION AND NUMBER
OF SIBLINGS

Has number of siblings affected the life chances of individuals in this country by significantly influencing the amount of education they have been able to attain? If so, where in the educational process has sibsize been most influential? What has been its relative importance compared to other background variables? Do the findings differ by age cohorts?

In this chapter, the first to consider empirical results, we will concentrate mainly on establishing the effect of sibsize in a variety of studies of adults and, in addition, within these studies demonstrate its relative importance compared to the major control variables to be used throughout the analysis.

Initially, we will discuss total years of educational attainment, and then we break down this experience into components—years of graded schooling (grades 1 through 12), proportions completing high school, proportions of high school graduates going to college, and years of college schooling.[1] For visual convenience, many of the findings are presented in charts, but the full tables may be found in appendix B. Since the educational losses with each increase in sibsize are obvious from the figures and appendix tables, our discussion will emphasize particular comparisons such as those between only children and children from two-sibling families; between children from two-sibling families and those from families of four siblings or more; and between only children and children from families of seven siblings or more.

SIBSIZE AND TOTAL YEARS OF EDUCATION

Figure 2.1 summarizes the bivariate relation between sibsize and total years of education for respondents in each survey. Numerical

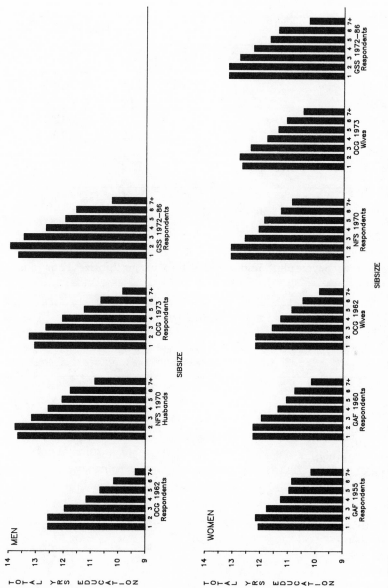

Figure 2.1 Total Years of Education (Unadjusted Means) by Sibsize, White Men and Women Age 25 and Over, Various Surveys.

Table 2.1. Comparison of Total Years of Education (Unadjusted Means) between Sibsize One and Sibsize Two, White Men and Women Age 25 and Over Who Grew Up in Intact Families, Various Surveys.

	Men		Women	
Survey	Sibsize One	Sibsize Two	Sibsize One	Sibsize Two
GAF 1955	—	—	12.5	12.4
GAF 1960	—	—	12.7	12.4
OCG 1962	12.9	12.8	12.3	12.3
NFS 1970	14.0	14.0	13.2	13.2
OCG 1973	13.4	13.5	12.9	13.0
GSS 1972–1986	14.2	14.2	13.4	13.5

Table 2.2. Comparison of Total Years of Education (Unadjusted Means) among White Men and Women Age 25 and Over for Sibsize One versus Sibsize Seven-plus, and Sibsize Two versus Sibsize Four-plus, Various Surveys.

	Years Difference as Percent of S.D.	
Survey	Sibsize One versus Sibsize Seven-plus	Sibsize Two versus Sibsize Four-plus
Men		
OCG 1962	94	73
NFS 1970	97	69
OCG 1973	89	68
GSS 1972–1986	95	72
Unweighted Average	94	70
Women		
GAF 1955	76	60
GAF 1960	89	63
OCG 1962	82	61
NFS 1970	96	70
OCG 1973	85	67
GSS 1972–1986	96	68
Unweighted Average	87	65

data supporting figure 2.1 are in table B.1 in appendix B. As is evident, except for the only child, there is a marked linear relationship between sibsize and total years of education attained. The somewhat less distinguished performance of the only child, versus those from sibsize two (in five instances) is due primarily to the effect of disproportionate numbers of broken families among only children, as may be seen from table 2.1, comparing only children and those from sibsize two who came from intact families. From table 2.1 we see that the only-child deficit is reduced in general, that it now appears in only three instances, and that it has been translated into an advantage in three instances.

The correlation ratios (etas) for the relationships in figure 2.1 range between .298 and .389. Table 2.2 indicates that the difference in educational attainment between only children and those from sibsize seven-plus is, in most surveys, close to a standard deviation. On average, taking all surveys combined, this difference is .94 of a standard deviation among men and .87 of a standard deviation among women. A less extreme comparison, contrasting respondents from sibsize two versus sibsize four-plus, table 2.2 shows that the difference is still very large—on average .70 and .65 of a standard deviation among men and women respectively.

Another way of looking at sibsize differences is to compare them with other types of variability in educational attainment to which we customarily attach importance, such as differences by race and age. During the mid-1970s in the United States, the black–white differential in years of education among men age 25 to 64 was 2.2 years and, among women, was 1.2 years (U.S. Bureau of the Census 1977). By age, the differential between those aged 25 to 29 and those aged 60 to 64 was 2.6 years among white men and 2.0 years among white women. During a comparable time period, our analysis of the surveys used here shows that, for example, in GSS 1972–1986 (table 2.3) the educational gap between white men who were only children and those from sibsizes seven-plus was 3.4 years. For comparable women, this gap was 2.9 years. The gaps for white men and women in the OCG 1973 study were 3.2 and 2.2 years respectively. In effect, the difference between the extremes of sibsize exceeded by a substantial margin the racial and age difference. A less sensational comparison of sibsizes, respondents from sibsize two versus sibsize four-plus families, shows the difference in educational attainment to be 2.6 years for men and 2.0 years for women

Table 2.3. Comparison of Adjusted and Unadjusted Means for Total Years of Education among White Men and Women Age 25 and Over for Sibsize One versus Sibsize Seven-plus, and Sibsize Two versus Sibsize Four-plus, Various Surveys.[a]

| | Years Difference Between: | | | |
| | Sibsize One versus Sibsize Seven-plus | | Sibsize Two versus Sibsize Four-plus | |
Survey	Unadjusted Means	Adjusted Means	Unadjusted Means	Adjusted Means
Men				
OCG 1962	3.2	1.6	2.5	1.2
NFS 1970	2.8	2.2	2.0	1.4
OCG 1973	3.2	1.6	2.5	1.2
GSS 1972–1986	3.4	2.2	2.6	1.4
Women				
GAF 1955	1.9	1.6	1.5	1.0
GAF 1960	2.2	1.9	1.5	1.1
OCG 1962	2.3	1.5	1.7	1.1
NFS 1970	2.2	1.8	1.6	1.2
OCG 1973	2.2	1.7	1.6	1.2
GSS 1972–1986	2.9	1.7	2.0	1.0

[a]All MCA equations control for father's SEI, farm background, respondent's age, and family intactness. In addition, except for OCG, GAF, and NFS women, and NFS men, father's education is also included as a predictor.

in the GSS 1972–1986 study, which is comparable to or exceeds racial differences or variability among the extremes of age.

Obviously, the variability in educational attainment by sibsize is not assignable entirely to the fact of sibsize alone. These differences are partly a function of other family characteristics known to be associated both with sibsize and with people's educational attainment. As discussed in chapter 1, we have controlled insofar as possible for the same background variables in each survey. Congruent with Featherman and Hauser's model (1978), we have used as controls the respondent's age, the parental family's socioeconomic status (as measured by the father's score on the Duncan

SEI index), the father's educational attainment, whether the family was intact, and farm background.

For total years of education, the adjusted means by sibsize for each survey are shown in figure 2.2 (appendix B, table B.2). Although the adjusted means control for the major background variables just discussed and, hence, reduce the sibsize differentials somewhat, the latter continue to be impressive. Table 2.3 compares the differences in the unadjusted and adjusted means for only children and those from families of seven or more; and for those from two-child families and those of four or more children. These results show that, even after adjustment, the difference for men between sibsize one and sibsize seven-plus is approximately 2 years of total education in relation to a grand mean of between 11 and 12 years, depending on the study. For women the corresponding difference is 1.5 to 1.8 years. In sum, with regard to total years of education alone, increases in number of siblings exert powerful downward pressure on schooling, and, as we have seen, coming from a large family is very common in the samples studied here. The large family disadvantage is perhaps best appreciated when compared to other handicaps we are more accustomed to considering. For example, even after taking account of family socioeconomic status, a white adult male in the mid-1970s from sibsize seven-plus was as disadvantaged educationally compared with sibsize one or two as a black male compared to a white one *taking account of no other differences between them.*

In the next section, we will see that the sibsize difference in total years of education tells only a small part of the story, since number of siblings affects the *process* of education in significant ways.

SIBSIZE AND THE EDUCATIONAL PROCESS

At what point, or points, in the process of acquiring an education does sibsize intervene most importantly? Because of free schooling and compulsory education in the United States, one might think that the dilution of family resources resulting from many children would make little difference to educational attainment through high school but that, after high school, sibsize would be a major determinant of who would go to college. Actually, our results are quite different from commonsense expectations. Sibsize has a major

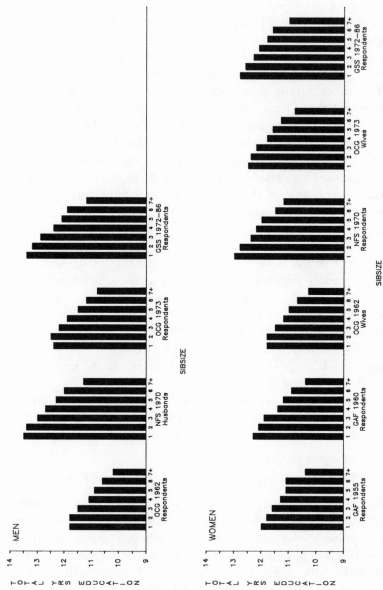

Figure 2.2. Total Years of Education (Adjusted Means) by Sibsize, White Men and Women Age 25 and Over, Various Surveys.

effect on educational attainment even during graded schooling (grades 1 through 12). In fact, as we shall see, in most studies attainment is more highly correlated with sibsize at the graded level of schooling than at the postsecondary level.

Consequently, another aspect of the importance of sibsize for educational attainment is that it has exerted its effects early in the schooling process. It has operated to select out a high proportion of students prior to high school graduation, thereby cutting them off from further academic advancement. This finding suggests that sibsize operates not simply by diluting parental economic resources for postsecondary schooling, but by impinging on basic education at the graded level in a manner that includes both economic and noneconomic effects.[2]

Years of Graded Schooling

Figure 2.3 shows, for all of the adult studies, the adjusted means for total years of graded schooling by sibsize (see also appendix table B.3). As between sibsize one and sibsize seven-plus, it is typical for respondents to have lost about a year or more of graded schooling even after taking account of family background. In judging the importance of such a deficit (all other factors in our analysis controlled), we must bear in mind that the loss of a year of graded schooling inevitably translates into large proportionate decrements in high school graduation. Hence, the loss of a year of graded schooling, on average, can be judged as very significant because of the great marginal importance of completing the last year of high school. We shall consider this next.

Proportions Graduating from High School

Figure 2.4 shows the adjusted percentages graduating from high school according to sibsize (see also appendix B, table B.4). Despite the theoretical importance of the background variables for which we have adjusted, it is clear that the sibsize differences in high school graduation remain large. Singleton boys are nearly half again as likely to graduate from high school as boys from families of seven children or more, and singleton girls are about half again as likely to do so as girls from families of seven children or more.

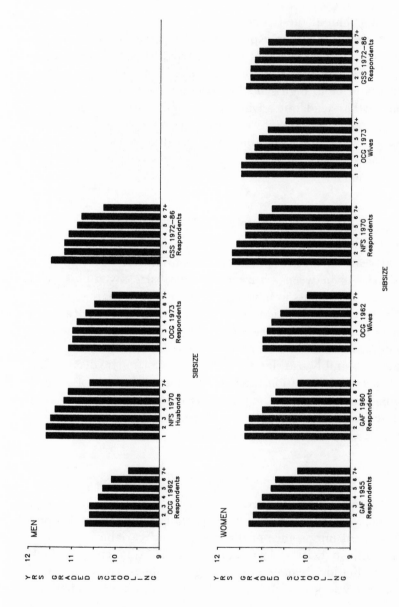

Figure 2.3. Years of Graded Schooling (Adjusted Means) by Sibsize, White Men and Women Age 20 and Over, Various Surveys.

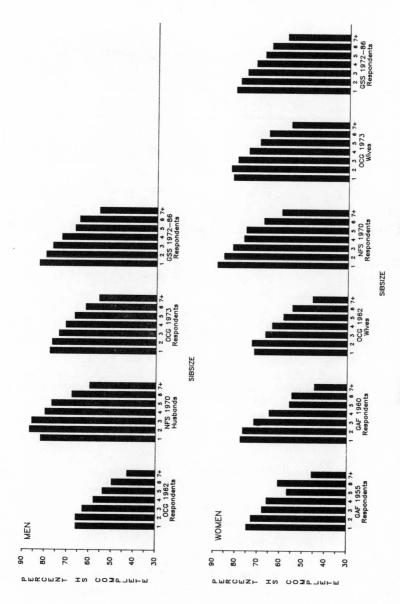

Figure 2.4. Percentage Who Graduated from High School (Adjusted Means) by Sibsize, White Men and Women Age 20 and Over, Various Surveys.

Table 2.4. Comparison of Adjusted and Unadjusted Means for Percentage Graduating from High School among White Men and Women, Age 20 and Over for Sibsize One versus Sibsize Seven-plus, and Sibsize Two versus Sibsize Four-plus, Various Surveys.[a]

| | Percentage Point Difference Between: | | | |
| | Sibsize One versus Sibsize Seven-plus | | Sibsize Two versus Sibsize Four-plus | |
Survey	Unadjusted Means	Adjusted Means	Unadjusted Means	Adjusted Means
Men				
OCG 1962	41	23	33	17
NFS 1970	27	22	21	16
OCG 1973	37	22	27	14
GSS 1972–1986	39	26	28	15
Women				
GAF 1955	33	29	25	18
GAF 1960	36	33	28	23
OCG 1962	36	26	28	18
NFS 1970	32	29	20	16
OCG 1973	33	26	25	19
GSS 1972–1986	39	24	27	14

[a]All MCA equations control for father's SEI, farm background, respondent's age, and family intactness. In addition, except for OCG, GAF, and NFS women, and NFS men, father's education is also included as a predictor.

The percentage point differences in high school graduation between sibsize one and sibsize seven-plus, and between sibsize two and sibsize four-plus, are summarized in table 2.4.

These data thus strongly reinforce the finding that total educational differentials by sibsize do not simply reflect relative advantage and disadvantage *after* high school graduation. Even in the graded schooling years, and with major parental background variables controlled, increasing sibsize has deleterious consequences for educational attainment.

In a later chapter we will document in detail the intense and early school dropout levels of men from large families. If the precocity of this school leaving seems strange to some readers, they should refer to an article by Suter that deals with part of the process by which such early school leaving comes about (Suter 1980). As Suter makes clear, the major reason historically so many men in the United States did not finish high school was because they fell behind (were "left back") early on—often in grade school. Even after the advent of compulsory schooling to ages 15–16 (depending on the state), such men did not simply drop out of high school, they dropped out of lower grades in which they had remained until the school-leaving age came around.

Postsecondary Education

Among the selected population of high school graduates, we see in figure 2.5 (and appendix B, table B.5) that attendance at college (percentage of high school graduates who went to college) is also influenced by sibsize (background factors controlled). Interestingly, however, among large sibsizes in particular (sibsizes six versus seven-plus), there is less difference than there is for proportions graduating from high school. This suggests that, among these large sibsizes, the high school selection left a population of "survivors" who had about equal chances of getting to college—in effect, that the differences in life chances between being from a six-child or a seven-plus–child family had already been taken into account at the high school level. We may also note that female-only children appear to be uniformly advantaged relative to females from other sibsizes in all of the surveys when it comes to *going* to college. This advantage does not persist, however, for years of college schooling (fig. 2.6).

If people have managed to enter college, does sibsize affect the number of years of college schooling they have been able to achieve? Figure 2.6 (appendix B, table B.6), for respondents and their wives in OCG 1962 and 1973, shows that the effects of sibsize are relatively small for this select group. That these effects exist at all, given the process of prior selection by sibsize that we have witnessed, is quite remarkable.

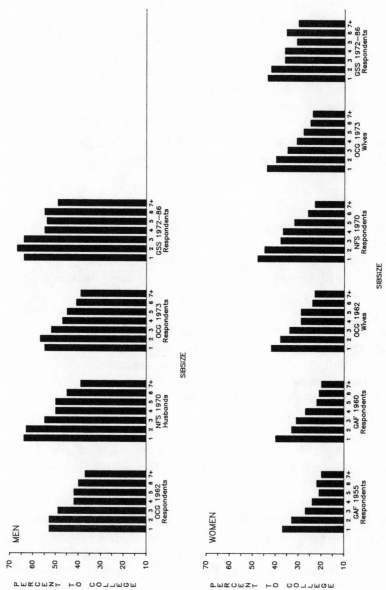

Figure 2.5. Percentage of High School Graduates Who Went to College (Adjusted Means) by Sibsize, White Men and Women Age 25 and Over, Various Surveys.

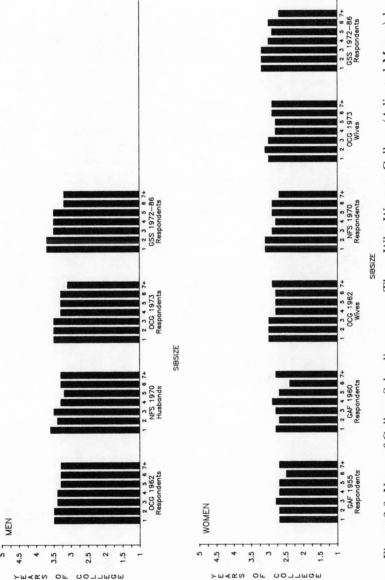

Figure 2.6. Years of College Schooling among Those Who Went to College (Adjusted Means) by Sibsize, White Men and Women Age 25 and Over, Various Surveys.

Table 2.5. Unstandardized Regression Coefficients for Sibsize by Four Levels of Education, White Men and Women, OCG 1962 and 1973, and GSS 1972–1986.[a]

| | | Educational Level | | |
Survey	Total Years of Education	Years of Graded Schooling	Years of College—HS Grads	Years of College—College Attenders
Men				
OCG 1962	−.199	−.136	−.072	−.037
	(.008)	(.006)	(.008)	(.009)
OCG 1973	−.215	−.132	−.098	−.057
	(.008)	(.006)	(.006)	(.008)
GSS 1972–1986	−.240	−.121	−.094	−.060
	(.015)	(.008)	(.014)	(.016)
Women				
OCG 1962	−.193	−.137	−.065	−.025
	(.008)	(.006)	(.006)	(.010)
OCG 1973	−.206	−.138	−.069	−.035
	(.006)	(.004)	(.005)	(.010)
GSS 1972–1986	−.171	−.106	−.067	−.058
	(.011)	(.006)	(.010)	(.015)

[a]Total Years of Education is based on respondents age 25 and over; Years of College on those age 20 and over; Years of Graded Schooling on those age 25 and over. All OLS equations control for father's SEI, farm background, respondent's age, and family intactness. In addition, except for OCG women, father's education is also included as a predictor. Figures in parentheses are standard errors.

The Relative Effects of Sibsize on Graded and Secondary Education

Our results so far, using multiple classification analysis, suggest that as the level of schooling rises the effect of number of siblings decreases. The truth of this is most succinctly exemplified by the unstandardized regression coefficients (slopes) for sibsize at each educational level. These are shown in table 2.5. From this table we see that the effect of sibsize diminishes with each level of schooling, the greatest effect being at the graded-schooling level. We have suggested that the selection against large families that occurs so early in the educational process is probably due to two factors: (1) outright school leaving (dropping out) among those from large families, and (2) being "left back" in high proportions among those from large families until dropping-out occurs at a legally permissible age. Here we may note for the first but not the last time, that this selection has important methodological implications for all research on the "effects" of number of siblings among juniors and seniors in high school, or among college populations. Such populations will have been already strongly selected *by* number of siblings at an earlier stage in the educational process.

The Importance of Sibsize Relative to Other Family Background Variables

In our introductory chapter, we pointed out that the effects of sibsize, relative to the effects of other family background variables, have tended to be understated by students of social stratification, who investigate the consequences of family background for educational opportunity.

One reason for investigators' underestimating the relative importance of number of siblings is that the influence of this variable is often incorporated into the overall influence of family background or "home" effects (so-called ascriptive influences) versus the respondent's own characteristics and performance (viewed as meritocratic). Thus absorbed into family background, number of siblings serves to overestimate the importance of parental "SES" and turn attention away from sibsize as an independent influence. For example, the following quotation from Alexander and Eckland is fairly typical of discussion of even those studies that have specifically included number of siblings as a predictor (Alexander and Eckland 1980, 34).

> More recent research, in revealing the range of advantages and liabilities conferred by the family of origin, serves only to broaden and deepen our appreciation of the residue of ascription in the supposed meritocracy (Blau and Duncan, 1967; Duncan, Featherman and Duncan, 1972; Hauser and Featherman, 1977).

> To what is this persistent importance of the family attributed? Largely, it appears, to the simple fact that children from high SES families tend to go further through school than their low SES counterparts, and hence reap the labor market benefits that advanced schooling accrues.

A second reason for underestimating the relative importance of number of siblings to an individual's attainment is that models of status attainment (including those used here) treat parental SES as exogenous—in no way influenced by parental reproductive behavior. Yet parental educational attainment and occupational achievement are not independent of parental age at marriage and childbearing, including number of children. Hence, to the extent that parental SES is itself influenced by numbers of children, the effect of the respondent's sibsize on measures of parents' education and occupation is not counted.

Additionally, insofar as investigators have studied the educational process among high school students (for example, the high school seniors in the Wisconsin Study, Sewell and Hauser 1980, or the National Longitudinal Study of the High School Senior Class of 1972, Eckland and Alexander 1980), the importance of number of siblings to postsecondary educational goals and attainment will appear relatively small (compared to other variables) because of the selection process by sibsize that has already taken place. Many youngsters from large families have already dropped out (or been held back) leaving a selected group of survivors from these families, whereas those from small families are less selected.

Finally, as a number of critics of the sociology of status attainment have noted (Spaeth 1976; Williams 1976; Scarr and Weinberg 1978), parental socioeconomic status is itself, in part, the translation of parental ability into socioeconomic currency. Were it possible to control for parental ability, the effect of parental SES on the son's achievement would probably be less and an additional effect of the parental ability transmitted to the child would be added. This point, which is increasingly being addressed by economists and sociologists (see, for example, Eckland 1967; Griliches 1970; Bowles 1972; Griliches and Mason 1972; Bowles and Gintis 1974; Bowles and Nelson 1974; Taubman and Wales 1974; Welch 1974; Griffin 1976; Hauser and Daymont 1977), will be discussed in more detail in chapter 4 on number of siblings and intelligence.

Here we will examine the relative effects of sibsize and other background variables for the adults in some of our samples. Table 2.6 shows, for OCG 1962 and 1973 as well as GSS 1972–1986, the standardized regression coefficients of the principal variables in our model for each level of the respondent's educational attainment. Standardized regression coefficients express the value of variables on the same scale so that their relative importance can be judged. The reader should be reminded that data on the father's education for the wives of the men in the 1962 OCG study are not available, and for these calculations we have made the two OCG studies comparable. To our knowledge, this is the first time that the standardized coefficients for disaggregated amounts of education (using the basic educational attainment model for adults) have been presented.

Among the variables in the model, all the surveys show (table 2.6) that the father's education is the most important influence on the son's total educational attainment. In this regard, the following quotation from Hauser and Featherman's analysis of total educational attainment in the two OCG studies is worth noting (1976, 105):

> We have not shown any standardized regression coefficients; some readers may be interested to know that in virtually every subpopulation we have looked at, father's education is relatively more important than any other background variable.

In both OCG 1973 and GSS 1972–1986, sibsize is second in importance and outweighs, in negative effect, the positive effect of the father's SEI (the third most important influence). In OCG 1962, sibsize is close to the father's SEI and probably would also exceed it in this study as well were it not for the anomalously high SEI (see, Hauser and Featherman 1976, 104).

Table 2.6. Standardized Regression Coefficients for Sibsize, Father's SEI, Father's Education, and Farm Background by Four Levels of Education, White Men and Women, OCG 1962 and 1973, and GSS 1972–1986.[a]

		Educational Level		
Survey and Predictor	Total Years of Education	Years of Graded Schooling	Years of College—HS Grads	Years of College—College Attenders
Men				
OCG 1962				
Father's Education	.228	.221	.119	.034[b]
Sibsize	−.183	−.178	−.102	−.074
Father's SEI	.213	.095	.263	.114
Farm Background	−.081	−.116	.018[b]	−.004[b]
R^2	.322	.269	.133	.029
OCG 1973				
Father's Education	.285	.265	.144	.069
Sibsize	−.178	−.155	−.128	−.089
Father's SEI	.151	.013[b]	.250	.146
Farm Background	−.094	−.127	.005[b]	.000[b]
R^2	.311	.212	.157	.052
GSS 1972–1986				
Father's Education	.286	.237	.206	.132
Sibsize	−.200	−.189	−.109	−.080
Father's SEI	.147	.010[b]	.195	.113
Farm Background	−.077	−.141	.017[b]	.065
R^2	.339	.283	.141	.053

Women

OCG 1962				
Sibsize	−.209	−.195	−.117	−.055
Father's SEI	.298	.193	.306	.165
Farm Background	.001[b]	−.048	.113	.001[b]
R^2	.206	.174	.107	.035
OCG 1973				
Sibsize	−.233	−.224	−.113	−.058
Father's SEI	.313	.153	.362	.192
Farm Background	−.006[b]	−.084	.116	.076
R^2	.232	.159	.140	.033
GSS 1972–1986				
Father's Education	.342	.250	.287	.186
Sibsize	−.177	−.186	−.092	−.087
Father's SEI	.152	.032	.180	.061[b]
Farm Background	−.066[b]	−.087	.078	.056[b]
R^2	.358	.272	.176	.057

[a]For Years of Graded Schooling, respondents age 20–24 were included. The coefficients for family intactness and age were also included in the regressions, but are not shown here. The first consistently ranks low in all of the equations, and age, used as a control, is discussed in a separate section.

[b]Not significantly different from zero at the 1-percent level.

Turning to the relative status of the variables in the disaggregated process of education, we find some interesting results. Among the educational levels, the relative influence of the father's education and sibsize is greatest for graded schooling, whereas the father's SEI is unimportant at this level. This finding might suggest that, given free schooling, whether the grades are completed depends more on the value placed on education by the parents and the child's ability (both native and as a consequence of socialization in the home) than on socioeconomic factors. However, the *dilution* of material resources is represented by sibsize at this level of schooling as is the corresponding ability of parents to sustain the direct and indirect costs of early schooling. How much the sibsize variable operates by influencing IQ and grades, and how much by influencing the direct and indirect costs of maintaining offspring in school, cannot be measured in these adult samples, since data are not available on either IQ or school performance. In later chapters, we shall see, however, that among samples of youngsters, the effects of sibsize on IQ are substantial, especially among samples of very young children. Hence, one can speculate that the early drop-out rate among men from large families was not due entirely to the diluting effect of sibsize on material resources but was due as well to sibsize effects on IQ, and the influence of the latter on school performance. It should be noted also that men whose fathers were farmers (farm background in the equations) experienced some relatively important negative effects at the graded-schooling level. Thus, although in general the father's occupational status was unimportant for graded schooling, having a father who was a farmer was a disadvantage.

Once a boy graduates from high school, table 2.6 shows that college attendance and years in college depend more on the father's SEI than on either his education or sibsize. By the college-going level, there are a number of reasons why father's SEI should move up in relative importance. One reason is that there has been a drastic selection out of school of children from larger families reducing, thereby, the relative importance of sibsize. Second, college involves not only indirect costs (the student's time and consequent loss of earnings) but usually substantial direct costs as well.

Among young women, although the father's education is not included for OCG 1962 and 1973, the patterns by educational level of the other variables are, with two interesting exceptions, the same as for men. First, in all of the surveys, farm background has a fairly substantial positive relative effect on whether a high school graduate goes to college. This difference is evident in the unstandardized coefficients as well. We may speculate that this effect is due to the traditional emphasis in land-grant colleges on applied subjects, nursing, and school teaching. Second, the GSS 1972–1986 data, table 2.6, based on female respondents and including the father's education, suggest that whether a girl goes to college and stays in college is relatively more dependent on her father's education than on his SEI—a finding that is also evident in the unstandardized coefficients (table 2.5)—and one that is different from men. It is thus probable that increased education among fathers is important in influencing the value placed on advanced education for women.

THE EFFECTS OF NUMBER OF SIBLINGS BY AGE COHORTS

The overall effects of family background on education by detailed cohorts have been discussed by Hauser and Featherman (1976) and Featherman and Hauser (1978) using the OCG samples for all races. Their analyses have shown that the influence of men's family backgrounds on total years of educational attainment has diminished somewhat over time. As they say (p. 241):

> As a block, the six aspects of social origin explain one-third of the variance ($R^2 = .33$) in schooling among cohorts born prior to World War I, but the same factors account for about one-quarter of the variance among men born during and after World War II.

Featherman and Hauser also emphasized that the results for total years of education are a composite of offsetting trends in background effects for graded and college schooling respectively (Featherman and Hauser 1978, 244–245). As the authors point out:

> Together, the five variables that denote social origins in Table 5.9 explain about 13% of the variance in graded schooling . . . for the younger cohort. . . . Among the oldest cohort . . . these variables account for 30% of the variance.

Table 2.7. Variance Explained by Basic Model of Educational Attainment by Age and Three Levels of Education, White Men and Women, OCG 1962 and 1973, and GSS 1972–1986.[a]

| | Educational Level | | |
Survey and Age	Total Years of Education	Years of Graded Schooling	Years of College— HS Grads
Men			
OCG 1962			
25–34	.276	.183	.166
35–49	.279	.201	.145
50–64	.291	.266	.075
OCG 1973			
25–34	.282	.144	.186
35–49	.298	.203	.152
50–65	.307	.238	.128
GSS 1972–1986			
25–34	.253	.135	.193
35–49	.273	.198	.129
50–64	.305	.226	.146
65 and over	.328	.297	.128
Women			
OCG 1962			
25–34	.189	.112	.139
35–49	.191	.147	.089
50–64	.164	.134	.080
OCG 1973			
25–34	.242	.135	.165
35–49	.210	.135	.147
50–65	.186	.151	.087
GSS 1972–1986			
25–34	.295	.142	.211
35–49	.337	.202	.209
50–64	.271	.209	.114
65 and over	.309	.263	.077

[a]For Years of Graded Schooling, respondents age 20–24 are also included. All equations control for father's SEI, farm background, respondent's (or wife's) age, and family intactness. In addition, except for OCG women, father's education is also included as a predictor.

In contrast to this trend, enrollment in college and continuation toward the college diploma show little systematic variation across cohorts in their association with social background. Where changes have occurred they have tended to increase the dependence of college attainment on social background. But in any case the association is modest at best, as given by the R^2 values that range between .186 and .235 in the "college" equations.

In effect, the society has become more "open" as far as years of graded schooling are concerned but, for the greatly augmented proportions who were thereby at risk of going to college, family background has *increased* as an influence on men's chances of a postsecondary education.

For the white men and women in OCG 1962 and 1973, as well as in GSS 1972–1986, table 2.7 shows the marked decline in the explanatory value of the basic model as one goes from older to younger age groups in each study when graded schooling is taken as the dependent variable. By contrast, there is an increase in explained variance when college schooling is examined. For *total* years of education, the explained variance is thus simply a composite of these offsetting effects at the graded and college levels. How has number of siblings contributed to this differential explanatory power of the model over time?

In order to examine this question, the unstandardized regression coefficients (slopes) for each variable by age group are presented in table 2.8. In addition, in the parentheses next to each unstandardized coefficient, the variable's rank order has been given, as determined by the standardized coefficients in each equation. The reader is thus able to compare, across age groups, the changes in the unstandardized coefficients, at the same time that he is aware of the relative importance of each particular variable in each equation. For example, the table shows that the father's education is the most important variable for men's total and graded schooling in virtually all equations. It is also clear that the number of siblings is the second most important variable in most cases for total and graded schooling and that the father's SEI ranks third or fourth in importance. By contrast, when college schooling is one's focus, the father's SEI moves to first place, the father's education to second, and sibsize to third in almost all equations.

Table 2.8. Unstandardized Regression Coefficients and Rank Order of Variables in Basic Model of Educational Attainment by Age and Three Levels of Education, White Men OCG 1962 and 1973, and GSS 1972–1986.[a]

Survey, Predictor, and Age	*Educational Level*		
	Total Years of Education	*Years of Graded Schooling*	*Years of College— HS Grads*
OCG 1962			
Father's Education			
25–34	.188 (3)	.101 (2)	.081 (2)
35–49	.191 (1)	.126 (1)	.066 (2)
50–64	.231 (1)	.191 (1)	.017[b](4)
Sibsize			
25–34	−.236 (2)	−.147 (1)	−.093 (3)
35–49	−.196 (3)	−.129 (2)	−.075 (3)
50–64	−.177 (3)	−.135 (2)	−.033[b](2)
Father's SEI			
25–34	.320 (1)	.065 (4)	.233 (1)
35–49	.315 (2)	.100 (4)	.205 (1)
50–64	.387 (2)	.191 (3)	.193 (1)
Farm Background			
25–34	−.306 (5)	−.377 (3)	.139[b](4)
35–49	−.715 (4)	−.713 (3)	.068[b](5)
50–64	−.579 (4)	−.557 (4)	.007[b](5)
Broken Family			
25–34	−.404 (4)	−.256 (5)	−.044[b](5)
35–49	−.665 (5)	−.523 (5)	−.100[b](4)
50–64	−.887 (5)	−.700 (5)	−.257[b](3)
OCG 1973			
Father's Education			
25–34	.251 (1)	.144 (1)	.092 (2)
35–49	.275 (1)	.188 (1)	.078 (2)
50–65	.300 (1)	.224 (1)	.065 (2)
Sibsize			
25–34	−.248 (2)	−.137 (2)	−.119 (3)
35–49	−.215 (2)	−.124 (2)	−.098 (3)
50–65	−.201 (2)	−.142 (3)	−.066 (3)

Table 2.8. *Continued.*

Survey, Predictor, and Age	Educational Level		
	Total Years of Education	*Years of Graded Schooling*	*Years of College— HS Grads*
Father's SEI			
25–34	.207 (3)	.017[b](5)	.218 (1)
35–49	.252 (3)	.026[b](5)	.205 (1)
50–65	.252 (3)	.052 (5)	.194 (1)
Farm Background			
25–34	−.229[b](5)	−.400 (3)	.215[b](5)
35–49	−.854 (4)	−.803 (3)	−.091[b](5)
50–65	−1.128 (4)	−1.060 (2)	−.019[b](5)
Broken Family			
25–34	−.711 (4)	−.273 (4)	−.345 (4)
35–49	−.936 (5)	−.635 (4)	−.196[b](4)
50–65	−1.044 (5)	−.875 (4)	−.042[b](4)
GSS 1972–1986			
Father's Education			
25–34	.220 (1)	.064 (1)	.131 (1)
35–49	.236 (1)	.092 (1)	.121 (1)
50–64	.223 (1)	.117 (1)	.093 (2)
65 and over	.328 (1)	.191 (1)	.078 (3)
Sibsize			
25–34	−.210 (2)	−.058 (2)	−.114 (3)
35–49	−.210 (2)	−.112 (2)	−.072 (3)
50–64	−.268 (2)	−.119 (2)	−.081 (3)
65 and over	−.219 (2)	−.127 (3)	−.073[b](4)
Father's SEI			
25–34	.171 (3)	.001[b](5)	.116 (2)
35–49	.215 (3)	.008[b](5)	.159 (2)
50–64	.261 (3)	.042[b](4)	.204 (1)
65 and over	.308 (3)	.181 (2)	.256 (1)
Farm Background			
25–34	−.174[b](5)	.300 (3)	−.068[b](5)
35–49	−.644 (4)	−.217 (4)	−.087[b](5)
50–64	−.920 (4)	−.402 (3)	.001[b](5)
65 and over	−.544[b](5)	−.030[b](5)	.724 (2)

Table 2.8. *Continued.*

Survey, Predictor, and Age	Educational Level		
	Total Years of Education	*Years of Graded Schooling*	*Years of College— HS Grads*
Broken Family			
25–34	−.735 (4)	−.110[b](4)	−.366 (4)
35–49	−.348[b](5)	−.438 (3)	−.383[b](4)
50–64	−.840 (5)	−.275[b](5)	.023[b](4)
65 and over	−.902 (4)	−.160[b](4)	.082[b](5)

[a]Although the respondent's age (within the age groupings) was included in the regressions, it is not shown here in the interest of saving space. It is not an important variable. In each age group, the standardized regression coefficients have been used to rank the variables.

[b]Not significantly different from zero at the 1-percent level.

Has the model's explanatory power declined for graded schooling because the effect of sibsize is less among younger than among older men? Not to judge from OCG 1962 and 1973 (table 2.8). In those studies, the effect (slope) of sibsize is virtually unchanged over the age groups, but the father's education, farm background, and SEI markedly lose explanatory power. In the GSS 1972–1986, sibsize also loses explanatory power over time, but the loss is not as great proportionately as is experienced by the other variables in the model. Hence, with regard to graded schooling for men, it appears that the main reason family background factors have explained less variability in men's graded schooling (as between younger and older men) is because of a decline in the explanatory power of father's education, farm background, and father's SEI, not because of a decline in the explanatory importance of number of siblings.

Turning to college schooling (table 2.8), the increases in the explanatory power of the model over time seen in table 2.7 reflect proportionate increases in the coefficients for number of siblings and father's education, as well as some increases in the effects of other variables. Because of the rising influence of sibsize over time at the college level, and the maintenance of influence at the graded level, the power of sibsize to explain total years of education seems to have increased rather than decreased over time. Put in substantive terms, comparing younger with older respondents large families have been a continuing drag on the society's ability to reduce family background effects on educational attainment at the graded-schooling level, and an increasing drag on our ability to reduce the influence of background factors at the college level. Even when society provided the resources increasingly to overcome a dependency on the father's background (education and occupational status), the reproductive choices that these respondents' parents made continued to exert an influence at the graded-schooling level.

Among women, the variance in total years of education explained by the model shows little sign of decreasing over the ages represented in the three studies considered here (table 2.7). Indeed, in the two OCGs the younger cohorts of women appear to be more bound by family factors than the oldest cohort. The time trend in total years of education is a result of the changes in the graded level and the college level as with men. At the graded level, the decline in the explanatory power of the model as between younger and older women is relatively modest in the OCGs, although more marked in GSS. At the college level, the model greatly increases in explanatory power; in the GSS 274 percent, in OCG 1973, 190 percent, and in OCG 1962, 174 percent. Which variables contributed most to the influence of the model on women's education chances over time?

Table 2.9 is identical to table 2.8 for men. For graded education in the OCG data, we may assume that the father's SEI is a good proxy for the father's education. Clearly, there is a marked proportionate reduction in SEI effects and father's-education effects (see the General Social Surveys, 1972–1986) on graded education over time. However, the proportionate reduction in the sibsize effect is generally less than for the other variables from older to younger age groups. At the college level, there are substantial increases in the effect of sibsize from the oldest to the youngest ages, suggesting that the increasing numbers of women from large families who complete high school have resulted in greater blockage at the next level of education if the young woman has many siblings.

A SEX/SIBSIZE INTERATION?

In considering the question of whether sibsize makes more difference for men than women when it comes to educational attainment, it is possible to think of two conflicting hypotheses. One could argue that girls may be at a particular disadvantage in large families

Table 2.9. Unstandardized Regression Coefficients and Rank Order of Variables in Basic Model of Educational Attainment by Age and Three Levels of Education, White Women, OCG 1962 and 1973, and GSS 1972–1986.[a]

Survey, Predictor, and Age	Educational Level		
	Total Years of Education	*Years of Graded Schooling*	*Years of College— HS Grads*
OCG 1962			
Sibsize			
25–34	−.184 (2)	−.125 (1)	−.075 (2)
35–49	−.193 (2)	−.141 (2)	−.056 (2)
50–64	−.209 (2)	−.151 (2)	−.066 (3)
Father's SEI			
25–34	.337 (1)	.119 (2)	.225 (1)
35–49	.374 (1)	.199 (1)	.185 (1)
50–64	.482 (1)	.307 (1)	.191 (1)
Farm Background			
25–34	−.013[b](4)	−.227 (4)	.332 (3)
35–49	−.157[b](4)	−.323 (3)	.306 (3)
50–64	.356 (3)	.036[b](4)	.706 (2)
Broken Family			
25–34	−.450 (3)	−.448 (3)	−.056[b](4)
35–49	−.474 (3)	−.363 (4)	−.103[b](4)
50–64	−.352[b](4)	−.291[b](3)	−.077[b](4)
OCG 1973			
Sibsize			
25–34	−.224 (2)	−.131 (1)	−.086 (2)
35–49	−.226 (2)	−.156 (1)	−.078 (2)
50–65	−.191 (2)	−.146 (2)	−.039 (3)
Father's SEI			
25–34	.355 (1)	.090 (2)	.268 (1)
35–49	.341 (1)	.118 (2)	.243 (1)
50–65	.439 (1)	.239 (1)	.209 (1)
Farm Background			
25–34	−.145[b](4)	−.448 (3)	.429 (3)
35–49	−.270 (4)	−.553 (3)	.430 (3)
50–65	−.010[b](4)	−.310 (3)	.520 (2)

Table 2.9. *Continued.*

	Educational Level		
Survey, Predictor, and Age	*Total Years of Education*	*Years of Graded Schooling*	*Years of College— HS Grads*
Broken Family			
25–34	−.596 (3)	−.322 (4)	−.284 (4)
35–49	−.610 (3)	−.436 (4)	−.129[b](4)
50–65	−.442 (3)	−.373 (4)	−.027[b](4)
GSS 1972–1986			
Father's Education			
25–34	.243 (1)	.068 (1)	.165 (1)
35–49	.237 (1)	.092 (1)	.154 (1)
50–64	.201 (1)	.110 (2)	.087 (1)
65 and over	.290 (1)	.224 (1)	.104 (1)
Sibsize			
25–34	−.141 (2)	−.061 (2)	−.082 (3)
35–49	−.168 (2)	−.106 (2)	−.055 (3)
50–64	−.193 (2)	−.168 (1)	−.081 (3)
65 and over	−.159 (3)	−.146 (2)	.009[b](4)
Father's SEI			
25–34	.139 (2)	.003[b](5)	.118 (2)
35–49	.185 (3)	.020[b](4)	.160 (2)
50–64	.162 (3)	.036[b](5)	.120 (2)
65 and over	.324 (2)	.091 (5)	.102 (2)
Farm Background			
25–34	.200[b](5)	−.123 (4)	.441 (4)
35–49	.035[b](5)	−.621 (3)	.193[b](5)
50–64	−.153[b](5)	−.826 (3)	.477 (4)
65 and over	.177[b](5)	−.744 (3)	.368[b](3)
Broken Family			
25–34	−.274[b](4)	−.175 (3)	−.187[b](5)
35–49	−.773 (4)	−.043[b](5)	−.372[b](4)
50–64	−.546 (4)	−.717 (4)	−.317[b](5)
65 and over	−.142[b](4)	−.759 (4)	.023[b](5)

[a]Although the woman's age (within the age groupings) was included in the regressions, it is not shown here in the interest of saving space. It is not an important variable. In each age group, the standardized regression coefficients have been used to rank the variables.

[b]Not significantly different from zero at the 1-percent level.

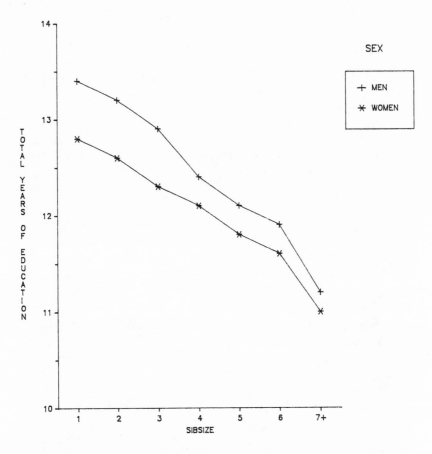

Figure 2.7. Total Years of Education (Adjusted Means) by Sibsize and Sex, White Men and Women, Age 25 and Over, General Social Surveys, 1972–1986.

where there will normally be some boys, and that in small families girls should fare approximately equally with boys. By this argument, sibsize might be more important for girls than for boys. However, it seems equally plausible that women's educational disadvantages have not inhered primarily in the dilution of parental resources but in a definition of sex roles that puts marriage and childbearing as the focus of girls' upbringing. By this reasoning one would expect sibsize to be less important for women than for men because of what might be called a "feminine override." Even if families are very small, girls will not, on average, have been reared like boys, and if families are very large the consequent relative disadvantage for girls will be less than for boys.

The regression coefficients in table 2.5 for the General Social Surveys, 1972–1986, allow us to begin to examine these hypotheses. The OCG data in the table are not useful for this purpose since the women in those samples are the wives of the male respondents and, hence, any comparison by sex is contaminated by the high probability that men and women with similar characteristics will marry. Table 2.5 suggests that the sibsize coefficients for women are somewhat lower at each level of education. Indeed, the results in figure 2.7 (also see appendix B, table B.2) imply that the relative positions of men and women who come from large families in the GSS 1972–1986 are closer in total years of schooling than the positions of men and women from small families. In effect, men seem to gain disproportionately out of coming from small families. We may thus entertain the hypothesis that there is a feminine role "override" that does not predispose parents of small families to encourage girls to attain (or the girls to seek) an educational advantage similar to that enjoyed by boys in the same situation. We shall return to this idea in chapter 6.

CONCLUSION

In this chapter, we have analyzed the effects of number of siblings on total years of education, years of graded schooling, proportions graduating from high school, proportions of high school graduates going to college, and years of college schooling. Even after controlling for family background variables, we have found differences by sibsize in level of total education that rival simple bivariate educational differences by race and age. Those from large versus small families lose about a year of graded schooling on average, which translates into large differences in proportions graduating from high school. Hence, although it seems logical to think that the deleterious effect of large families centers on chances for postsecondary education, the actual fact is that the greatest impact is early in people's schooling—in the grades. Since, as we shall see, there are marked negative effects on IQ of increasing sibsize, it is possible that IQ, as well as the dilution of material resources among many children, affects the drop-out rates among those from large families.

Sibsize influences college attendance much less than it influences graded schooling. We believe that this finding reflects the biases introduced by the high drop-out rates among those from large families at the graded-schooling level. Those children from large families who have made it through high school are a sample of survivors. They are quite probably highly selected for IQ, motivation, performance, and whatever other factors contribute to college attendance.

If sibsize is important as a predictor of educational attainment, how does its importance rank relative to that of our predictors in the family background model? For total years of education and years of graded schooling, the father's education ranks first and sibsize second. The father's SEI ranks third for total years, but it is unimportant for graded schooling. By contrast, college schooling depends more on the father's SEI than on his education or on sibsize. These results may be surprising for some students of educational mobility, since there has been a tendency to lump sibsize along with parents' education and father's occupation under the category "socioeconomic background," and to assume, thereby, more importance for socioeconomic effects in the "macro" sense than seems justified. As we shall discuss, it is one thing to look at socioeconomic effects *controlling* for sibsize, and another to *aggregate* a major predictor like sibsize into the overall effects of socio-economic status.

In their analysis of educational opportunity by age cohorts, Featherman and Hauser found that the society was somewhat more open for younger than for older cohorts when total years of education were under consideration. But this overall finding was actually a result of offsetting influences of family background for graded and college schooling respectively—graded had become more egalitarian and college more ascriptive. Here we asked how number of siblings contributed to these trends in the explanatory power of the whole model. We found that the declining power of the model to explain graded schooling was, in general, not due to declining effects of sibsize but to declining effects of the other variables. And, with regard to college schooling, the influence of sibsize increased over the age cohorts along with father's education. Thus, we find that large families have been a *continuing* drag on the society's effort to provide openness in graded schooling, and an *increasing* drag on our ability to provide equal opportunity at the college level.

3

EDUCATIONAL ATTAINMENT BY SIBSIZE, RELIGION, ETHNICITY, AND SOCIAL STATUS

If dilution of resources makes large families educationally less advantageous than small ones, we would expect this effect to differ according to the amount of social support for large families, as well as according to families' own internal resources. Since there is an upper limit on the educational benefits that can be provided a child, parents who have access to more resources may provide this limit for all (or most) children even if the family is large.

In this chapter, we will examine the effect of sibsize on educational attainment for major subgroupings of the white population—religious, ethnic, and social status. We begin with religious groups since, in the United States, they have differed in their support for large families, as well as in their educational attainment. Then we turn to ethnicity among Catholics, for American Catholics are exceptionally diverse in ethnic origin. Moreover, Catholic ethnic groups arrived in this country in different "waves," and their involvement with Catholic education and the church generally has not been uniform. Finally, we will investigate whether the effects of sibsize vary among the social status groupings of respondents' fathers.

NUMBER OF SIBLINGS, RELIGION, AND EDUCATIONAL ATTAINMENT

Other things equal, one would expect the negative effect of large families to be experienced most forcibly in those groups that provided the least *non*familial support for high fertility, believing that each couple should produce only the number of children it can support. We would thus expect that non-Catholics (as compared with Catholics) would experience the most negative educational effect from large sibsizes.

By contrast, given the strong Catholic church commitment to large families (Blake 1966, 1984), one might expect that coming from a large Catholic family would not be as inimical to educational attainment as coming from a large non-Catholic one. Indeed, although in general, parochial schools have placed a great financial burden on Catholics, it is also true that such schools have provided a more supportive environment for the children of prolific parents than attention solely to tuition charges might suggest. As Greeley and Rossi have pointed out (1966, 273), parochial schools at times charged on a per family rather than a per child basis. Such schools are also known to charge less for each succeeding child in large families and to be generous with scholarships for those in need. In addition, families in Catholic parishes "network" with regard to children's clothing and other child-oriented resources. During the Depression, parochial schools often accepted the children of the unemployed without charge (Sanders 1977, 184–185). The parish frequently pitched in and helped the schools with whatever resources were at their disposal. In Sander's words (p. 184):

> The voluntary labors of willing parishioners, many out of work anyway, helped maintain the buildings. With practically free labor, the schools functioned at minimal cost. Further, the entire congregation, not just the parents, supported the meager expenditures.

Moreover, the church's emphasis on Catholic schools for Catholic children (in part because public schools frequently had strong Protestant overtones and were often overtly anti-Catholic) appears to have made schooling itself salient among Catholics, except perhaps among southern Italians who did not participate in parochial schools.[1] As Glazer and Moynihan (1963, 276) have said:

> There is nothing in the history of organized religion comparable with the effort of the American Catholic Church to maintain a complete, comprehensive educational system ranging from the most elementary tutelage to the most advanced disciplines. The effort absorbs so much of the energies and resources of the faithful as to prompt the remark of a New York Jesuit that a Catholic diocese is a school system here and there associated with a church.

Additionally, Catholic schools were in-group affairs to which im-poverished and poorly clad children could be sent without fear of ridicule or shame by outsiders. Finally, Catholic charities were devoted to helping poor children, orphans, and those with health and learning problems.

> In other fields of educational endeavor [over and above elementary schools], the same dedication prevailed. Catholics punctuated Chicago history with the founding of secondary schools, universities, nursing schools, and educational institutions for the dependent, delinquent, and deprived. They launched settlement houses, vacation schools, and adult and continuing education programs in bewildering variety. The histories of all these varied activities, from the elementary school to the university, from the settlement house to the adult education center, from the parish library to the boy scout troop, lead to one indisputable conclusion. The Church attempted to construct a Catholic educational island within Chicago. (Sanders, p. 12)

For this analysis, we will use white males in the General Social Surveys, 1972–1986, the only adult sample extending over all ages for which we have data on religion and ethnicity.

Our theoretical concern in this chapter is complicated by two analytical problems. On the one hand, we wish not simply to examine *whether* interactions exist, but to see as well what the sibsize distributions look like within religious, ethnic, and social status groups. On the other hand, the simple expedient of examin-ing the results of separate regression equations for different groups turns out to be far from simple. The groups in question more often than not differ quite drastically with regard to characteristics such as age or farm background, and a number of these characteristics have offsetting effects on educational attainment within the separate groups. For example, Catholics and non-Catholics differ markedly in farm background, and this difference seems to affect the sibsize influence in diverse ways. Among Catholics, farm background was a major negative for education, since it separated the flock from the urban nexus of the church's educational support. Among non-Catholics, although farm background had some negative effect on education, this effect was minor compared to the effect among Catholics and, among large non-Catholic families, farm back-ground may actually have been somewhat helpful because of land-grant colleges and other supports for the American farmer. Hence, if we wish to answer questions like the following—"Had those from different sibsizes among Catholics and non-Catholics not differed as to family background and period of growing up, would sibsize have had less of a negative effect for Catholics than non-Catholics?"—we need to control for family background and age across, as well as within, religious groups.

Accordingly, in this chapter we will make extensive use of the pattern variable option in multiple classification analysis (see, Andrews, et al., 1973, 20–22). This option allows us to create a categorical interaction variable to use in a single multivariate equation. In this case, the 16-category variable was constructed as follows:

Religion	Sibsize	Category Number
Catholics	1–2	1
	3–4	2
	5–6	3
	7+	4
Mainline Protestants	1–2	5
	3–4	6
	5–6	7
	7+	8
Fundamentalist Protestants	1–2	9
	3–4	10
	5–6	11
	7+	12
Jews	1–2	13
	3–4	14
	5–6	15
	7+	16

The variable was included in a model along with the usual additional controls of father's education and SEI, family intactness, farm background, and age.[2] We can, therefore, consider the educational attainment of Catholics and non-Catholics by sibsize assuming that the controls are constant over the 16 categories of religion and number of siblings.

Table 3.1 gives some background information for the Catholics and non-Catholics in the sample. We see that Catholic fathers were much less likely to have been farmers than mainline Protestant fathers, but, in spite of being more urban, Catholic fathers were less educated than mainline Protestants and had higher fertility. Jews had the most educated fathers, were virtually 100 percent nonfarm, and came from the smallest families. Fundamentalist fathers were the least educated, the most likely to have been farmers, and had the most children of all the religious groups. Clearly, the average educational attainment of Catholics and mainline Protestant respondents is most similar being 12.38 years and 12.77 years respectively. The education of fundamentalists is markedly lower—11.45 years, whereas the average educational attainment of Jews is 15 years.

Table 3.2 gives the results of the multiple classification analysis. It shows mean total years of education for the white male respondents in the four religion-by-sibsize groups, adjusted for father's education and SEI, farm background, whether the family was intact, and respondent's age. Given these controls, are Catholics less influenced by the negative educational effects of large families than non-Catholics? We see that they are marginally less influenced than mainline Protestants and fundamentalist Protestants, but it is Jews that are least affected. We believe that the lack of effect for Jews is due to the fact that large Jewish families are almost invariably orthodox. Thus, these families will have had not only a strong external support system but a major emphasis on education as well. As for Catholics, it is worth noting that although Catholics, on average, have less education than mainline Protestants, those Catholics who came from families of seven or more siblings have slightly more education than similarly situated mainline Protestants. In sum, taken as a group, Catholics are not strikingly protected from the effects of large families on total years of education, but there is some suggestion of a small effect. Let us now see if a division of Catholics by ethnicity provides additional information.

CATHOLICISM, ETHNICITY, AND SIBSIZE

Although Catholics in the United States have not been divided by sects, they have been split very markedly by ethnicity. As is well known, these ethnic divisions were not only of major importance

Table 3.1. Average Family Background Characteristics and Educational Attainment of Respondents by Religion, White Men Age 25 and Over, GSS 1972–1986.[a]

Family Background and Education	Religion in Which Brought Up			
			Non-Catholic	
	Catholic	Mainline Protestant	Fundamentalist Protestant	Jewish
Sibsize	5.20	4.54	5.67	3.31
	(3.16)	(2.85)	(3.27)	(1.94)
Father's Education	9.17	10.06	8.36	10.63
	(4.47)	(4.06)	(4.09)	(4.95)
Father's SEI	34.10	35.78	28.64	52.35
	(23.52)	(24.96)	(21.37)	(23.19)
Farm Background (%)	12.37	23.04	31.92	0.60
Intact (%)	78.94	80.53	77.47	88.27
Respondent's Age	46.04	49.23	47.05	49.61
	(15.64)	(16.18)	(15.83)	(16.47)
Respondent's Total Years of Education	12.38	12.77	11.45	15.00
	(3.52)	(3.34)	(3.64)	(3.64)
N	1,793	2,168	1,501	179

[a]The numbers in parentheses are standard deviations.

Table 3.2. Adjusted Total Years of Education by Sibsize and Religion for Catholics and Non-Catholics, White Men Age 25 and Over, GSS 1972–1986.[a]

| | | Religion in Which Brought Up | | |
| | | | Non-Catholic | |
Sibsize	Catholic	Mainline Protestant	Fundamentalist Protestant	Jewish
1–2	13.42	13.50	12.89	14.69
3–4	12.67	12.99	12.18	14.58
5–6	11.99	12.23	11.87	13.00
7+	11.46	11.37	10.89	13.24
Percentage difference between				
1–2 and 7+	14.6%	15.8%	15.5%	9.9%
N	1,793	2,168	1,501	179
Grand Mean	12.38	12.77	11.45	15.00

[a]The adjusted means are derived from a single MCA equation which adjusts for respondent's age, family intactness, farm background, father's SEI, and father's education across and within each of the four religion groups.

Table 3.3. Adjusted Total Years of Education by Sibsize, Religion and Ethnicity among Catholics, White Men Age 25 and Over, GSS 1972–1986.[a]

		Ethnicity and Religion in Which Brought Up				
			Catholic			
					Polish/	
Sibsize	Non-Catholic	German	Irish	Italian	East European	Other
1–2	13.32	12.70	13.80	13.44	12.97	13.73
3–4	12.75	12.30	13.23	12.61	12.79	12.66
5–6	12.08	12.37	11.95	12.39	12.03	11.40
7+	11.13	11.91	11.57	11.15	11.64	11.24
Percentage difference between						
1–2 and 7+	16.4%	6.2%	16.2%	17.0%	10.3%	18.1%
N	4,282	249	258	311	307	461
Grand Mean	12.34	12.46	13.31	12.10	11.92	12.11

[a]The adjusted means are derived from a single MCA equation which adjusts for respondent's age, family intactness, farm background, father's SEI, and father's education across and within each of the six religion and ethnicity groups.

culturally but were correlated with time of arrival in this country—
the Irish and Germans during the middle and later nineteenth
century, the Italians and other southern and eastern Europeans
primarily during the last years of the nineteenth century and the
early years of the twentieth (Easterlin et al. 1982, 16–17).

Table 3.3 compares the educational attainment by sibsize of
Catholics divided by ethnicity and of non-Catholics as a group. As
with the analysis in table 3.2, this one controls over the separate
religion–ethnic–sibsize groups for the family background variables
in the model. Considering first the grand means, the Catholic
ethnic groups differ in educational attainment, with earlier-arriving
groups more educated than later-arriving ones. The Irish are the
most educated among Catholics and have almost a year more
education than non-Catholics. Germans are next in educational
attainment, and the Italians and Poles/Eastern Europeans are last,
having less education than the Irish and Germans as well as less
than non-Catholics. We thus see that, for earlier-arriving Catholics,
a main effect of the church's educational emphasis and support is
reflected in the *overall* levels of education of the Irish and Germans
compared with late-arriving Catholics and non-Catholics.

As for the adjusted coefficients (coefficients which control for
family background) by sibsize, we see that Irish Catholics have
more education in almost all sibsize categories than non-Catholics.
We interpret this finding to mean that Irish Catholics benefited
greatly as a group from the church's support for education and the
family (both large and small) but that small families were able to
benefit the most from such support. In addition, the Irish Catholic
leadership in Catholic higher education doubtless gave the Irish an
edge over later-arriving non-English-speaking immigrants, and
even over early-arriving non-English speakers such as Germans
(see, for example, Glazer and Moynihan 1963, passim; Weisz 1976,
passim; Sanders 1977, passim; Franklin in Ravitch and Goodenow
1981, passim; Sanders in Ravitch and Goodenow 1981, passim).

However, except for Germans and Poles/Eastern Europeans, the
ethnic groups suffer relatively as much from large families as do
non-Catholics. This is because whatever external support the Catholic church provided also benefited those in small families, thereby
making the drop from small to large families as steep for Irish
Catholics, for example, as for non-Catholics. On the other hand,

for Germans, Italians, and Poles (whose educational attainment was equal to or less than that of non-Catholics), sibsizes of seven or more attained more education than non-Catholics. This suggests that influences relating either to Catholicism or ethnicity particularly favored large families as compared to non-Catholics. Therefore it is worth some detailed consideration of the ethnic groups separately.

German Catholics were an "old" immigrant group like the Irish but well below them educationally. Why, unlike the Irish, did German Catholics gain so little out of having small families? Although more educated, on average, than non-Catholics, Italians, Poles/Eastern Europeans, and other ethnic groups combined, Germans from sibsizes one through four have less education than those in the same sibsize in the other ethnic groups respectively—in some cases markedly less. We can offer some informed speculation in this regard but no more. First of all, for German Catholics small families were more unusual than for the other ethnic groups, and families of seven or more were the most typical. For example, 14 percent of German Catholics were only children or had one sibling, whereas this was true of 20 percent of the Irish. Thirty percent of German Catholics came from families of seven or more siblings, whereas this was true of 20 percent of the Irish. We may surmise, therefore, that small sibsize among German Catholics indexes a problem that we cannot measure at this time. Second, German Catholics were intensely nationalistic from both a linguistic and general cultural point of view. As McCluskey (1968) has said:

> The German immigrant tended to lump together his language, his culture, and his religion. Moreover, he was suspicious and resentful of attempts to dilute his *Deutschtum*, whether by Americanizing bishops or Americanizing public schools. (p. 77)

It may very well have been, therefore, that small families or large, German Catholic parents encouraged children to remain within the German Catholic fold and provided little incentive or encouragement for higher education outside of the context of "German-ness." This interpretation has some credibility since Catholic higher educational institutions were primarily Irish. On the other hand, the German attachment to Catholic education was exceptionally strong at the parochial school level and into high school, and Germans had managed to establish German-speaking parochial schools (Greeley and Rossi 1966, 3; Tyack 1974, 86–87; Sanders 1977, 119; Franklin in Ravitch and Goodenow 1981, 57; Sanders in Ravitch and Goodenow 1981, 127), but German Catholics, being a minority among Germans in this country, did not have the clout to put the stamp of German culture on a broad range of education. German Catholic parents could thus educate their children through high school with the help of the church, as did the Irish, but beyond high school further education would have represented a venture into alien territory.

An additional hypothesis to explain the lack of a sibsize effect among German Catholics is that German Catholic fathers were disproportionately involved in craft occupations that were likely to have been family businesses. These fathers were bakers, brewers, carpenters and cabinetmakers, plumbers, restaurateurs, and so forth. It is possible, therefore, that men from small families were less likely to advance educationally than might have been expected because they were the only sons available to inherit the business. This is an attractive hypothesis, but one that goes beyond our analytical capabilities here, since we do not have data on class of worker for fathers. We should point out, however, that a comparison of the actual occupations of the fathers of Catholic and non-Catholic Germans in the General Social Surveys data shows that non-Catholic German fathers were also concentrated in the kinds of crafts and trades that suggest the possibility of family-owned businesses. And, a similar damper on the educational attainment of German non-Catholics in small families is evident as well. For example, the average educational attainment of German mainline Protestants is 13.23 years of schooling, compared with 12.74 years for other mainline Protestants, and 12.38 for Catholics. Yet, in spite of relatively high average educational attainment, German mainline Protestants in sibsizes one and two achieve 13.05 years of education, compared to 13.51 years among other mainline Protestants and 13.40 among Catholics in the same sibsizes (all other background variables in our model controlled).

Turning to late-arriving ethnic groups, the Italians, although Catholic, were culturally unique. As we have already noted in this chapter, their attachment to the church, and particularly to parochial schools, was minimal compared with other Catholic ethnic groups. By the time the Italians had arrived, most of the really big battles over Catholic education had ended, and the Irish had captured a dominance over Catholic education at all levels (Covello 1944, passim; Glazer and Moynihan 1963, passim; Weisz 1976, passim). Italians entered the public rather than the parochial school system from the beginning of their sojourn in this country—a system that had changed greatly since the Irish and Germans first arrived—and confronted essentially Protestant common schools that were, more often than not, explicitly anti-Catholic. How is it, therefore, that Italians with less education on average than non-Catholics could equal or exceed them educationally at larger sibsizes (five or more)? Although Italians were not closely tied in with the church, they were supported by an exceptionally strong, cohesive, and ramified kinship structure and fierce male pride in providing for the family. We must assume that this intense southern Italian and Sicilian familism functioned as an equivalent to the Irish dependence on the church in helping Italians to cope successfully with large families. However, we also know that Italian parents and elders of peasant origin were deeply threatened by a school system that acculturated and educated their children so far beyond parental levels (Covello 1944; Glazer and Moynihan 1963; Weisz 1976). The cultural pressure to maintain parental authority and family cohesiveness at all costs militated for some time against the pursuit of ambitious educational objectives for children.

The Poles and Eastern Europeans were deeply religious Catholics who sent their children to parochial schools and were closely involved with the church. However, these groups had major language problems, and, in addition, viewed the purpose of education as being the retention of the cultural, linguistic, and religious values of the ethnic group (Franklin, in Ravitch and Goodenow 1981, 55–57)—a purpose that did not mandate a great deal of education. Over time these groups became heavily concentrated in the industrial working class—in steel mills and other heavy industry, as well as in apparel manufacture. Hence, although they were in the fold of the Catholic church, their late arrival, language problems, and concentration as blue-collar workers (often in company towns) was not conducive to having their children rival the Irish educationally. Nonetheless, in spite of their disadvantages, those in large families in these ethnic groups have done better educationally than non-

Catholics and, in general, the sibsize effect among Polish/Eastern Europeans is well under that for non-Catholics.

To sum up our results so far, we have seen that Catholics, taken as a group, do not enjoy much less of a sibsize effect than Protestants—mainline or fundamentalist. The maintenance of a sibsize effect among Catholics is due, in part, to the fact that church support for the family helps small sibsizes as well as large ones, and small sibsizes can reap additional advantages as well. Hence, among Catholics there is a gradient from small sibsizes to large that is almost as great as the one among Protestants. On the other hand, we have seen that although Catholics have less education than mainline Protestants on average, those Catholics who came from sibsizes of seven or more have slightly more education than mainline Protestants from similar sibsizes.

The importance of the Catholic church's role becomes clearer when we consider Catholics by major ethnic group—Irish, German, Italian, and Polish/Eastern European. Here we find that among early-arriving ("old") immigrants such as Irish and Germans, the overall level of education is higher than that of mainline Protestants, and this disparity is particularly marked for the Irish who dominated Catholic educational institutions in the United States. Nonetheless, it is also true that the Irish maintain as strong a sibsize effect as non-Catholics, apparently because the Catholic church's support helped families of all sizes. By contrast, German Catholics evince very little sibsize effect, due to the fact that this group has gained little educational advantage out of having small families. German Catholics from small families do less well than other Catholic ethnic groups whose overall educational level is inferior (for example, Italians, Poles, and other groups). We have attempted to offer explanations for why German Catholics—of all Catholics the most committed to parochial schools—would have hit an educational threshold beyond which they did not advance.

Late arriving immigrants—Italians and Polish/Eastern Europeans—differed greatly in their attachment to the Catholic church. The Italians were alienated, sent their children to public school, and did not do as well educationally with large families as the Polish. On the other hand, in spite of late arrival and language handicaps, Italians equaled or exceeded non-Catholics in educational attainment among large families. We interpret this fact as

Table 3.4. Average Family Background Characteristics and Educational Attainment of Respondents by Four Paternal Educational/SEI Groupings, White Men Age 25 and Over, GSS 1972–1986.[a]

Family Background and Education	Father's Social and Economic Status			
	Educ Low/SEI Low	Educ Low/SEI High	Educ High/SEI Low	Educ High/SEI High
Sibsize	5.91	4.63	4.36	3.73
	(3.22)	(2.80)	(2.51)	(2.19)
Farm Background (%)	41.51	2.60	26.04	0.00
Intact (%)	88.49	90.04	88.59	90.53
Respondent's Age	51.39	50.09	41.50	40.40
	(15.09)	(14.72)	(14.41)	(13.81)
Respondent's Total Years of Education	10.90	12.69	13.27	14.71
	(3.41)	(3.19)	(2.94)	(2.71)
N	1,850	693	868	1,616

[a]The numbers in parentheses are standard deviations.

being due to the unusual strength of the Italian immigrant family—an offset against the group's cultural disadvantages in a strange country, as well as its alienation from the protective mantle of the church.

Thus, we feel that this analysis tells us something important. Groups in our society that did very well educationally in spite of large families (like the Irish), or that did disproportionately well with large families in particular (like the Germans, Poles, and Italians), were either closely integrated with an external support system like the Catholic church or, if not, had unique familial strengths like the peasants of southern Italian and Sicilian origin. Without such powerful and structured offsets to the drain of large families, high fertility groups such as, for example, fundamentalist Protestants remain at relatively low overall educational levels and do not do well educationally with their large families. We will now turn to sibsize effects on education among respondents from different social and economic groups.

SOCIAL STATUS, RELIGION, AND SIBSIZE

In this section, we ask whether the negative effects of increasing sibsize differ according to whether the respondent's family of birth was of low or high socioeconomic status. Since we do not require data on religious affiliation to answer this question, we can make use of the studies, Occupational Changes in a Generation, 1962 and 1973, as well as the General Social Surveys. We divide respondents into four groups on the basis of their fathers' education and SEI. We divide fathers' SEI scores approximately at the median, and we divide fathers' educational attainment into eight years or less and nine years or more. We thus have a pattern variable (identical in form to the pattern variable for religion and sibsize) for four paternal status categories each divided by sibsize, which is part of a model including respondent's age, farm background, and whether the family was intact when the respondent was growing up. The importance of keeping the four social status groups in the same equation is well illustrated by the diversity of their ages and farm backgrounds, as may be seen in table 3.4 showing results for the General Social Surveys, 1972–1986. The averages for OCG 1962 and 1973 (not shown) are similar.

Table 3.5. Adjusted Total Years of Education by Sibsize and Paternal Educational/SEI Groupings, White Men Age 25 and Over, GSS 1972–1986, and OCG 1962 and 1973.[a]

	Father's Social and Economic Status			
Survey and Sibsize	Educ Low/SEI Low	Educ Low/SEI High	Educ High/SEI Low	Educ High/SEI High
OCG 1962				
1–2	11.07	12.55	12.44	13.94
3–4	10.44	11.91	12.09	13.30
5–6	9.90	11.31	11.20	12.70
7+	9.03	10.51	10.54	12.25
Percentage difference between 1–2 and 7+	18.4%	16.3%	15.3%	12.1%
N	6,581	3,209	1,529	2,976
Grand Mean	9.64	11.60	11.59	13.44
OCG 1973				
1–2	11.67	12.82	13.09	14.14
3–4	10.98	12.29	12.71	13.67
5–6	10.20	11.33	12.32	12.98
7+	9.27	10.57	11.69	12.37
Percentage difference between 1–2 and 7+	20.6%	17.6%	10.7%	12.5%
N	8,207	4,135	2,417	5,465
Grand Mean	9.96	12.01	12.45	13.92

GSS 1972–1986

1–2	12.48	13.78	14.08	14.91
3–4	11.97	12.87	13.35	14.51
5–6	11.09	12.34	12.76	14.15
7+	10.24	11.48	12.18	13.14
Percentage difference between 1–2 and 7+	17.9%	16.7%	13.5%	11.9%
N	1,850	693	868	1,616
Grand Mean	10.90	12.69	13.27	14.71

[a]The adjusted means are derived from a single MCA equation which adjusts for respondent's age, family intactness, and farm background across and within each of the four paternal educational/SEI groups.

From the multiple classification analysis in table 3.5, we see that there is a difference in sibsize effects according to the father's social status. The sibsize effects decline as the father's social status increases and, for each survey, there is a consistent difference in sibsize effects between those whose fathers had low education and SEI and those whose fathers had high education and SEI. For OCG 1962, the sibsize decrements in table 3.5 are 18.4 percent for fathers in low/low and 12.1 percent for fathers in high/high. For OCG 1973, comparable decrements are 20.6 and 12.5 percent, and, for the GSS 1972–1986, they are 17.9 and 11.9 percent.

These results accord with the dilution hypothesis, which posits that advantaged parental socioeconomic status should mitigate the negative effects of increasing sibsize. However, it is also evident that sibsize effects remain even among the most advantaged. In this group (high/high) an average of 1.75 years of education are lost between sibsize one–two and seven-plus for the three surveys—two surveys losing 1.77 years and one survey losing 1.70 years. In the next chapter we shall see that part of the explanation for sibsize educational deficits even in privileged families may be that, regardless of other resources available, parental interaction and attention are diluted when there are many children, and such dilution affects IQ.

Let us here pursue the social status difference in educational attainment further, and combine a consideration of paternal social status differences with Catholic/non-Catholic religious differences, again using only GSS 1976–1986. We will ask the following questions: "Does the differential sibsize effect by social status persist among Catholics and non-Catholics? And will Catholicism provide an extra mitigation of sibsize effects within social status categories of Catholics and non-Catholics?"

The results of the multiple classification analysis shown in table 3.6 confirm that the differential sibsize effect by father's social status persists within the two religious groups. Moreover, within comparable social status categories, sibsize has less of an effect among Catholics. In particular, in spite of the fact that, within each paternal status group, Catholics on average achieved less education, Catholics in large sibsizes (seven-plus) have more education than non-Catholics in three out of four of the paternal status categories. This difference is particularly notable in the high/high social status group, where Catholics from sibsizes of seven or more achieve over a half a year more education than similarly situated non-Catholics.

Table 3.6. Adjusted Total Years of Education by Sibsize, Religion and Paternal Educational/SEI Groupings, White Men Age 25 and Over, GSS 1972–1986.[a]

Religion and Sibsize	Father's Social and Economic Status			
	Educ Low/SEI Low	Educ Low/SEI High	Educ High/SEI Low	Educ High/SEI High
Catholic				
1–2	12.24	13.02	13.86	14.73
3–4	11.92	12.70	13.12	14.19
5–6	10.58	11.91	12.99	14.03
7+	10.41	11.47	12.17	13.45
Percentage difference between 1–2 and 7+	15.0%	11.9%	12.2%	8.7%
N	453	187	245	455
Grand Mean	10.89	12.46	13.31	14.53
Non-Catholic				
1–2	12.57	13.98	14.29	14.96
3–4	12.11	12.94	13.48	14.65
5–6	11.34	12.49	12.76	14.12
7+	10.25	11.38	12.38	12.90
Percentage difference between 1–2 and 7+	18.5%	18.6%	13.4%	13.8%
N	1,226	437	563	1,041
Grand Mean	10.93	12.77	13.33	14.79

[a]The adjusted means are derived from a single MCA equation which adjusts for respondent's age, family intactness, and farm background across and within each of the eight paternal educational/SEI and religion groups.

In sum, consistent with the dilution hypothesis, if their sibsize is large, men who come from more privileged families suffer less educational loss than men from less privileged families. Moreover, if, to parental advantage, we add the support for high fertility of an external agency such as the Catholic church, we find extra protection against the negative effects of large sibsize. In spite of lower education on average than non-Catholics, Catholic respondents from large sibsizes whose fathers were in the high/high category are over a half a year more educated than non-Catholic respondents with similarly situated fathers. Indeed, in general Catholic men from large families receive more education than non-Catholic men. It is nonetheless true that coming from a large family has educational effects even among Catholics from high status families who lose 1.28 years of education as between small and large sibsizes. Among high status non-Catholics the loss is 2 years, and among low status ones it is 2.32 and 2.60 years.

THE EFFECT OF FATHER'S STATUS BY SIBSIZE

Up to now we have examined the differential effect of sibsize according to status categories of the respondents' fathers. In this section, we will turn the question around and consider whether the effect of having a high or low status father differs according to sibsize. In other words, we will consider whether the stratificational system was more open for men from small than from large families because men from small families were less affected by their social origins.

Table 3.7 uses the basic data from table 3.5 and percentages them across fathers' status categories rather than down sibsize categories. We see from table 3.7 that the educational loss for those in the smallest families as one moves from fathers in low/low to high/high statuses is consistently lower than for those in large families. Indeed, among the three surveys, the effect of the father's status (comparing low/low with high/high) is 37, 45, and 64 percent greater if the respondent comes from a sibsize of seven-plus than from a sibsize of one–two. Turning to the addition of Catholic/non-Catholic religion in the pattern variable from the prior table (table 3.8), we see that when we compare the effects of the father's social status within sibsizes, Catholics and non-Catholics from small sibsizes experience just about the same effect of social status on educational attainment. But, among large sibsizes Catholics experience

Table 3.7. Percentage Gain in Respondent's Total Years of Education among Separate Sibsize Groups due to Gains in Father's Status, White Men Age 25 and Over, OCG 1962 and 1973, and GSS 1972–1986.[a]

	Percentage Gain in Respondent's Total Years of Education Comparing Father Low/Low with Father High/High		
Sibsize	*OCG 1962*	*OCG 1973*	*GSS 1972–1986*
1–2	25.9%	21.2%	19.5%
3–4	27.4%	24.5%	21.2%
5–6	28.3%	27.3%	27.6%
7+	35.7%	33.4%	28.3%

[a]Percentages are derived from the adjusted years of education shown in table 3.5. For example, the gain in education among sibsize one–two for OCG 1962 is 2.87 years (13.94 years—11.07 years) which represents a 25.9% increase over the level achieved for father's status low/low (11.07).

Table 3.8. Percentage Gain in Respondent's Total Years of Education by Religion among Separate Sibsize Groups due to Gains in Father's Status, White Men Age 25 and Over, GSS 1972–1986.[a]

	Percentage Gain in Respondent's Total Years of Education Comparing Father Low/Low with Father High/High	
Sibsize	*Catholic*	*Non-Catholic*
1–2	20.4%	19.0%
3–4	19.0%	21.0%
5–6	32.6%	24.5%
7+	29.2%	25.9%

[a]Percentages are derived from the adjusted years of education shown in table 3.6. For example, the gain in education among sibsize one–two for Catholics is 2.5 years (14.73 years—12.24 years) which represents a 20.4% increase over the level achieved for father's status low/low (12.24).

somewhat more of a social status effect. The greater social status effect for Catholics among large sibsizes is due to the ethnic concentrations among large sibsizes in the different status groups of fathers. For example, the Irish are clustered in the high/high group and the Italians in the low/low group.

To summarize, this section suggests that coming from a large sibsize exacerbated the effects of father's social status differences on son's education, compared to coming from a small sibsize. Or, to put the matter another way, the social system was more "open" with regard to education for those born into small families.

CONCLUSION

Our interest in this chapter has been primarily theoretical and has focused on questioning whether the postulated dilution effect of increasing family size on educational attainment was mitigated by forces either external to, or within the family. We have concentrated on Catholic–non-Catholic religious affiliation, breaking non-Catholics down into mainline and fundamentalist Protestants and Jews, and Catholics into major ethnic groups. We have also examined sibsize effects by paternal social status groupings.

This analysis suggests that the negative educational effects of large families can be somewhat offset—by a powerful external force such as the Catholic church, by an exceptionally persistent carryover of kin cohesion, by high parental socioeconomic status, or by a combination of these influences. This finding thus adds some weight to our interpretation of the sibsize influence as a dilution effect, because we see that the negative influence of increasing sibsize is responsive to augmented resources. The evidence is complex since, in some cases (the Irish being a prime example) the offset to relatively large average family size has been one of substantially raising the educational level of the entire religioethnic group. Yet, because church backing for education and the Irish Catholic family has also helped small families, the sibsize gradient among Irish Catholics has remained large. The importance of Catholicism to the educational attainment of large families is also indicated by the fact that, even when Catholic ethnic groups have lower overall educational levels than non-Catholics, those in large Catholic families achieve more education than those in large non-Catholic families. In particular, we may contrast the relatively poor performance of fundamentalist Protestants with that of Catholics—even of Catholics who arrived in this country late and whose native language was not English.

Although supportive forces can mitigate the effect of large families on education, our analysis shows that a sizable sibsize gradient tends to persist. Indeed, where such a gradient is slight, as in the case of German Catholics, this occurs because some force is negatively affecting the performance of small families, not because this group has totally overcome the disadvantage of large ones. Our analysis of German Catholics has raised a question that cannot be answered here for lack of appropriate data but that nonetheless may be relevant to the educational position of the only child. This question is whether, when there was a family business, being an only child (or an only son) may actually have militated against the pursuit of more than minimally "necessary" education. It may be that occasionally there are offsets to the advantages of small families!

Our analysis also bears on another interesting issue relating sibsize and achievement. This concerns the indisputable fact that there are numerous Americans from large families who are highly educated and economically successful. We will see in a later chapter that the existence of such individuals is due in part to the overrepresentation of those from large families in the population generally, but it is also due to the remarkable efforts of those immigrant groups, like the Irish, who, for the first time in their history, were supported not only by the church but by a benign government and a successful economy as well.

Finally, our analysis has suggested that the smaller the family, the less men's educational attainment was influenced by their social origins. In effect, the system of social stratification (itself affected most importantly by educational attainment) has been more open for those from small families than for those from large.

4

SIBSIZE AND INTELLIGENCE

If differential parental background does not eliminate the effect of sibsize on educational attainment, what additional types of influence must be considered? Perhaps sibsize operates through intervening variables such as intellectual ability, parental support and encouragement, and personality and motivation. In the ensuing chapters we will examine sibsize effects on these variables. For this effort, we will turn to the samples of young people described in our introductory chapter—Cycles II and III of the Health Examination Survey, high school sophomore boys from the survey Youth in Transition, and high school sophomores and seniors from the High School and Beyond surveys. Before doing that, however, we will examine some of the voluminous literature on the subject of sibsize and intelligence.

Parenthetically, no data on birth order will be presented here, since the analysis by birth order is reserved for the next chapter. The fact is that for all the data sets available to us, statistically significant birth order effects on IQ are rare once controls have been instituted for sibsize and familial background factors. Moreover, our extensive review of other studies, in which birth order effects appear to have occurred, indicates that such effects are invariably a result of systematic confounding factors.

PRIOR RESEARCH ON INTELLIGENCE AND SIBSIZE

In 1956 Anne Anastasi summarized the research to date on sibsize and intelligence (Anastasi 1956). The results of 110 studies showed that customarily the relation was inverse. In deviant cases, confounding factors and selection biases were clearly operating.

The Verbal Component

More recent research has uncovered important refinements in the relation of components of IQ to educational attainment, and of sibsize to such components. Turning first to the influence of IQ on educational attainment, much research (including longitudinal studies) has reinforced the importance of intelligence to years of schooling completed (Lavin 1965; Griliches and Mason 1972; Alexander and Eckland 1975; Parnes and Rich 1980; Sewell and Hauser 1980). An opposing view from a Marxist perspective is presented in Bowles and Gintis (1974).

Additionally, research has increasingly brought to light the specific effect on knowledge acquisition and education of verbal ability—particularly vocabulary. The importance of vocabulary to other types of reasoning has led many psychologists to regard it as a good indicator of overall measured intelligence (Matarazzo 1972; Jensen 1980; Heyns and Hilton 1982; Sternberg 1985). Although vocabulary tests are strongly influenced by achievement (acquired knowledge), Sternberg and others believe that vocabulary is a good indicator of intelligence because vocabulary measures the ability to acquire knowledge in everyday contexts, rather than skills that have been developed through formal schooling or instruction. While emphasizing the importance of cultural environment, and particularly the vocabulary of parents to youngsters' vocabularies, Sternberg thinks that the ability to acquire knowledge is distinct from knowledge per se—different people exposed to the same environmental content will acquire different amounts of knowledge and at different speeds. Along these lines, Cynthia Deutsch (1973) has an excellent review of the literature on social class in relation to verbal ability; and Golden and Birns (1976) review numerous studies showing social class differences in verbal scores among infants up through age three (see, also Feagans and Farran 1982). These studies also show that such verbal measures are highly correlated with the children's later performance on intelligence tests.

The importance of verbal ability to overall IQ scores and to later academic performance has led, naturally, to efforts to identify what, in the early environment of the child, seems to influence verbal ability. Such efforts have attempted to isolate, within and across SES groupings, aspects of parental behavior and interaction with

children—so-called "process variables"—that affect verbal and linguistic ability. Research in this area (which will also be discussed
in a later chapter) suggests strongly that the child's interaction with
adults "in cognitively and motivationally stimulating settings"
(Whiteman and Deutsch 1968) is of primary importance. Similar
findings are reviewed by Bloom (1964), Marjoribanks and Walberg
(1975), Golden and Birns (1976), and Bradley and Caldwell (1978).
Although efforts to isolate aspects of interaction with adults as a
major influence on verbal ability have constituted a breakthrough
compared to older research on overall SES differences in ability,
these efforts have been criticized by Willerman (1979) as still far
from adequate as regards the direct measurement of parental behavior.

A special instance of efforts to implicate the family environment
as an influence on ability is represented by the "confluence model"
proposed by Zajonc (1975, 1976; Zajonc and Bargh 1980*b*). Zajonc
believes that the family environment can be thought of as embody-
ing the intellectual levels of the parents and the children in some
mathematical relationship. Put simply, as children are added, the
intellectual environment diminishes because babies are born with
a value of zero as far as the intellectual level of the household is
concerned. So, a number of closely spaced young children results
in a diminution of the intellectual level in the family and, hence,
affects the abilities of the children involved in such families. This
model has been severely criticized in the mechanistic form proposed
by Zajonc, since it is hard to operationalize a notion that appears
to assume that intelligent parents with a number of small children
become less intelligent, or that babies or young children can ever
be thought of as having zero or low intellectual levels (unless the
children are subnormal).

What Zajonc seems to mean, and what he comes close to saying
occasionally, is that a household with only two parents and a number of relatively young children becomes numerically "tipped" in
the direction of youth, and the adult component of conversation
and styles of interaction becomes swamped and engulfed by the
activities and concerns of children. This process can very well mean
that instead of children being brought up in an adult world, adults
are inexorably "brought down" into the world of their children. In
effect, the adult component of the family is diluted, not simply

because of a limitation on interaction between parent and individual child, but because the parents operate at the children's verbal and developmental levels more of the time than would be the case if fewer children were involved. If this is what Zajonc "really" means, we would agree that he has had an important insight, and that this insight is a dimension of environment "dilution" that requires consideration.

As for the relation of sibsize to intellectual components, Nisbet in a monograph entitled *Family Environment* (1953*b*), proposed the hypothesis that the negative association of sibsize and IQ is primarily an association between sibsize and verbal ability. Nisbet believed that this hypothesis, if it could be shown to have merit, would establish a direct relationship between sibsize and IQ through verbal ability, because children in large families had less interaction with their parents. In the 1953 monograph, Nisbet assembled a variety of evidence supporting his hypothesis, and in 1967 he and Entwistle published more systematic research on children (for various periods between 1960 and 1965 in Aberdeen) that showed verbal abilities to be more highly correlated with family size than nonverbal abilities. The authors also demonstrated that the relationship of verbal abilities to sibsize held within social class groups.

Following up on Nisbet's results, Davie, Butler, and Goldstein using 16,000 school children in England, Scotland, and Wales produced similar findings (1972). These investigators found large verbal ability differences by sibsize and relatively small nonverbal ones, as have Kellaghan and Macnamara (1972) in Ireland.

Do children in large families in fact spend less time interacting with parents? A recent analysis by Hill and Stafford (1974) based on the University of Michigan Time Use Survey shows that the answer is affirmative for two reasons. First, women with large numbers of children spend less time per child regardless of the women's own education. Second, women who are more educated spend more time per child than poorly educated women. Hence, since women who are less educated have larger families on average, children from larger families receive less attention both because their mothers are less educated and because the family is large. However, Lindert (1978), using time-input data from the Cornell survey on child-care in 1967–1968, concludes that as regards child-care time the number and ages of siblings far exceeds in importance the characteristics of the parents (see also Wolfe 1982). Lindert thus disagrees with those who find that mother's education is significantly related to per-child time spent in care (Hill and Stafford 1974; Leibowitz 1977). In any event, it seems clear that number of siblings has been found, in at least two systematic studies, to be strongly related to parental attention and interaction.

Confounding and Selection

Anastasi's review cautioned that before one can interpret the negative relation of sibsize and IQ as causally meaningful, one has to rule out two possible confounders—the negative association of sibsize with socioeconomic characteristics of the parents, and the possibility that large families are more prevalent among genetically less able couples. Both of these points are important, but the study of sibsize and IQ is, unfortunately, beset by some additional problems as well. One of these, which clouds much research is selection bias. First, we will discuss the problem of a possible genetic explanation for the negative relation of sibsize and IQ. Next, we will examine confounding effects of parental socioeconomic status and then turn to the problem of selection bias.

The genetic explanation.   We do not believe that a compelling case can be made for regarding the association of sibsize and IQ as being caused primarily by a negative association between parental IQ and fertility—the belief that parents who have larger families have lower IQ. Our position rests both on the fact that heritability coefficients for parent–child IQ have been greatly reduced in recent research, and on the tenuousness of information concerning a negative association between parental IQ and parental fertility.

With regard to heritability, a number of points can be made. First, all heritability estimates are population characteristics and allow for a wide range of response to different environments by individuals.

Second, recent reviews of the literature on heritability of IQ (Lewontin 1975; Horn, Loehlin, and Willerman 1979; Vernon 1979; Plomin and De Fries 1980; Bouchard and McGue 1981) suggest much lower estimates than earlier reviews (for example, Erlenmeyer-Kimling and Jarvik 1963). Recent correlations between parents and offspring who were reared together average .42 and, for offspring reared apart, .22 (Bouchard and McGue, 1981). These correlations are down from older estimates which were as high as .80.

Third, recent reviewers are much more sensitive to the methodological problems with all of the heritability studies. For example, after deleting Burt's apparently fraudulent data, there are few observations on identical twins reared apart. Even among those data available, the disparity of environment is typically suspect. Comparisons of identical and fraternal twins, respectively, reared together are flawed by assumptions concerning the similarity of environments for identical versus fraternal twins (see, for example, Jencks and others 1972; Lewontin 1975; Goldberger 1977). A case can be made that identical twins are more likely to be treated alike than fraternal twins. The other design option, adoption studies, is increasingly recognized as containing flaws of selective placement and delays in adoption, together with genotype–environment interaction and correlation. These problems make it relatively risky to partition explained variance in IQ (so much for inheritance, so much for environment) in the seemingly scientific manner that was once believed possible (Plomin and DeFries 1985).

Fourth, if the major sibsize effect is on the verbal component of IQ, and the effects on nonverbal components are much more modest, this fact suggests that the sibsize–ability association relates to environmental influences primarily.

Fifth, if (as will be the case in our analyses) controls for parents' education are introduced, this precaution exercises some control over parental IQ, since it is generally believed that the correlation of IQ and educational attainment is around .50 (Jensen 1980).

Finally, one study that contains data on the IQ of parents and children (Scarr and Weinberg 1978) finds no reduction in the effect of sibsize on youngsters' IQ when parental IQ is added to the regression equation.

With regard to the negative association between parental IQ and parental fertility, the evidence is weak. A study by Williams (1976) demonstrates a very low correlation between the IQ of parents and the number of their children. A frequently cited (see, Heer, 1985) additional study that includes data on parents' IQ as well as the IQs of their children (Higgins, Reed, and Reed 1962), finds that parents' IQ and the number of their children are related with the exception of the largest family sizes, which occur among both high IQ and low IQ parents. No controls were introduced for socio-economic status. Perhaps more important, the type of IQ test is not discussed, the ages at testing are vague, and the derivation of the sample, plus the possible selection biases accruing over a 50-year period, introduce uncertainties that are unimaginable. To give the reader a flavor of the types of data upon which conclusions about the relation between parental IQ and family size are based, we reproduce (without further comment) the account given by Higgins, Reed, and Reed (1962).

> A careful study of the genealogies and social characteristics of the families of over 500 patients at the Minnesota State School and Hospital for the mentally retarded was made almost 50 years ago. A subsample of these families which excluded 200 with epileptic involvement, was selected for a follow-up study. The large family constellations which resulted from inclusion of all descendants of the grandparents of the original 300 patients include something in the neighborhood of 85,000 persons. It will be readily apparent that most of this huge population were not closely related to the original patients and many were related only by marriage. IQ values have been obtained for everyone possible. They were obtained from the widespread school testing programs within the states where the families had attended school. Many of them were obtained from many Department of Public Institutions and Welfare. . . . We are well aware that the accuracy and value of a single intelligence quotient may be slight. However, in a large collection of IQ values the errors in the individual tests should largely cancel out, and the striking differences to be presented are certainly not the result of testing errors.

> Families for whom IQ values were obtained for both parents and for one or more of their children were selected from our large pool of data. These families were in most cases a generation or two removed from the original patients.

When all of these points are taken into account, the burden of proof would seem to be on those who desire to establish primacy for a genetic explanation. This is not to deny that individuals differ in IQ, nor to deny that such differences may have genetic as well as environmental antecedents. The problem we face in this analysis, however, is that genetic studies of heritability are too flawed methodologically and too imprecise to cast light on the sibsize–IQ relationship. While we recognize that such studies involve major, perhaps insuperable, logistical difficulties, this fact simply explains why the research is so unscientific and flawed.

Controls for SES and other "home" effects. Although fertility of parents has varied inversely with socioeconomic status for a much longer period of time than researchers have studied the sibsize–IQ relationship, it is still not always true that parental background variables are controlled when children's IQ is analyzed. Indeed, it is not always clear that even such a critical factor as race has been taken into account. Less obvious, is the need to control for whether or not the family is intact. Although controls for family intactness have some effect on the IQ scores of all sibsizes, such controls are particularly important with regard to the only child who is more likely to come from a broken family. As we shall see later in this chapter, it is probably also necessary to recognize that some only children may have this status because they have defects (intellectual or otherwise) that led parents to discontinue reproduction. Numerous "inconsistent," puzzling, and anomalous results concerning sibsize and IQ may be laid to the door of a lack of control for differences in the social status, or crucial other characteristics, of the home or the child. This problem of controls relates to the within-families versus between-families differences frequently discussed by psychologists.

It is appropriate here to mention a study by Brackbill and Nichols (1982) which claims to show that father-absence does not make a difference to IQ levels among very young children (age 4) once SEI is accounted for. Unfortunately, no controls were introduced in this study for the presence or absence of supplemental day care and, in addition, among such young children (who normally spend most of their time with mothers rather than fathers even if the father is "present"), the differences may not be overly visible. In an additional effort to discount the "dilution" hypothesis, Brackbill and Nichols also explore the effects of adding adults to the household of intact families. The researchers find that such additions do not enrich the youngsters IQs. However, since it is not clear whether the additional adults are typically aged parents who may *require* care, rather than giving it, and since not all of the adults were relatives (they could have been roomers who paid no attention whatever to the children), this research does not seem to be a conclusive refutation of the "dilution" hypothesis.

Selection bias.   As our early chapters will have by now warned the reader, selection bias cannot fail to plague the researcher on sibsize and IQ. This bias is obvious in the endless reports by casual observers of this or that group—a professor's college class and so on. Less obvious is the bias lurking in well-executed random samples of particular classes in the educational system (for example, high school seniors), or the full annual complement of national tests, such as SATs and the like. In essence, given the drop-out rates selective for large sibsize before high school entry, to say nothing of after entering high school, all research on high school and college students, and on tests for college entry (for example, Breland 1974; Velandia, Page, and Grandon 1978; Page and Grandon 1979; Galbraith 1982*b*) is severely biased by the fact that disproportionate numbers of youngsters from large families have already dropped out. This bias will have the effect of favoring scores for the remaining youngsters from large families and penalizing scores for those from small ones because dropping out of school has been so extreme among those from large families and so minimal among those from small ones. Sibsize "effects" will be minimized in such samples and consideration of relative positions of various sibsizes will not infrequently turn up anomalous results, especially when compared with other samples that have not undergone such selection, or that have undergone a different type of selection.

Research Since Anastasi's Summary

Since Anastasi's summary, research both in the United States and Europe (some on exceptionally large data sets) has confirmed the inverse relation of sibsize and various measures of ability or achievement (Belmont and Marolla 1973; Breland 1974; Claudy, Farrell, and Dayton 1979; Nisbet 1953*a* and *b*; Nisbet and Entwistle 1967; Davie, Butler, and Goldstein 1972; Douglas 1964; Maxwell

1954, 1961, and 1969*a* and *b*; Scottish Council for Research on Education 1949, 1953, 1958; Illsley 1967; Gille et al. 1954; Vallot 1973).

In a set of unusual research papers, Marjoribanks, and Marjoribanks and Walberg, have made additional contributions to this issue (Marjoribanks 1972*a* and *b*; Walberg and Marjoribanks 1973; Marjoribanks and Walberg 1975; Walberg and Marjoribanks 1976). Controlling for the parents' socioeconomic status, these researchers have measured directly what they call "family environment" variables of school children (pressure for achievement, activeness, intellectuality, and independence, as well as mother and father dominance). The family environment variables were negatively related to sibsize and positively related to ability—particularly verbal ability. The Marjoribanks–Walberg research indicates that sibsize is related to ability through the family environment variables, and that the relation is specific for verbal ability.

However, some recent large-scale studies (notably Velandia, Grandon and Page 1978; Page and Grandon 1979; Galbraith 1982*b*) claim not to have found a sibsize effect on IQ and, in some studies, the only child appears to constitute an exception to the linear relationship. First, we will discuss two major cases (Belmont and Marolla 1973; Breland 1974) in which the only child constitutes an exception, and then we will go on to those studies in which sibsize appears to have little effect.

Among the studies listed above, in two major instances (where the inverse relation exists generally), the only child constitutes something of an exception because it performs less well than do children of other small- or medium-sized families. These two cases merit some detailed discussion because they illustrate some of the confounding and selection problems involved in research on sibsize and IQ. These instances are the Dutch data on 19-year-old males analyzed by Belmont and Marolla, and the cohort of National Merit Scholarship test takers (in 1965) analyzed by Breland. The Belmont and Marolla and the Breland results by sibsize are presented in figure 4.1 along with data from the French and Scottish studies of young children that do not indicate an only-child deficit.

In considering the Dutch and American results for only children, we must emphasize that the studies did not control for selective factors peculiarly affecting such youngsters. Regarding the Belmont

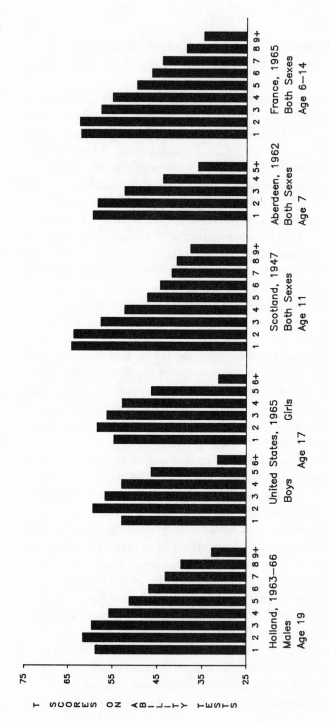

Figure 4.1. T–Scores on Various Cognitive Ability Tests by Sibsize for 19-Year-Old Dutch Males, 11th-Grade U.S. National Merit Scholarship Qualifying Test Takers, Scottish, Aberdeen, and French Grade School Children. Data from Belmont and Marolla (1973); Breland (1974); Illsley (1967); Scottish Council for Research in Education (1949); Vallot (1973).

and Marolla findings on young Dutchmen born during the period 1944 to 1947, probably the most acute selection, as I have discussed in detail elsewhere, concerns the effects of the famine in Holland on all last-born and apparently last-born children, including only children (Blake, 1981a). In brief, since the famine drastically affected fertility, fetal mortality, and infant deaths, being an only child or other last-born child was a status that would occur selectively in those families worst hit by the famine (those families in which the woman could not become pregnant or stay pregnant to term or in which a next-born child would die). Moreover, since the adult death rate was adversely affected as well, many only and last-born children born during the 1944–1947 period were partially or completely orphaned by the famine and, hence, remained "last-born." Again, on average this adult mortality would occur in those families worst affected by the famine. Since severe starvation in childhood is known to affect intellectual functioning adversely, it is hardly surprising that only and other last-born children in the Dutch data demonstrate an unexpectedly sharp drop in performance on the Raven Progressive Matrices test.

Although the selective effects of the famine were quite probably crucial in the Dutch data, overriding other effects, the fact is that all of the data sets I have analyzed indicate that only children suffer disproportionately from some particular familial handicaps relative to children from other small families. As we have seen, only children invariably come from broken families in higher proportions than do children from other sibsizes. The disruption of their parents' marriages is doubtless the reason, in many cases, that these children are singletons. Moreover, since most of the children reside with their mothers when the family is disrupted, the family's income level is adversely affected compared to children from other small families that remain intact. Additionally, since unusually high proportions of only children are born to older parents (who are from cohorts in which education was not as high as in more recent years), the parents of singletons tend to be somewhat less educated than the parents of children in other small families (the two- and three-child families with which the only child is usually compared). Finally, the incidence of infant and child health problems (particularly low birth weight and its possible sequelae) is greater among only children than among those in two- to three-child families. As we shall see when we present our own analysis, controls for such characteristics of the parent as educational attainment, income, and intactness of the family affect the results of ability/achievement testing on the sibsize results, and markedly affect the results for only children.

Turning to Breland's findings on the approximately 800,000 participants in the National Merit Scholarship Qualifying Tests in 1965 (figure 4.1), we may note that there were no controls for background characteristics, including race. This point is often misinterpreted in discussions of the Breland article since he also mentions, but does not present, sibsize data for a small sample of finalists in 1962, where some parental background data were apparently available. Thus, the somewhat less distinguished performance of the only child in the 1965 data is easily accounted for by the overrepresentation among only children of broken families, less educated parents, lower income, and a disproportionate number of blacks. Moreover, since only children are being compared with those of other sibsizes, we must remember that singletons are disproportionately likely to finish high school and be encouraged to go to college and, hence, are less selected for academic performance by the age of the NMSQTs than are children from larger sibsizes, among whom many have been weeded out by age 17. It is perhaps unnecessary to add that the NMSQT-takers are then additionally selected out of the population of 17-year-olds in high school.

We may now turn briefly to three recent studies that appear to have failed to show an association between sibsize and IQ or achievement. These are Page and Grandon (1979); Galbraith (1982*b*); and Velandia, Grandon, and Page (1978). All three studies are of samples of either high school graduates or college students. Additionally, the samples are of groups among whom other selective mechanisms appear to be important.

Turning first to Page and Grandon, this analysis was based on the second followup of the National Longitudinal Survey of the High School Class of 1972. The original sample, a stratified random sample of U.S. high school graduates in 1972, numbered 22,000 in all. However, what with losses to followup (cases that were never found at later stages of the survey) and missing data, the Page and Grandon analysis is based on 10,662 cases. The Page and Grandon analysis is thus victimized by selection in two ways. One, it is of high school graduates, among whom (as we have seen from the data on adults) there has been drastic selection by sibsize, but, additionally, losses to followup and missing information have also been very large. We are not told anything about the biases involved in these losses. In any event, it is hardly surprising, knowing what we know about dropping out among those from large families prior to high school graduation, that Page and Grandon do not find a strong relationship between sibsize and ability measures. Page and Grandon also consider an interaction between the sibsize achievement relation and SES which we will discuss in a later section devoted to this interaction.

Galbraith's analysis began with 15,000 students (class undesignated) at Brigham Young University in Utah, a Mormon institution. Data limitations reduced the sample to 10,925. Family size was found to have either neutral or slightly positive effects on ACT (College Testing Program Examination) scores. No Ns are included in the tables, but we are told in a footnote that the tables are based only on those respondents for whom information was available on all of the variables—presumably a count lower than 10,925. Thus the analysis is based first of all on college students of unknown year in college (itself a major sibsize selector), the students are Mormons (among whom high fertility is religiously enjoined, whose families are strongly supported in daily activities by the temple and the community, and who are generally exceptionally prosperous and well educated with unusually stable family situations), and we have no idea how many cases are involved in the actual analysis—that is, how selected this highly selected original sample has become due to data problems. Although it could be argued that youngsters from Mormon families are not selected by sibsize for high school graduation and college entry like other American children, we have no empirical reason to believe that Mormons are an exception. Given the above, we cannot be sure what Galbraith's data show.

Velandia, Grandon, and Page's analysis is based on verbal and mathematical aptitude scores of over 36,000 college applicants in 1974 in the country of Colombia. On a bivariate basis, the authors find that students in families of three rank highest, and those from families of one or two children rank somewhat lower. Beyond the three-child family, scores go down continuously up to the largest families of ten children. Why do students in one- and two-child families rank lower than children in three-child families, and lower than even students in four-child families? A hint is provided by the authors themselves (although not heeded by them) in their description of the sample.

> The Colombian educational system, like those of many other countries succeeds with only a minor fraction of the students. . . . For a complex of reasons, most students have dropped out of elementary school by the third grade, and graduates from secondary school number only around 5% of their age-mates. Of those who finish, called *bachilleres*, virtually all desire entrance into higher education.

In addition to this drastic selection, one may mention as well that there probably are some special reasons why, in a high fertility society, some families have only one or two children. In any event, the importance of selection *according to sibsize,* is suggested by an additional facet of the authors' own analysis. Here they divide their admittedly upper-class sample into SES quartiles. For the bottom quartile, they find virtually no difference in scores by sibsize, but for the top quartile they find a marked decline of scores with sibsize. For the middle 50 percent of the SES continuum, the authors find a negative relation with sibsize as well after the third child. The authors themselves suggest the interpretation that these results may be due to the fact that young people are much less selected by sibsize at the upper end of the SES continuum, but this interpretation is rejected by them because they do not feel that it is "parsimonious." Thus, this "exception" to the negative relation between IQ and sibsize turns out to be readily explicable in terms of both selection and the fact that most of the family-size continuum is in conformity with expectations.

In sum, a long history of research, based primarily on bivariate relationships between IQ and number of siblings, has found the association to be inverse. Recent work has begun to investigate what aspect of intelligence seems most implicated in the IQ–sibsize association. This work stresses the role of verbal ability, and the principal proponent of this view (Nisbet 1953a, 1953b, 1967) has suggested that children in smaller families have more verbal ability because they spend more time interacting with their parents. We have seen, however, that a number of confounders must be dealt with before we can assume that number of siblings bears a causal relation to IQ. We need controls for parents' socioeconomic status because this is associated both with their children's IQ and with the number of offspring the parents have. We also need to be assured that the data used to study this relationship are not strongly selected *by sibsize* (because of school drop-outs) as occurs when late high schoolers and college students are the subjects. Finally, we need to pay some attention to parental IQ as an influence on differential sibsize IQ. We have no evidence that genotypically more intelligent parents have smaller families. We do know, however, that recent heritability estimates for IQ have been greatly lowered and that they provide considerable room for environmental influence. Indeed, methodological examination of heritability estimates does not inspire confidence. We have noted, as well, that controls for parents' education can provide some control for parents' IQ. We have reviewed a number of major recent studies of IQ and sibsize which have shown some anomalies in the inverse relationship. We believe that these anomalies can be explained by an absence of control for parental characteristics and/or a strong selection by sibsize in the samples. We now turn to our own analysis of the sibsize–IQ relationship.

THE ANALYSIS

We concentrate in this chapter on data from the Health Examination Surveys (Cycles II and III; ages 6 through 17), from the study Youth in Transition (high school sophomore boys), and from the High School and Beyond base surveys (high school sophomores and seniors). Since the dependent variables are various components of the aptitude and achievement tests in these surveys, we shall discuss these tests first.

The Aptitude/Achievement Tests

Each of the studies analyzed here used a different battery of aptitude/achievement tests. However, each included in its battery, tests of verbal ability, quantitative ability, and nonverbal ability.

The health examination surveys.   Both Cycle II and Cycle III of the Health Examination Survey employed a short form of the Wechsler

Intelligence Scale for Children (WISC). The WISC was first published in 1949 as an extension, to children, of the already well-known Wechsler test for adults. The Wechsler tests had their inception in their author's broad view that "intelligence" implies a global ability to act purposively, think rationally, and deal with the personal environment effectively (Wechsler 1958; Glasser and Zimmerman 1967; Matarazzo 1972; Kaufman 1979). The test, consisting of 12 subtests, endeavored to take account of more than purely logical (what, today, might be called "left-hemisphere") functioning, and to recognize that cognitive functions are an integral part of personality in general. For these reasons, unlike the Stanford-Binet, the subtests are not ranked hierarchically but accorded equal weight.

Six of the subtests measure verbal abilities and six measure what Wechsler called "performance." The latter is roughly equivalent to what psychologists now call perceptual organization (spatial organization, and the like). An important additional difference from the Stanford-Binet is that the Wechsler has abandoned the Binet notion of mental age and evaluates test performance on the basis of distributions of representative samples of persons of comparable chronological age. The WISC scores presented here are standardized for age and sex and have a mean of 100 and a standard deviation of 15. The subtest scores have a mean of 50 and a standard deviation of 10. It is thus easy to translate score differences into standard deviations. For example, a 5 point difference in scores equals one-half a standard deviation on the subtests.

In spite of Wechsler's vision concerning a more inclusive and holistic approach to intelligence testing, the Wechsler tests are, in content, lineal descendants of the Binet. As a consequence, the Wechslers are criticized today (as is the Stanford-Binet) for not including more material that reflects intuitive, right-hemisphere functioning. This criticism is voiced especially regarding their use for testing blacks. An additional problem with the Wechsler for clinical purposes is that it is insensitive at the extremes of intellect— exceptionally gifted and exceptionally handicapped children are somewhat underestimated relative to the Stanford-Binet. Nonetheless, the WISC correlates highly with the Stanford-Binet (correlations that fluctuate around .80) in most studies.

Does the WISC measure "ability" or "achievement?" Sidestepping what has become a raging controversy, Wechsler maintained that it measures accrued achievement, plus such personality factors as drive and persistence. Its purpose is to predict future learning, and it is very good at that, especially for white, non-Hispanic young people. However, subtests of the WISC are designed to tap into different kinds of achievement, and to depend on different sorts of past influence in the subject's life. They are also differentially predictive of future academic attainment. In particular, the Vocabulary subtest of the Verbal battery appears to be deeply influenced by the home environment and cultural influences within it, as well as outside reading and school learning. A number of the Performance (perceptual-organization) subtests, such as Block Design, are regarded as less dependent on past levels of personal and cultural enrichment, and more influenced by personality characteristics such as field dependence and independence, as well as ability to work under time pressure. For English-speaking Caucasian young people (called Anglos in this study), the Vocabulary subtest is the single best predictor of future academic achievement (Kaufman 1979). The test is not adequate for bilingual Hispanic or black children.

Although, for clinical purposes, it is desirable to use the full complement of subtests (in addition, of course to numerous other diagnostic tools), it is not uncommon to use "short forms" of the WISC to describe the intellectual level of groups (National Center for Health Statistics 1973; Kaufman 1979). A short form, made up of various combinations of two or more subtests, is used to estimate the Full Score. A large number of studies of special populations (gifted, mentally retarded, etc.) have found high correlations between the Vocabulary and Block Design combination and the Full Scale. A special study of school children by Mercer and Smith (performed in Riverside, California, under contract to the National Center for Health Statistics) found that for Anglo children, the Vocabulary and Block Design subsets were the optimal combination to estimate the Full Score. For Anglo children, the Vocabulary/Block Design combination had a .867 correlation with the Full Scale (National Center for Health Statistics, 1972). It is worth noting as well that a number of investigators have confirmed Wechsler's own data indicating that Vocabulary and Block Design are the most reliable subtests of the WISC scale. It has also been reported that these subtests are the most indicative of the so-called general factor of intelligence in factor analyses of the WISC. In the light of this evidence, and of the time constraints of the Cycle II and Cycle III examinations, the Vocabulary and Block Design dyad was used for both Cycle II and III of the Health Examination Surveys. The total WISC scores presented are the unweighted sum of the dyad of subtests.

Clearly, the two cycles of the Health Examination Survey for young people provide an extraordinary range of information in addition to sibsize. These data, for example, make it possible to analyze dependent variables according to sibsize controlling for a number of important "background" variables of the parents, as well as for many additional predictors such as infant health (including birth weight), current health, and mother's and father's age at birth. The Wechsler data to be discussed here were analyzed using the following predictors: Sibsize, mother's education, father's education, family income, mother's labor force activity, intactness of family, and region and community size.

Youth in transition.   The University of Michigan's study of male sophomores in public high schools, Youth in Transition, used a number of tests of intellectual achievement/ability. One, the Quick Test, was individually administered, and the remainder were group tests. The tests measured a range of abilities. We will use three.

The Quick Test of intelligence is a widely used instrument that consists entirely of a word list graduated in difficulty (Ammons and Ammons 1963). Essentially a test of vocabulary, it does not depend on verbalization or reading ability. It is, along with other tests of vocabulary, regarded by psychologists as reflecting principally non-school-related influences (Page and Keith 1981).

In addition, a number of tests dealt with abstract reasoning and spatial ability. Among these was a Matrices test (an update and modification of the Raven Progressive Matrices test) which is essentially a measure of reasoning ability. The test attempts to be culture-fair. Also, the Hidden Patterns test is regarded as a measure of cognitive style and field dependence or independence. For more detailed discussion of all of these tests as used in the Youth in Transition study, the reader should consult Bachman and associates (1969, chap. 4). The tests are also discussed in Cronbach (1969).

1972	1980	Testing time (minutes)
	Senior Battery	
Vocabulary (15)*	Vocabulary, Part 1 (identical with 1972 test)	5
	Vocabulary, Part 2 (12 new items with broader range in difficulty)	4
Picture Number (30)	Picture Number (15 of original 30 items)	5
Reading (20)	Identical	15
Letter Groups (25)	Omitted	
Mathematics (25)	Mathematics, Part 1 (19 items the same as 1972, 6 easier)	15
	Mathematics, Part 2 (8 more-difficult items)	4
Mosaic Comparisons (116)	Mosaic Comparisons (89 of original 116 items)	6
	Visualization in Three Dimensions (16 items)	9
	Sophomore Battery	
No sophomores in sample	Vocabulary (9 from 1972 senior test and 12 new items increasing range)	7
	Reading (8 from 1972 senior test and 12 new easier items)	15
	Mathematics, Part 1 (18 from 1972 senior test and 10 new items increasing range)	16
	Mathematics, Part 2 (10 emphasizing achievement)	5
	Science (20)	10
	Writing (17)	10
	Civics Education (10)	5
* The number of items is shown in parentheses.		

Figure 4.2. Origins of Items and Subtests for *High School and Beyond*. From Heyns and Hilton (1982, 92).

High school and beyond.　　The tests used in High School and Beyond were developed by the Educational Testing Service specifically for that study. The objectives were dual—to provide continuity with the National Longitudinal Study of the High School Class of 1972, and to enable investigators to compare the seniors and sophomores who would form the basis of the High School and Beyond sample. In general, the tests for seniors were essentially the same as the 1972 battery, with the exception that two additional tests of vocabulary and mathematics were included (Vocabulary 2 and Mathematics 2), both having a greater range of difficulty than their original versions. To make room for these additions, Picture Number and Mosaic Comparisons were shortened. Additionally, a test used by Project Talent in 1960, Visualization in Three Dimensions, was substituted for Letter Groups, a test that had not been found useful by analysts of the 1972 study.

For the sophomores, there were no analogues with 1972 since sophomores did not appear in that study. Hence, the tests for sophomores were essentially versions of the senior tests scaled back in difficulty. Additionally, sophomores were tested on writing, civics education, and science. Picture Number, Letter Groups, and Mosaic Comparisons were dropped from the sophomore battery. Figure 4.2 (from the article by Heyns and Hilton, 1982) summarizes relevant information on the senior and sophomore batteries.

Three shorter tests were also devised that provided a joint appraisal of the seniors and the sophomores (these tests contained items common to both classes). These joint tests were used by Coleman and colleagues (1981) in their report to the National Center for Education Statistics, *Public and Private Schools.* Here we will not use the short joint tests at all but concentrate our analysis on the tests for each class separately.

In general, Vocabulary and Reading may be regarded as measures of verbal ability, although, as we have noted in connection with other studies, Vocabulary has a unique status as a test that is more likely to measure home influences than school influences (Page and Keith 1981). The two Mathematics tests may be taken as measuring quantitative aptitudes; Picture Number, and Visualization in Three Dimensions and Mosaic Comparisons, measure nonverbal mental abilities. Detailed discussions of the High School and Beyond tests may be found in Page and Keith (1981) and Heyns and Hilton (1982).

Sibsize and Aptitude/Achievement

Does the inverse relation of educational attainment and sibsize reflect, in part, a similar relation of intellectual ability or achievement and sibsize? In attempting to answer this question, we obviously want to avoid, as much as possible, interpreting relationships that have been confounded by the association of parental background characteristics and fertility, or by selection of various kinds. For this reason we will employ similar, in most cases identical, controls for parental background characteristics in each of the studies, as well as controls for whether the family is intact, region of the country, and, where possible, size of community. We use multiple classification analysis throughout so that exceptions to a regularly decreasing relationship with increasing sibsize will be visible. Additionally, in a final section of this chapter, we will deal with some "special effects" on the relation of sibsize and ability/achievement tests.

The controls used in this chapter markedly influence the shape of the relationship of sibsize and ability/achievement tests, as will be seen by comparing adjusted and unadjusted means in those cases where we present both. This analysis thus underscores the importance of such controls—controls that capitalize on our knowledge of the relation of parents' characteristics and their fertility.

For Cycles II and III of the Health Examination Surveys, figures 4.3 and 4.4 show both the unadjusted and the adjusted means by sibsize for the components of the WISC, Vocabulary and Block Design; the supporting data are in appendix C, table C.1.

Beginning with Cycle II, among the unadjusted means we see that Vocabulary is clearly the most important component for the relation with sibsize among this sample of children age 6 to 11. The difference between sibsize one (score of 53) and sibsize seven-plus (score of 43) is a standard deviation. In effect, 74 percent of the children taking the test had a score better than the average score obtained by children from sibsizes seven-plus. For Block Design there is only four-tenths of a standard deviation difference between sibsizes one and seven-plus. Adjustment for major background variables reduces the Vocabulary relation with sibsize somewhat, but it remains very strong. Even in the adjusted data it amounts to seven-tenths of a standard deviation. Controls substantially reduce the effects of sibsize on Block Design. There is clearly no only-child deficit.

In Cycle III, figure 4.4, the findings are essentially the same as for Cycle II except that the effects of sibsize are slightly less. It is notable in Cycle III that the only child clearly does the best on Vocabulary in both the unadjusted and adjusted data.

It should be noted, with regard to both Cycle II and Cycle III, that controls were introduced for the mother's labor force activity—whether she was working full-time, part-time, or had no job. No significant effect on the WISC, or either of its components, was evident. This result is not surprising since, as will be discussed in a later chapter, the literature on the effects on children's achievement of mother's labor-force participation rarely suggests much impact.

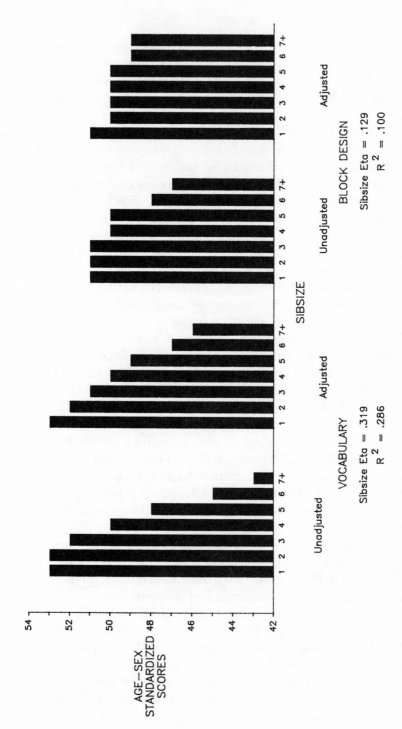

Figure 4.3. Age–Sex Standardized Scores on Vocabulary and Block Design Components of the Weschler Intelligence Scale for Children (WISC), Adjusted and Unadjusted for Parental Characteristics, White Boys and Girls, HES, Cycle II.

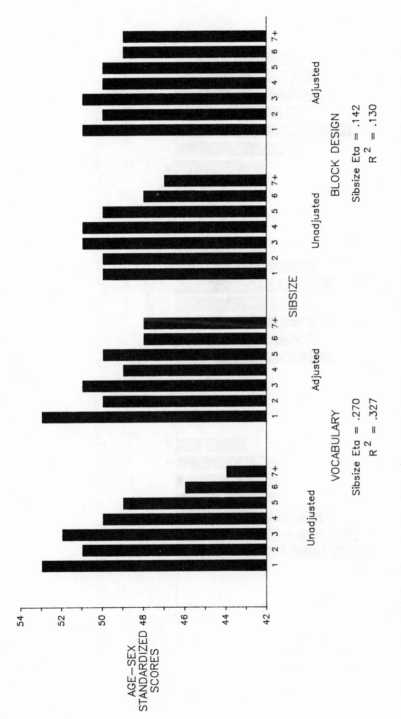

Figure 4.4. Age–Sex Standardized Scores on Vocabulary and Block Design Components of the Weschler Intelligence Scale for Children (WISC), Adjusted and Unadjusted for Parental Characteristics, White Boys and Girls, HES, Cycle III.

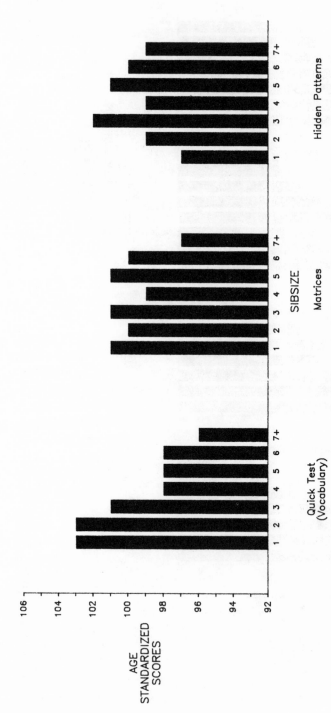

Figure 4.5. Age Standardized Achievement Test Scores by Sibsize, White Boys, YIT, High School Sophomores, Adjusted Means.

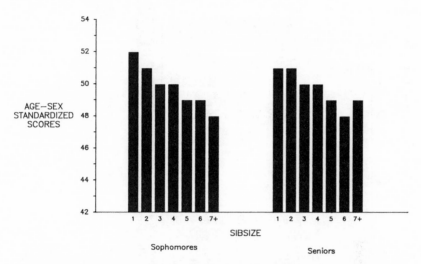

Figure 4.6. Age–Sex Standardized Vocabulary Test Scores by Sibsize, White Boys and Girls, HSB, Sophomores and Seniors, Adjusted Means.

One reason for the lack of effect appears to be that mothers who work spend almost as much time with their children as mothers who do not, and other relatives (including fathers) act as alternative child-care suppliers.

When we turn to the Youth in Transition high school sophomores, figure 4.5 (and appendix C, table C.2), and the High School and Beyond sophomores and seniors, figure 4.6 (and appendix C, table C.2), the relationship of verbal ability and sibsize is less than in the younger samples, quite probably because the high school samples have already been selected by sibsize (as we have seen in our analysis of the experience of adults). The relationship with sibsize for the other tests either disappears (figure 4.5 for Youth in Transition and table C.2 for High School and Beyond) or suggests that those from large families do slightly better. The persistence of verbal differences is noteworthy, however.

In sum, it seems clear that the most important aptitude/achievement influence of sibsize is on the vocabulary component of tests even after controls for parental background. These findings thus help to validate the earlier research we have discussed (by Nisbet, and by Davie et al.) and assist in explaining the strong association of sibsize and educational attainment. The findings are also impor-

Table 4.1. Age–Sex Standardized Vocabulary Scores by Sibsize and Grade Levels, White Boys and Girls, HES, Cycles II and III, Adjusted Means.[a]

Survey and Grade	Sibsize							Eta	Sibsize Difference as Percent of S.D.[b]
	1	2	3	4	5	6	7+		
Cycle II									
K and 1st	54	53	49	49	48	46	46	.361	79
2nd and 3rd	52	52	51	50	48	47	47	.303	50
4th and 5th	53	52	51	51	50	47	46	.335	74
6th and 7th	56	54	53	51	51	50	50	.244	68
Cycle III									
6th through 8th	53	50	51	49	49	47	46	.331	70
9th and 10th	54	51	51	50	50	49	49	.198	53
11th and 12th	54	52	52	52	52	50	51	.168	35

[a]Scores have been adjusted, through multiple classification analysis, for mother's and father's education, family income, family intactness, and region. Tests have a mean of 50 and a standard deviation of 10. The number of cases in each grade level varies beween 604 and 1,601.

[b]This is the difference in scores between those from only-child families and those from families of seven or more shown as a percent of the standard deviation for each test.

tant in suggesting that not all components of aptitude/achievement are much affected by sibsize, something about which we have had little information. This finding casts some doubt on claims that the sibsize–IQ relation is based on the possibility that parents of smaller families are genotypically more intelligent. Quite clearly, children from large families only suffer certain kinds of ability deficits—those that are known to be particularly associated with low levels of parent–child interaction. Unfortunately, since verbal ability is the principal cognitive predictor of educational success, this particular deficit has significant educational consequences for youngsters from large families.

It is worth mentioning that the diminution of vocabulary effects as students advance in school classes can be seen *within* the Cycle II and III samples (table 4.1) when these youngsters are tabulated by grade level. For high school students in Cycle III, we see a marked diminution of sibsize effects on Vocabulary compared with youngsters in lower grades. The discontinuity between the sixth- and seventh-grade scores in Cycle II and the sixth- through eighth-grade scores in Cycle III is due to the fact that each sample is standardized within itself. It is particularly clear from these data that as the grade levels increase, the scores of youngsters from large families improve proportionately much more than the scores for students from small families. We believe that these results are a consequence of school leaving (or being held back) by the less able students.

Although we know that school leaving (and being held back) among students from large sibsizes greatly changes the relation between sibsize and ability as youngsters go up the educational grade levels, a critic could argue that the diminution of sibsize effects is due simply to the fact that these effects are ironed out in the schooling process. Youngsters from large families make up the verbal deficit in school, and gain from school what youngsters in small families gained at home. Logically, this is a compelling point, and it would be more compelling if we did not already know that, in fact, there is a large differential drop-out rate by sibsize. Nonetheless, it is possible that both mechanisms are operating—selective drop-out *and* improvement.

One way of casting some light on the issue of a persistence of verbal deficiency by sibsize is to consider the results of a vocabulary

Table 4.2. Scores on Vocabulary Tests among Different Sibsize Groups by Respondents' and Mothers' Education, White Men and Women, GSS 1972–1986.[a]

Respondent's and Mother's Education	*Sibsize*			
	1–2	*3–4*	*5–6*	*7+*
Respondent—Grade Sch				
Mother—Grade Sch	5.06(31)	4.35(82)	4.52(100)	4.18(272)
Respondent—HS Inc				
Mother—Grade Sch	5.92(51)	5.69(122)	5.31(88)	4.57(200)
Respondent—HS Comp				
Mother—Grade Sch	6.55(139)	5.96(224)	6.03(185)	5.91(213)
—HS Inc	6.14(78)	5.73(128)	5.98(81)	5.68(66)
—HS Comp	6.29(215)	6.11(356)	6.03(195)	5.85(153)
Respondent—College				
Mother—Grade Sch	7.65(101)	7.17(141)	7.11(95)	6.79(99)
—HS Inc	7.69(83)	7.44(100)	7.08(40)	6.77(30)
—HS Comp	7.79(392)	7.38(506)	7.14(189)	7.12(104)
—College	8.01(96)	8.05(118)	7.50(36)	7.25(16)

[a]The number of cases for each cell is shown in parentheses. Omitted categories of respondent's and mother's education are due to the relative rarity of certain combinations of education and sibsize.

test that adult respondents in the General Social Surveys take at the end of the interview session. In table 4.2, we have tabulated these test scores for individual sibsize groups by respondents' mothers' education (as an indicator of family environment) and by respondents' own education. From this table, it is evident that at each level of education for respondents and for mothers, there is a significant verbal deficit for respondents from large families compared to those from small ones. Even when respondents have gone to college, the deficit between small and large sibsizes remains, and it remains at each level of the mother's education among the college-educated.

To sum up our findings so far, it is clear that verbal ability (especially vocabulary) stands out in its relation with sibsize among all of the studies. Only-children excel in verbal ability—there is no only-child deficit. Moreover, there are important relationships with

sibsize even after adjusting for major family background characteristics. On other tests, the relationship with sibsize is much more
modest, suggesting that a genetic interpretation of the relationship
is unlikely. Finally, as we move from young children to high schoolers, the sibsize relation diminishes suggesting strong effects of selection by sibsize such as we have seen among our adult respondents.
Although children from large families, if they stay in school, may
gain some of the verbal ability that they did not get from parent–
child interaction, a vocabulary test of adults in the General Social
Surveys suggests a persistence of verbal deficits among those from
large families.

The Interaction with Parents' Socioeconomic Status

A number of researchers have suggested that sibsize–IQ effects are
evident only among low socioeconomic groups—that is, that there
is an interaction between the sibsize–IQ relationship and parental
socioeconomic status. Among advantaged groups, the connection
is said to be nonexistent (Kennett 1973; Page and Grandon 1979;
Ernst and Angst 1983) or attenuated (Heuyer, et al., 1950; Gille
et al., 1954; Douglas 1964; Nisbet and Entwistle 1967). In other
studies, however, the connection has been claimed within socio-
economic-status groups (for example, Maxwell 1954; Davie et al.,
1972). We have just seen, as well, that in the study of college
applicants in Colombia by Velandia, Grandon, and Page, the relationship of sibsize and IQ among the applicants was greatest for
the least-selected and highest socioeconomic group.

Given the association of sibsize with intelligence, and particularly with that type of intellectual ability that is dependent upon
the home environment, it is natural to expect that there might be
some interaction of the sibsize–intelligence relationship and differences in the home environment. Perhaps the most likely expectation
is that the strength of the relationship would differ according to the
parents' educational levels. In examining all of the studies on
youngsters, it is clear that verbal ability (among all of the test
components) is the most closely associated (see the correlation
ratios—etas) with parents' education (table 4.3), and particularly
for the youngest respondents. Moreover, among young respondents, the mother's education is more closely associated than the

Table 4.3. Association between Achievement/Ability Test Scores and Mother's and Father's Educational Attainment, White Boys and Girls, HES, Cycles II and III, YIT, High School Sophomores, and HSB, Sophomores and Seniors.[a]

Survey and Test	Eta		Beta	
	Mother's Education	Father's Education	Mother's Education	Father's Education
HES, Cycle II				
Vocabulary	.449	.426	.240	.157
Block Design	.287	.266	.172	.098
HES, Cycle III				
Vocabulary	.473	.457	.253	.235
Block Design	.303	.299	.155	.154
YIT				
Quick Test	.261	.277	.136	.137
Matrices	.147	.161	.080	.075
Hidden Patterns	.079	.124	.025	.074
HSB, Sophomores				
Vocabulary	.295	.316	.173	.208
HSB, Seniors				
Vocabulary 1	.238	.251	.151	.171
Vocabulary 2	.235	.237	.157	.153
Picture/Number	.085	.085	.058	.058
Mosaic Comparisons 1	.061	.077	.035	.059
Mosaic Comparisons 2	.079	.090	.046	.067
Visualization—3 Dimensions	.137	.166	.081	.120

[a] The beta coefficients have been adjusted for all of the predictors, including sibsize, used in each study shown in tables 4.1 and 4.2.

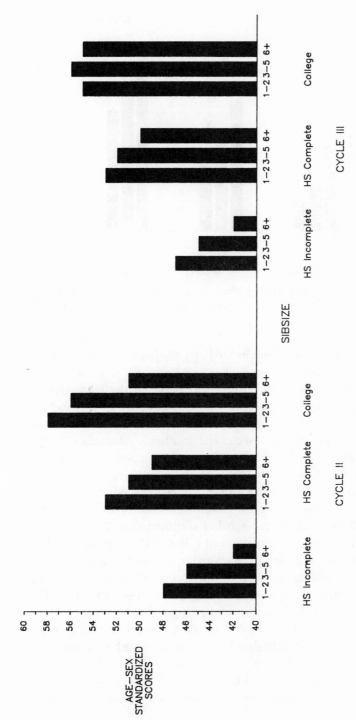

Figure 4.7. Age–Sex Standardized Vocabulary Scores by Sibsize and Three Levels of Mother's Education, White Boys and Girls, HES, Cycles II and III, Adjusted Means.

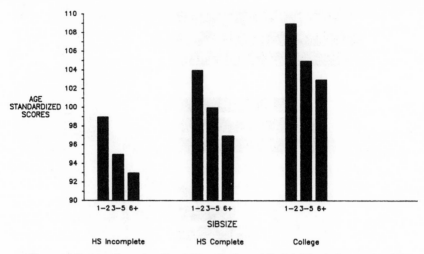

Figure 4.8. Age Standardized Vocabulary (Quick Test) Scores by Sibsize and Three Levels of Mother's Education, White Boys, YIT, Adjusted Means.

father's (compare betas—standardized coefficients—for mother's and father's education).

In examining a possible interaction between the sibsize/verbal ability relationship and parental background, we have chosen to use the mother's education (rather than the father's) for two reasons. First, as we have seen, the mother's education is more closely associated with verbal ability, and, second, since children from broken families tend to live with their mothers, we have more complete data on the mother's than the father's education.

For Cycles II and III, figure 4.7 shows us the WISC Vocabulary scores by three levels of the mother's education—high school incomplete, high school complete, and college. The means have been adjusted for the other family background characteristics we have been using including mother's education within the groupings. From these figures, we see that the sibsize effect in Cycle II is evident at each level of mother's education. For the older children in Cycle III, there is a sibsize effect among youngsters whose mothers had less than a high school education and who completed high school, but no effect is evident among those whose mothers had been to college. Figure 4.8 from Youth in Transition, for the Quick Test among boys, shows sibsize effects at all levels of mothers' education. Results are similar for the students in High School and Beyond (not shown). These results suggest that verbal ability deficits among children from large families are not solely confined to those from the most disadvantaged homes.

An Interaction by Sex?

In considering whether an interaction exists between sex and sibsize regarding IQ, we need to turn briefly to the issue of sex differences in IQ and in the components of cognitive ability. As is well known, the question of whether there are sex differences in cognitive ability has been a deeply argued one in psychology. With regard to general intelligence (as distinct from specific abilities) a diminution of sex differences was built into standardized testing by balancing items according to whether boys or girls (women or men) performed well or poorly on the items in question (Matarazzo 1972, 352–353). Measures of general intelligence aside, all major reviews of the psychological literature on gender differences in cognition conclude that there are sex differences in specific tested cognitive abilities and that these differences are fairly consistent (Terman and Tyler 1954; Tyler 1965; Maccoby 1966; Maccoby and Jacklin 1974; Wittig and Peterson 1979). The large-scale Maccoby and Jacklin review, which has been criticized for systematically understating sex differences in all domains (see Block 1976), still points out that girls excel in verbal ability and boys in visual–spatial and mathematical ability, and that the differences show up most consistently late, rather than early, in childhood. SAT scores in the United States (self-selected high school seniors who intend to go to college) show boys as superior to girls in mathematics and slightly superior in verbal ability. Boys have also been found to score higher than girls on the National Merit Scholarship Qualifying Tests (Breland 1974). There is some evidence that girls have improved in cognitive tests relative to boys in recent years (Deaux 1985).

Internationally, the large-scale studies to which we have frequently referred in this volume are far from clear-cut concerning sex differences. Seven-year-olds tested in England, Scotland, and Wales show that girls score higher in reading ability (Davie et al. 1972). Seven to eleven year olds in France tested in a 1954 study (using a mosaic test) showed no difference between the sexes (Gille and others 1954). Six to thirteen year olds in 1965 in France also evinced no sex differences (Vallot 1973).

One thing seems clear in both the national and international testing: the variance for boys is greater than for girls. Boys do both extremely poorly and extremely well to an extent that exceeds the dispersion for girls. Just why this is true is certainly far from clear, although some investigators tend to relate it to a personality difference that is frequently found between the sexes—girls are more conforming and "socialized" than boys, who are found to be more aggressive, restless, ranging, distractive, and nonconforming (see, for example, Davie et al. 1972). The dispersion may also be due to the fact that boys appear to have more health problems (for example, neurological problems) that bear on cognitive testing (Maccoby and Jacklin 1974).

In considering the data we have analyzed by sibsize on cognitive ability, we shall adhere to our concentration on the issue of whether the effect of sibsize differs by sex. The Cycle II Vocabulary test, restandardized on age alone, suggests that boys are slightly more sensitive than girls to sibsize, but the remainder of the surveys, similarly standardized, evidence little interaction by sex. (In the interest of space, we do not show these findings.) With regard to mathematical ability (where boys typically exceed girls), the findings are mixed. Using the Arithmetic component of the WRAT scores in Cycles II and III of the Health Examination Survey, and the Mathematics 1 and 2 scores for sophomores and seniors in High School and Beyond, we find, except for Cycle II, no significant sibsize differences by sex in the scores, although in the High School and Beyond data there is some tendency for sibsize to make more of a difference among girls. However, the direction of the relationship is inconsistent in that coming from a larger family sometimes results in higher scores in mathematics (for both boys and girls) and sometimes in lower scores. In Cycle II, there is an appreciably larger sibsize difference for boys than for girls—the difference between the only child and the child in a family of seven children is 3.8 points for boys and 1.5 points for girls (each sex having a mean of 50 and a standard deviation of 10). By contrast, there is no sibsize difference between the sexes in Cycle III. We must conclude, therefore, that not only are sex differences in cognition relatively small but that sibsize differences do not greatly alter this conclusion. Just why the Cycle II data show the differences on arithmetic that they do cannot be interpreted by us with the data at hand.

The Riddle of the Only Child

Although only children presumably enjoy undiluted parental attention and resources, we have seen that singletons do not always do better educationally, and in terms of ability, than children from other small families. We have also seen that, when parental background characteristics are controlled, much of the only-child deficit, usually all of it, is removed, and only children do better than those from any other sibsize. In this section, we will examine the hypothesis that only children may be onlies because their problems led parents to stop reproducing. In effect, in some cases, parents may stop having more children because their first child has—or had as a baby—major health, ability, or developmental problems.

In Cycles II and III of the Health Examination Surveys, it has been possible to combine the results of a number of questions into indexes of problems that the children have experienced. These indexes are necessarily fairly crude since the data themselves do not allow us to weight the items in terms of importance. However, even in their relatively crude form, the indexes provide us with important information.

For Cycle II, the indexes were formed by dichotomizing responses from a variety of items into "problems/no problems" and then adding the scores. The composition of each index is schematized in the following outline, which lists the "problems" in parentheses (all other responses were coded as "no problem"):

Ability/Achievement Problems Index
1. Age-sex standardized WISC (scores below 90)
2. Grades repeated (affirmative response or indication of transfer to special education)
3. Slow learner (recommendation for help by school authorities)
4. Teacher's judgment of child's intellectual ability for age ("Clearly below average")
5. Teacher's judgment of child's academic performance ("Clearly below average")

6. Recommendation for help with mental retardation (help recommended by school authorities).

Infant Health Problems Index
1. Weight at birth (below 5.5 pounds)
2. Length of infant's stay in hospital after birth (one week or more)
3. Anything wrong with baby at birth? (Mother says "Yes")
4. Health of baby at one year (Mother says "Poor" or "Fair")
5. Anything wrong with child as baby? (Mother says "Yes")

Developmental Problems Index
1. Age when child first walked (more than 18 months old)
2. Age when child spoke first word (more than 18 months old)
3. Mother's judgment about learning speed on items like feeding self ("Slower than other children")
4. Thumb sucked at present time (Mother says "Yes")
5. Bed wetter at present time (Mother says "Yes")
6. Speech problems (Mother says "Yes")

In the case of each index the summed scores were used to construct a code for each child as follows:

0 No problems
1 One problem
2 Two problems
3 Three problems
4 Four to five problems

For Cycle III the same procedures used above to form the Ability/Achievement Problems Index and the Infant Health Problems Index were again employed, except that some of the items differed. The composition of each index is presented below:

Ability/Achievement Problems Index
1. Age–sex standardized WISC (scores below 90)
2. Teacher's judgment of child's intellectual ability for age ("Clearly below average")

3. Teacher's evaluation of child's academic performance ("Clearly below average")
4. Mother's evaluation of rate of mental development ("Too slow")

Infant Health Problems Index
1. Weight at birth (below 5.5 pounds)
2. Anything wrong with baby at birth? (Mother says "Yes")
3. Any health difficulty with child before one year? (Mother says "Yes")

For each index, a code was formed listing "no problems," "one problem," and so forth, as for Cycle II.

Table 4.4 shows the indexes, by sibsize, for ability/achievement problems, development problems, and infant health problems in Cycle II, and for ability/achievement problems and infant health problems in Cycle III. We then show ability/achievement problems (Cycles II and III) and development problems (Cycle II) adjusted for parental background characteristics *and* the infant health problems index.

Looking first at the unadjusted data in Cycle II, clearly only children have more problems of all three kinds, particularly infant health problems, than children from other small families. With regard to infant health problems, only children are more disadvantaged than those of any other sibsize. However, when we control both for parental background characteristics and infant health problems and look at ability/achievement problems and development problems, the position of the only child changes quite markedly. As for ability problems, it has substantially fewer than any other sibsize, and its development problems are essentially equal to children in two-child families who, in turn, are below other sibsizes.

Turning to Cycle III, the unadjusted data show only children to have fewer ability/achievement problems than any other sibsize but, again, more infant health problems. With regard to ability/achievement problems, we must assume that the sample of older children represented by Cycle III may, itself, be more selected than Cycle II. Children with severe ability and health problems may have died, or been institutionalized, by ages 12 to 17 and, hence,

Table 4.4. Indexes of Ability, Development, and Infant Health Problems, White Boys and Girls, HES, Cycle II, and Ability and Infant Health Problems, HES, Cycle III.

Problem Index	Sibsize							$\bar{X}$	(S.D.)
	1	2	3	4	5	6	7+		
Cycle II				Adults					
Unadjusted Means									
Ability/Achievement	.57	.51	.52	.75	.97	1.03	1.45	.74	(1.28)
Development	.38	.34	.40	.45	.57	.48	.63	.45	(.72)
Infant Health	.63	.46	.45	.40	.37	.39	.41	.43	(.79)
Adjusted Means[a]									
Ability/Achievement	.49	.59	.61	.78	.90	.90	1.15		
Development	.34	.35	.41	.45	.56	.48	.61		
Cycle III									
Unadjusted Means									
Ability/Achievement	.48	.57	.55	.62	.79	1.00	1.09	.68	(1.00)
Infant Health	.31	.24	.23	.20	.21	.20	.19	.22	(.50)
Adjusted Means[a]									
Ability/Achievement	.41	.63	.61	.69	.75	.90	.90		

[a]Scores have been adjusted, through multiple classification analysis, for mother's and father's education, family income, family intactness, mother's labor force participation, region, child's age and sex, and infant health problems. Ns for Cycle II range between 4,006 and 4,498, and for Cycle III between 2,868 and 3,006. The higher the index number the more the problems.

have been unavailable for this sample. Children with less severe problems may have improved with therapy. In any event, when the ability/achievement problems index is adjusted for parental background and infant health problems, the ability/achievement problems among only children relative to other children are seen to be markedly less.

Bearing in mind that there are multiple reasons why a woman might not continue to a second birth, or that an only child may be in this category because a sibling has died, it is still instructive to ask whether we can get more direct evidence concerning ability/achievement problems as an influence on selection for being an only child. For example, are such problems more evident among only children born of mothers whose pregnancy came at the typical childbearing age (and, hence, who could have readily continued reproduction, other factors being equal), or are they more common among only children of women in their thirties at childbirth (who could well have been impeded by age, in many cases, from further reproduction). And, are the problems more evident among only children than among the firstborns of other small families?

For this comparison, we will look at Cycle III, where we can rely that families are reasonably complete at smaller sibsizes. From table 4.5, we see that, indeed, the only children of younger mothers have more ability/achievement problems than the firstborns of women who went ahead to have a second child. In addition, the only children of mothers who were younger at childbirth have a great many more ability/achievement problems than the only children of mothers who were in their thirties at childbirth (who have *fewer* such problems than the firstborns of mothers who went ahead to have a second and a third child). These results thus suggest that only children, in addition to having the advantages of undiluted parental resources, are also in some measure selected for problems—health problems and ability problems.

This surmise is made more telling when we divide into two classes the WISC scores for only children, by the ages of their mothers at childbirth—under 29 and 29 to 39 (table 4.6). We see, first of all, that only children born to older mothers have consistently higher scores than do those born to younger mothers. Moreover, when youngsters who are subnormal are excluded the scores for the children of mothers who were younger at childbirth rise

Table 4.5. Index of Ability/Achievement Problems among Only Children and Firstborns in Two- and Three-Child Families Whose Mothers Were under 29 and 29 to 39 at the Birth of the Children, White Boys and Girls, HES, Cycle III.

	Sibsize Among Firstborns		
Mother's Age at Birth of Child	*1*	*2*	*3*
Unadjusted Means			
< 29	.60	.50	.48
29–39	.34	.41	.42
Adjusted Means[a]			
< 29	.52	.53	.52
29–39	.33	.45	.42

[a]Scores have been adjusted through multiple classification analysis, for mother's and father's education, family income, region, and family intactness. The number of cases for firstborns in small families is 645 for women under age 29 at the birth of the child, and 187 for women age 29 to 39 at the birth of the child.

more markedly than do the scores for children whose mothers were older when they were born. So much is this the case, that the differences between the children of younger-at-birth and older-at-birth mothers are essentially obliterated.

Obviously, conclusive evidence regarding selective mechanisms affecting only children must come from prospective studies, and prospective studies that are so perfectly executed that selection bias does not again prevail. We believe, however, that we have established here fairly compelling evidence for the existence of such selective mechanisms regarding only children. These mechanisms call into doubt the wisdom of interpreting only-child deficits exclusively, or even primarily, in terms of socialization disadvantages, before we have asked the prior question of why a child does not have siblings.

CONCLUSION

This chapter has addressed the question of whether the inverse relation of sibsize and educational attainment reflects in part an

Table 4.6. Age–Sex Standardized WISC Scores for Only Children and Only Children Excluding Subnormals by Age of Mother at Birth of Child, White Boys and Girls, HES, Cycles II and III, Adjusted Means.[a]

	Age of Mother at Birth			
Survey and Child's Age	Under 29	(N)	29–39	(N)
Cycle II				
Children of all Ages				
All Only Children	102	(84)	106	(76)
Subnormals Excluded	107	(68)	109	(67)
Children Age 9–12				
All Only Children	102	(36)	105	(44)
Subnormals Excluded	109	(27)	109	(38)
Cycle III				
Children of all Ages				
All Only Children	102	(81)	107	(103)
Subnormals Excluded	108	(62)	109	(96)

[a]Scores have been adjusted by multiple classification analysis, for mother's and father's education, family income, region, and family intactness. Subnormals are those who score below 90 on the WISC.

inverse relation of cognitive ability and number of siblings. Our analysis has used the cognitive testing data from the surveys of young people discussed in our introductory chapter, and has controlled for parental background characteristics. Additionally, it has made use of the distinction between verbal and nonverbal abilities that has, in prior research, been found to be of importance when relating sibsize and cognitive ability.

In all of the studies, verbal ability is found to be related negatively to sibsize and nonverbal ability is seen to bear little or no relation. The strongest relationship between verbal ability and sibsize—close to a standard deviation difference between those from small and large families—is among the children who have been least selected by the educational process (those in Cycle II of the Health Examination Survey). In an effort to test whether the diminution of a sibsize effect on verbal ability among high school students might be due simply to the fact that deficits among those from large families are made up by the educational process, we analyzed data for adults from the General Social Survey. The survey administers a vocabulary test to the adult respondents interviewed. This retrospective approach overcomes the selection biases involved in sampling high school students. Controlling for both the respondent's and the respondent's mother's education, we found a significant verbal deficit among adults from large families. This finding suggests that individuals from large families do not make up the deficit over time and that the diminution of the sibsize/verbal ability relationship among advanced high school students is probably due primarily to selection.

Two features of our results have important methodological implications for the claim that the negative relation of sibsize and ability merely reflects the fact that more intelligent parents have smaller families. First, we have controlled for parental education, which is a partial control for parental IQ. Second, the fact that sibsize is specifically associated with verbal but not nonverbal ability also casts doubt on the claim that the association is due primarily to inherited IQ. We should note as well that verbal ability is known from prior research to be related to interaction with adults and, as well, is a strong predictor of educational success.

In sum, we have evidence of a strong relationship between sibsize and an aspect of cognitive ability that is both responsive to differential parental attention and predicts educational attainment. Moreover, because we have instituted partial controls for parental cognitive ability, and because our analysis indicates that only a specific aspect of a youngster's intellectual ability is responsive to sibsize differences, we do not believe our interpretation is spurious.

Finally, we have addressed the question of why the only children in some data sets do not do as well as might be expected given the fact that they are the sole object of parental attention. We have already documented that the only child sometimes suffers from coming from a broken family with its attendant loss of income and advantages. In this chapter, we examined whether some only children may not be singletons because of problems peculiar to themselves. In particular, we have found that only children in our samples appear disproportionately to have had health problems in infancy. We also have found that ability/achievement problems were particularly prevalent among only children whose mothers were young enough at their birth to have been able, other things equal, to continue childbearing. These results concerning the only child, coupled with those indicating selectivity by parental characteristics (such as marital disruption), suggest that, insofar as only children are seen to have "problems," it may be gratuitous to ascribe such difficulties to socialization. The relatively few only children who do not excel would appear to be singletons as a consequence of selection that is often related to the problems under consideration.

5

BIRTH ORDER, INTELLECTUAL ABILITY, AND EDUCATIONAL ATTAINMENT

If family size bears a negative relation to both cognitive ability and educational attainment, is this effect mitigated, on average, by birth order? Are there systematic birth-order effects (over and above sibsize effects) that would lead us to modify our results so far? In this chapter, we will consider intellectual ability and educational attainment separately in relation to birth order. This separate treatment is necessary because our theoretical expectations differ somewhat as between the two dependent variables, the confounders are not identical, and our measures of intelligence are for children whereas our educational data are for adults. In each case—intellectual ability and educational attainment—we will first discuss what we expect theoretically, and then present an outline of frequent and important confounding factors as they have related to prior research. We will then turn to our own analysis.

THEORETICAL EXPECTATIONS ABOUT THE RELATION OF BIRTH ORDER AND IQ

There have been numerous reviews of the research on birth order and intelligence, as well as other dependent variables (Jones 1931; Sampson 1965; Kammeyer 1967; Adams 1972; Schooler 1972). All of these reviews emphasize that the literature on birth order is not distinguished by systematic theoretical expectations. Rather, much of it has involved the unexpected "discovery" of some birth-order difference and, then, an ad hoc effort to explain it (Kammeyer 1967). Thinking in terms of intellectual ability or achievement (as distinct from personality characteristics, or psychological variables), have we any reason to expect birth-order differences? This attempt to outline possible reasons takes as a given that the data are not for actual siblings. Rather, the data sets must be thought of as pertaining to individuals from different families.

Reasons for Expecting Birth-Order Differences in Intelligence

I. *Purposive differences in parental treatment*

This reason presupposes that parents would intentionally treat children of different birth orders differently so that the results would be systematic over samples of populations. In modern circumstances, it is difficult to imagine that this would occur and, hence, it seems improbable to expect that the oldest child, for example, would be systematically favored, or a younger one ignored, to a degree that would affect IQ.

II. *Patterned circumstantial differences, over the family cycle, in parents' biological capacity for reproduction, in dilution by other children of parents' resources, or in siblings treatment of each other.*

   i. *Biological capability of parents.* Later-born children occur to older parents who may have some DNA impairment, or other impairment associated with prior childbearing or age. In addition, being older, parents may have less energy for interaction and stimulation of later-born children.

   ii. *Dilution by other children of parents' resources.* Children of particular birth orders may be uniquely favored or disfavored regarding, in particular, parental attention and interaction and, hence, motivation to learn.

Birth Position	Advantages	Disadvantages
Oldest	1. An only child for a period of time.	1. Parents inexperienced.
	2. Parents at peak of enthusiasm if child wanted at that time.	2. Parents may be harried and irritable if child not wanted so soon after marriage.

		3. Child is being reared during all or most of remaining pregnancies and arrivals of other siblings.
Middle	1. Parents have experience.	1. Younger siblings are arriving and requiring care from parents.
		2. Parental enthusiasm may have lessened somewhat.
Youngest	1. Child may experience some of advantages of only child as far as parental interaction is concerned. 2. Parents are very experienced.	1. Parents may be bored with reproduction and be unwilling to pay much attention.

iii. *Contribution of siblings to the child's environment.* Clearly, siblings cannot be thought of only as detractors from parental resources. Having brothers and sisters may constitute a positive contribution to a child's environment and learning, and this contribution may vary systematically according to the child's position in the birth-order hierarchy.

Birth Position	*Advantages*	*Disadvantages*
Oldest	1. May gain an advantage from teaching younger children. 2. No older siblings to short-circuit learning by "telling."	1. No older siblings to act as mentors.
Middle	1. Same as oldest (above).	1. Older siblings may short-circuit learning by "telling."

	2. Older siblings may teach.	
Youngest	1. Older siblings may teach.	1. Same as middle (above).

Even this brief outline of superficially reasonable expectations about birth-order effects on intelligence points up how conflicting and mutually offsetting many of these possible effects may be. If we were to add expectations concerning possible sex differences to our outline, it does not take much imagination to recognize that we have no very good reasons for expecting highly patterned ability differences by birth order. Insofar as investigators derive such expectations from *a priori* hypotheses, such a derivation comes from systematically ignoring or overlooking countervailing expectations that could be considered equally plausible. It is hardly surprising, therefore, that most thinking about birth order and ability has emanated from adventitious "discoveries" of birth-order differences in empirical data.

POSSIBLE CONFOUNDERS IN THE ANALYSIS OF BIRTH-ORDER DIFFERENCES IN INTELLIGENCE

The analysis of birth-order differences in intelligence is not only beset by weak theory regarding the determinants of this presumed association, but it is also subject to weak theory concerning a large number of potential (and powerful) confounders when an apparent association is discovered. Although these confounders are not uniquely mysterious and arcane, they have frequently been overlooked because of the relatively casual and ad hoc approach to birth-order effects already noted in our discussion of predictors of birth-order differences. Investigators become interested in birth order when an "effect" turns up and happens to be startling. It is then relatively simple to weave an "explanation" out of some assortment of the advantages and disadvantages we have just discussed. It is seldom appreciated by researchers that expanding the sibsize distribution to a sibsize–birth-order matrix involves a level of specificity regarding, for example, the ages of parents and the periods of their lives during which particular children are born and reared that may be averaged out when one looks at sibsize alone.

It is hardly surprising, therefore, that research on birth order and intelligence has produced perplexing disagreements concerning *whether* a birth-order effect exists and, if there is such an effect, what is its nature (for example, see, Jones 1931; Anastasi 1956; Sampson 1965; Adams 1972; Schooler 1972; Berbaum, Markus, and Zajonc 1982; Galbraith 1982*a*, 1982*b*, 1982*c*; Ernst and Angst 1983). As we shall see, it is easy to be victimized by confounding factors, and exceptionally difficult, given the data available, to avoid all of them. As a start, we shall attempt to systematize some of the major confounding elements in the study of birth-order effects. A share of these confounders have been recognized in a scattered fashion in the literature, but some, I believe, have not been noted before.

Outline of Confounding Factors in the Analysis of Birth Order

1. The prevalence fallacy
2. Absence of controls for sibsize
3. Period effects
4. Parental background differences by birth order
5. Parental background differences by sibsize
6. Differences in child-spacing
7. Selection biases:
    a. Age truncation biases
    b. School-grade attrition biases (for example, seniors in high school do not include high school drop-outs who may differ from seniors in sibsize and birth order)
    c. Other selection biases.

We may now consider each of these confounders in detail.

The Prevalence Fallacy

Probably the most obvious problem with some of the more striking findings on birth order is the bias introduced by looking at the proportionate *prevalence* of a particular birth order, or birth orders, in a selected group—for example, people of eminence or great talent, students taking a particular test, or those entering college at a particular time (for a discussion, see, Price and Hare 1969; Schooler 1972). All such research concludes that "*x* percent of persons who have a particular characteristic (eminent men, or college entrants, or students having IQs of 140 or over) are of a given birth order (firstborn, last born, and so forth) and that, therefore, this birth order is highly desirable." Such prevalence studies with results sufficiently startling to report are subject to the bias of an excess of the birth order in question in the underlying population. Thus, to take college entrants in 1965, for example, a marked excess of firstborns is due to at least two major biases: On average, these students will be 18 years old and hence have a high probability of having been born in 1947—a year of the highest proportion of first-order births in our recorded past. Moreover, college students come from small families (disproportionately) and, hence, from families in which first-order births make up a high proportion of all births. So, not only will college entrants in 1965 share a disproportionate "firstborn-ness" with all 18-year-olds, but the small sibsize bias among middle- and upper-class young people will further potentiate the birth-order bias. As Schooler (and likewise Price and Hare) emphasize, the problems of bias in such prevalence studies remove all such "findings" from serious consideration.

From here on out, therefore, our discussion will relate to studies that involve the computation of values of a dependent variable by birth order and that compare the results for different birth orders. However, even when we thus avoid the prevalence fallacy, we are far from out of the woods regarding confounders.

Absence of Controls for Sibsize

As with many areas of scientific inquiry, knowledge is far from linear in birth-order research. Although it has long been recognized that, without a control for sibsize, birth-order effects will be confounded with sibsize effects (Jones 1931), this error continues to be made from time to time. For some recent examples, the reader may refer to Record, McKeown, and Edwards (1969) and King and Lillard (1983), in which sibsize effects are interpreted as birth-order effects.

Period Effects

The fact that children of different birth orders appear and are reared at different times in the parents' lives may mean that such children are subjected to markedly different economic and social conditions as they mature. This may be particularly true for children from large families, but it can occur in small families as well during periods of rapid social and economic change. It seems reasonable to assume that such marked differences in environment might affect children through effects on their parents and on the latter's ability to provide a good learning environment. For example, if in 1968 one decides to study a sample of 18-year-olds, those from families of, say, six children will have experienced quite different periods in the U.S. economy depending on whether they are the oldest or the youngest. The oldest in one family, born in 1950, will come from a family that started its childbearing and childrearing during boom times economically—from 1950 onwards. But the youngest from another family—also born in 1950—will come from a family that started its childbearing and rearing around 1930—during the Depression. The following diagram may help to clarify this point.

Test date is 1968, subjects are eighteen years old

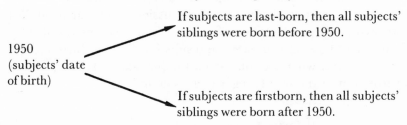

1950
(subjects' date
of birth)

If subjects are last-born, then all subjects' siblings were born before 1950.

If subjects are firstborn, then all subjects' siblings were born after 1950.

On the one hand, the confounding effects of a specific period are, of course, exaggerated in studies where individuals of only one age (or a very narrow age range) have been included—age truncation bias—since everyone has been subjected to the same historial event (being of the same age and the same cohort). On the other hand, the period effects are easier to isolate (once the investigator is aware of them) when the age range of the subjects is narrower. Nonetheless, the exact pinpointing of period effects may be difficult unless one has fairly precise information on child-spacing and the interval between the parents' marriage and the birth of the first child.

A good example of what appear to be systematic period effects interpreted as birth-order effects may be found in the data from Breland's study of National Merit Scholarship Qualifying Test takers and Belmont and Marolla's data on young Dutch males

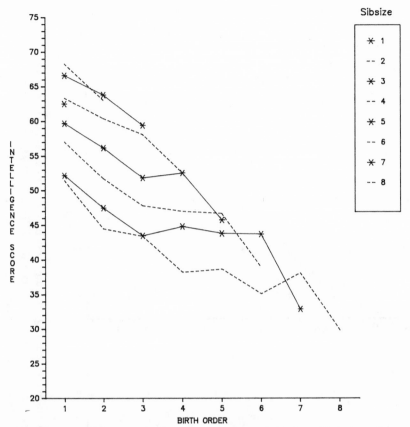

Figure 5.1. T-Scores on Raven Progressive Matrices Test by Sibsize and Birth Order among 386,114 19-Year-Old Dutch Males Who Were Survivors of Children Born during 1944–1947. Data from Belmont and Marolla (1973). Scores have been restandardized with a mean of 50 and standard deviation of 10.

(both of which have been referred to previously). Both studies show a marked decline in intellectual performance by birth order within sibsize (figs. 5.1 and 5.2).[1] A share of this decline is doubtless due to differences in parental education by birth order (to be discussed shortly). In addition, the last-born children in the Dutch study suffered unique problems (also to be discussed). But, a share is also quite probably due to period effects to which both studies are particularly vulnerable since both concentrate on a highly restricted

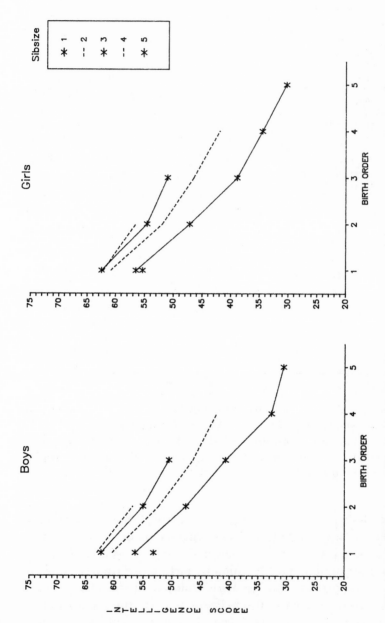

Figure 5.2. T-Scores on National Merit Scholarship Qualifying Test by Sibsize and Birth Order among 794,589 Eleventh-Grade Boys and Girls, United States, 1965. Data from Breland (1974). Scores have been restandardized with a mean of 50 and standard deviation of 10.

age grouping (17-year-olds in Breland's case and 19-year-olds in the Belmont and Marolla case). In fact, since the Breland youngsters were, on average, born in 1948, and the young Dutch men were born in 1944–1947, the economic period effects were similar. The oldest (firstborn) children were born to families that were beginning after the Depression, and as World War II was ending or over. On average, the families thus enjoyed improving circumstances as the youngsters were growing up. The later-born children (particularly those in large families) were born to parents whose reproduction started many years earlier—at the beginning of (or during) the Depression. Thus, most of the childbearing and rearing of the families of these later-born children occurred in unfavorable circumstances. It is unlikely that such circumstances left these families in a highly advantaged position to do well by their youngest children. Thus, as we see in figures 5.1 and 5.2, higher-order births do less well than lower-order ones—for period reasons among others.

Parental Background Differences by Birth Order within Sibsize and over All Sibsizes

The introduction of birth order as a variable necessitates controlling for differences in parental age (and, hence, most probably parental educational attainment) by birth order within sibsize. For example, in a group of 18-year-olds, all of whom are being studied in 1968, those who are the oldest of a family of six siblings were born to parents who *started* childbearing when the subject individual was born—1950. The youngest child in a family of six among these 18-year-olds was born to parents who *completed* childbearing in 1950, and who may have started it 20 years earlier, in 1930. Since, in most Western countries including the United States, educational levels of the population were rising over that time period, these young people's parents represent very different educational cohorts. If one does not control for the parents' educational levels among birth orders one may be simply measuring the effects, not of birth order, but of parents' educational differences within the same sibsize. Again, since parents' socioeconomic status was not controlled in either the Breland or the Belmont and Marolla data, the marked decline by birth order within sibsize of the intellectual scores would appear to be in part a result of differential parental education—especially among children from large sibsizes. This differential may be added to the period effects already noted.

As has been noted previously, there are important parental background differences by sibsize. In looking at birth order, it is not sufficient to control for parental background differences by birth order *within* each sibsize; one has to control over all sibsizes as well. In other words, one must control for parental background differences among second-born children across all sibsizes containing such children, and the same is true of third-born, fourth-born, and so forth, rather than solely controlling for background differences between birth orders within each sibsize. If this is not done, the relative values by sibsize will be affected and, in particular, the position of the only child may be downgraded relative to children from other small families. The lack of controls for parental socioeconomic status over sibsizes in both the Breland and the Belmont and Marolla data may account for the unusual position of the only child in both studies, as we have already noted.

Differences in Child-spacing

Theoretically, child-spacing differences may be confounded with birth-order differences, if systematically biased variations in child-spacing by birth order occur. For example, this confounding would take place if last-born children characteristically appeared after a longer interval than children of other birth orders. In practice, it seems unlikely that such systematic spacing differences by birth order would occur over large samples. This is particularly true for younger subjects in the United States since child-spacing itself has become much less variable than in the past. Infant mortality and breastfeeding (which created "spaces" in the past) have declined, and family planning has led to a purposive concentration of childbearing with a sharply defined ending point (Whelpton, Campbell, and Patterson 1966; U.S. Bureau of the Census 1976; Bumpass, Rindfuss, and Janosik 1978). Women have begun childbearing in their late teens and early twenties, and most have curtailed it before age 30. However, insofar as differential child-spacing does exist, certain kinds of samples may lead to systematic child-spacing effects that can show up as birth-order effects. This problem is evident in age-truncation biases to be discussed in the next section.

Selection Effects

We have already seen, with regard to the only child (considered as a sibsize), that selection effects can be important in affecting the relative position of children from a particular sibsize. We have also seen that selection effects, such as when seniors in high school are studied, can influence relative sibsize standings on IQ tests or National Merit Scholarship Qualifying Test findings. This is because less able young people in large families are more likely to have dropped out of high school than less able young people in small ones, and this differential drop-out rate has biased the IQ–sibsize relationship. Now we must consider how selection can affect birth-order findings.

The reader should consider this discussion to be illustrative only, since there are probably as many selection effects as there are research designs.

Age-truncation biases.   The problem of age truncation (sampling a single age or a very restricted age group) occurs quite frequently in birth-order research on intelligence because young people are being sampled. For example, if one has sampled 11-year-olds, those who are the oldest and from large families *must* come from closely spaced families because all of the children in the sibsize must have been born during an 11-year period. The youngest 11-year-olds from large families have not necessarily come from such closely spaced sibsizes. Thus, it is not at all uncommon to find that, among youthful samples, there may be an upturn for later-born children in the dependent variable (say, in IQ), an upturn that cannot be interpreted out of hand as a birth-order effect. The upturn at later birth orders in IQ testing is a not-infrequent result among age-restricted samples of young people, as figures 5.3 through 5.5 illustrate.[2]

We should emphasize here that in general very wide spacing in large families (six or seven or more siblings) is not possible. For example, women beginning childbearing at age 20 and having a child every five years would be limited to five children even assuming that their last child was born when the woman was 40. It is thus not practical to think of wide spacing in families of six or seven or more as a generally compensatory mechanism allowing parents to provide more attention to each child—although obviously an individual child, or even two children, can be widely spaced in an

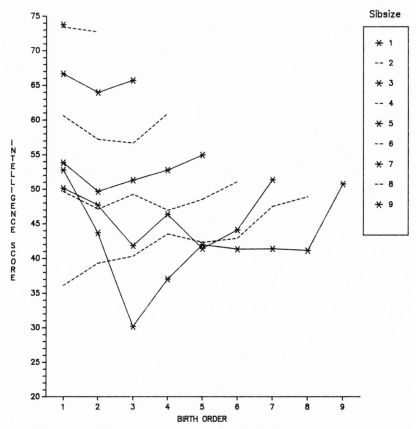

Figure 5.3. T-Scores on Group Test of Intelligence by Sibsize and Birth Order among Scottish School Children Age 11 in 1947. Data from the Scottish Council for Research in Education (1949). Scores have been restandardized with a mean of 50 and standard deviation of 10.

otherwise closely spaced family. Although extremes in spacing are uncommon, it would be desirable to know more about spacing in data sets such as we have been using because such information would provide an important test of the dilution hypothesis. Other things equal, we would expect widely spaced youngsters to have characteristics associated with smaller family size.

School-grade attrition biases.   Just as youngsters from large sibsizes may be selected out of school at an early age, it is also not improbable that youngsters of particular birth orders may stay in school

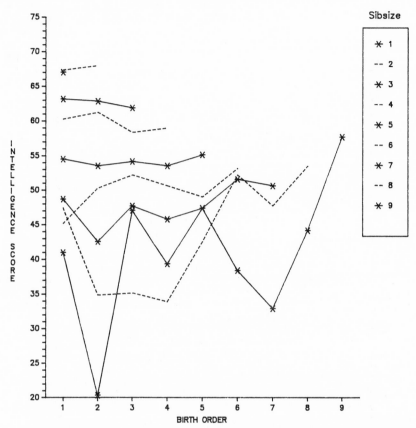

Figure 5.4. T-Scores on Benedetto Test of Intelligence by Sibsize and Birth Order among 100,000 French School Children Age 6–14 in 1965. Data from Institut National d'Etudes Demographiques (1973). Scores have been restandardized with a mean of 50 and standard deviation of 10.

or drop out early, particularly in large families. For example, we shall see in a later section that, in large families, youngest and next-to-youngest children seem to stay in school the longest, whereas "early" middle-born children in such families (for example, third-born in families of six, seven, and eight or more) seem to be most deprived. It would appear, therefore, that sampling seniors in high school (and college students) for ability tests may well be selecting students from large families by birth order as well as by sibsize. Since last-born and later-born children appear to enjoy some economic advantages in large families (to be discussed), such

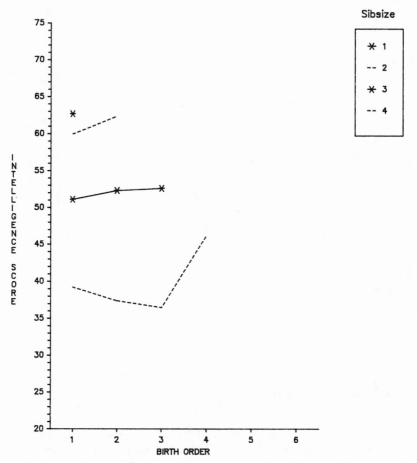

Figure 5.5. T-Scores on Moray House Picture Test by Sibsize and Birth Order among 9523 Aberdeen School Children Age 7 in 1962. Data from Illsley (1967). Scores have been restandardized with a mean of 50 and standard deviation of 10.

children may be less selected intellectually, other things equal, than earlier-born children in large families and, hence, on this count test less well as high school seniors (or college students) than youngsters from large families of other birth orders.

Other selection biases.   The difficulty of distinguishing selection effects from birth-order effects is again illustrated from the Belmont and Marolla data on 19-year-old Dutchmen. As may be seen in figure 5.1, not only do the results by birth order decline within each sibsize, but the last-born child in each sibsize takes a particularly sharp drop. The acute drop for each last-born child is quite different from the curves by birth order in any other data (figs. 5.2 through 5.5). It seems highly probable that this systematic drop in scores for all last-born children is related to the effects of the catastrophic famine in Holland during 1944 and 1945 (Smith 1947*a* and 1947*b*; Stein and others 1972 and 1975; Blake 1981*a*). In brief, since the famine drastically affected fertility, fetal mortality, and infant deaths, being an only child or other last-born child was a status that would occur selectively in those families worst hit by the famine (those families in which the woman could not become pregnant or stay pregnant to term or in which a next-born child would die). Moreover, since the adult death rate rose as well, many only and last-born children who were born during the 1944–1947 period, were partially or completely orphaned by the famine and, hence, remained "last-born." Again, on average this adult mortality would occur in those families worst affected by the famine. Since severe starvation in childhood is known to affect intellectual functioning adversely, it is hardly surprising that only and other last-born children in the Dutch data evidence an unexpectedly sharp drop in performance on the Raven Progressive Matrices test. The sharp drop among youngest children in the Dutch data led Zajonc (1976) to speculate that it was occasioned by a "teaching deficit." According to Zajonc, youngest children lagged intellectually because they (along with only children) had no siblings to whom they could act as mentors. In fact, I think it can be shown that this acute effect in the Dutch data is due to selection bias and that it is inadvisable to construct ad hoc substantive explanations for it.

To summarize our discussion so far, we have seen that theoretical expectations for birth-order differences in ability are weak and conflicting. We have no systematic, clear-cut reasons for expecting such effects. Moreover, when birth-order effects are found in empirical data, we have suggested that such effects are probably a consequence of one or more confounders—that the interpretation of effects as due to birth order may well be spurious. Different confounders will produce different "effects," and it is, therefore, hardly surprising that birth-order curves are so varied and difficult to interpret.

Before turning to our own empirical analysis of whether there are birth-order differences in cognitive ability, we will consider in some detail the use, by Zajonc, of birth-order data to interpret the trend in SAT scores in the United States.

BIRTH ORDER AND SAT SCORES, OR SIBSIZE AND SAT SCORES?

Since the publication in 1976 of an article by Robert Zajonc, "Family Configuration and Intelligence," the topic of birth order and cognitive ability has achieved renewed prominence. In that article, Zajonc used data on birth order as a proxy for information on spacing or birth interval, because, according to his confluence model (already discussed in chapter 4), he believes that short birth intervals decrease the intellectual environment in the family. This decrease in intellectual environment with short birth intervals occurs, according to Zajonc, because as infants are born (with an intellectual level of zero), they reduce the overall intellectual equation in the family. Close spacing implies a high proportion of infant and childlike abilities in the family in relation to the abilities of adults and older children. Zajonc (1976) emphatically denies that birth order per se is an important variable, it is only influential insofar as it is accompanied by close spacing.

> In itself birth order is not an important variable. The model predicts that its effects are mediated entirely by the age spacing between siblings. . . . Hence, with large enough age gaps between siblings (allowing sufficient time for the earlier born to mature), the negative effects of birth order can be nullified and even reversed. (p. 227)

Using average birth order by year for the United States, Zajonc reasoned (on the basis of the confluence model) that one could predict the SAT scores in the United States and account for their decline, as well as project a future rise. The average annual birth order is simply an average of the distribution of annual births according to whether they are first births, second births, third births, and so on. In the 1976 article, Zajonc predicted, on the basis of what he felt was a past association of SAT scores and average birth order, that the scores would rise after about 1980, since average birth orders were declining. The figure from Zajonc's 1976

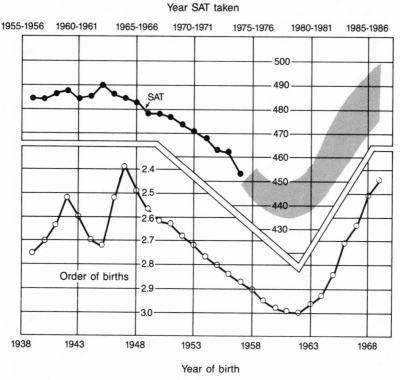

Figure 5.6. Average Order of Live Births in the United States, 1939 to 1969, and Average SAT Scores for the First Eighteen Cohorts. Future SAT averages are predicted to lie within the shaded area. Data from Zajonc (1976).

article is reproduced here as figure 5.6. In figure 5.7 we have extended the data on average birth order and SAT scores backward in time to the year of the first published scores, and forward in time to the scores for 1985. We also show the verbal and math scores separately.

When this entire range of SAT scores and average birth orders is presented, it is evident that average annual birth order is not as felicitous a predictor of SAT scores as it appeared to be in the incomplete figure presented by Zajonc. For example, although the SATs are at a high point in the early 1950s, the average birth order was as high among these test takers (those born 17 to 18 years

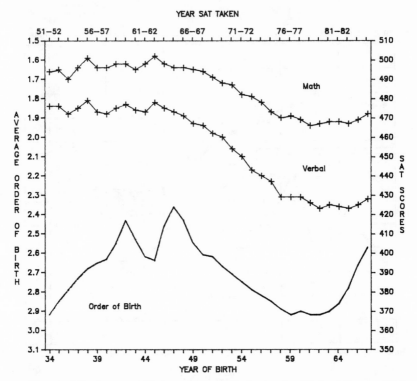

Figure 5.7. Average Order of Live Births in the United States 1934–1967, and Verbal and Mathematics SAT Scores 1951–1952 through 1984–1985. SAT scores are from Eckland (1982) and personal communication with the College Entrance Examination Board. Order of birth data are derived from National Center for Health Statistics (1950) and each respective year 1948–1968 (Vital Statistics Natality Volumes).

previously in 1934) as it was for test takers born in the early 1960s. This means that the average birth order was identical for the birth years of the SAT takers who were at both the high and the low points of the SAT scores.

Why does average annual birth order work so poorly as a predictor of SAT scores? At least two factors are operating. One concerns problems with average annual birth order as an indicator, and the other is differential selection bias among the SAT takers.

To understand why average annual birth order is a poor indicator, one must first be clear about why Zajonc (1976) believes it is a good proxy for birth-spacing.

High values of average order of births for a given year indicate that children born that year have on the average more older siblings and come from larger families . . . [average order of births] combines two important factors of intellectual development, family size and birth rank. (p. 232)

Implicit in his reasoning is that, on average, large families involve closer spacing. But, is average order of annual births a good indicator of either family size or spacing? The answer regarding family size is, of course, negative because although being of a higher birth order must mean that one comes from a large family (as Zajonc recognized), the converse is not true—being from a lower birth order in any given year tells us nothing about the individual's sibsize. Any number of children can be born after the first or the second, and so forth. Nor, assuming one knows family size, could one predict spacing from that knowledge because, as we have discussed already, although larger families inevitably constrain shorter spacing, on average, than smaller families, small families may be spaced closely out of parental choice, as has been true in the recent fertility experience of the United States.

However, if one believes (as we do) that family size is important for ability because of the dilution of parents' resources (as well, perhaps, because of a heavy representation of very young "intelligences" in large families, as Zajonc assumes), then one can obtain an accurate direct measure of the average family size of women who gave birth in each of the years in question (these are the birth years for 17-year-olds taking the SAT between 1952 and 1985). This is possible because, in each of the years, we know that the women giving birth had to be in the reproductive ages and, hence, we can date their birth cohorts and use the cohort fertility tables for the United States to read off the completed family size of women who were having children in those years. In actual practice, since most births (approximately three-quarters) in each year occurred to women age 20–34, we can use the completed family size data for those age groups in each year. The data, plotted in figure 5.8, thus represent the completed family size of women age 20–24, 25–29, and 30–34 in each year of birth of the SAT takers (1934, 1935, 1936, etc.) averaged into one curve (for women 20 to 34). An additional curve has been computed for more recent years in which information for 20- to 25-year-old mothers was not available. These

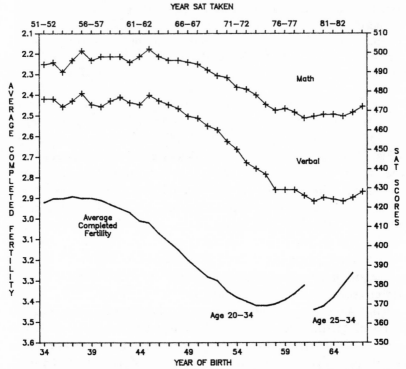

Figure 5.8. Average Completed Fertility (at Age 40–44) of American Mothers Who Were Age 20–34 or 25–34 in the Year of Birth of the Test Takers, and Verbal and Mathematics SAT Scores 1951–1952 through 1984–1985. SAT scores are from Eckland (1982) and personal communication with the College Entrance Examination Board. Fertility data are derived from Heuser (1976) and National Center for Health Statistics (1980).

curves involve weighting the completed fertility for each age group of women according to the group's importance as a contributor to the reproduction of that year.

It is evident from figure 5.8 that there is a close correspondence between the completed family size of the women who gave birth in each of the years 1934 through 1966 and the SAT scores of the youngsters born in those years. In particular, the family-size curve conforms rather well to the verbal SAT scores. However, for the most recent dates, family size goes down more sharply and sooner than the SAT scores rise. This difference may result from differen-

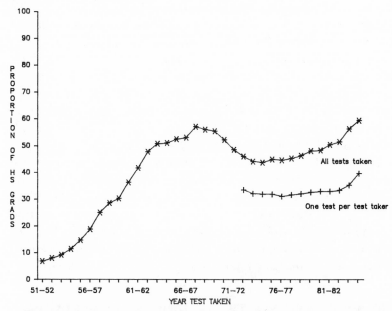

Figure 5.9. Percentage of High School Graduates Who Took SATs in Each of the Years 1951–1952 through 1984–1985. (The complete series is based on all SATs taken in a given year regardless of grade level of the test taker, or whether test takers repeated the test in that year. These data are from a personal communication with the Educational Testing Service. The series from 1971–1972 onward is based on only one test per student. These data are from Educational Testing Service [1984] and personal communication with the CEEB. Data on high school graduates are from Plisko and Stern [1985].)

tial selection bias among the SAT test takers, to be discussed in a moment. At this point, we may simply emphasize that an understanding of the inverse relation of the SAT scores and the family size of the test takers does not require a resort to data on birth order.

Although the family size and SAT curves are tantalizingly congruent over much of the period in question, one should be skeptical about overinterpreting this apparent association. SAT takers have been a highly variable percentage of high school graduates over the years as may be seen from figure 5.9. Prior to 1971, we have no direct information on the socioeconomic biases involved and none concerning family-size selection over time. Indirect analysis, using

1960 Project Talent data and 1972 National Longitudinal Survey data, has suggested that the socioeconomic backgrounds of the test takers declined during the 1960s so that SES compositional effects on the SAT declines during that period appear clear (Eckland 1982). Some SES compositional effects appear to have continued during the 1970s, but these are not sufficient to explain the poor results after 1973. It is possible, therefore, that family size (itself correlated with SES) may be implicated. When we bear in mind, however, that high school graduates are themselves selected by sibsize, the further selection among high school graduates of SAT takers makes it remarkable (perhaps too remarkable!) that the family size/SAT curves conform as well as they do. Rather than overstating the importance of this congruence, we would caution that widespread interest in the causes of variability in SAT scores should lead to the acquisition of actual information on the socio-economic background *and* family sizes of the SAT takers.

EMPIRICAL ANALYSIS OF BIRTH-ORDER DIFFERENCES IN INTELLIGENCE

We may now ask whether apparent birth-order effects on ability disappear if we control for at least some of the confounding discussed in the previous section. Of the studies used in this book, we have data on birth order and IQ testing from Cycles II and III of the Health Examination Surveys and from the sophomore boys in the Youth in Transition study. Consequently, we can control for sibsize, for parental background differences by sibsize, and for such differences by birth order within sibsize. We can also control for period effects in Cycles II and III to some extent because such effects average out when data involve subjects from a broader age range, and this age range also obviates much age-truncation bias. However, Youth in Transition data are more vulnerable to both period effects and age truncation bias since the youngsters are all sophomores in high school. Moreover, the children in Cycle II are still so young that age-truncation biases may also still be operating.

For the statistical analysis of birth order within sibsize, we needed to control, over all sibsizes and birth orders, for the parental background variables used in our analysis so far (parents' education, family intactness, etc.). In effect, we did not wish simply to do

a regression on each sibsize separately using the background predictors and adding birth order, because this would only have controlled, *within each sibsize,* for background differences among the different birth orders of that sibsize. We would still not have equated,
with respect to background variables, subjects who were born third
in three- and six-child families, for example, or only children with
children of other sibsizes and birth orders (for example, Steelman
and Mercy, 1980 and 1983).

Consequently, we used a two-stage analytical technique.[3] First,
we removed the effects of major background variables (mother's
and father's education, family income, mother's usual activity,
family intactness, community size, and region) on the dependent
variable through multiple regression (multiple classification
analysis). Employing the resulting residuals, we were then able to
do an analysis of birth order and ability within each sibsize. For
this purpose, we used one-way analysis of variance. In sum, we
controlled over the whole sample for background factors, and then
were free to examine birth order within sibsize.

These calculations, for all three samples and using both verbal
and nonverbal test scores, resulted in statistically significant birth-
order differences between only three comparisons (of two birth
orders each) out of 56 possible comparisons. However, although
the birth-order differences are inconsequential, the disparities between unadjusted and adjusted scores are of interest because of
what adjustment does to the relative position of the only child and
because of the shape of the curves. The unadjusted and adjusted
Vocabulary results for Cycle II are shown in figure 5.10. Quite
clearly, adjustment for the background characteristics markedly
improves the position of the only child to one of preeminence, and
it is also clear that the shape of the curves is more like those in the
Scottish and French data than in the Dutch or National Merit
Scholarship data (figs. 5.1 through 5.5). The upward tilt of the
curves may be due to age-truncation bias (since many of the children are very young), but this same pattern is manifested in the
Youth in Transition results for 16-year-old sophomores in high
school (fig. 5.11). It is also noteworthy that, except occasionally for
the oldest child, the curves for birth order by family size do not
often overlap, indicating that the negative effect of family size is
not offset by birth order.

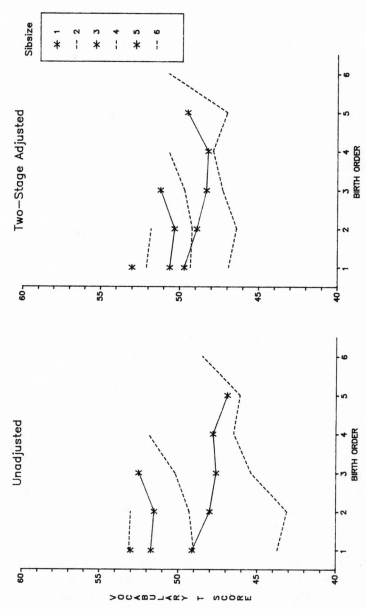

Figure 5.10. Unadjusted and Two-Stage Adjusted Age–Sex Standardized T–Scores by Sibsize and Birth Order on WISC Vocabulary, White Boys and Girls, HES, Cycle II.

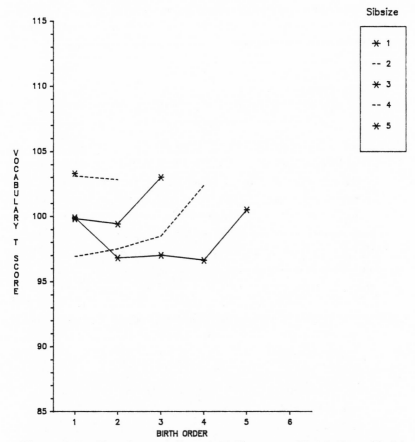

Figure 5.11. Two-Stage Adjusted T–Scores on Vocabulary (Quick Test) by Sibsize and Birth Order, White Boys, YIT, High School Sophomores.

THEORETICAL EXPECTATIONS ABOUT THE RELATION OF BIRTH ORDER AND EDUCATIONAL ATTAINMENT

When we turn to the educational attainment of adults, even assuming no major differences in intellectual endowment by birth order, we may have somewhat better reasons for expecting systematic birth-order effects than was the case with IQ. Educational attainment involves family financial resources over a protracted period of time. It is thus possible that birth order could interact with the family life cycle (and the trajectory of family economic commitments) in such a way as to have some systematic effect on the educational attainment of adults by birth order. We may again, as with intelligence, outline possible reasons for expecting birth-order differences in educational attainment.[4]

Reasons for Expecting Birth-Order Differences in Educational Attainment

I. *Purposive differences in parental treatment*

As with intelligence, it seems unlikely that parents would purposely favor or discriminate against children of a particular birth order. Given an absence of rules of inheritance and succession (and the importance of jobs versus the inheritance of fixed assets, such as land, in the modern world), it seems unlikely that we would find a systematic favoring of an oldest son relative to other sons, for example, when it comes to educational attainment. It is possible, however, given sex-role definitions, that parents might favor boys over girls in providing educational opportunities and that these sex differences in parental treatment might interact with birth order in a systematic fashion.

II. *Patterned circumstantial differences in parental treatment (or life chances) that result from the fact that children appear at, and live through, different points in the family cycle*

i. *Dilution by other children of parents' resources.* Children of particular birth orders may be uniquely favored or disfavored regarding financial resources and encouragement to continue through high school or on to college.

Birth Position	Advantages	Disadvantages
Oldest	1. Has first chance at parents' resources and may be able to continue with education at expense of children immediately following.	1. Grows up while other children are being born and growing up—a period of heavy demands. May be pressed into pseudo-parental "sacrificing" role.

Middle	1. Has a chance at resources before youngest child.	1. Parents are at peak of family demands and child may have to "sacrifice" to help.
Youngest	1. Older siblings may no longer be competing for resources.	1. Parents may have exhausted resources, or be in debt because of help to older children.
	2. May be brought up during peak income years for parents—father's income at its highest and mother may be able to work.	2. Parents are older and may begin to need help themselves. Child may get "stuck" at home as parental caretaker.
	3. Family may have consolidated consumption position—mortgage paid off, furnishings bought, etc.	

ii. *Contributions of siblings to life chances*

Birth Position	Advantages	Disadvantages
Oldest	1. None. Unlikely to get help from younger siblings.	1. May have to quit school to help support younger siblings.
Middle	1. May get help from older siblings, especially if middle is much younger.	1. May be called upon to help with younger siblings. May need to quit school.
Youngest	1. Does not need to help younger siblings and may receive help from older ones.	1. None.

In sum, although the expectations are far from clear-cut, we have some reason to think that, on average, the oldest and youngest children may have a better chance at educational attainment than middle children in large families. In two- and three-child families, it seems unlikely that systematic birth-order differences in educational attainment would be found, since children in small families are brought up in similar periods of the parents' life cycle and, as well, tend to be relatively close in age. It is possible, however, that boys will be favored over girls at any birth order when it comes to educational chances.

POSSIBLE CONFOUNDERS IN THE ANALYSIS OF BIRTH ORDER BY EDUCATIONAL ATTAINMENT

In general, we would expect to see most of the same confounders in the analysis of educational attainment as in the analysis of intelligence. We would, however, expect some changes. First, is a greater importance of period effects on educational attainment, since a person's educational chances may depend heavily on when some external event (such as a depression) impinges on the family and its ability to help with education. As we have indicated, such period effects are difficult to analyze in relation to educational attainment, but we will hope to average them out by using the wide age ranges available in our adult samples. Second, it is probably particularly important to control for parental background variables by birth order and sibsize, since the parents are a major component of the individual's life chances. Third, there will not be truncation effects by age since adults are the ones who are interviewed. And finally, there may be marked effects according to the sex compositions of the other siblings and their birth order. For example, an only boy in a family of four may have quite different educational chances, regardless of birth order, than one of four boys.

In performing this analysis, we will first present data for all cohorts combined (thereby hoping to average out period effects). We will control for parental background factors (father's education, father's SEI, farm background, and family intactness) and respondent's age, but we will not deal initially with the sex composition of the respondent's siblings in relation to birth order. Then, we will examine the data by selected age cohorts and, in addition, do some

Table 5.1. Correlation Coefficients for Birth Order with Total Years of Education by Sibsize, White Men Age 25 and Over, OCG 1962 and 1973.[a]

	Sibsize				
Survey	4	5	6	7	8
OCG 1962	.000	.714	.958	.796	.854
OCG 1973	.447	.919	.795	.903	.978

[a]For this analysis, residuals were created which are free of the effect of all background variables used for each data set. Then, a quadratic equation was fitted to the relation between birth order and total years of education (residuals) within each sibsize.

analysis of the surveys by sex composition of the birth orders within selected sibsizes. These analyses will give some sense of how much difference period and sex composition effects may make to birth-order analysis.

EMPIRICAL ANALYSIS OF BIRTH-ORDER DIFFERENCES IN EDUCATIONAL ATTAINMENT

We have data on birth order and educational attainment for three major data sets—Occupational Changes in a Generation, 1962 and 1973, and the National Fertility Study, 1970. In the interest of space, we will not present our analysis of the National Fertility Study because it completely parallels the findings from the other two analyses. As mentioned above, we have controlled for parental background factors in the same way as for the analysis of birth order and intelligence. First we created residuals that are free of the effect of background factors, and then we ran analyses of variance (ANOVAs) of birth order (within sibsize) against the dependent variable.

Turning first to Occupational Changes in a Generation, 1973 (the largest data set having information on birth order), figure 5.12 plots the adjusted means by birth order within sibsize for total years of education, as well as percentages having at least a high school education. The figure suggests a number of important points. First, on the one hand, at small sibsizes the birth-order effects

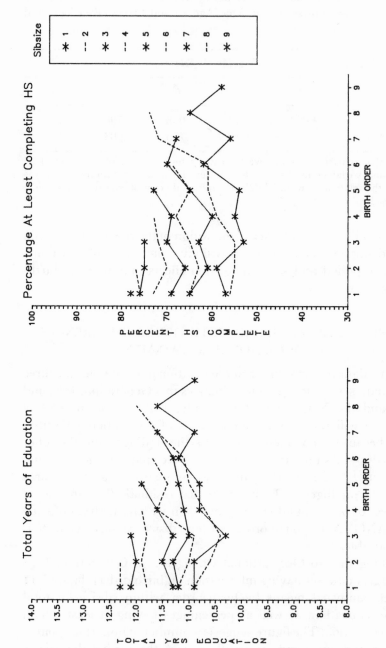

Figure 5.12. Two-Stage Adjusted Total Years of Education and Adjusted Percentages Who Have at Least a High School Education by Sibsize and Birth Order, White Men, OCG 1973.

appear negligible. Indeed, the ANOVAs indicate that, even given the very large numbers, the differences between any two birth orders in families of one to four children are not statistically significant. Second, and on the other hand, the shape of the birth-order distributions (even in small families) conforms to theoretical expectations—last-borns do better than middle-borns. Third, among large families, the parabola is very clear.[5] In fact, it is not unusual for last borns and next-to-last borns to do considerably better than firstborns. Consequently, if we fit a quadratic equation to the birth-order data within sibsize (among families of four or more siblings), we find a high correlation of birth order and educational attainment, see table 5.1.

The high correlation of birth order with total years of education and the position of later birth orders in large families suggests that, in such families, birth order can somewhat mitigate the effects of sibsize. For example, as may be seen from figure 5.12, last-born and next-to-last-born children in large families may do better educationally than children in somewhat smaller families. However, those from small families (one, two, and even three children) are obviously in a class apart. The particularly positive effect on youngest and next-to-youngest children in large families suggests that it is help from older siblings that makes a major difference, and not merely that older siblings may no longer be a drain. To achieve this last-child and next-to-last-child effect, the family size must be sufficiently large to give time for older siblings to be mature enough to help. It is probably also true that the parents in these very large families were traditional and familistic and, hence, enforced strong norms of family assistance by older children to younger ones.

This analysis also highlights the fact that we must specify the idea of the "middle" child more carefully than, for example, was the case in the Blau and Duncan (1967) analysis of the OCG 1962 data. In large families, it is not merely being "in the middle" that is detrimental, it is being in the middle at an early stage of parental family building. Actually, among large sibsizes in the OCG 1973 data, the third child is in the trough. Conditions begin to improve from fourth children onward, so that many later-born "middle" children do as well or better than firstborns.

One way of dramatizing the effect of differential birth order in

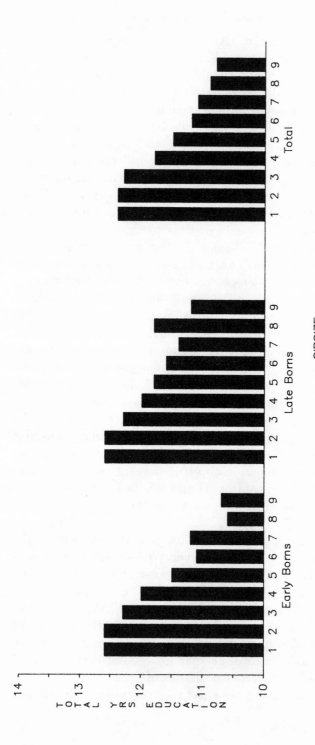

Figure 5.13. Total Years of Education Achieved by Sibsize Contrasting Early and Late-Born Children, White Men Age 25 and Over, OCG 1973. (Early borns were computed by using the only child, two children and three children and the first three children in each remaining sibsize. Late-borns were computed by using only children, two children and three children, and the last two children born in each remaining sibsize.)

large families is to look at the *sibsize* relation to total years of education but, for sibsizes larger than three, to include only the first three birth orders. This tabulation may be contrasted with the sibsize tabulation including all birth orders, and with a tabulation of education by sibsize that includes only the two last-born children in each sibsize (fig. 5.13 presents all three tabulations). As may be seen from figure 5.13, the sibsize differential is widened if one considers only the first three children in each sibsize. If, however, one looks at only the last two children in each sibsize, the sibsize differential is mitigated. It is clear that the negative effects of large sibsize on educational attainment can be partially overcome if one is among the two last-born children.

Before proceeding to Occupational Changes in a Generation, 1962, we may ask whether the adjusting process changed the shape and position of the birth-order curves for OCG 1973. Looking at figures 5.14 and 5.15 for OCG 1973 (which contasts the unadjusted and adjusted findings) we see that it did. At the smaller family levels (four and under), the adjustment corrected for depressants to the status of the only child and reversed a downward tendency of values by birth order within sibsize. At the larger sizes of family, the adjustment sharpened the parabolic tendency, getting rid of some of the depressants to the upward movement of the curve.

Turning to OCG 1962, figures 5.16 and 5.17 summarize the same analysis on this data set that we did for OCG 1973. It is evident that the results of the 1973 analysis are replicated very closely. Moreover, in table 5.1, we again find that when a quadratic is fitted to the data for birth orders within larger families, a high correlation is achieved between birth order and total years of education within each sibsize.

Although our findings concerning birth order and educational attainment in OCG 1962 and 1973 accord with the more aggregated analysis for OCG 1962 by Blau and Duncan (1967), it is worth noting that Hauser and Sewell (1985) have found no birth-order effects on education in their analysis of the followup data for respondents who were Wisconsin high school seniors in 1957 (and in a derived sample of their siblings). When study designs differ radically, it is never easy to pinpoint the causes of differing results.[6] However, we may mention a few relevant points.

First, the Hauser and Sewell data originate from a sample of

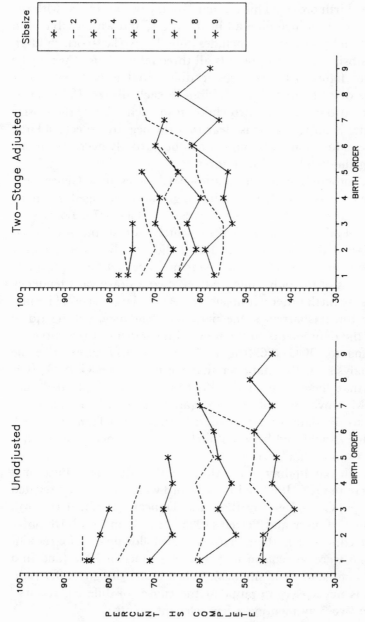

Figure 5.14. Comparison of No Adjustment and Two-Stage Adjustment, Percentages Who Have at Least a High School Education by Sibsize and Birth Order, White Men Age 20 and Over, OCG 1973.

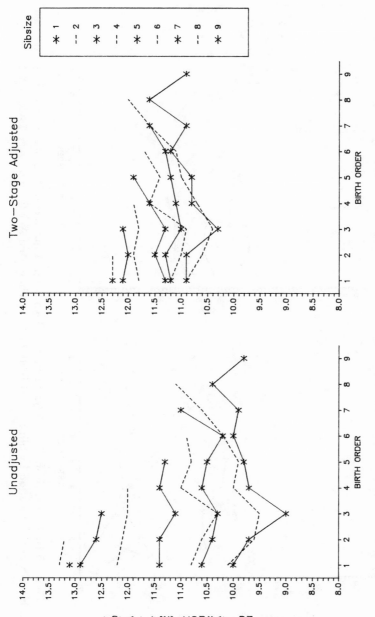

Figure 5.15. Comparison of No Adjustment and Two-Stage Adjustment, Total Years of Education by Sibsize and Birth Order, White Men Age 25 and Over, OCG 1973.

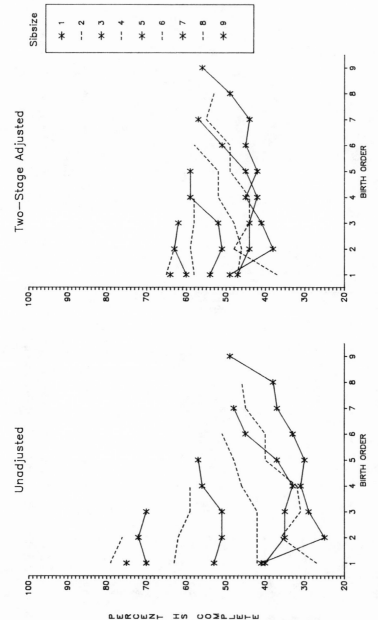

Figure 5.16. Comparison of No Adjustment and Two-Stage Adjustment, Percentages Who Have at Least a High School Education by Sibsize and Birth Order, White Men Age 20 and Over, OCG 1962.

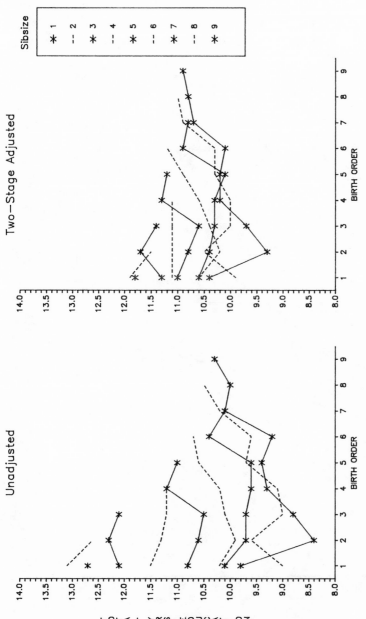

Figure 5.17. Comparison of No Adjustment and Two-Stage Adjustment, Total Years of Education by Sibsize and Birth Order, White Men Age 25 and Over, OCG 1962.

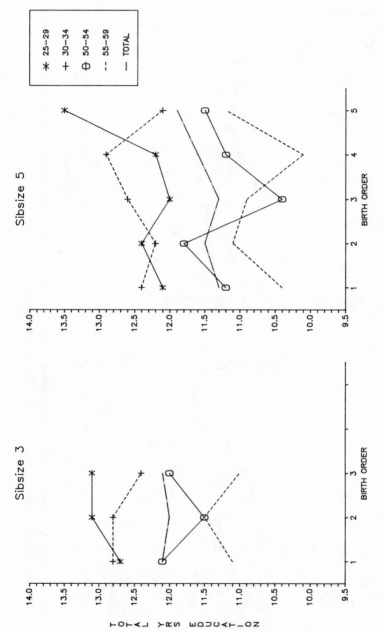

Figure 5.18. Two-Stage Adjustment for Selected Cohorts, Total Years of Education, Sibsizes Three and Five, by Birth Order, White Men Age 25 and Over, OCG 1973.

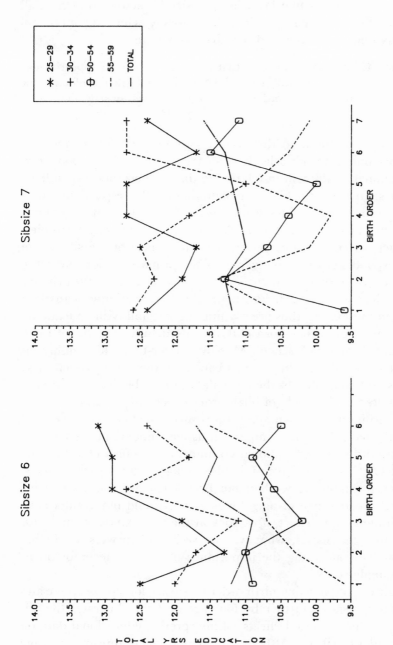

Figure 5.19. Two-Stage Adjustment for Selected Cohorts, Total Years of Education, Sibsizes Six and Seven by Birth Order, White Men Age 25 and Over, OCG 1973.

graduating seniors in 1957 whose sibsize is skewed toward small families because the respondents had already achieved high school graduation. As Hauser and Sewell (1985) state:

> The combination of the facts that respondents tend to appear in low birth orders and are all high school graduates further confounds the interpretation of birth order effects on mean levels of schooling.

Second, in addition to the overall selectivity of the sample, the authors find a strong selectivity in large families of respondents' educational attainment in relation to that of their (nonrespondent) siblings. In effect, the high school graduates (the respondents) who came from large families were more different from their siblings than the high school graduates who came from small families. Further, as Hauser and Sewell point out, most of the siblings of the respondents were younger than the primary respondents (the high school graduates), many substantially so. In sum, the primary respondent who had achieved high school graduation was an older child in most cases, thus greatly limiting variability in educational attainment for earlier born children. By definition, most of them graduated from high school. Moreover, later-born children invariably had an older sibling who had achieved this status. Given these biases and anomalies in the basic data, it may be that they are not well suited to the study of birth-order effects on education.

Returning to our own analysis, as mentioned earlier, we expect period effects to be very important as confounders in the analysis of birth order and educational attainment, but our findings for the entire OCG samples have probably averaged out the period effects. However, supposing we had not been fortunate enough to have such a broad range of ages for analysis, would our results have been different? In effect, if we look at the same kinds of curves for separate age cohorts, what will we see? The answers are highly instructive concerning the importance of period effects for birth-order analysis.

Figure 5.18 (showing birth order by sibsize for sibsizes three and five disaggregated further by four age groups) illustrates the difficulties, due to period effects, of interpreting educational data on birth order by sibsize. Although the period effects appear to average out when a wide age range of subjects is considered, period effects create marked differences in the curves when the latter are examined by *cohort*—in this case, those ages 25–29, 30–34, 50–54, and 55–59. It is tempting to interpret these cohort curves in relation to depressions, wars, economic booms, and the like. But such a level of specificity strains the data beyond their limits. At minimum for such an interpretation, one would want to use data by single years of age, but given the size of the sibsize–birth-order matrix, this requirement would transcend the resources of even a sample as large as OCG 1973. The complexity of the period effects is again illustrated in figure 5.19, which plots education by birth order for sibsizes six and seven among the four age groups. It is clear as well, that assumptions about spacing could introduce considerable bias into one's thinking, but some such assumptions would have to be made if one were to match up birth orders with periods in order to attempt to understand how the periods impinged on various points in the individual's educational cycle.

Do period effects undo the curvilinear relationship we have seen for large families? Figure 5.19 shows that the well-defined parabola for larger sibsizes that was evident when all age groups were averaged together is less clear-cut in age groups taken separately. However, the tendency for younger children to benefit at the expense of older children is obviously present in some (but not all) of the age-specific curves.

This consideration of separate age cohorts is thus a sobering check on interpretations of data that may be highly period-specific instead of spanning a broad range of periods as do both the OCG samples.

In sum, this analysis, which involves unusually adequate controls for family background and period effects, suggests that among large sibsizes the relation of birth order to the achievement of adults is curvilinear. A curve fitted to this parabola gives a high correlation of birth order with educational attainment after major background factors have been controlled. This correlation is evident in three major data sets, two of which are shown here. The correlation accords with a reasonable set of expectations regarding how educational attainment should be related to sibsize and birth order, and, hence, offers a fairly strong challenge to disproof.

The curvilinear relationship among birth orders in the largest families suggests that the youngest and next-to-youngest children can benefit educationally by having many siblings and, as a consequence, frequently bring their performance up to levels comparable with those in four-child families (figs. 5.12, 5.16, and 5.17). However, this accomplishment is at the expense, as it were, of siblings at earlier birth orders who are left far behind in the educational race. Additionally, not even the youngest in large families can equal the educational performance of those in family sizes one through three.

Among birth orders in small families, statistically significant effects are not evident. However, controls for background factors serve to raise the values for only children relative to other birth orders and sibsizes.

BIRTH ORDER AND SEX COMPOSITION OF THE FAMILY

Did it make a systematic difference to men's education in the OCG samples what the sex composition of their sibsize was and where the men stood in the birth order/sex composition matrix? Again, our expectations in this regard are far from consistent. One could argue that being the only boy (and, perhaps, the youngest) in a family of girls might put a boy in a better position than being the oldest, or in the middle, in a family containing a similar number of boys. Presumably, parents of one boy who appears after a long succession of girls might make particular efforts to ensure his education, in contrast to a situation where the family was made up of all boys (whose education might have equal claim), or where the family contained more than one boy (but not necessarily all boys).

A counter to this "only boy" expectation could be that, regardless of parental motivation, a family that is predominantly girls may be less able financially than one that is predominantly boys. Typically, parents are more protective of girls and, hence, girls may not be able to earn as much from early on as boys. Moreover, boys may be able to contribute longer than girls, because (at least in the past) if girls married and did not participate in the labor force, and had little control over resources, they would not be able to contribute much to their families of orientation. Thus, their greatest "contribution" might be to marry and cease being a financial burden to their parents. Hence, a family of all boys, or predominantly boys, might be able to help younger boys more effectively.

The reader should bear in mind that our analysis is silent (due to lack of data) regarding the position of the girls versus the boys in mixed-sex families. Relative to girls, boys might receive favored treatment in such families, although, other things equal, they might still not have the advantages of boys in an all-boy family. Clearly, if one were convinced that birth order/sex composition was a systematic predictor of educational attainment, the data requirements for a full-scale and meaningful analysis of this issue are formidable.

Figure 5.20 plots total years of education by birth order/sex configuration for OCG 1962 and 1973 side by side for sibsizes two, three, and four. In each case, the configuration is plotted against the average birth-order values for that sibsize so that the reader can see what difference the particular configuration makes in contrast to the average by birth order for the sibsize group.

Since the patterns are so heterogeneous between the two surveys, the results do not lead us to believe in highly structured, systematic differences in educational attainment as a consequence of the birth order/sex configuration of the family. Being an only boy of any particular birth order in these families suggests no clear-cut advantage or disadvantage compared to boys of other configurations in the same sibsize. From the data, one could argue for an advantage inhering in the "all-boy" configuration, but sibsize three in OCG 1962 is an exception. Thus, although men from different birth order/sex configurations assuredly differ in many cases from the average birth-order curves, the pattern of these differences, if one exists, is far from obvious.

One pertinent question regarding a birth order/sex configuration influence is whether it has a bearing on the advantaged position of last-born and next-to-last-born boys in very large families—an advantage that we have already seen to exist? In other words, when the sibsize is at a known average disadvantage, but a particular birth order within it is advantaged, does this advantage depend on a unique birth order/sex composition?

In an attempt to answer this question, we confine ourselves to OCG 1973, which has the largest number of cases. Even so, if we focus on sibsizes seven and eight, there are not enough cases to isolate families with only one boy, or with all boys, for analysis. As a compromise, we have grouped "one-boy" configurations with families that are predominantly girls, and "all-boy" configurations

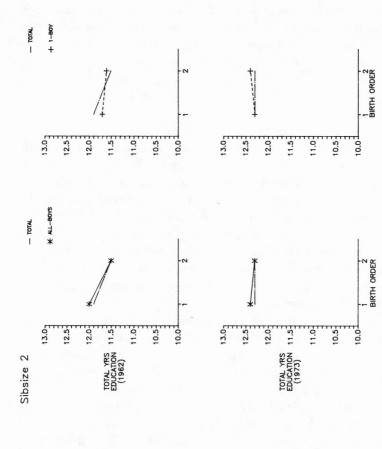

Figure 5.20. Total Years of Education by Birth Order for All Respondents Versus Individual Sex Configurations of the Sibsize, Sibsizes Two through Four, White Men age 25 and Over, OCG 1962 and 1973.

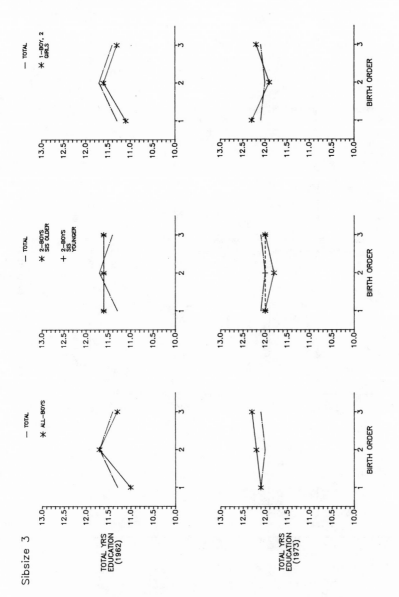

Figure 5.20. Continued.

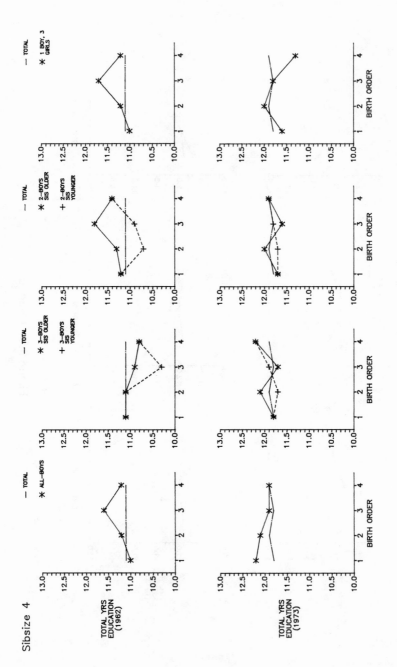

Figure 5.20. Continued.

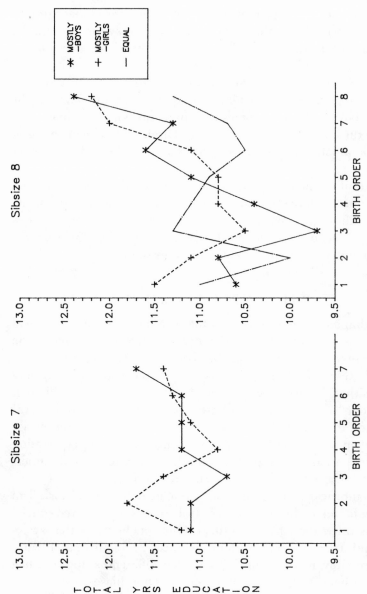

Figure 5.21. Total Years of Education by Birth Order and Sex Configuration of the Sibsize, Sibsizes Seven and Eight, White Men Age 25 and Over, OCG 1973.

with families that are predominantly boys, thereby allowing us to contrast the curves for men who came from large families that were mostly (or all) boys, and families that were mostly girls. The results for sibsizes seven and eight (with the influence of background factors removed as for the other curves) are shown in figure 5.21. Both curves for "mostly boys" and "mostly girls" are parabolic in form with troughs in the middle, and the last two children do better than either firstborn or middle children. However, the last-born boy seems to take a particularly sharp upward turn among the "mostly boys" families, suggesting that, indeed, there may be a unique educational advantage in large families to being a youngest child (or among the youngest children) in a long line of older brothers.

The results concerning education by birth order in large families thus tend to reinforce the "dilution" hypothesis. In large, primarily male families, the last-born children may, on average, have a number of pseudo-fathers and, hence, may be able to achieve disproportionately from an educational point of view.

SUMMARY AND CONCLUSION

In this chapter, we have seen that there are no clear-cut theoretical expectations regarding birth order and cognitive ability. Hence, the research literature on this topic has been, as the saying goes, "data driven." Research "findings" have been subject to a wide variety of biases that, in turn, have produced many, varied and conflicting, birth-order "effects." The latter are reported in the research literature when they are noteworthy and startling and, apparently, ignored when they are not. Among these biases are the interpretation of sibsize, period, parental background, child-spacing, and numerous types of selection effects as birth-order differences.

Our empirical analysis has not pretended to control for all of these confounders, but we have controlled for some and recognized and illustrated the effects of others. Our conclusion is that systematic and patterned birth-order differences in cognitive ability are quite probably nonexistent. Where such differences appear, they are consequences of confounding and selection biases.

We have given particular attention to Robert Zajonc's claim that national data on average annual birth order in the United States can be used to predict the course of SAT scores. We have shown that the full series of birth-order and SAT data (as distinct from the truncated series used by Zajonc) do not correlate well, but that the SAT scores do appear to be associated over time with completed cohort fertility per woman (a measure that is very different from annual average birth order). However, we have cautioned against overinterpreting any such series of aggregated data.

Turning to birth-order effects on educational attainment, we have (following Blau and Duncan) outlined a variety of reasons for expecting oldest and (particularly) youngest children in large families to achieve the most education, and for middle-born children to receive the least, but we have little reason to expect systematic birth-order differences in education among individuals in small families. Our expectations for large families are based on the notion that, relative to middle-born children, oldest children have the advantage of growing up while the family is smaller, whereas middle-born children (especially early middle-borns) experience the full force of large sibsize, and last-born (or next-to-last-born) children have the advantage of being reared in a family where there may be a number of older wage-earners among the siblings and, at worst, where many older siblings have left home for marriage or work elsewhere. Moreover, the youngest child or children are being reared during a period of the parents' lives when the latter are probably at a peak income level and have established themselves in terms of housing and consumer durables.

Our actual analysis of OCG 1962 and 1973 data (and of data from the 1970 National Fertility Study, not shown) indicates no statistically significant birth-order differences in education among small families but a definite parabola among large families. Moreover, the last borns and next-to-last borns in large families frequently do better than firstborns. As well, the data suggest that it is not simply being in the "middle" that is most detrimental, but rather that being a middle-born child early in the sequence of offspring presents the greatest disadvantage. Later-born middle children may do as well as or better than firstborns.

In order to illustrate how varied and marked are period effects on the birth order/education relationship, we have redone the analysis of the OCG data using separate age groups of respondents. It is evident from this disaggregation that, had the birth-order analysis of the OCG data been for one restricted age group (instead of the wide range of ages that is actually the case), our interpretations would have been profoundly affected by period influences. A reanalysis of the data according to the sex configuration of the respondents' families in OCG 1973 illustrates, as well, that selection biases according to sex configurations could have profound effects. We also have been able to document that had we not used the special two-stage analysis of sibsize and birth order (an analysis that removed family background influences prior to the birth-order calculations) our findings would have differed. In this regard, the position of the only child, relative to other birth orders, would have been a notable sufferer. Our analysis has thus made it possible to account for the puzzling disadvantages apparently suffered by only children relative to those of other birth orders in larger families.

6

FAMILY BACKGROUND, SIBSIZE, AND EDUCATIONAL EXPECTATIONS

In this chapter, we continue our effort to understand how family background and sibsize operate to affect educational attainment. Here our object will be to learn how these aspects of the family get translated into differential postsecondary educational goals among young people.

Although the sibsize effects on educational expectations in the pages that follow are modest, we have included this analysis for a number of reasons. First, the effects are consistent in direction, generally significant, and typically as important (or almost as important) as the father's SEI or family income. Additionally, the analysis, following in the theoretical tradition of the Wisconsin data, suggests ways in which the effects of sibsize on educational goals could be studied among young people at a considerably earlier age. Obviously, such research would require the employment of a more realistic set of dependent variables than college expectations, the relevance and validity of which doubtless decline rather rapidly as one moves down the age range. Nonetheless, our analysis here, like similar analyses in the past, suggests the importance of focusing research regarding the determinants of educational objectives on much younger groups of students than appear in this chapter.

Why analyze factors affecting youngsters' educational goals? The answer, in brief, is that the postsecondary goals of high school students have been found to be a major predictor of years of schooling completed (Alexander and Eckland 1975; Sewell and Hauser 1980). In fact, Sewell and Hauser believe that if you can explain educational aspirations you are well on your way to explaining attainment (Sewell and Hauser 1980, 64). In this chapter, we will use (with some changes to be discussed) that part of the Wisconsin model of status attainment that focuses on educational aspirations as its principal dependent variable. The full model (see, Sewell and Hauser, ibid.) considers the determinants of occupational aspirations, educational and occupational attainment, and income as well.

THE MODEL

Sewell's thinking about the Wisconsin model took off from the fact, by then well-documented, that educational aspirations among young people are positively related to socioeconomic background (Sewell and Shah 1968*b*). The researchers wished to understand the mechanisms by which differential family background is translated into differential educational goals. A major hypothesis was that high socioeconomic status (SES) results not only in more intellectual ability and better performance in school, but that high status parents provide more encouragement of, and psychological support for, postsecondary education than do low status parents. In the words of Sewell and Hauser (1980):

> We then extended our analysis using a path model to determine and compare the direct and indirect effects of socioeconomic status, measured intelligence, and parental encouragement on college plans. We assumed that parental encouragement would be influenced by the socioeconomic status and measured ability of the child, and that all three variables would have direct effects on college plans. This analysis revealed that for both sexes, the effect of socioeconomic status on parental encouragement is greater than that of ability. . . . The direct effect of parental encouragement on the college plans of both sexes is greater than the direct effect of socioeconomic status or of ability.

Since, as we shall see, sibsize is also related to young people's educational goals or expectations, our interest in this chapter focuses on the mechanisms by which variability in sibsize affects these goals. Are most of its effects indirect, operating through ability, grades, and differential parental expectations and encouragement? Or, does it have fairly substantial direct effects even after taking these intervening variables into account? Insofar as sibsize has indirect effects, what intervening variables does it impinge on the most? These questions were not raised by the Wisconsin researchers in their work on high school seniors, since sibsize was not part of the original model. Only recently, at a much later stage of the longitudinal analysis, has this variable been added and, by this time, the interest of Sewell and his colleagues had shifted somewhat from a concentration on goals to a concentration on outcomes.

In employing the Wisconsin approach to educational goals, we are using the most updated specification of the model, a specification that differs from the early work of Sewell and his colleagues (see, Sewell and Shah 1968*a* and *b*; Sewell, Haller, and Portes 1969; Sewell, Haller, and Ohlendorf 1970). The changes made by Sewell and colleagues (see, Sewell and Hauser 1980, for a summary of the changes) in this recent version relate principally to a disaggregation of the parental SES index in order to consider separately mother's and father's education, father's occupation, and father's income. Additionally, the updated version of the model views the young person's intellectual ability as an intervening rather than a predetermined variable. This change was in response to a recognition of the influence of parental characteristics on the young person's abilities.

We have also made some changes of our own in the model. An important change concerns the measurement level of the dependent variable—educational goals. The Wisconsin model used a dichotomous dependent variable—whether or not the youngster expected to go to college. All of our data (as will be discussed in more detail shortly) relate to years of expected postsecondary education. As for the remainder of the model, the Wisconsin approach did not include sibsize (although the followup analysis of actual educational attainment did add this variable). The Wisconsin model of educational goals included a measure of ability, grades in school, and an index of parental, peer, and teacher expectations of the student as perceived by the youngster. In the Wisconsin formulation, parental goals or expectations are regarded as indicative of parental support (or lack of it) for postsecondary schooling. Our model deletes peer expectations, because recent research has suggested that once one takes account of the selectivity of peers for one another, the effect on students' educational aspirations is small (for a review of this literature, see Cohen 1983). As for teacher effects, it is unfortunate that

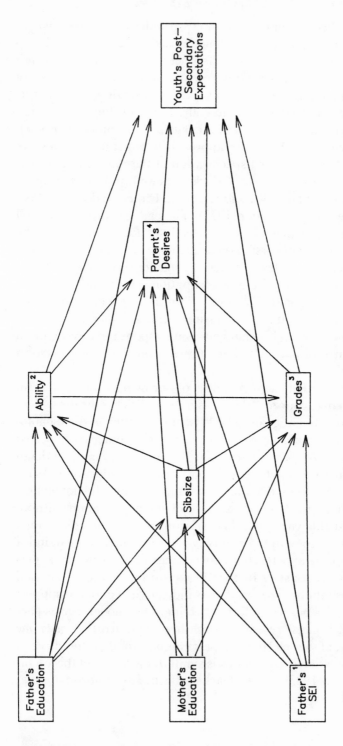

Figure 6.1. Diagram of the Basic Path Model of Youth's Postsecondary Expectations. (1) In Cycle III, family income. (2) In Cycle III, WISC; in HSB, WISC. (3) In Cycle III, Vocabulary. (3) In Cycle III, WRAT. (4) In Cycle III, data are from parent; in HSB, they are from the student concerning the parent.

the data sets analyzed here have high proportions of missing data on this issue and, hence, this variable has been excluded. Our model retains parental desires or goals for the student, and this variable, like the student's expectations, is coded in terms of years of postsecondary schooling desired. Moreover, as will be discussed, in the High School and Beyond study (HSB), the data on the parents are from the student (as in the Wisconsin model) reflecting the student's perception of parent's goals. In Cycle III of the Health Examination Survey, the data on parent's desires are from the parent directly, providing some check on the criticism (of the Wisconsin research) that to obtain parents' views from students, and then regress these views on students' expectations, involves a degree of circularity that may guarantee a high level of explained variance (R^2). The diagram for the basic model is shown in figure 6.1.

What expectations have we concerning the nature of the relationships, the placement of the variables, and their relative importance in the model? For reasons that by now do not require explanation, the model assumes some inverse relation of fertility by the parent's socioeconomic background. We also expect a positive effect of background on ability and a negative effect of sibsize. Holding ability constant, the model assumes that parents' background will affect grades positively because higher-educated parents will place more emphasis on academic achievement and create home situations that are conducive to study and concentration. Children of higher-SEI fathers may need to work less at odd jobs as well. We expect large sibsize to be negatively related to grades because of distraction and crowding at home, and to more emphasis on community and family activities than upon academic achievement. Based on past research, we expect ability to be the major influence on school performance for both sexes and for all classes in school. Although we believe that parental desires for children probably influence ability and grades, we have adhered to the placement of both prior to parental desires in this model. Our reasoning is twofold. First, we are dealing with high school students and the postsecondary goals of the parents. At this relatively late stage in the young person's education, it seems reasonable to think of the parents' postsecondary desires as responsive to ability and grades. Second, there is an advantage to having continuity with the Wisconsin model. For a study that treats parental encouragement and grades in a nonrecursive model, see, Hout and Morgan (1975).

We expect that parents' characteristics will have significant direct effects on their educational desires for both sexes, but that the mother's education will be more important than the father's education for girls, and that the reverse will be true for boys (Sewell, Hauser, and Wolf 1980). We also expect, as already discussed, that grades and ability will be important for parents' desires, but that the relative importance of grades will be greater for boys than for girls congruent with research by Sewell and others (ibid.). We expect the relative negative importance of sibsize for the parents' desires to approximate the positive importance of the father's SEI, primarily because sibsize seems rather consistently to have a negative effect on educational variables that approximates the positive effect of the father's SEI. Moreover, we expect that parental background and sibsize influences on the parents' desires will be mediated primarily through ability (rather than school performance), because parents will be more strongly influenced by a life-long experience with a child than by his or her grades in school.

Regarding the student's own expectations, we expect family background effects to be more heavily mediated than is the case for the parents' desires, because students' expectations are conditional on parental support and encouragement. We also see no reason to doubt that sibsize will continue to be a negative offset to the father's SEI. We believe that for the students' goals, grades will be more important than ability, in contrast to the parents, because grades are so strongly supported normatively among students as indicating how they "stack up" against peers. Since a major finding of the Wisconsin analysis is that parents' desires have the most important effect of all the variables in the model, we expect to find this relationship as well.

It is worth noting that, in addition to our focus on sibsize, the analysis in this chapter represents a detailed consideration of the revised Wisconsin model using educational goals as the principal focus of interest. As we have mentioned, by the time that Sewell and colleagues finally revised the overall model, their major concern had shifted from educational goals to a concentration on educational and occupational attainment and income.

Since the principal function of path models is to make explicit theoretical assumptions and interconnections, this is an appropriate place to discuss the causal status of family size and parents' educa-

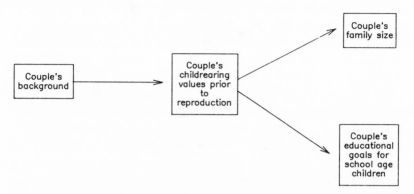

Figure 6.2. Hypothetical Model of Parent's Childrearing Values as Antecedent to Both the Number of Children They Have and Their Educational Goals for Their Children.

tional goals for children. It can be argued, of course, that insofar as parents of different numbers of children have different educational goals, the association is not a *consequence* of family size but a *cause* of it. According to this argument, sibsize per se does not give rise to differential parental educational goals for children, but rather sibsize is a consequence of the couple's goals *prior* to reproduction which continue after the children are actually present. Holding constant marital intactness and control over fertility (both fecundity and control over unwanted births), this reasoning is diagrammed in figure 6.2.

Is this possible confounding theoretically so compelling as to rule out the relevance of the basic model we have suggested? There are a number of reasons for believing that the answer is negative. First, parental concern about the educational quality of children (or lack of such concern) is not the only determinant of family size. Leaving aside marital disruption, couples may have different family-size goals for reasons quite other than a concern about child quality— reasons relating to the couples' interest in children as social investments, as economic investments, as political power investments, and so on (Blake 1979; Blake and Del Pinal 1982).

In addition, family-size goals are also related to other consumer goals of parents—the parents' quality of life rather than the quality of the child. Further, not all fertility is explicable by reference to couple's family-size goals. A share is due to differential fecundity

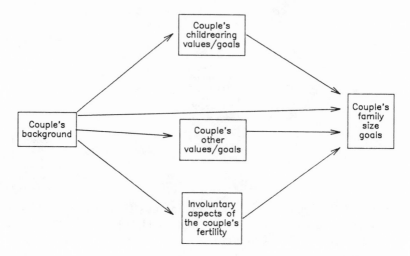

Figure 6.3. Hypothetical Model of the Determinants of Family-Size Goals.

and differential efficiency and effectiveness of birth control practice. However, insofar as concern about the educational quality of children affects family size, our controls for parents' background characteristics take this fact into account—at least partially. This is especially true since we have no evidence that, after controlling for major background factors, couples have different child-quality goals. In sum, the determinants of family-size goals can be modeled as shown in figure 6.3.

Finally, the analysis to be presented in this chapter will show that parents' schooling desires for children are influenced more by the child's ability and performance than by either parental background or sibsize, and we have seen in a prior chapter (using younger children) that sibsize is an important influence on IQ. In sum, we have reason to believe that, through a variety of channels, both indirect and direct, sibsize genuinely influences parents' educational goals.

Consequently, although a share of parents' educational expectations for school-age children may be a result of couples' prereproductive educational goals for prospective children (even after controls for parental background have been introduced), we shall proceed in this chapter as if this possibly confounding effect did not exist. We believe that if the presumed confounding could be measured, it would not change the basic argument of our model, although it would certainly add a dimension to our understanding.

Although we know that even prior to high school a number of students from large sibsizes and low socioeconomic status drop out of school, the analysis of our basic model allows us to view the educational selection process in high school populations, as well as among a sample of somewhat younger children from Cycle III of the Health Examination Survey. These samples can help us to understand how parental background and sibsize get translated into more proximate influences on young people's expectations of postsecondary educational attainment—influences such as intellectual ability, grades, and parental desires.

THE DATA

The data for the analysis in this chapter concern high school sophomores and seniors studied in the survey High School and Beyond (HSB), and youngsters age 12 to 17 in Cycle III of the Health Examination Survey. From HSB, we have used as predictors the mother's and father's education in years, the father's occupation coded according to the Duncan SEI, sibsize, the age standardized vocabulary test as an indicator of ability, the students' average grades during the past year, and the responses from students to a question about the post–high school education desired by the mother. The dependent variable is the student's estimate of the years of schooling he or she expects to achieve. The codes for mother's desires and student's expectations were as follows:

11 Less than H.S. graduation (sophomores only)
12 H.S. graduation only; vocational-trade
13 College, less than two years
15 College, two years or more
16 Finish college
18 Master's degree
22 Ph.D., M.D., etc.

Mother's desires for youngster's postsecondary education were favored over father's because the latter could not be scaled in years and would have resulted in a dichotomous dependent variable.

The Cycle III predictors were father's and mother's education coded in years, family income (no data were available on the father's occupation), sibsize, the age-standardized WISC as a measure of ability, the age-standardized WRAT (see appendix A for a detailed discussion of the WRAT) as a measure of school-related performance, and data derived from the parent (primarily the mother) concerning years of schooling desired for the child. The dependent variable was the youth's expectations about the years of schooling he or she would achieve. The codes for parent's desires and youth's expectations were as follows:

11 Quit school as soon as possible
12 Finish high school
14 Get some college
16 Finish college
18 Finish college and take further training

It will be remembered that a major difference between the HSB and the Cycle III data is that the HSB refers to the student's estimate of the mother's desires. The Cycle III data are based on information from the parent directly. Also, Cycle III contains a wider age range than does HSB. Whereas HSB relates to sophomores and seniors, Cycle III (including as it does youngsters who were age 12 to 17) involves those who are in grades 6 through 9 as well as those who are in grades 10 through 12.

It is worth emphasizing here that the principal data on educational expectations analyzed in this chapter are from young people who have already "survived" critical states in the schooling process. As we know from adult experiences, youngsters who are high school students, and especially those who are seniors, are a selected group of survivors (that is, their characteristics differ from the drop-outs). This process of selective school leaving occurs during grade school, between grade school and high school, and during the first shock of the transition into high school. Furthermore, as may be seen from table 6.1, the selection is specific for sibsize. Average school performance is higher at the higher grades than at the lower ones, and this is particularly true for those from large families. For example, among youngsters from sibsizes five-plus in Cycle III, the age-standardized WRAT scores for tenth- to twelfth-graders are approximately one-half a standard deviation higher than the scores for sixth- to ninth-graders, whereas the differences in WRAT scores by grade is relatively small for those from small families. Moreover, the increase in scores at the higher grades is accompanied by a decrease in variance as can be seen from a comparison of the standard deviations. The same increase in school performance and homogeneity of school performance is evident in the HSB data as well. As a consequence of this selection by sibsize, the sibsize effects on educational expectations to be discussed in this chapter are not large. It may also be true that among those students who suffer family background disadvantages (such as coming from a large family), schooling has a marginally greater effect on school performance than among more advantaged students—*if* the student can manage to remain in school and at grade level. Hence, both selection and the differential value that is added by schooling may contribute to greater homogeneity at the higher class levels. Documentation of this process may be found in Alexander and others (1985).

STUDENTS' EDUCATIONAL EXPECTATIONS

We begin with the sophomores and seniors in the High School and Beyond study. Table 6.2 shows the decomposition of our basic model of student's educational expectations into total effects, indirect effects, and direct effects. For readers who are not familiar with the jargon of path analysis it is worthwhile for us to go over the logic briefly. Initially, it should be noted that since path analysis compares effects of variables in a model, standardized regression coefficients are used throughout. The parents' SES variables are predetermined—that is, they are given in the model and are assumed to appear without further explanation. Hence, the *total* effects of parental SES are the standardized regression coefficients for SES variables taking account only of their intercorrelations. The *direct* effects of each of the parent's background variables are the standardized coefficients taking into account, in addition, the effects of the subsequent variables in the model—sibsize, vocabulary, grades, and mother's desires. Consequently, the *indirect*-effects coefficients for the mother's education, for example, indicate how

Table 6.1. Average School Performance Measures for Lower and Higher Classes in School by Sibsize and Sex, White Boys and Girls, HSB, Sophomores and Seniors, and HES, Cycle III, Grades 6–9 and 10–12.[a]

Survey, Sex, and Sibsize	$\bar{X}$	(S.D.)	N	$\bar{X}$	(S.D.)	N	Percent Change between Grade Levels
HSB		Sophomores			Seniors		
Boys							
1–2	5.5	(1.53)	1,498	5.8	(1.48)	1,043	5.5%
3–4	5.4	(1.65)	2,595	5.7	(1.45)	1,702	5.6
5+	5.0	(1.62)	1,312	5.4	(1.43)	870	8.0
Girls							
1–2	6.1	(1.46)	1,485	6.3	(1.32)	1,106	3.3
3–4	5.9	(1.53)	2,760	6.3	(1.31)	1,874	6.8
5+	5.6	(1.54)	1,341	6.0	(1.45)	952	7.1
HES, Cycle III		Grades 6–9			Grades 10–12		
Boys							
1–2	101.9	(14.20)	242	104.5	(13.28)	200	2.6%
3–4	101.9	(14.47)	391	103.0	(13.23)	234	1.1
5+	95.8	(14.48)	286	102.1	(13.03)	120	6.6

Girls							
1–2	102.7	(13.49)	184	103.7	(12.83)	157	1.0
3–4	102.0	(13.69)	361	104.3	(13.73)	198	2.3
5+	94.7	(16.37)	227	101.2	(12.93)	133	6.8

[a]For HSB, school performance has been measured using the student's self-reported grades for the previous year. The response categories for this variable range from 1 = mostly below Ds to 8 = As mostly. For HES, no measure of grades was collected so here we have used the age-standardized WRAT scores as an indicator of school-related performance.

Table 6.2. Direct and Indirect Effects of Parental Background Variables, Sibsize, IQ, Grades, and Mother's Educational Desires on Students' Educational Expectations by Sex, White Boys and Girls, HSB, Sophomores and Seniors.

Sex, Class, and Predictors	Total Effect	Indirect Effects:				Direct Effect	R^2	R^2 without Mother's Desires
		Sibsize	Vocab	Grades	Mother's Desires			
Boys								
Sophomores								
Fa Educ	.261	.004	.053	.022	.066	.116		
Mo Educ	.161	.008	.043	.017	.068	.026		
Fa SEI	.122[a]	.005	.027	.016	.036	.036		
Sibsize	-.104	.	-.026	-.018	-.027	-.034		
Vocab	.298	.	.	.125	.077	.095		
Grades	.331	.	.	.	.100	.231		
Mo Desires	.508	.	.	.	.	.508	.574	.289
Seniors								
Fa Educ	.332	-.003	.046	.041	.113	.135		
Mo Educ	.079	.001	.029	.008	.052	-.011[a]		
Fa SEI	.132	.013	.025	.000	.057	.036		
Sibsize	-.116	.	-.023	-.005	-.038	-.050		
Vocab	.307	.	.	.117	.094	.096		
Grades	.330	.	.	.	.097	.233		
Mo Desires	.566	.	.	.	.	.566	.644	.398

Girls

Sophomores

Fa Educ	.203	.005	.048	.010	.067	.074
Mo Educ	.190	.003	.030	.014	.089	.053
Fa SEI	.076	.005	.029	.004	.034	.005[a]
Sibsize	-.077	.	-.021	-.008	-.030	-.019[a]
Vocab	.280	.	.	.104	.082	.094
Grades	.246	.	.	.	.083	.163
Mo Desires	.601	.	.	.	.	.601
					.575	.275

Seniors

Fa Educ	.222	.000	.047	.012	.070	.093
Mo Educ	.167	.004	.029	.007	.104	.023[a]
Fa SEI	.095	.006	.008	.005	.050	.026[a]
Sibsize	-.087	.	-.016	-.014	-.032	-.026[a]
Vocab	.282	.	.	.090	.118	.074
Grades	.250	.	.	.	.096	.154
Mo Desires	.641	.	.	.	.	.641
					.617	.290

[a]Not significant at the 5-percent level.

much of the total effect of mother's education operates through sibsize, vocabulary, grades, and mother's desires respectively. Readers should satisfy themselves that the coefficients for indirect and direct effects for each variable sum to the coefficient for total effects (except for small differences due to rounding). Turning to sibsize, the total effect is, again, the standardized coefficient taking account of the effect of prior variables in the model (the parents' background); whereas the direct effect of sibsize is the coefficient taking account, in addition, of the effects of vocabulary, grades, and mother's desires; with the indirect effects of sibsize operating through these variables shown in-between. The reasoning is the same for the remainder of the variables: *Total effect* is the standardized coefficient taking account of prior variables in the model (or concurrent variables as with parents' background), *direct effect* takes account of the influence of prior and subsequent variables, and *indirect effect* shows how, beginning with predetermined variables, subsequent variables absorb some of the total effects.

We may note first of all (table 6.2) that, for both high school classes, the model explains a high proportion of the variance in student's postsecondary expectations—between 58 and 64 percent. This fit compares most favorably with the Sewell and Shah analysis (1968*b*), which had an R^2 (variance explained) for Wisconsin senior boys of 37 percent and for girls of 41 percent. The improved fit is probably because our analysis is based on years of schooling (for both the mother's desires and the youngster's expectations) rather than an ordinal variable, and includes sibsize and school performance, which the Sewell and Shah (1968*b*) analysis did not. Second, it is clear that a major increment to explanation rests with the variable "student's perception of mother's schooling desires." This finding accords with the analyses by Sewell and Shah (1968*b*).

As for direct effects, most of the total effects of parental background and sibsize are mediated—primarily through ability and the mother's desires. Thus, most of the influence of parental background and sibsize has been translated into differential ability and the youngster's perception of parental wishes. Consequently, since the direct effects of background and sibsize have been diminished, and ability operates through grades, grades remain unchallenged as the only major direct effect after the mother's expectations (which are far and away the most important variable). However, as between boys and girls, the relative importance of grades compared to the mother's desires is consistently greater for boys. For example, among senior boys, the effect of grades is 41 percent of mother's desires, but for girls, only 24 percent. In addition, comparing the relative effects of ability versus grades by sex, it is evident that the relative importance of grades compared to ability is greater by far for boys than for girls. So, boys are more influenced by grades compared either to ability or the mother's desires than are girls. Since the relative importance of ability compared to the mother's desires is less for girls than for boys (in addition to the relative importance of grades being less), it turns out that girls are relatively more dependent on their mother's educational hopes and wishes than are boys, and less stimulated by their own performance (or their own ability operating through their performance). This finding corresponds with the recent analysis of Wisconsin data by Sewell and his colleagues (Sewell, Hauser, and Wolf 1980).

Although the results for seniors and sophomores are very similar, it should be noted that the direct effects of both ability and grades (compared to the mother's desires) are relatively more important for sophomores. We would argue that this quite probably reflects the differential selection that occurs between the tenth and twelfth grades. In particular, by the senior year, students have higher and more homogeneous school performance.

Turning to indirect effects of family background and sibsize, we have seen that the principal mediating channel is the mother's desires and that next comes ability. Relating to the selection noted above, it is worth mentioning that although the mother's desires are the most important mediating channel for both sophomores and seniors, ability and grades have relatively more importance in mediating parental SES and sibsize among sophomores than among seniors. This further documents the mechanism of selection at younger ages in high school. Moreover, when (as in table 6.3) the effects of parental SES and sibsize through ability are decomposed (see, Alwin and Hauser 1975), we see that, for both younger and

Table 6.3. Decomposition of the Indirect Effects of Father's and Mother's Education, Father's SEI, and Sibsize through IQ on Student's Educational Expectations by Sex, White Boys and Girls, HSB, Sophomores and Seniors.

Sex, Class, and Predictors	Ability Directly	Indirect Effect through:		Total Indirect Effect through Ability
		Ability through Grades	Ability through Mother's Desires	
Boys				
Sophomores				
Fa Educ	.017	.022	.014	.053
Mo Educ	.014	.018	.011	.043
Fa SEI	.009	.012	.007	.027
Sibsize	-.008	-.011	-.007	-.026
Seniors				
Fa Educ	.014	.017	.014	.046
Mo Educ	.008	.011	.009	.029
Fa SEI	.008	.010	.008	.025
Sibsize	-.007	-.009	-.007	-.023
Girls				
Sophomores				
Fa Educ	.016	.018	.014	.048
Mo Educ	.010	.011	.009	.030
Fa SEI	.010	.011	.008	.029
Sibsize	-.007	-.008	-.006	-.021

Seniors				
Fa Educ	.012	.015	.020	.047
Mo Educ	.008	.009	.012	.029
Fa SEI	.002	.002	.003	.008
Sibsize	-.004	-.005	-.006	-.016

older students, the indirect effects through ability directly and, by that route, through grades are greater than the effects through mother's desires. For example, for sophomore boys, 42 percent of the effect of background and sibsize through ability is then through grades, but only 26 percent is through the mother's desires. Among senior boys, the differential between indirect-ability effects through grades and through mother's desires is less (38 percent for grades and 31 percent for mother's desires). We have, of course, already seen that when it comes to direct effects, sophomores are relatively more sensitive to ability and grades in their educational expectations (compared to the mother's desires) than are seniors. The overall analysis thus points to some of the mechanisms whereby students select themselves out of school over time, or decide to truncate their educations at critical stopping points like high school graduation.

This analysis of HSB thus seems to justify some straightforward conclusions. By the time youngsters are this far along in school, family background, sibsize, and ability operate primarily to create two major stimuli for boys' postsecondary expectations—performance in school and the perception of parental support for more (or less) postsecondary education. Moreover, differential performance provides a stimulus to differential parental support. By and large, boys from socially disadvantaged and large families have absorbed the impact of these influences into personal characteristics—less ability, lower grades, and lower educational expectations, and these boys perceive a home environment that reinforces their own views. With regard to girls (tables 6.2 and 6.3), the results are similar to those for boys, but with some important exceptions. The relative effect of the mother's education is greater than for boys, the relative effect of grades compared to the mother's desires is much less than for boys, and the relative effect of the mother's desires is generally markedly greater for girls than for boys. In sum, girls appear to be more dependent on their mother's education and their perceptions of parental hopes for them, and less influenced by their own performance, than are boys (see Sewell and Hauser 1980; Sewell, Hauser, and Wolf 1980).

Turning to Cycle III of the Health Examination Survey (table 6.4), it is clear that whether the parents' views are recounted by the student (as in HSB), or stated by the parent herself or himself (in Cycle III), parental expectations and desires are singularly important in explaining young people's educational expectations. However, as might be expected, increments to R^2 from adding the parents' views are generally larger when these views are given by the student than by the parent independently. It is nonetheless true that this increment ranges between 27 and 65 percent of R^2 (without the parent's views) in Cycle III, and that the coefficient for the parent's expectations is far and away the most important for this data set, as is the case for HSB.

Rather than embark upon a discussion of the entire path analysis for Cycle III, we shall concentrate here upon those features of it that are similar and dissimilar to the HSB findings. Looking first at direct effects on students' expectations, we see that, among boys, the mother's education is not significant either for younger or older children, but for older girls mother's education does have a significant influence, whereas father's education is unimportant for girls in general. These results are broadly similar to those for HSB. Equally, the relative effects of the school performance measure, WRAT, versus the importance of the parents' desires is somewhat greater for boys than for girls. As with HSB, for both boys and girls, the parents' desires are clearly the most important among the predictors. Turning to indirect effects, the most important mediating influence for background variables and sibsize is the parents' schooling desires, except for the mother's education, which is most frequently mediated through the WISC. As between the WISC and the WRAT, background effects and sibsize are more frequently mediated through the WISC. However, much of the effect of background and sibsize on expectations through the WISC actually goes through performance (WRAT) as in HSB, and not through the mother's desires (table 6.5).

PARENTS' EDUCATIONAL EXPECTATIONS FOR CHILDREN

The importance of the parents' educational goals for students' own postsecondary ambitions leads us to ask how sibsize affects parental goals. The model, figure 6.1, states that sibsize has an effect on parents' educational desires (or the student's perception of these desires) even after taking account of the effect of the parents' SES

Table 6.4. Direct and Indirect Effects of Parental Background Variables, Respondent's Age, Sibsize, WISC, WRAT, and Parents' Educational Desires on Youth's Educational Desires by Grade Level and Sex, White Boys and Girls, HES, Cycle III.

Sex, Grade, and Predictors	Total Effect	Indirect Effects:				Direct Effect	R^2	R^2 without Mother's Desires
		Sibsize	WISC	WRAT	Mother's Desires			
Boys								
Grades 6–9								
Fa Educ	.266	.004	.049	.001	.058	.153		
Mo Educ	.039	.034	.041	.021	.005	−.061[a]		
Fam Income	.175	.017	.015	.002	.023	.118		
Sibsize	−.151	.	−.019	−.006	−.022	−.104		
WISC	.196	.	.	.139	.032	.025[a]		
WRAT	.210	.	.	.	.072	.138		
Par Desires	.313	.	.	.	.	.313	.338	.267
Grades 10–12								
Fa Educ	.213	−.001	.054	.042	.078	.039[a]		
Mo Educ	.046	.018	.033	.008	.021	−.033[a]		
Fam Income	.208	.003	.028	.009	.102	.066[a]		
Sibsize	−.110	.	−.006	−.005	−.058	−.041[a]		

	1	2	3	4	5	6	7	8
WISC	.253			.169	−.003	.086	.428	
WRAT	.306				.168	.139		.264
Par Desires	.495				.	.495		

Girls

Grades 6–9

	1	2	3	4	5	6	7	8
Fa Educ	.129	.007	.041	.002	.017	.062[a]	.294	
Mo Educ	.155	.010	.044	.018	.040	.043[a]		.178
Fam Income	.145	.005	.021	.009	.048	.062[a]		
Sibsize	−.067	.	−.022	−.003	−.049	.007[a]		
WISC	.177	.	.	.096	.047	.035[a]		
WRAT	.152	.	.	.	.031	.122		
Par Desires	.380	.	.	.	.	.380		

Grades 10–12

	1	2	3	4	5	6	7	8
Fa Educ	.234	.016	.049	.016	.058	.095[a]	.399	
Mo Educ	.192	.011	.061	.006	.010	.105		.268
Fam Income	.084	.006	.005	.007	.058	.008[a]		
Sibsize	−.174	.	−.007	−.006	−.056	−.106		
WISC	.225	.	.	.112	.067	.046[a]		
WRAT	.190	.	.	.	.087	.104		
Par Desires	.424	.	.	.	.	.424		

[a]Not significant at the 5-percent level.

Table 6.5. Decomposition of the Indirect Effects of Father's and Mother's Education, Father's SEI, and Sibsize through IQ on Youth's Educational Desires by Grade Level and Sex, White Boys and Girls, HES, Cycle III.

Sex, Grade, and Predictors	Ability Directly	Indirect Effect through:		Total Indirect Effect through Ability
		Ability through Performance	Ability through Parent's Desires	
Boys				
Grades 6–9				
Fa Educ	.006	.035	.008	.049
Mo Educ	.005	.029	.007	.041
Fam Income	.002	.011	.003	.015
Sibsize	−.003	−.014	−.003	−.019
Grades 10–12				
Fa Educ	.019	.036	−.001	.054
Mo Educ	.011	.022	.000	.033
Fam Income	.010	.019	.000	.028
Sibsize	−.002	−.004	.000	−.006
Girls				
Grades 6–9				
Fa Educ	.008	.022	.011	.041
Mo Educ	.009	.024	.012	.044
Fam Income	.004	.011	.006	.021
Sibsize	−.004	−.012	−.006	−.022

Grades 10–12				
Fa Educ	.010	.024	.014	.049
Mo Educ	.013	.031	.018	.061
Fam Income	.000	.002	.001	.003
Sibsize	-.001	-.003	-.002	-.006

(education and the father's SEI). The model says that this total effect of sibsize may be reduced, however, if we recognize that sibsize influences ability and grades and that some of its total effect on the parents' desires may operate indirectly through these channels. That is, parents of small families have smarter and higher-performing children, and it is these factors that lead to higher parental goals. The same type of reasoning operates for the family background variables of mother's and father's education and father's SEI. Do these variables have direct influences on the mother's expectations, or are their effects mediated through sibsize, ability, and grades? What do the data show? We shall begin with the HSB.

Table 6.6 presents the total effect, the indirect effects, and the direct effects of the variables in the model on the mother's educational desires (as perceived by the student) for sophomore boys and girls in HSB. First we may note that this model leaves a lot of variance unexplained, and this is particularly true for girls. At best the model explains 25 percent of the variance (senior boys), and at worst 17 percent (sophomore girls). So, there are other influences beside the variables in the model (including poor measurement) that affect the schooling the mother desires, and perhaps particularly the student's perception of these desires. We may remind the reader, however, that the model performs as well as the one used in the Sewell and Shah analysis of the Wisconsin data (Sewell and Shah 1968*b*).

Considering direct effects first, we see that high percentages of total effect remain for both family background and sibsize even after considering ability and grades. By and large, the remaining direct effects run between 70 and 80 percent of the total effects for these variables and all are significantly different from zero at the .01 level. This finding means, therefore, that insofar as high status and small family size influence the mother's educational goals, this influence is affected relatively little by the child's ability or school performance. Among family background variables and sibsize, we see in addition that sibsize consistently ranks fourth, but close to the father's SEI. Another point of interest is that, among boys, the father's education is equal to or greater than the mother's education in its effect but, among girls, the mother's education predominates over the father's as an influence. In sum, girls are more dependent on having educated mothers than are boys when it comes to maternal support for higher education.

The fact that family background and sibsize affect the mother's schooling desires without a great deal of mediation by ability and grades does not, of course, mean that ability and grades are not important in the mother's calculations. As can be seen from the column on direct effects, the importance of ability and grades generally outweighs that of family background or sibsize on the mother's desires, although the mother's or father's education sometimes competes for a dominant place. It is interesting as well that, among boys, the direct effect of grades on the mother's desires exceeds the effect of ability but, among girls, ability either ranks above grades or is equal to them in importance.

We may now turn from direct effects to indirect ones. Although the effects of family background and sibsize are not mediated a great deal by ability and grades, there is some mediation. That is, some of the total effect of family background and sibsize is indirect. So we may ask, to the extent that this mediation takes place, which variable is more important as a mediator—ability or grades? The answer seems clear from table 6.6—ability. That is, insofar as status and sibsize influence mothers in their educational desires, and insofar as this influence depends on ability and/or grades, it appears that ability predominates as an influence.

Although this answer seems straightforward, it is not as ironclad as it could be because we have not explored the possibility that the indirect effect of parents' SES and sibsize on ability may actually be operating primarily through grades. For example, it may be that high parental status and small families lead to higher ability, and higher ability gets translated into higher grades, which are what really influence the mother's desires. From table 6.7 we can see that most of the effect of parental SES and sibsize through ability remains, it is not lost to grades, although some of course is lost. Hence, the original message of table 6.6 holds. Inasmuch as parental background and sibsize have effects on the mother's desires, and inasmuch as these effects are mediated by ability and grades, ability is the predominant mediating path.

Finally, we may note that the mediation through sibsize of parental background variables is very small and not statistically significant (table 6.6). This means, of course, that if high or low status parents have differential educational desires, these differences are *not* due to the influence of status on sibsize and, by that path, on parents' goals. We shall return to this point in a moment.

Table 6.6. Direct and Indirect Effects of Parental Background Variables, Sibsize, IQ, and Grades on the Students' Mothers' Educational Desires by Sex, White Boys and Girls, HSB, Sophomores and Seniors.

Sex, Class, and Predictors	Total Effect	Indirect Effects:			Direct Effect	R^2
		Sibsize	Vocabulary	Grades		
Boys						
Sophomores						
Fa Educ	.187	.003	.040	.013	.130	
Mo Educ	.182	.006	.033	.010	.133	
Fa SEI	.105	.004	.021	.010	.071	
Sibsize	-.082	.	-.020	-.011	-.052	
Vocab	.226	.	.	.074	.152	
Grades	.197	.	.	.	.197	.232
Seniors						
Fa Educ	.252	-.002	.034	.021	.200	
Mo Educ	.117	.001	.021	.004	.091	
Fa SEI	.130	.010	.019	.000	.101	
Sibsize	-.087	.	-.017	-.002	-.068	
Vocab	.226	.	.	.061	.165	
Grades	.171	.	.	.	.171	.246

Girls

Sophomores

Fa Educ	.155	.004	.034	.005	.111
Mo Educ	.180	.003	.021	.008	.148
Fa SEI	.084	.004	.020	.002	.057
Sibsize	-.069	.	-.015	-.004	-.050
Vocab	.195	.	.	.059	.137
Grades	.138	.	.	.	.138
					.172

Seniors

Fa Educ	.155	.000	.040	.007	.108
Mo Educ	.194	.003	.025	.004	.162
Fa SEI	.092	.005	.006	.003	.078
Sibsize	-.071	.	-.013	-.008	-.050
Vocab	.238	.	.	.054	.184
Grades	.150	.	.	.	.150
					.203

Table 6.7. Decomposition of the Indirect Effects of Father's and Mother's Education, Father's SEI, and Sibsize through IQ on Mother's Educational Desires by Sex, White Boys and Girls, HSB, Sophomores and Seniors.

		Indirect Effects through:	Total Indirect
			Effects through
		Ability through	Ability
Sex, Class, and Predictors	Ability Directly	Grades	
Boys			
Sophomores			
Fa Educ	.027	.013	.040
Mo Educ	.022	.011	.033
Fa SEI	.014	.007	.021
Sibsize	−.013	−.006	−.019
Seniors			
Fa Educ	.025	.009	.034
Mo Educ	.015	.006	.021
Fa SEI	.014	.005	.019
Sibsize	−.012	−.005	−.017
Girls			
Sophomores			
Fa Educ	.024	.010	.034
Mo Educ	.015	.006	.021
Fa SEI	.014	.006	.020
Sibsize	−.010	−.005	−.015
Seniors			
Fa Educ	.031	.009	.040
Mo Educ	.019	.006	.025
Fa SEI	.005	.001	.006
Sibsize	−.010	−.003	−.013

We will now consider the results for Cycle III (table 6.8). It is convenient to begin by concentrating on those students who are in grades 10 through 12, and looking at the similarities with and differences from the HSB results.

Regarding similarities, among boys the direct effects of the mother's education are not only relatively less important than the father's, they are not even statistically significant. Very little of family income or sibsize effects are mediated, and father's education retains approximately two-thirds of its total effect. Insofar as the father's education is mediated, the path through the WRAT (our indicator of school performance) is somewhat higher than the WISC. Considering the direct effects of the WISC and the WRAT, not only is the WRAT the most important variable explaining the mother's desires, but most of the effect of ability (the WISC) is mediated through the WRAT. Hence, consistent with HSB for boys are the greater relative importance of the father's education (compared to the mother's), the modest amount of mediation affecting family background variables and sibsize, and the overriding importance of school performance as an effect on the mother's desires.

For tenth- through twelfth-grade girls, we find that little of family income and sibsize are mediated and that 60 percent of the total effect of the father's education remains direct. The main mediating path for father's education is through the WISC. Further emphasizing the importance of the WISC for girls, we see that the direct effect of the WISC is close to the direct effect of the WRAT (although the WRAT is higher) whereas for boys the effect of the WISC was entirely mediated through the WRAT. Thus, as with HSB for girls in Cycle III, family background and sibsize are relatively unmediated, and the relative importance of ability versus school performance for the mother's desires is repeated.

Let us now turn to some differences from HSB. One major difference is that for both boys and girls the model fits better—the amount of variance explained is considerably higher than it was for HSB. We can only surmise why this should be true, but we believe that a major reason is that the family background data were derived from the parent in Cycle III, whereas they came from the student in HSB. We have already discussed the data problems with HSB and so there is no further need to elaborate on this point. The data on the parent's desires also come from the parent in Cycle III, so there is less slippage all the way around.

An interesting methodological point is that although Cycle III explains the *parent's* schooling desires better than HSB, the HSB explains the *student's* schooling goals better than Cycle III. Given the substantive difference between the two data sets (Cycle III obtains the parent's views from the parent, and HSB obtains them

Table 6.8. Direct and Indirect Effects of Parental Background Variables, Respondent's Age, Sibsize, WISC, and WRAT on Parents' Educational Desires for Their Children by Grade Level and Sex, White Boys and Girls, HES, Cycle III.

Sex, Grade, and Predictors	Total Effect	Indirect Effects:			Direct Effect	R^2
		Sibsize	WISC	WRAT		
Boys						
Grades 6–9						
Fa Educ	.252	.003	.064	.001	.184	
Mo Educ	.116	.023	.053	.023	.017[a]	
Fam Income	.108	.011	.020	.002	.075	
Sibsize	−.103	.	−.025	−.007	−.071	
WISC	.253	.	.	.153	.100	
WRAT	.231	.	.	.	.231	.265
Grades 10–12						
Fa Educ	.242	−.001	.039	.047	.157	
Mo Educ	.095	.021	.024	.008	.042[a]	
Fam Income	.239	.004	.020	.010	.205	
Sibsize	−.127	.	−.004	−.006	−.117	
WISC	.182	.	.	.187	−.005[a]	
WRAT	.339	.	.	.	.339	.328

Girls

Grades 6–9

Fa Educ	.102	.016	.040	.001	.045[a]	
Mo Educ	.181	.022	.043	.010	.106	
Fam Income	.163	.012	.020	.005	.126	
Sibsize	−.152	.	−.022	−.002	−.129	
WISC	.174	.	.	.051	.124	
WRAT	.081	.	.	.	.081[a]	.188

Grades 10–12

Fa Educ	.227	.014	.060	.017	.137	
Mo Educ	.114	.009	.075	.006	.024[a]	
Fam Income	.154	.005	.006	.008	.136	
Sibsize	−.146	.	−.008	−.007	−.131	
WISC	.278	.	.	.121	.157	
WRAT	.204	.	.	.	.204	.265

[a]Not significant at the 5-percent level.

from the student), this result should not be too surprising. When the parent's wishes are the primary dependent variable, the data are more accurate if they come from the parent. When the student's schooling goals are the primary dependent variable, and the parent's views are regarded theoretically as "support and encouragement" provided to the student, then there is less inaccuracy if the student's perception of the parent's wishes is used, as in HSB. Clearly, however, as noted already, even when the parent's desires are obtained from the parent (as in Cycle III), these desires are perceived with some accuracy by the student, as is indicated by the large increment to explained variance (R^2) when the parent's perceived desires are included.

Another difference between Cycle III and HSB is that for girls in Cycle III, even the total effect of the father's education is twice that of the mother's education, and the influence of the mother's education is almost entirely mediated—primarily through the WISC. Hence, unlike HSB, the mother's education is not relatively more important than the father's education as an influence on the parent's schooling desires for Cycle III high school girls. One speculation concerning this difference is that the Cycle III data were gathered at a time when wives' characteristics were more likely to be submerged into husband's and, hence, independent effects on many women's views about girl's education might be obscured in the earlier data set.

When we focus on the younger boys and girls in Cycle III, our interest centers on how the results are similar to or different from the Cycle III high school students. As for similarities, and considering boys first, we see that (except for the mother's education) very little of the total effect of family background and sibsize are mediated. The direct effect of the mother's education, however, becomes insignificant. The relative direct effect of the WRAT is still the most important of all effects in the model, and most of the WISC is mediated through it. It is also true that the direct effect of sibsize offsets the effect of family income. As for differences from older students, among younger boys the WISC is relatively more important than among older students in explaining parents' post-secondary desires, in addition to being important as a mediator for the mother's education.

Among younger girls, as among older ones, we see the direct

relative importance of the WISC, family income and sibsize are essentially exact tradeoffs and, insofar as background and sibsize are mediated, this occurs through the WISC. Different from older girls is the fact that the direct effect of the mother's education is relatively more important than the father's (the father's becoming statistically insignificant), and the fact that the direct effect of the WISC is actually greater than the effect of the WRAT.

In sum, although there are a number of important similarities between how the model of parents' schooling desires works for younger and older students, an interesting difference is that for both younger boys and girls ability enters in more forcefully (relative to indicators of school performance) in the parents' calculations. It may be that the parents of younger students put more weight on their own sense of the child's ability (high or low) than on school performance measures. For example a child who is experienced as very bright but at present not a high performer, may nonetheless be thought of as having high educational potential, whereas a child who is experienced as fairly dull but who "tries hard," may not be singled out by the parent for college.

We may ask why the model is less predictive among younger than among older students. We believe that the reason is fairly straightforward. A question on parents' postsecondary desires for offspring is less relevant to parents of younger students than older ones. While it is a question that probably can be answered readily by parents of very young students at the extremes of ability and performance, for many other parents the question, as stated, may be premature.

As between boys and girls, the mother's education seems to be clearly more important an influence on parental desires for girls than it is for boys. In addition, there is a fairly consistent tendency for grades to be relatively more influential when it comes to desires for boys, whereas ability is more so when it comes to girls. The greater dependence of educational aspirations for girls versus boys on the mother's education is hardly surprising in view of past research (Sewell, Hauser, and Wolf 1980), but the greater emphasis on grades and school performance for boys as influences on parents educational desires requires some explanation. It may be that competitive school performance is part of parents' role definition of successful male behavior and future success in life generally. It is probably more rare for parents to emphasize competition for grades when they think of educating their daughters. In fact, being intensely competitive with boys for grades in school is often regarded by parents as a negative for girls. Hence, parents of girls may be more likely to think of postsecondary education for daughters if the latter are bright enough to be able to go to college, but not necessarily because of the daughter's competitive grade-point average.

SUMMARY AND CONCLUSION

This chapter has asked how aspects of family background, including sibsize, get translated into differential postsecondary goals among young people. Our concentration on this dependent variable is justified on the basis of past research by others showing that postsecondary goals of high school students are a major predictor of years of schooling completed. This chapter uses (with some changes) that part of the Wisconsin model of status attainment that focuses on educational aspirations as its dependent variable. Important novel components of our analysis are that we repeat the analysis on three national data sets of boys and girls, two of which concentrate on young people prior to their senior year. Moreover, one of the data sets contains information on parents from parents, whereas the other two derive information on parents from youngsters (like the Wisconsin data). We are thus able to see whether the high degree of importance attached to parental influence on youngsters in past research is primarily a function of circularity in the data-gathering procedure. Finally, we have done a detailed analysis including sibsize, not included as a variable at the time that the Wisconsin analysts were focusing on youngsters' educational goals.

A major emphasis in the chapter concerns the mechanisms by which differential sibsize affects educational goals. Are most of its effects indirect, operating through ability, grades, and differential support and encouragement? Or, does it have substantial direct effects even after taking these intervening variables into account? Insofar as it has indirect effects, what intervening variables does it impinge on the most?

With regard to student's expectations in the HSB data, we find that most of the total effects of parental background and sibsize are indirect—mediated through ability and the mother's schooling desires. Differential ability influences grades, so that the net of this analysis is that mother's desires and grades become the most important direct influence on the students' expectations. As between grades and the mother's desires, younger students (sophomores) are more sensitive to grades relative to the mother's desires than are seniors. Our analysis thus suggests a mechanism by which younger students begin to select themselves out of school on the basis of externally validated performance.

The students' expectations in Cycle III of the Health Examination Survey are exceptionally valuable in showing that even when the parents' desires have been stated by the parent, parental desires are still the most important influence on students' expectations. The Cycle III results are otherwise broadly similar to the HSB results.

Because of the demonstrated importance of the parents' expectations to the students' expectations, we analyzed how sibsize affects parents' expectations specifically. Our main question was whether sibsize operates through ability and grades to influence parents' expectations, or whether it has an effect over and above the fact that youngsters from smaller families are smarter and do better in school. We found that insofar as parental status and sibsize influence parents' educational goals, this influence is primarily direct— that is, it is independent of the child's grades or ability. However, although background and sibsize are not mediated very much, it is nonetheless true that the most important direct influence on parental expectations is ability and grades, not parental background and sibsize. These findings were essentially replicated for Cycle III. However, a major difference from HSB is that the model fits better, presumably because the data on parents are from the parent directly and not from the youngster. There are also noteworthy differences between how the model works on younger and older students. Among younger students, ability is more important to parental expectations than it is among older students where grades weigh more heavily. We interpreted this to mean that among younger children, parents put more weight on their own observations of the child's talents but, as the youngster moves along in school, external validation must be recognized. It is also true that the model is less predictive among younger students. We believe this may be due to the fact that postsecondary expectations may be less salient and realistic for parents of younger than older students, especially the large body of such students who are neither very bright nor very dull.

In sum, young people from higher-status families and small sibsizes appear to have higher educational goals primarily because these influences operate on ability and grades and thence through parental expectations. Regardless of how the data on parents' expectations are obtained, or whether these data pertain to seniors or younger children, parents' expectations are the most important influence on youngsters' expectations. These results tend to confirm past research using the Wisconsin model, except that they add considerable detail concerning the relative importance of sibsize compared with other family background variables. And we have been able to show that the importance of parental expectations is not simply a methodological artifact of questioning students about their views of their parents' views.

7

SETTINGS, TREATMENTS, AND SOCIAL AND PERSONALITY CHARACTERISTICS BY SIBSIZE

Sociologists have become increasingly concerned with identifying the familial behavior that is indicated by, or results from, family background measures such as parental education, occupation, income, and marital cohesion. Spaeth (1976) has suggested that differential parental socioeconomic status is an indicator of variability in cognitively stimulating home environments. He has also suggested the usefulness of making a heuristic distinction between "settings" and "treatments" as aspects of the home environment— settings being the various cognitively stimulating features of the environment that are available to be engaged but do not actively engage the child, such as books, musical instruments, and so forth; and treatments being purposive parental interventions in the child's intellectual development, such as active teaching, correcting, encouraging, goal setting, and the like. The importance of environmentally stimulating settings to the development of intellectual ability has been a focus of much research by psychologists (Milner 1951; Dave 1963; Bloom 1964; Wolf 1964; Hess and Shipman 1965; Lewis and Goldberg 1969; Hess 1970a and b; Marjoribanks 1972a and b; Williams 1976). Sociologists have demonstrated the significance of differential treatments, in the instance of differential parental encouragement to educational achievement among high school students (Sewell and Hauser 1980, for example). We have just discussed parental encouragement in Chapter 6.

If the home environment contributes (or fails to contribute) cognitive stimulation at an early age and continuing through adolescence, the school increasingly takes over this function as the child advances in age. It is hardly surprising, therefore, that considerable interest has been generated in the character of the school environment, and particularly in the types of extracurricular activities engaged in by young people in high school.

Finally, it is fruitful to ask about aspects of young people's characteristics that seem relevant to educational attainment, and the ability to engage progressively more stimulating situations and challenges.

In sum, this chapter will present information from surveys concerning (1) the cognitive stimulation of two types of settings (home and school); (2) what we call parental "treatments"—specific parental interactions relevant to cognitive stimulation; and, finally, (3) personal characteristics of young people that would seem relevant to successful educational advancement. Our focus will be on sibsize differences in these elements. Very little data gathering has been directed to the topics of cognitively relevant settings and treatments by sibsize, although there are, by contrast, numerous questions on psychological characteristics and moods. The purpose of this chapter is not, therefore, to present a definitive picture. Rather, it should be viewed as a stimulus to research of all kinds to fill in the enormous gaps in our knowledge.

To make a hard and fast distinction between stimulation that is simply "passive" and stimulation that is actively directed toward the child by a parent would not be productive. Parents may make a great deal of effort to provide settings that are stimulating. There is nonetheless a worthwhile distinction to be made between stimulation that is a constant, undirected feature of simply living in a particular setting, and stimulation that involves targeted interaction by the parent with regard to the child's behavior—what we will call "treatments."

SETTINGS AT HOME

After controlling for parents' socioeconomic characteristics, do the types of cognitively stimulating "settings" in the home differ by sibsize for the young people in our samples? We will use the 6- to 11-year-olds in Cycle II of the Health Examination Survey, the 12- to 17-year-olds in the same survey, the high school sophomore boys in Youth in Transition, and the sophomore and senior boys and girls in High School and Beyond. The data differ among the studies, and some of the information might be considered as equally relating to "treatments" and "settings."

Although much heat has been expended on the unsociability and loneliness of the only child (see, Bossard 1954; Bossard and Boll 1956; Terhune 1974; Thompson 1974; Claudy, et al. 1979; Blake 1981*b*), little systematic research has been done on the differential environments of only children, and children from other small families, compared to children from large families. One could entertain the hypothesis, therefore, that some of the widespread perception of only children as "less sociable" may actually be a function of their class position and intellectual levels.[1] Such children tend to come from milieus that value privacy, time alone, and intellectually demanding uses of time—reading, listening to music, playing an instrument, and so on. And, on average, such children have the intellectual ability to respond to these environments, as well as the desire.

Claudy and colleagues (1979) have addressed the issue of differential uses of discretionary time in their analysis of only children and children from two-child families in the Project Talent Study. They have controlled for indicators of the parents' socioeconomic status, but not for IQ in these particular tabulations. They found that only children participated to a greater extent than children with siblings in extracurricular activities generally—in reading for pleasure, in collecting, hobbies, raising animals and pets, in acting, singing, and dancing, and in music, photography, and clubs. Children with siblings participated more in sports and other team activities, high school leadership roles, hunting/fishing, woodworking, crafts, and cooking. In effect, only children were engaged in activities that were often solitary, intellectual, and artistic; whereas "non-onlies" were engaged in group-oriented and practical activities.

Another study of the effect of the family settings of youngsters, by number of siblings, is represented in the work of Heise and Roberts (1970). Studying children in elementary school, the investigators were concerned with children's extent of knowledge of common family and community roles and with the correlates of role knowledge. Of relevance here is the counterintuitive finding that an increase in number of siblings was negatively correlated with role knowledge, and that this negative correlation increased with the age of the child. Interestingly, the negative effect of siblings was greatest for what the investigators called "peer focus" roles (filial roles, sibling roles, and a role-complex called "High School Boy"). The investigators interpret this finding as being a consequence of the parochialism of children in large families. Such children are more inclined to confine their playing and their interaction to within the family because the family is a more self-sufficient unit. It turns out, therefore, that children with numerous siblings do learn peer-focus roles, but ones that have little social currency or validation. In effect, these roles have been *mis*learned by paying too much attention to the behavior of family members exclusively. The authors caution that their findings, based on intensive study of 93 children, are suggestive only. However, their results are worth citing to represent a level of theoretical sophistication that is relatively rare in available research on the effects of family size.

A principal source of our data on family settings is Cycle II of the Health Examination Survey. The Cycle II data are particularly important because early childhood has been targeted by psychologists as a critical time for cognitive and linguistic development (Passow, Goldberg, and Tannenbaum 1967; Jensen 1968; Whiteman and Deutsch 1968; Gewirtz 1969; Bernstein 1970; Bijou 1971). Moreover, it would seem that as children get older the influence of the family is diluted by that of schools and peer groups (Campbell 1969).

Cycle II obtained information from parents on a variety of the child's (age 6 to 11) uses of time—Scouts, sports, cultural activities, watching television, listening to radio, reading newspapers, reading books, and playing by him or herself. The reader is cautioned that these parental replies are not systematic time-use data. Their value inheres in the fact that they add to a body of prior information (for example, the Project Talent data analyzed by Claudy), and they provide a stimulus to future, more rigorous, data gathering.

Taking all formalized extracurricular activities (Scouts, sports, church groups, music and other cultural pursuits) as a group, we have coded the children in terms of whether they engaged in any or none. Table 7.1 indicates that children from small families, including only children, are more likely to be involved in one or more such activities even after controls for the child's age and sex, parents' education, family income, family intactness, region of the country, community size, and the mother's usual activities. Among

Table 7.1. Formalized Extracurricular Use of Time by Sibsize, White Boys and Girls Age 6 to 11, HES, Cycle II, Adjusted Means.[a]

Sibsize	Extracurricular Activities (None/One or More)		Music, Painting, Cultural[b]	
1	0.58	(184)	1.55	(92)
2	0.53	(951)	1.44	(509)
3	0.49	(1,171)	1.43	(608)
4	0.46	(952)	1.38	(423)
5	0.44	(490)	1.30	(198)
6	0.44	(261)	1.27	(109)
7+	0.48	(502)	1.23	(167)
Grand Mean	0.49	(4,511)	1.39	(2,106)
S.D.	—		0.60	
R^2	.153		.143	

[a]The means have been adjusted for the child's age, sex, mother's and father's education, family income, family intactness, region of the country, community size, and mother's labor force participation. The number of cases for each group is shown in parentheses.

[b]The means here are calculated using only those respondents who indicated participation in any activity and are coded with 1 = no activities in the specific group to 4 = 3 or more activities in the group.

those engaging in such activities, table 7.1 shows the results for music and other cultural pursuits. Respondents were coded "1" if they participated in no activity in each category, and up to "4" if they participated in three or more activities in each category. We see that children from small families are more participatory. In the unadjusted data, children in small families also participated more in sports and Little League. However, the difference disappeared where data were adjusted.

For watching TV, listening to radio, and reading books, responses ranged from zero to six or more hours per day, and reading newspapers ranged from zero to four or more hours per day (see table 7.2). There are no sibsize differences in TV watching, but time spent listening to radio, reading newspapers, and reading books shows declines as sibsize increases. Only children, in particular, spend the most time on these pursuits. The same table shows that "playing by self" (zero to six or more hours a day) is related to sibsize, and is particularly marked for only children.

Table 7.2. Informal Use of Time by Sibsize and Sex, White Boys and Girls Age 6 to 11, HES, Cycle II, Adjusted Means.[a]

Sibsize	Hours Per Day			
	Listening to Radio		Reading Newspapers	
1	0.45	(173)	0.30	(171)
2	0.25	(914)	0.22	(918)
3	0.22	(1,122)	0.22	(1,130)
4	0.26	(925)	0.23	(924)
5	0.27	(474)	0.23	(470)
6	0.14	(250)	0.14	(245)
7+	0.13	(470)	0.20	(465)
Grand Mean	0.24	(4,328)	0.22	(4,323)
S.D.	0.63		0.37	
R^2	.041		.078	
	Reading Books		Playing by Self	
1	0.66	(173)	1.35	(172)
2	0.62	(887)	0.76	(910)
3	0.60	(1,104)	0.71	(1,114)
4	0.54	(907)	0.52	(909)
5	0.54	(465)	0.59	(467)
6	0.50	(246)	0.64	(245)
7+	0.50	(476)	0.28	(457)
Grand Mean	0.57	(4,258)	0.64	(4,274)
S.D.	0.66		1.04	
R^2	.095		.068	

[a]The means have been adjusted for the child's age, sex, mother's and father's education, family income, family intactness, region of the country, community size, and mother's labor force participation. The values represent mean hours per day spent on the activity as stated by the parent.

These results, while bearing out the Claudy findings that were confined to differences between only children and those from two-child families, suggest that preferences for relatively solitary and/or intellectual, as well as cultural and artistic, uses of time characterize the entire small end of the sibsize continuum versus those from large families.

Is this intellectual/solitary tendency of children from smaller families a function of being less popular and well liked by other

Table 7.3. Teacher Assessments of Child's Popularity by Sibsize, White Boys and Girls Age 6 to 11, HES, Cycle II, Adjusted Means.[a]

Sibsize	*Teacher's assessment of frequency child is chosen when other children choose sides*[b]	
1	2.24	(149)
2	2.21	(796)
3	2.22	(984)
4	2.19	(770)
5	2.14	(410)
6	2.23	(200)
7+	2.09	(401)
Grand Mean	2.19	(3,710)
S.D.	0.61	
R^2	.032	

[a]The means have been adjusted for the child's age, sex, mother's and father's education, family income, family intactness, region of the country, community size, and mother's labor force participation.

[b]The values here represent means on a scale with 1 = almost always last, 2 = intermediate, and 3 = almost always first. The Ns are somewhat reduced here due to the fact that teacher's evaluations were not available for all children.

children? The data do not justify such a conclusion. Table 7.3 shows the teacher's evaluation of the frequency with which the child is chosen when other children are choosing sides. These results suggest that only children and those from small families are, if anything, more popular than children from larger families. Parent responses to questions concerning shyness and getting along with other children show no difference by sibsize.

If enforced isolation due to unpopularity does not account for differences in children's activities by sibsize, does the association of higher ability with sibsize (as well as with reading, playing by oneself, and other intellectual and cultural activities) account for the sibsize association with these activities. Controls for intellectual ability not shown here reduce somewhat, but do not eliminate, the sibsize difference in reading shown in table 7.2, suggesting that the intellectual-ability differences by sibsize conjoin with discretionary use of time to set young children from small families on a path toward academic success. Moreover, although playing alone is asso-

Please read down this list and check the things you have done at least one time in your life:

1. Danced	24. Worked part-time
2. Smoked	25. Worked full-time
3. Gone swimming	26. Owned a wrist watch
4. Ice skated	27. Had a bank account
5. Made a long distance phone call	28. Made minor house repair
6. Driven a car	29. Had a driver's license
7. Taken a taxi	30. Heard a live symphony
8. Bought a book	31. Acted in a play
9. Visited a zoo	32. Sent an entry blank to a contest
10. Cashed a check	33. Put together a picture puzzle
11. Attended a summer camp	34. Belonged to a sports team
12. Visited Europe	35. Sent away for a radio offer
13. Played ping pong	36. Collected stamps or coins
14. Bought a magazine	37. Attended a professional sporting event
15. Visited a museum	38. Bought a phonograph record
16. Flown on an airplane	39. Ridden in a rowboat
17. Gone alone to a different city	40. Ridden a horse or pony
18. Attended a live opera	41. Baby-sat for a neighbor
19. Attended a live ballet	42. Had a friend who attended college
20. Seen a live circus	43. Taken out a library book
21. Visited a farm	44. Belonged to scouts or other club
22. Ridden on a merry-go-round	45. Played a musical instrument
23. Stayed overnight in a hotel	46. Written letter to someone

Figure 7.1. Items Included in Index of Richness of Past Experience (Youth in Transition).

ciated positively with intellectual ability, using the WISC as a control does not reduce the overall relationship of playing alone with sibsize—a relationship that is obviously enforced by the absence of siblings among only children and the ubiquitousness of siblings in large families. Since studying and other intellectual activities typically require concentrated periods of solitude, the development of a tolerance for being alone at an early age may also be helpful to the academic development of children from small families.

Finally, the picture that emerges from these data may account for some of the popular prejudice against only children, especially, as overprivileged, asocial, and royally autonomous. These children clearly are something of an intellectual and social elite, as well as being relatively less numerous than the mass of children from larger families. Cumulated over a number of activities and uses of time, young children from small families, and only children particularly, appear to lead rather different personal lives from those residing with numerous siblings. Children born into large families who complain of lack of privacy and the constant need to adjust to other people may well be told by their parents that conditions in small families "spoil" children, making them self-centered, aloof, and overly intellectual. Since so many more people come from large

Table 7.4. Adjusted Means for Indexes Measuring the Value of Social Skills, Anomie, Resentment, and Richness of Past Experience by Sibsize, White Boys, YIT, High School Sophomores.[a]

Sibsize	Value of Social Skills	Anomie	Resentment	Richness of Past Experience
1	5.12	2.40	2.48	33.2
2	5.08	2.48	2.47	33.4
3	4.97	2.54	2.51	33.1
4	5.02	2.53	2.54	32.8
5	4.99	2.53	2.56	32.4
6	5.04	2.51	2.59	32.3
7+	4.90	2.60	2.60	31.5
Grand Mean	5.02	2.52	2.52	32.8
S.D.	.64	.66	.71	6.59
R^2	.010	.018	.005	.103
N	1,856	1,823	1,873	1,912

[a]Means have been adjusted for mother's and father's education, socioeconomic status, community size where youth was brought up, and family intactness. The values for the first three indexes represent the average over 7 items scored using a scale from 1 = very bad to 6 = very good for the value of various social skills; and 1 = never true to 5 = almost always true for feelings of anomie and resentment. The values for richness of past experience represent the mean number of items checked. See figure 7.2 for a list of the possible items.

families than from small ones, it is not too surprising that prejudices against small families have been widely transmitted.

Turning to the Youth in Transition study, tenth-grade boys were asked to respond to a 46-item Index of Richness of Past Experiences, answering whether they had or had not done each of the itemized activities at least once in their lives (see fig. 7.1). Although some of the items would seem to favor children from large families (such as having a part-time or full-time job), an analysis of the overall index of richness of past experience (see table 7.4) indicates that those from small families have had richer and more varied lives. Other information from this survey, although indirect, suggests that only children and those from small families experienced socially stimulating and "upbeat" home environments. Nothing in our data suggests depression, isolation, sadness, hopelessness, and the like. For example, table 7.4 gives results for a social skills index

Table 7.5. Frequency of Being Read To as a Preschooler by Sibsize and Sex, White Boys and Girls, HSB, Sophomores and Seniors, Adjusted Means.[a]

	Frequency of Being Read To as a Preschooler			
Class and Sibsize	Boys		Girls	
Sophomores				
1	10.88	(312)	13.92	(326)
2	9.68	(1,458)	13.17	(1,581)
3	9.32	(1,768)	12.13	(1,974)
4	8.64	(1,306)	11.53	(1,462)
5	8.25	(707)	12.08	(769)
6	8.21	(431)	11.38	(471)
7+	8.55	(573)	11.58	(724)
Grand Mean	9.08	(6,555)	12.21	(7,307)
S.D.	10.22		11.24	
R^2	.027		.037	
Seniors				
1	10.99	(295)	13.17	(276)
2	10.29	(1,038)	14.09	(1,177)
3	9.94	(1,216)	12.30	(1,397)
4	8.87	(909)	11.92	(1,069)
5	8.22	(532)	11.40	(632)
6	7.80	(281)	12.14	(319)
7+	7.67	(385)	10.70	(435)
Grand Mean	9.36	(4,656)	12.42	(5,305)
S.D.	10.02		11.00	
R^2	.042		.048	

[a]Means have been adjusted for father's and mother's education, father's occupation, and family intactness. The values represent mean times per month that the event occurred.

(boys were asked to place a value on various skills that help people get along with others); an anomie index (8 items measuring respondent's feeling that the world is uncaring and "going to the dogs"); and a resentment index (7 items measuring feelings of being cheated, getting a "raw deal," and that others "get the breaks"). All show relatively small differences by sibsize, but differences favoring those from small families.

Table 7.6. Average Score on Music and Dance Lessons, and Travel Outside the United States, by Sibsize, White Boys and Girls, HSB, Sophomores, Adjusted Means.[a]

| | Score on Music/Dance Lessons and Foreign Travel | | | |
| | Boys | | Girls | |
Sibsize				
1	1.08	(321)	1.56	(329)
2	1.06	(1,496)	1.54	(1,602)
3	1.05	(1,826)	1.46	(1,997)
4	0.99	(1,357)	1.37	(1,495)
5	0.97	(732)	1.33	(786)
6	0.97	(454)	1.28	(482)
7+	0.87	(595)	1.24	(736)
Grand Mean	1.01	(6,781)	1.42	(7,427)
S.D.	0.82		0.94	
R^2	.100		.171	

[a]Means have been adjusted for father's and mother's education, father's occupation, and family intactness. The values represent mean occurrence of the three possible activities scored as 0 = No on three, 1 = Yes on one, 2 = Yes on two, and 3 = Yes on three.

Both the sophomores and the seniors in High School and Beyond were queried concerning various aspects of the home environment. Among these aspects was whether and how frequently they were read to before they started attending school. The code went as follows:

0	=	Never
.5	=	Less than once a month
2.5	=	One to four times a month
14.0	=	Several times per week
30.0	=	Every day

Table 7.5 demonstrates for sophomores and seniors of both sexes that reports of being read to are associated negatively with number of siblings, even after controls for parents' educations, father's occupation, and whether the family was intact. Only children and children from small families were allegedly more likely to have been read to before they started school than were children from larger families, and the relationship, although not large, is quite linear.

We must remember that by the time children become sophomores and seniors in high school, there has been selective dropping out that may well affect the strength of this relationship. In any event, this type of cognitive enrichment is negatively associated with number of siblings, in spite of the fact that a potential contribution of large families might be the presence of older siblings who could read to younger ones. These results do not, therefore, offer support to Zajonc's notion that older siblings in large families provide substitutes for parents.

Sophomores were questioned concerning whether they had had a variety of advantages—music lessons, dance lessons, and travel outside the United States. Children from small families were more likely to have had one or more of these advantages, whereas those from large families were more likely to have had none. Table 7.6 shows the adjusted mean average score on the three activities by sibsize for boys and girls. The difference between boys and girls results from a lower frequency among all boys with regard to taking dance lessons. There is a substantial and linear sibsize difference even after controlling for family background.

SETTINGS IN SCHOOL: EXTRACURRICULAR ACTIVITIES

Discretionary behavior in school can be regarded as an extension of the settings/treatments dichotomy to another phase of the life cycle. In this case, as Spaeth (1976) has suggested, youngsters are participating actively in choosing settings in which to place themselves and in the self-administration of "treatments." At least two studies have found a relationship between educational attainment (years of school completed) and participation in extracurricular activities in high school independent of parental SES, academic ability, and academic performance (Spady 1970; Otto 1975). Extracurricular activity has also been suggested as a mechanism by which parental SES is transmitted to offspring (Otto 1975). Otto has postulated that extracurricular activity provides socialization for attitudes and skills that "pay off" later in life.

A rather different perspective has been offered by Coleman in *The Adolescent Society* (1961). Coleman concentrates on the *types* of activities in which students are engaged (rather than on the level of participation), and on the degree to which activities are congruent with high levels of academic achievement and scholarship. Our own analysis will lean more toward the Coleman type of research question. Are there sibsize differences in the *types* of activities in which young people are engaged after controlling for major family background characteristics? Are young people from small families, including only children, more likely to engage in extracurricular activities that are intellectually and culturally stimulating, in contrast to community-oriented activities, vocationally oriented activities, or sports? In considering the results we will present, the reader should bear in mind that extracurricular activities—especially school activities—are not always perfect indicators of students' principal interests and diversions. Some activities require particular talents and cannot be enjoyed passively, and some may be selected as a change of pace from the student's usual activities, or as an experiment. However, as will be seen, our analysis attempts to deal with this problem.

We will concentrate our analysis on seniors in the High School and Beyond data. Students were asked the questions in figure 7.2. Although it is possible to distinguish between students who had no extracurricular activities during the past school year and those who had one or more such activity, it is not possible to count activities because, in the initial questions, items were grouped (for example, types of sports were grouped, as were activities like debating or drama, chorus or dance, and so on). We thus turned our attention to the types of activities in which students were engaged according to sibsize, rather than to the number of activities.

As a beginning, students could be grouped into those who had no activity, only sports, only nonsports, and both sports and nonsports. For boys and girls, the percentage distributions in these categories are shown in table 7.7. Clearly, few seniors have no activity. Most boys are engaged in sports, or sports and another activity, and girls are engaged modally in a nonsport activity.

The next question was whether the activities of students checking more than one nonsport category formed a pattern. For example, we believed that the activities of dance, band and orchestra, and drama would go together; and that student government, service on school newspapers and magazines, and membership in honor clubs would be cognate. We also saw a congruence between church activi-

Have you participated in any of the following types of activities either in or out of school this year? (MAKE ONE OVAL FOR EACH LINE)

		Have not participated	Have participated actively (but not as a leader or officer)	Have participated as a leader or officer
a.	Varsity athletic teams	0	0	0
b.	Other athletic teams - in or out of school	0	0	0
c.	Cheer leaders, pep club, majorettes	0	0	0
d.	Debating or drama	0	0	0
e.	Band or orchestra	0	0	0
f.	Chorus or dance	0	0	0
g.	Hobby clubs such as photography, model building, hot rod, electronics, crafts	0	0	0
h.	Honorary clubs, such as Beta Club or National Honor Society	0	0	0
i.	School newspaper, magazine, yearbook, annual	0	0	0
j.	School subject-matter clubs, such as science, history, language, business, art	0	0	0
k.	Student council, student government, political club	0	0	0
l.	Vocational education clubs, such as Future Homemakers, Teachers, Farmers of America, DECA, FBLA, or VICA	0	0	0
m.	Youth organizations in the community, such as Scouts, Y, etc.	0	0	0
n.	Church activities, including youth groups	0	0	0
o.	Junior Achievement	0	0	0

Figure 7.2. Questions Asked of Seniors Concerning Extracurricular Activities (High School and Beyond).

ties and youth organizations such as Scouts and the "Y." A factor analysis showed that we could combine students engaged in sports and nonsports with nonsports only.[2]

The analysis showed that we could divide the various nonsport activities into five factors: (1) "Intellectual," (2) "Artistic and Cultural," (3) "Community," (4) "Hobbies," and (5) "Vocational." These factors were then used to assign students to one of the five groups. Students with one nonsport activity were assigned to the relevant group, students with more than one such activity were assigned to the group in which they had the most activities. And if number of activities in all groups was equal, then the student was assigned to the group with which any given activity had the highest correlation. The final distribution is shown in table 7.8.

Among those who have activities (table 7.8), the single most important type of nonsport pursuit for both boys and girls is some form of community involvement—church, youth groups, and so

Table 7.7. Percentage Distribution of Students by Extracurricular Activities, White Boys and Girls, HSB, Seniors.

Activity Group	Boys	Girls
No Activity	13	10
Sports Only	11	3
Sports and Nonsports	50	37
Nonsports Only	26	50
Total	100	100
N	4,692	5,324

Table 7.8. Percentage Distribution of Students by Extracurricular Activities, Showing Distribution by Types of Nonsports Activities, White Boys and Girls, HSB, Seniors.

Activity Group		Boys		Girls
Intellectual		16.7		11.6
Only	4.2		6.2	
Sports and Intellectual	12.5		5.5	
Artistic/Cultural		9.8		24.4
Only	4.2		13.1	
Sports and Art	5.6		11.3	
Community		24.8		29.8
Only	6.2		16.4	
Sports and Community	18.6		13.4	
Hobby		15.3		3.5
Only	6.2		2.2	
Sports and Hobby	9.1		1.3	
Vocational		9.7		18.0
Only	4.9		11.9	
Sports and Vocational	4.8		6.1	
Only Sports		10.7		2.8
No Activity		13.0		9.9
Total		100.0		100.0
N		4,692		5,324

forth. After community activities, boys and girls divide quite markedly. Boys are more likely to be engaged either in intellectual activities (school newspapers, student government, yearbook, etc.) or in hobby clubs. Girls are more likely to be involved in artistic and cultural activities, or in vocational pursuits. There is a particularly sharp gender discrepancy with regard to hobby clubs and artistic and cultural pursuits—the one almost exclusively a male activity, the other primarily a female activity. It is also true that very few girls are engaged solely in sports, whereas this is true for 11 percent of the boys.

If we assume that the pursuit of "intellectual" activities (and intellectual activities plus sports) provides students with training and experience that will help to further their academic careers, are there sibsize differences between those who engage in such activities versus those who engage in sports only, community only, or community and sports; vocational only, or vocational and sports; or no activity at all? Turning first to boys, the top tier of table 7.9 shows the results of four multiple classification analyses (MCAs). The dependent variable in each case is a dichotomy—"1" for intellectual activities, and "0" for only sports, or for community, vocational, or no activity, respectively. The proportions shown have been adjusted for the parents' education, the father's occupation, and whether the family is intact. We see that, in general, boys from small- and medium-size families are more likely to engage in intellectual activities (versus any of the other activities) than are those from large families (sibsizes five and over). Relative to community and vocational activities, only children are particularly likely to engage in intellectual pursuits. The findings are similar if we combine artistic/cultural activities with intellectual activities and redo the MCAs as in the second tier of table 7.9. Boys from small- and medium-size families are also more likely to engage in intellectual (and artistic) activities than no activities at all. However, in this case, only children are slightly less participatory than children from two-child families.

As for girls, since artistic and cultural activities are modal, we have in table 7.10 performed the same analysis as for boys (table 7.9) using Artistic (which includes cultural) in the top tier instead of Intellectual, and combining both Intellectual and Artistic in the second tier. As between artistic and community activities, only

Table 7.9. Proportions Engaged in Intellectual (or Intellectual and Artistic) Activities as Contrasted with Other Extracurricular Activities by Sibsize, White Boys, HSB, Seniors.

	Mean Proportions[a]			
Sibsize	*Intellectual versus Only Sport*	*Intellectual versus Community*	*Intellectual versus Vocational*	*Intellectual versus No Activity*
1	0.62	0.48	0.67	0.57
2–4	0.63	0.41	0.64	0.59
5+	0.54	0.36	0.58	0.48
Grand Mean	0.61	0.40	0.63	0.56
R^2	.040	.007	.123	.108
N	1,284	1,950	1,244	1,391
	Intellectual and Artistic versus Only Sport	*Intellectual and Artistic versus Community*	*Intellectual and Artistic versus Vocational*	*Intellectual and Artistic versus No Activity*
1	0.72	0.59	0.76	0.67
2–4	0.73	0.52	0.74	0.70
5+	0.66	0.49	0.69	0.61
Grand Mean	0.71	0.52	0.73	0.67
R^2	.028	.005	.095	.085
N	1,741	2,407	1,701	1,848

[a]Means have been adjusted for the mother's and father's education, father's occupation, and family intactness. The dependent variable is coded one for "intellectual" or "intellectual and artistic," and zero for "sport," "community," "vocational," and "no activity," respectively.

children are clearly more likely to engage in artistic pursuits, whereas there is no difference among the other family sizes. The same pattern appears if we include intellectual activities in the dependent variable. Interestingly, however, only girls are slightly more likely to engage in no activities (than artistic or artistic/intellectual activities) compared with those from families of two to four children. In this respect, only children appear somewhat more like children from large families than those from two- to four-child families.

Table 7.10. Proportions Engaged in Artistic (or Artistic and Intellectual) Activities as Contrasted with Other Extracurricular Activities by Sibsize, White Girls, HSB, Seniors.

	Mean Proportions[a]		
Sibsize	Artistic versus Community	Artistic versus Vocational	Artistic versus No Activity
1	0.56	0.56	0.69
2–4	0.45	0.57	0.73
5+	0.44	0.59	0.66
Grand Mean	0.45	0.58	0.71
R^2	.004	.041	.074
N	2,885	2,254	1,827
	Artistic and Intellectual versus Community	Artistic and Intellectual versus Vocational	Artistic and Intellectual versus No Activity
1	0.64	0.64	0.76
2–4	0.55	0.67	0.80
5+	0.54	0.68	0.74
Grand Mean	0.55	0.67	0.78
R^2	.005	.049	.072
N	3,508	2,877	2,450

[a]Means have been adjusted for the mother's and father's education, father's occupation, and family intactness. The dependent variable is coded one for "artistic" or "artistic and intellectual," and zero for "community," "vocational," and "no activity," respectively.

Children from large families are the most likely to have no activity (when this category is compared with artistic and intellectual).

In sum, only children are particularly unlikely to engage in "community" type activities relative to young people from other sibsizes, and those from small families generally are more likely to engage in intellectual and artistic pursuits than are those from large families. Children from large families are more likely to have no activity at all than an intellectual or artistic one, and only children are very slightly more likely to have no activity (compared to an intellectual and artistic one) than those from two- to four-child families. Except for this last-mentioned anomaly among only children, it thus appears that coming from a small family versus a large one is associated with extracurricular activities that are congruent with and facilitative of academic and developmental skills. By contrast, those from large families are more likely to engage in sports only, in church activities, youth groups and other community efforts, in vocational activities (boys only), and in no activity at all.

Turning to whether students participate (or do not participate) at all in extracurricular activities, are there major sibsize differences in this behavior? Theoretically, we expect that school grades and type of school program will be major determinants of participation since both schools and parents tend to limit involvement when students have low grades, and schools that are heavily oriented toward vocational and general programs may have limited opportunities for extracurricular activities. It is also true that youngsters from farm families (although often in vocational and general tracks) tend to have uniquely high levels of extracurricular participation because of their involvement in church, community, and farm-related vocational and hobby activities. Those from farm backgrounds also come from larger families.

Accordingly, we limited our multiple classification analysis to senior boys and girls from nonfarm families, and included as predictors high school program, grades, parents' education, father's occupation, whether the family is intact, and sibsize. In addition, we introduced a control for ability as measured by the age-standardized vocabulary test. No major sibsize differences in overall participation for either boys or girls were evident (results not shown here). The principal determinants of participation/nonparticipation are grades and high school program. The major program difference is between academic (higher participation) and other programs (all other variables in the model equal), and there is marked variability in participation by grade performance. The relative importance of program (other variables controlled) is slightly greater than the relative importance of grades. Given controls for grades and program, parents' education is not salient, nor is family intactness.

PARENTAL "TREATMENTS"

What do we already know about sibsize and parental behavior toward children as these relate to intellectual development? Actually, very little work has been done that considers sibsize as an influence on parental behavior, and the latter in turn as an influence on intellectual achievement. It is nonetheless worthwhile to trace out some of the theoretical and empirical background for our own effort. This background stems primarily from educational psychology, social psychology, and sociology.

Beginning with the work of Bloom at Chicago (1964) and Plowden in Britain (1967), there has developed a major research literature on the relation of intrafamilial environments to children's cognitive development. This research has concerned active parental interventions (treatments) in the process of the child's intellectual development such as expressed and reinforced aspirations and expectations, rewards for intellectual development, pressures for language development (correcting diction and grammar, presenting opportunities to enlarge vocabulary), as well as providing opportunities for learning (settings). An informative review of this literature and the various theoretical frameworks involved is provided in the first two chapters of Marjoribanks's *Families and Their Learning Environments* (1979). In general, this literature suggests that specific measures of environmental influences—"treatments" as well as "settings"—are important in explaining intellectual development, and are more powerful than the simple use of parental social status as an indicator of family environment. In particular, these intrafamilial environmental measures have been strongly associated with verbal performance scores, moderately associated with mathematics scores, and minimally associated with scores on nonverbal intelligence.

Rather than asking how background variables (parents' education, occupation, income, etc.) and sibsize affect parental behavior, most research in the intrafamilial-environment tradition has concentrated on examining the importance of environmental measures (settings and treatments) *versus* the importance of family background and number of siblings. However, an exception may be found in an article by Marjoribanks and Walberg (1975) which, unlike much of their other work, deals specifically with whether sibsize affects the social-psychological environment in the family. Using some of the usual "environmental" measures (in this case, treatments) like press for achievement, press for activeness, press for intellectuality, press for independence, and so on, Marjoribanks and Walberg found correlations ranging from −.30 to −.45 between these variables and sibsize, indicating that as sibsize goes up parental interaction and attention declines.

Sociologists have had a major interest in differential socialization practices and values of parents (what the intrafamilial environment school would call "environmental influences"), but the sociological focus has been very largely on the social-structural *antecedents* of parents' childrearing behavior. One school of thought has actually derived the characteristics of presumed parental treatments of children from differential family size. Another school has derived a very similar kind of paradigm from the influence on parents of the demands of their occupations. It is worthwhile to consider each briefly.

Bossard (1953) and Bossard and Boll (1955) explicitly emphasized the role of family size in how parents actively relate to their children. Parents of small families are characterized as driven by ambition for their children, exhibiting great overt concern for performance in school, and as expressing strong affect in response to the child's successes and failures in relation to standards of excellence. The large family, by contrast, is described as emphasizing cooperation, obedience to parental authority, conformity, and self-reliance in situations of self-caretaking (but not in situations relating to standards of excellence). Competition and rivalry in such families is said to be discouraged by parents as divisive and disruptive to the family group. More recently, a number of researchers have suggested that parents in small families are less restrictive of children's autonomy and more encouraging of inquiry and self-direction (Rosen 1961; Elder and Bowerman 1963; Clausen 1965; Nye, Carlson, and Garrett 1970; Clausen and Clausen 1973).

Clearly, this literature relating family size and parental concerns for achievement implicitly assumes that achievement-oriented parents are motivated to have fewer children in whom they will invest enormous effort *and* that large families structurally *require* that children be less individuated and more obedient and conforming. In effect, no matter how achievement-oriented parents in large families might be, life in such families tends to involve more conformity and less self-direction than life in small families, and less of a tendency to pressure any given child for achievement. Hence, whatever antecedent factors affect both family size and achievement orientation of parents, this formulation sees life in small and large families as having an independent, structural effect on parental behavior (if not parental values).[3]

A very different chain of reasoning concerning the relation of self-direction versus conformity as parental values for children is represented by the work of Melvin Kohn. Kohn's research, resting on a long tradition in sociology of deriving childrearing values from the values that are salient in the parents' socioeconomic status (Duvall 1946; Kohn 1959, 1963, 1969, 1971, 1976, 1977; Miller and Swanson 1960), is based on a scale measuring self-direction versus conformity in parental values. Kohn's main thesis is that individuals' orientations to life—and, as a consequence, the values they emphasize in childrearing—are a result of socialization in the occupations they perform. Middle-class job conditions involve self-direction and autonomy, whereas working-class job conditions socialize people to value conformity over autonomy. Although other investigators working in this area have increasingly emphasized that factors such as education and religion may actually be more important than jobs (Lenski 1961; Wright and Wright 1976; Alwin and Thornton 1984), Kohn believes that the association of these variables with self-direction and conformity is still simply due to the principal "cause"—the association with occupation, and consequently with job conditions. All investigators following the Kohn tradition, insofar as they are interested in family size, simply control for all background variables related to parental values, and they report that family size has no effect (see Kohn 1969; Alwin and Thornton 1984). Actually, Alwin and Thornton (1984) have found a very small effect of all background variables, education, occupation, religion, and so forth, on the "thinks/obeys" scale (a modification by Lenski of the Kohn scale, autonomy versus conformity).

We should note parenthetically, as well, that the self-direction–conformity items in the Kohn scale may be suffering some contamination as a consequence of the popularization of the developmental childrearing literature since the items were first constructed. We shall come back to this point shortly. It is also true that the self-direction versus conformity scale is related to but not identical with achievement motivation.

In connection with sibsize influence on parental attention and interaction with children, an important effort at estimating the sibsize effect on time spent with children has been made by Peter Lindert (1978). Lindert used the basic data from the Cornell–Syracuse time-budget study of 1296 Syracuse families in 1967–1968. Lindert's analysis of these data is ingenious and described in detail in his book. Here we will simply note that a major finding is that the total amount of time parents spent on children was primarily a function of the ages and numbers of children, rather than of parental characteristics such as education, woman's labor force participation, mother's age, or father's socioeconomic status. These background variables turned out to be statistically insignificant when it came to time inputs. Hence, although parents of higher socioeconomic status and education spent more time *per child,* this was because such parents had fewer children.

Finally, in this section on parental "treatments" (parental interventions in the child's cognitive development) by sibsize we should mention that the intensive research by many psychologists on this topic (and on birth order) has been primarily concerned with the affective rather than the cognitive consequences of differential family size. Numerous psychologists have been interested in the changing emotional quality of interactions with children, shifting constellations of power, and also affection among families of different size. Studies of the process of interaction suggest that as additional children are born constellations do change. For some of the more recent studies of such processes see M. E. Lamb and B. Sutton-Smith (1982). However, these studies also suggest that it is difficult to characterize the changes in ways that psychiatrists might once have suggested—dethronement of the oldest child, hostility toward the new born, and so on. Rather, siblings have wide-ranging types of interactions and relationships—both outgoing and social as well as ambivalent and hostile. In effect, systematic studies of process do not lead us to think that the period of family-building is one so strongly characterized by particular types of sibling relationships that they inevitably lead to permanent personality changes or imprints on individuals depending on number of siblings, or ordinal position. We will see in our last section that there seem to be few, if any, major personality differences by sibsize.

*Analysis of Family Size and Parents' Valuation of Intellectual Curiosity
versus Obedience*

As has been suggested, one possible reason for the higher educational attainment of those in small families is that parents in small families may place a greater value on intellectual curiosity versus obedience than parents in large families. We should note here that given the data available, the discussion will be confined to expressed values, rather than behavior. Hence, the analysis will approach only marginally the issue of whether family size constrains and shapes behavior in spite of values.

Here we do not wish to engage the overall issue of self-direction versus conformity, but rather we will concentrate on those items in the Kohn scale relating to intellectual curiosity and obedience. These data are available from the General Social Surveys for selected years (1973, 1975, 1976, 1978, 1980, and 1983). Out of a range of 13 items characterizing a child of undesignated age and sex (items including "keeps neat and clean," "is considerate of others," "is a good student," "is honest," "has good manners") respondents were asked to pick the one most desirable, the three most desirable, the three least important, and the one least important. The results for each item were then coded as follows:

1   Mentioned as the one least important
2   Mentioned as one of three least important
3   Not mentioned
4   Mentioned as one of three most desirable
5   Mentioned as the one most desirable

The items, "Is interested in how and why things happen" and "Obeys parents," have been tabulated by family size of the parents in the GSS. This family-size variable was calculated from a combination of two items in the surveys—actual and expected number of children. (Respondents who had no children and expected none were excluded. For each respondent who had children and expected more, the expected number of additional children was added to the actual number already born. If a respondent expected no additional children over those already born, then the actual existing number was used. Finally, for childless respondents who expected children, the expected number was used.) Among 76 percent of respondents

Table 7.11. Percentage Distribution of the Importance of Intellectual Curiosity and Obedience to Parents as a Quality in a Child by Family Size, White Men and Women, GSS 1972–1983.

Item and Family Size[a]	Importance of Quality[b]			Total	(N)[c]
	Least Important	Not Mentioned	Most Important		
Intellectual Curiosity					
1–2	39	43	18	100	(2,140)
3–4	42	44	14	100	(1,521)
5–6	48	43	9	100	(345)
7+	44	45	11	100	(146)
Total	41	44	15	100	(4,152)
Obedience to Parents					
1–2	7	64	29	100	(2,140)
3–4	6	65	29	100	(1,523)
5–6	6	56	38	100	(345)
7+	3	58	39	100	(146)
Total	6	64	30	100	(4,154)

[a]Actual and expected number of children (excludes respondents who have and expect to have no children).

[b]The categories in the headings are 1 and 2, 3, and 4 and 5 of the following code:
   (1) The least important quality.
   (2) Among the three least important qualities.
   (3) Not mentioned.
   (4) Among the three most important qualities.
   (5) The most important quality.

[c]In constructing the family size variable it was necessary to exclude respondents interviewed in 1973 and 1980 since they were not asked future expected childbearing. In addition, the battery of questions on importance of specific child qualities was only asked in 1973, 1975, 1976, 1978, 1980, and 1983. This reduces the sample available for analysis even further.

no additional children were expected, and among 24 percent the total family size has been estimated by combining actual and expected fertility.

With regard to intellectual curiosity, the bivariate relation with parents' family size appears very weak (table 7.11). However, since Lenski (1961) and Alwin and Thornton (1984) have emphasized an interaction with religion on the "thinks/obeys" polarity, it is worth examining the relationship between family size and intellectual curiosity for separate religious groupings. Accordingly, we have analyzed the data (not shown) by the following groupings: Catholics; Episcopalians, Jews, and None; Lutherans and Presbyterians; and Baptists and Methodists. This division serves not only to separate Catholics from non-Catholics, but to divide non-Catholics into those having similar levels of secularism and fundamentalism. We will summarize the analysis without showing the detailed findings.

Family size bears no bivariate relation to parents' valuation of intellectual curiosity among Catholics. However, within each non-Catholic group, those having smaller families are more likely to choose intellectual curiosity as desirable and less likely to choose it as unimportant. In addition, members of the grouping "Episcopalians, Jews, and None" are markedly less likely than any other group to regard this quality as unimportant, and markedly more likely to regard it as important, whereas Baptists and Methodists are at the other extreme, having the lowest proportion regarding intellectual curiosity as important and the highest proportion singling it out as unimportant.

As for obedience to parents we can see (table 7.11) that there is no overall relation with family size. There is also none among Catholics, but the item does show a relationship within the other religious groups. Those having large families are consistently more likely to pick this trait as desirable. There is also a noteworthy difference between Episcopalians, Jews, and None versus Baptists and Methodists in their evaluation of obedience as a desirable quality. Seventeen percent of the former but 35 percent of the latter single out this quality as desirable, while 10 percent of the former but only 5 percent of the latter see it as not important.

Parenthetically, we may now note that for one of the items from the Kohn scale, "Is a good student," tabulation (not shown) indicates no overall bivariate relation with family size and none among Catholics. There is however some association with family size among other religious groups, but it is in the *opposite* direction to our expectations—those having small families are the most likely to regard this trait as *un*important. This trait is selected as desirable by a small fraction of all religious groups, and specifically mentioned as not important by between 37 and 45 percent (depending on the group). The group having the largest percentage holding this quality *not* important is Episcopalians, Jews, and None. A possible interpretation of this anomalous finding is that, for developmentally oriented parents, emphasis on being a good student may be regarded as excessively directive and demanding—in effect, the opposite of what was intended by the item. It is also possible that, with few items in the scale innocuous enough to choose as unimportant, being a good student may seem like an acceptable or inoffensive candidate. This item clearly is not (or is no longer) measuring along the same dimension as the one on intellectual curiosity.

A final item in the Kohn scale worth mentioning is "Tries hard to succeed." This item is not associated with family size even at a bivariate level overall, or within any religious group.

Would the relationship between family size and intellectual curiosity versus obedience to parents be maintained if we controlled for possible antecedent influences on both family size and childrearing values—influences such as age, education, occupation, farm–nonfarm background? From table 7.12 we can see that the answer is negative. In this table, we show the R^2 (adjusted for degrees of freedom) for a multiple classification analysis within each religious group using intellectual curiosity and obedience to parents as dependent variables, together with a listing of the two most important predictor variables in order of relative importance. Quite clearly, the model explains only a modest amount of variation in the dependent variables and, in addition, the most important sources of explanation are education and age. Only among Episcopalians, Jews, and None does family size maintain a relation with obedience to parents after controls, but the relationship is modest. These results thus suggest that the apparent association of family size and different childrearing values emphasized by Bossard and Bell is really a result of the joint influence of education and generation on both family size and values.

It is also worth noting (see table 7.13) that our suspicion that a high score on the Kohn item "Is a good student" will be perceived as directive and nondevelopmental, rather than a companion to "intellectual curiosity," seems to be born out by a multiple classification analysis. As may be seen from the table, it is the less educated

Table 7.12. Explained Variance and Listing of the Two Most Important Predictors from Multiple Classification Analysis of Intellectual Curiosity and Obedience to Parents as Important Qualities in a Child by Religion, White Men and Women, GSS 1972–1983.[a]

	Dependent Variables	
Religious Affiliation	*Intellectual Curiosity*	*Obedience to Parents*
Catholics		
R^2	.027	.057
Predictors	Age	Age
	Education	Education
Episcopalians, Jews, and None		
R^2	.077	.116
Predictors	Education	Education
	Age	Family Size
Lutherans and Presbyterians		
R^2	.026	.070
Predictors	Education	Education
	Age	Age
Baptists and Methodists		
R^2	.040	.043
Predictors	Age	Education
	Family Size	Occupation

[a]The multiple classification analysis included respondent's age, education, occupation (if a man), spouse occupation (if a woman), actual and expected family size, and farm–nonfarm background.

and the older respondents who place a high value on being a good student, and the younger and more educated respondents value this quality the least.

Finally, this discussion of differential parental values has some methodological implications for our prior analysis of adult educational achievement in relation to sibsize. The discussion suggests that our controls for the socioeconomic status (father's education and SEI) of men's and women's parents, and the respondent's own

Table 7.13. Adjusted Means for the Importance of Being a Good Student as a Quality in a Child by Age, Education, and Religious Affiliation, White Men and Women, GSS 1972–1983.[a]

Predictors	Religious Affiliation[b]				Total
	(1)	*(2)*	*(3)*	*(4)*	
Age					
20–29	2.5	2.4	2.4	2.4	2.4
30–39	2.7	2.5	2.5	2.5	2.5
40–49	2.6	2.5	2.5	2.6	2.6
50–59	2.6	2.6	2.5	2.7	2.6
60–69	2.7	2.6	2.6	2.6	2.6
70–79	2.8	2.7	2.8	2.7	2.7
80+	2.8	2.4	2.8	3.0	2.8
Education					
Grade School	2.8	2.7	2.7	2.6	2.7
HS Inc	2.8	2.6	2.5	2.6	2.6
HS Comp	2.6	2.5	2.5	2.6	2.5
College Inc	2.6	2.4	2.4	2.5	2.5
College Comp	2.4	2.5	2.4	2.5	2.5
Masters, Ph.D.	2.6	2.6	2.5	2.5	2.5
Grand Mean	2.6	2.5	2.5	2.6	2.6
S.D.	.75	.74	.75	.71	.73
R^2	.035	.010	.043	.029	.032
N[c]	2,001	921	986	1,958	7,154

[a]In addition to age and education, variables included in the model were actual and expected family size, occupation, and farm–nonfarm background. The values represent mean response on a scale ranging from 1 = least important to 5 = most important.

[b]Religious Affiliations are:
    (1) Catholics
    (2) Episcopalians, Jews, and None
    (3) Lutherans and Presbyterians
    (4) Baptists and Methodists

[c]The total N is larger than the row sum because it includes respondents who specified other Protestant denominations or no denomination or other religions.

age (as an indicator of the period during which he or she was brought up), will serve to control to some extent for unmeasured differences among respondents' parents in the kinds of childrearing values they espoused. As we have just seen, parents' childrearing values do not appear to be associated with the number of children they bear, once antecedent variables like education and age are controlled. This finding strengthens our interpretation of the independent effect of sibsize on education. We appear to have been measuring relatively pure sibsize effects, and not the influence of major unmeasured parental differences associated with the decision to have large versus small families.

Family Size and Parents' "Interventions"

Have we information on the amount of direct parental intervention in the lives of the children in the surveys under analysis? This type of information is not ideally collected from surveys and, hence, we do not have a wealth of data to present. We can, however, draw some insight from relatively indirect information concerning parental attention to youngsters' health and dental maintenance through visits to doctors and dentists.

Cycle II contains two questions relating to the last time the child had been to the dentist and the doctor. The results from each were coded as follows:

1   During past twelve months
2   One to two years ago
3   More than two years
4   Never

Table 7.14 shows the adjusted means by sibsize. The reader should note that, in addition to controls for background characteristics, visits to the doctor were controlled for an overall health status variable. In the case of doctor visits, sibsize was relatively the most important variable and, in the case of visits to the dentist, it ranked second to mother's education. There is a standard deviation difference between only children and those from families of seven or more in the unadjusted means; the difference remains substantial in the adjusted values for doctor visits, and approximately half a standard deviation for visits to the dentist. If we take these two

Table 7.14. Mean Time Elapsed Since Child Has Been to a Doctor or Dentist by Sibsize, White Boys and Girls Age 6 to 11, HES, Cycle II, Adjusted Means.[a]

Sibsize	Recency of Visits to:	
	Dentist	*Doctor*
1	1.47	1.20
2	1.56	1.29
3	1.60	1.36
4	1.67	1.41
5	1.91	1.54
6	1.94	1.67
7+	1.99	1.78
Grand Mean	1.69	1.43
S.D.	1.13	0.72
R^2	.275	.168
N	4,487	4,485

[a]Means have been adjusted for child's age and sex, mother's and father's education, family income, region, community size, family intactness, and mother's labor force participation. In addition, current health status was added to the model for doctor visits. The code ranges from 1 = during past 12 months to 4 = never.

parental behaviors as indicative, parents of fewer children appear to intervene more actively with regard to their children's physical welfare (at the cost of both time and money) than do parents of large numbers of children. These data tell us nothing, of course, about whether parents of small versus large families also intervene more in matters relating to cognition, but the data do support some speculation that this might be the case.

SOCIAL AND PERSONALITY CHARACTERISTICS BY SIBSIZE

As mentioned in the introduction to this chapter, our concern in this section will focus on those aspects of our subjects' personalities and temperaments that could prove important to educational attainment *and* about which systematic data are available. Specifically, we will concentrate on aspects of achievement motivation, on over- and underperformance in school, and on self-confidence in ability. Although the relation of such variables to achievement outcomes may be in doubt (see Featherman 1972; O. D. Duncan, Featherman, and B. Duncan 1972; G. J. Duncan 1983; and Hill et al. 1983), many researchers are not convinced of the irrelevance of such variables to actual achievement.

Our focus on variables presumably related to educational attainment may leave some readers with a sense of dissatisfaction, since so much of what has been written in the past about number of siblings and personality has concentrated on how people from different sibsizes relate to and interact with others. In the section on "settings" we addressed the issue of whether only children (and those from small families generally) are more asocial, unpopular, lonely, and depressed. Our evidence has suggested just the opposite. Recent systematic research concerning the allegedly "spoiled," demanding, selfish, unsociable characteristics of only children, or of those from small versus large families, seems to provide virtually unequivocal answers. Either there are no differences by number of siblings, or the differences favor the only child and the small family (Claudy 1976; Falbo 1977; Blake 1981*b*; Grotevant and Cooper 1982; Lamb and Sutton-Smith 1982; Ernst and Angst 1983).

The emphasis in this chapter on antecedents and correlates of cognitive development may be justified not only on the basis of the importance of this aspect of personality for educational advancement, but because there is widespread agreement in psychology that cognitive development is, in turn, an important predictor of future social development (see, for example, Kohlberg 1981*a* and *b*; Loevinger and Knoll 1983; Mussen 1983; Parke and Asher 1983; Cairns and Valsiner 1984; Fischer and Silvern 1985).

Why are the results concerning the emotional and interactional aspects of personality by sibsize so unproductive of the effects that are most likely to be the focus of popular expectations? One reason, as suggested earlier, is that systematic studies of actual processes of interaction in families do not document the existence of the types of structured behavior (by sibsize) that "armchair" deduction from psychoanalytic theory presupposed. Moreover, in contrast to psychoanalytic theorizing, recent research in developmental psychology and sociology has abandoned the rigidity of "infant determinism" (see, Sewell 1952; Mischel 1969; Havighurst 1973; Brim and Kagan 1980). It is becoming clear that personality is more plastic and changing over the life cycle than was previously believed. Varying childrearing practices, within a normally benign range, do not seem to be productive of major differences in personality development. It does seem clear, however, that deviantly "bad" parents (intense parental conflict, criminality, neglect, etc.) retard and disrupt development (for a summary, see Kohlberg 1981).

Here we may also point out structural reasons for a possible historical diminution in the personality effects of sibling number and birth order. First, children are increasingly exposed to a wide variety of emotionally engaging influences outside of the family, as well as to the influence of nonfamilial peers. Second, since occupations are ever more divorced from the family, both work activities and anticipations of these activities are more independent of siblings. Whereas in the past many people continued their sibling relationships into adult working life, the declining importance of family farms and family businesses means that this is rarely the case today. Long before young people leave home for college or work, they are thinking and dreaming about what they will do occupationally. Rarely does this fantasy include familial continuity in work relations. Finally, and as an extension of these points, under modern American conditions, such inheritance as there is appears either to be divided among children equally (Brittain 1978; Menchik 1980) or to be apportioned in a manner that is inversely related to the wealth of the sibling recipients (Becker and Tomes 1976; Griliches 1979; Tomes 1981), with no special advantage to a child of a particular birth order, such as the oldest. It is also no longer incumbent upon younger siblings to wait for their marriages until older siblings have been wed. Thus, as familial control over both occupation and marriage has declined, birth order has lost its saliency as a basis for role differentiation in the family (see, Schooler 1972, for a discussion of this point in relation to the oldest child).

Number of Siblings and Achievement Motivation

The issue of whether certain groupings in the population are characterized by more or less "achievement motivation" is probably most familiar to the reader as a consequence of the literature on the "culture of poverty" or the "underclass" (see, for example, Banfield 1970; Rainwater 1970; Schiller 1976; Gecas 1979; Auletta 1982). One alleged component of the so-called culture of poverty is less achievement motivation, a component that is believed to be transmitted through the socialization process from parents to children, and which is said to perpetuate people as an underclass over generations.

We do not wish to engage the issue of the "underclass" here. Of relevance, however, is the analogous reasoning involved in the hypothesis that family size is of major motivational importance. This hypothesis is seen, for example, in the notion that small and large families are essentially different "systems" (see, Bossard 1953; Elder and Bowerman 1963). The small family system is said to be striving and achievement oriented, in contrast to the less compulsive and ambitious character of the large family system. If this hypothesis is correct, it could relate, of course, to differences in educational attainment by number of siblings.

Before we attempt to bring data to bear on this issue, a brief discussion of achievement motivation is in order. Following Atkinson and Birch (1978) we will distinguish the components of motivation into motives/incentives and expectancies. A motive is said to be a generalized disposition to approach or avoid a class of incentives. For example, the needs for achievement, power, or affiliation are classed as motives. An expectancy is the individual's assessment of the probability that his or her behavior will lead to a desired outcome. Both motives and expectancies are involved in overall motivation—people must need to achieve in order to take action (to try to bring about a result that would not occur without effort), but if the outcome does not seem remotely achievable to them, then action may not be initiated. Motives are believed to be strongly influenced by early socialization and relatively impervious to change during the life course. Expectancies, by contrast, are dynamic because they are influenced by a daily round of environmental cues, or more correctly, by people's *perception* and *interpretation* of environmental cues.

The notion of individuals being in situations of structured deprivation or opportunity involves, therefore, not simply whether such situations affect the development of particular motives, but whether the situations sensitize people to perceive and interpret environmental cues in ways that contribute to achievement or failure, to action or inaction (Hyman 1953; Knupfer 1953). For this reason, the issue of deprived "cultures" (or, in essence, a structured situation of deprivation) cannot be dichotomized simply as leading to "flawed character" versus "restricted opportunity" (Schiller 1976). People who have been reared in situations of restricted opportunity may have strong needs to achieve ("unflawed characters"), but their rearing and the ordinary circumstances of their lives are such that "opportunities" are not perceived or interpreted correctly. There is an absence of the kind of "paradigm," to use Kuhn's terminology, that would enable them to sort environmental cues into a message that signals "opportunity." For purposes of simplicity, we will leave aside any discussion of the complexities involved when individuals transform blocked expectancies in the legitimate world into achievement through the use of negatively sanctioned means.

In chapter 6, we analyzed expectancies regarding educational levels. With regard to motives, our data are replete with the standard measures of achievement motives, both positive and negative (need for achievement and fear of failure). The variables are listed in figure 7.3. The results by number of siblings are easy to summarize. We find neither bivariate effects with sibsize nor suppressed effects that emerge when other components of the respondents' background are added. In an effort to go beyond the standard data relating to achievement motives, we have created a derived measure that relates to achievement motivation—"under-" or "overperformance" in school.

School performance by sibsize and "under-" and "overperformance." The most common measure of school performance is grades. Our data for young people include self-reported grades in the prior year (for the Youth in Transition and High School and Beyond samples) and teacher evaluations of school performance (for Cycles II and III of the Health Examination Surveys). We have already seen that grades are negatively related to sibsize in all of the samples. This finding is hardly surprising since IQ is negatively related to sibsize, and IQ is an important determinant of grades.

More indicative of achievement motivation is whether students perform in school at a level that would be expected given their

YOUTH IN TRANSITION

Need for Success

Compared with other boys your age, how important is it for you to do things where you might win or achieve success?
1. Much more important than average
2. A little more important than average
3. About average importance
4. A little less important than average
5. Much less important than average

Need to Avoid Failure

Compared with other boys your age, how important is it for you to avoid doing things where you might fail?
         Same code as need for success

Self-Development

Compared with other boys your age, how important is it for you to try improve yourself?
         Same code as need for success

Self-Utilization

Compared with other boys your age, how important is it for you to be doing things you're really good at?
         Same code as need for success

Index of Test Anxiety

Index is composed of 16 items (true/false) relating to how the respondent feels during test taking.

     Examples: I get to feel very panicky when I have to take a surprise exam.

              During a final exam, I often get so nervous that I forget facts that I really know.

Index of Effort at Self-Development

Index is composed of 8 items (true/false) relating to the respondent's desire for self-development.

     Examples: I look for opportunities to better myself.

              When I have set myself a certain level in anything I do, I set myself a higher level and try to reach it.

Index of Avoidance of Non-Self-Development

Index is composed of 7 items (true/false) relating to the respondent's desire to avoid stultifying situations with regard to self-development.

     Examples: I try to stay out of situations where I don't see any chance for progress or advancement.

              I would be unhappy in a job where I didn't grow and develop.

Figure 7.3. Indicators of Achievement Motivation (Youth in Transition, High School and Beyond, Health Examination Survey—Cycle III).

YOUTH IN TRANSITION (continued)

Index of Effort at Self-Utilization

Index is composed of 5 items (Almost always true to Never true) relating to respondent's desire to use skills.

Examples: When I have mastered something, I look for opportunities to do it.

I'd like to bring my usual performance in line with the best I've done.

Index of Avoidance of Non-Self-Utilization

Index is composed of 4 items (Almost always true to Never true) relating to respondent's desire to use avoid skill degradation.

Examples: It upsets me when I get worse at something I was good at.

When the work I'm doing doesn't give me the chance to do the things I'm good at, I am dissatisfied.

HIGH SCHOOL AND BEYOND

Both seniors and sophomores were asked the following questions related to achievement motivation:

How important is each of the following to you in your life?

Being successful in my line of work:
1. Not important
2. Somewhat important
3. Very important

Being a leader in my community:
Same code

Being able to give my children better opportunities than I've had:
Same code

HEALTH EXAMINATION SURVEY--CYCLE III

How important do you think it is for a young person to have each of the following qualities or characteristics listed below?

To be ambitious:
1. Extremely important
2. Important
3. Slightly important
4. Unimportant

ability, or whether they "underachieve" or "overachieve" in relation to ability, and how such behavior relates to sibsize. Following Lavin's methodological discussion of "overperformance" and "underperformance" in school (Lavin 1965), we have regressed grades on ability to obtain expected performance levels at each level of ability and, then, created a new variable that shows (in standard deviation units) respondents who perform below, at, and above what would be expected given their ability.

Table 7.15 shows predicted underperformance and overperformance in school for the youngsters in Cycles II and III of the Health Examination Surveys, the tenth-grade boys in Youth in Transition, and the tenth- and twelfth-grade boys and girls in High School and Beyond. It is worth noting first how similar are the overall proportions (the total lines) at predicted underperformance and overperformance levels among the surveys. Second, there seems to be a fairly consistent, but not invariant pattern of underperformance among those from large families. This pattern is more marked among girls than among boys. A comparison of seniors (High School and Beyond) versus sophomores (both Youth in Transition and High School and Beyond) suggests that school-leaving by underperforming boys from large families may contribute to the reversal of the sibsize/underperforming relation. Third, with regard to overperformance, it is rare for male only-children to exhibit this characteristic, but female singletons are somewhat more inclined to do so. Indeed, male only-children quite frequently underperform in relation to their abilities. Finally, children from sibsizes two to four are generally more likely to overachieve than those from sibsizes five or more. None of these differences are large, and many are not statistically significant. However, their appearance in so many different surveys generates some interest.

Are the tendencies to underperformance by those from large families due to the fact that they are more likely to come from educationally less-advantaged homes? Table 7.16 breaks down the data from table 7.15 into three educational groups for the youngsters' fathers. Since all of the surveys show a similar pattern, we present here only HES Cycle II and sophomores and seniors in HSB. With regard to underachievement, the dominant pattern among the surveys is for there to remain a higher-than-average underperformance value among children from sibsizes five or more.

As for overperformance, the differences by sibsize either disappear, or there is a tendency for those from small families to be only slightly more overperforming. Quite clear is a decline in underperformance with an increase in father's education (total lines), and an increase in overperformance as father's education goes up. Hence, the intuitive impression, such as by Bossard and Boll, of children from small families as overperforming (and/or not underperforming) is compounded by the association of father's education with small families, and by the association of both father's education and small families with less underperforming and somewhat more overperforming. Indeed, as we have suggested, some of the prejudice against children from small families (and especially only children) may actually be a reflection of the dual advantages such children have enjoyed (higher class and small family size) on the part of those who have suffered dual disadvantages (lower class and large family size). Insofar as being an only child seems particularly to lead to feminine overperformance, a further complication is added. However, there is a persisting tendency for singleton boys to underperform in relation to ability. A fairly obvious interpretation of underperformance in relation to grades by singleton boys and overperformance by singleton girls is that the boys feel totally without competition for their parents' approval and (being on average very bright) do not see fit to overextend themselves. Girls are also without actual competition, but many may feel symbolic competition—comparison with what they may believe to be their parents' vision of how well a boy would have done in their place. It is evident that there is much more to be learned about the effects of being an "only" on young people's achievement pressures. It is certainly clear that only boys, on average, are not feeling intense pressure to uphold extreme parental desires for achievement.

Confidence in ability.   As Ernst and Angst (1983) have noted, most psychoanalytic expectations of self-confidence and self-esteem by birth order have been that only children and firstborns would rank lower on these qualities. However, among the numerous studies cited by Ernst and Angst, most of which control neither for social class nor number of siblings, there is typically either no difference by birth order or firstborns score higher. The Project Talent data analyzed by Claudy, Farrell, and Dayton (1979) controlled for

Table 7.15. Youths' Academic Performance by Sibsize, White Boys and Girls, HES, Cycles II and III, YIT, High School Sophomores, and HSB, Sophomores and Seniors.

	Academic Performance					
	Percentage of Youths Under and Over Predicted[a]					
Survey, Class,	Boys			Girls		
and Sibsize	Under	Over	(N)	Under	Over	(N)
HES, Cycle II						
1	20	29	(69)	18	30	(54)
2–4	26	29	(1,344)	28	32	(1,266)
5+	33	27	(505)	30	28	(493)
Total	27	29	(1,918)	28	31	(1,813)
HES, Cycle III						
Grades 6–9						
1	27	30	(44)	24	38	(29)
2–4	29	34	(529)	26	35	(462)
5+	32	28	(252)	40	27	(193)
Total	30	32	(825)	30	33	(684)
Grades 10–12						
1	36	27	(44)	34	39	(41)
2–4	31	29	(352)	28	32	(275)
5+	30	35	(112)	26	32	(119)
Total	31	30	(508)	28	33	(435)
YIT						
1	27	38	(77)	—	—	—
2–4	30	34	(1,098)	—	—	—
5+	34	27	(390)	—	—	—
Total	31	32	(1,565)	—	—	—
HSB						
Sophomores						
1	29	29	(203)	26	34	(181)
2–4	27	35	(3,527)	27	35	(3,712)
5+	35	27	(1,166)	30	32	(1,194)
Total	29	33	(4,896)	27	34	(5,087)

Table 7.15. *Continued.*

| Survey, Class, and Sibsize | Academic Performance Percentage of Youths Under and Over Predicted[a] | | | | | |
| | Boys | | | Girls | | |
	Under	Over	(N)	Under	Over	(N)
Seniors						
1	39	29	(160)	31	38	(143)
2–4	28	37	(1,991)	28	36	(2,184)
5+	30	30	(660)	33	36	(733)
Total	29	35	(2,811)	29	36	(3,060)

[a]Predicted values are from a regression of vocabulary on grades and school performance. For each sibsize, the percentage of students who are at predicted levels (neither under- nor overperforming) equals 100 minus the sum of over- and underperformance percentages. For HSB, the tabulations are only for intact families in order to be congruent with table 7.16. See footnote to that table.

Table 7.16. Youths' Academic Performance by Sibsize and Father's Education, , White Boys and Girls, HES, Cycle II and HSB, Sophomores and Seniors.

| | Academic Performance Percentage of Youths Under and Over Predicted[a] | | | | | | | | |
| | HES, Cycle II | | | HSB Sophomores | | | HSB Seniors | | |
Sex, Father's Education, and Sibsize	Under	Over	(N)	Under	Over	(N)	Under	Over	N
Boys									
HS Inc									
1	38	27	(26)	34	12	(56)	58	14	(36)
2–4	32	26	(434)	35	26	(588)	33	29	(317)
5+	38	26	(258)	41	23	(326)	38	24	(179)
Total	34	26	(718)	37	24	(970)	36	27	(532)
HS Comp									
1	3	30	(30)	28	31	(94)	44	28	(71)
2–4	25	27	(503)	30	33	(1,566)	30	34	(836)
5+	29	30	(137)	34	25	(547)	27	28	(261)
Total	25	28	(670)	30	31	(2,207)	30	32	(1,168)
College									
1	*	*	*	28	42	(53)	19	41	(53)
2–4	19	36	(404)	22	40	(1,373)	25	42	(838)
5+	24	28	(105)	29	35	(293)	27	38	(220)
Total	20	34	(522)	23	40	(1,719)	25	41	(1,111)
HS Comp									

Girls

HS Inc									
1	27	27	(26)	25	31	(36)	*	*	*
2–4	34	19	(405)	32	30	(710)	30	33	(399)
5+	36	23	(253)	32	28	(380)	37	34	(208)
Total	34	21	(684)	32	29	(1,126)	32	34	(630)
HS Comp									
1	*	*	*	27	35	(85)	38	33	(72)
2–4	27	36	(463)	28	33	(1,616)	29	36	(935)
5+	25	30	(138)	29	33	(504)	35	36	(306)
Total	26	35	(618)	28	33	(2,205)	31	36	(1,313)
College									
1	*	*	*	25	35	(60)	19	39	(48)
2–4	23	40	(392)	22	38	(1,386)	25	38	(850)
5+	23	40	(96)	29	36	(310)	26	38	(219)
Total	23	39	(498)	23	38	.(1,756)	25	38	(1,117)

[a]Predicted values are from a regression of Vocabulary on grades and school performance. Asterisks indicate that there were fewer than 25 cases for analysis. For HSB, only intact families are included because students from broken families were highly unreliable concerning their father's educational attainment.

parental background and showed no significant difference in self-confidence between only children and those from two-child families. A recent study by Falbo (1981), of undergraduates in college who responded to an advertisement, did control for number of siblings and social class. This research used an index of self-esteem (a short form of the Texas Social Behavior Inventory) that measures social self-confidence. Only one barely significant difference by birth order was found—between firstborns and last-borns, favoring firstborns.

Here we will focus our research question on an issue that would seem to be relevant to the educational process: Given that children from small families are known to have higher intellectual abilities than children from large ones, how does their confidence in their ability relate to their measured ability? To attempt to address this issue, we will have to confine our efforts to the Youth in Transition data set. Unfortunately, questions on confidence were not asked of sophomores in the High School and Beyond study and, among seniors in that study, only four items on the Rosenberg self-esteem scale were asked. The overall variability of response was slight, and there were no differences by sibsize even at the bivariate level. Equally, no questions on confidence were asked in either of the Health Examination Surveys.

The Self-Evaluation of School Ability index in the study Youth in Transition was composed of three questions to which the boy could respond on a six-point scale ranging from (1) "Far below average" to (6) "Far above average." The questions were:

1. How do you rate yourself in school ability compared with those in your grade in school?
2. How intelligent do you think you are compared with other boys your age?
3. How good a reader do you think you are compared with other boys your age?

Table 7.17 shows the adjusted means of the index of confidence in school ability by sibsize. These means result from a multiple classification analysis controlling for parents' education and socioeconomic status, family intactness, and size of the place where the youth was brought up. There is a marked and linear difference in

Table 7.17. Index of Confidence in School Ability by Sibsize, White Boys, YIT, High School Sophomores, Adjusted Means.[a]

Sibsize	Index of Confidence in School Ability	
1	4.36	(105)
2	4.26	(428)
3	4.19	(475)
4	4.18	(384)
5	4.05	(236)
6	4.00	(119)
7+	3.91	(158)
Grand Mean	4.16	(1,906)
S.D.	0.74	
R^2	.111	

[a]The means have been adjusted for mother's and father's education, socioeconomic status, family intactness, and community size where youth was brought up. The values represent the mean of three items in which students were asked to rate themselves on a 5-point scale ranging from 1 = Far below average to 5 = Far above average.

results by sibsize, with only children being over half a standard deviation (from the grand mean) higher than children in families of seven or more even after adjustments.

However, since boys from small families have higher IQs on average and higher grades than boys from large families, one would expect higher levels of self-confidence from those with few siblings. Hence, we may now ask whether boys from small families are more confident, and those from large families less so, than would be predicted on the basis of their IQs? The lowest tier (the total) of table 7.18 shows that this is indeed the case. Boys from small families are more confident than would be predicted, and those from large families less so. When the results are broken down by three levels of the father's education in table 7.18 (in an effort to control for the association of family background with both confidence and sibsize), we see that the relationship between sibsize and confidence disappears for those where the father has completed high school, but that among those with college-educated fathers overconfidence is a particularly marked characteristic of boys from

Table 7.18. Youths' Self-Concept of School Ability by Sibsize and Father's Education, White Boys from Intact Families, YIT, High School Sophomores.

| | Self-Concept | | |
| | Percentage of Youths Under and Over Predicted[a] | | |
Father's Education and Sibsize	Under	Over	N
HS Inc			
1	21	33	(24)
2–4	31	25	(334)
5+	41	23	(166)
Total	34	25	(524)
HS Comp			
1	25	28	(36)
2–4	30	32	(428)
5+	24	30	(123)
Total	28	32	(587)
College			
1	*	*	*
2–4	21	44	(290)
5+	35	23	(79)
Total	24	39	(383)
Total			
1	22	32	(76)
2–4	28	33	(1,097)
5+	34	25	(391)
Total	29	31	(1,564)

[a]Predicted values are from a regression of Vocabulary (Quick Test) on self-concept. Asterisks indicate that there were fewer than 24 cases for analysis.

small families, and underconfidence particularly characterizes those from large families. Moreover, coming from a large family provides no more overconfidence if the father is college educated than it does if he has not completed high school. These data thus suggest that family size is not only negatively related to ability but also to confidence in such ability, and that this relationship is particularly evident among boys from the highest and lowest levels of parental education.

CONCLUSION

Do children from different-size families have home environments that vary in ways that may influence their cognitive development and academic achievement? Do extracurricular school activities diverge by sibsize in a manner that may have cognitive and academic implications? Do young people from different-size families have distinctive personality characteristics, such as achievement motivation and self-confidence, which may help to account for the educational deviations that we have seen to exist? And, finally, do parents of small versus large families have disparate childrearing values that may function as unmeasured antecedent variables explaining unequal educational achievement by sibsize? This chapter is devoted to providing some answers to these questions.

Our examination of the home environment makes a distinction between environments as "settings" and as "treatments." Following Spaeth, "settings" refer to the passive aspects of the environment—features that are available to be engaged but do not actively engage the child. "Treatments" are parental behaviors that are directed toward the child and that represent active interventions—encouragement, correction, goal setting and the like. We have regarded this distinction as heuristic and tentative, not ironclad, since many of the environmental features we discuss can be regarded as both passive and active. Using the Health Examination Survey (Cycle II) of young people, we have looked at quantitative data on the amount of time spent by young children (six to eleven year olds) in a variety of informal activities such as reading books, reading newspapers, TV watching, playing alone, and engaging in sports, Little League, and similar activities. We find that children from small families are more likely to engage in intellectual and cultural pursuits, and children from small families (particularly only children) spend much more time playing alone. However, data on popularity suggest that children from small families are more popular. Hence, the fact that such children spend a fair amount of time alone is not due to enforced isolation because of unpopularity. It does seem, however, that such children have the opportunity to develop the ability to be alone and to use such time profitably. Nothing from any of the surveys suggests that children from small families, especially only children, are lonely, depressed, or hopeless.

An interesting finding from the High School and Beyond data concerns whether the respondents were read to as children. Children from small families report themselves as having been more likely to have been read to as children than those from large families, in spite of the fact that, in many cases, children from large families presumably had siblings who could have performed this service. These data thus indicate that although siblings might theoretically provide help and instruction, children's chances of actually receiving such attention are enhanced if parents can provide it. The data do not support Zajonc's hypothesis concerning the teaching role of older siblings. In the same study, youngsters from small families were more likely to have experienced selected advantages such as having music or dance lessons or to have traveled outside the United States. In effect, our analysis suggests that children from small families and only children have more intellectually stimulating settings and a broader range of stimuli.

Among teenagers, our analysis by sibsize of the types of extracurricular activities in high school engaged in by seniors is also instructive. A factor analysis allowed us to divide nonsports activities into five types—intellectual (student government, school newspapers, etc.), cultural and artistic (drama, orchestra, etc.), community (youth groups, church groups, "Y," etc), vocational (farm clubs, carpentry, etc.), and hobby. Youngsters from small families are more likely to engage in intellectual and cultural activities (with or without sports) than are those from large families, and those from large families incline more toward community, vocational, and hobby activities. This is true even after we have removed youngsters from farm families (which are both larger than others and also have high rates of participation in community and vocational kinds of activities).

Turning to parental treatments, do parents of small versus large families conform to the speculation that small families are hard-driving and competitive, emphasizing external standards of excellence, whereas large families emphasize obedience, conformity and assimilation? Although there does seem to be some bivariate association between parental values for offspring and the number of children parents have, this association disappears when education, age, and religion are held constant. These results provide further backing to our contention that many of the personality characteristics that have been associated with small versus large families are actually characteristics related to education and class rather than family size.

Turning to respondents' personality characteristics, we have been concerned with those aspects of personality that seem important for academic and intellectual advancement, and about which we have information. We have concentrated on over- and underperformance in school and on confidence in one's own intellectual ability.

With regard to over- and underperformance (defined as receiving school grades above or below what would be expected given the student's ability), differences by sibsize are not large, but children from sibsizes two to four are more likely to overperform than those from sibsizes five or more. Large families show a fairly consistent pattern of underperformance as well.

Information on confidence in one's own intellectual ability is available from Youth in Transition. Not only do youngsters from small families have more confidence in their ability than those from large families, but they have more confidence than would be expected on the basis of their ability scores. By contrast, boys from large families have less confidence than would be expected on the basis of such scores.

It thus appears that with regard to personality characteristics, young people from small families, including only children, seem to have none of the adverse traits often associated with an absence of many siblings. Moreover, children from small families are likely to overperform rather than underperform in school (although the differences on overperformance are not large), and to have a great deal of confidence in their own ability. Children from large families are more likely to underperform, and lack confidence in such objectively verified abilities as they have. We are thus led to believe that the prevalent notions about negative traits of only children and those from small families stem in part from the highly advantaged position that such children have, relative to children from large families—advantaged socioeconomically and in terms of the lack of dilution of such resources as exist. Since many more people have come from large families than from small ones, such people have "carried the day" in labeling those from small families as overindulged or spoiled by advantages.

Finally, this chapter has provided additional information relating to the causal interpretation advanced in this volume—that there are independent effects of sibsize on child achievement. As discussed in detail in our introduction, the alternative explanation of sibsize effects is that both sibsize and differential environment are the result of unmeasured antecedent parental characteristics that affect both the number of children parents have and the environments they provide. In effect, it is argued that sibsize effects are spurious. The results in this chapter supplement the data presented in our introduction concerning whether parents of small versus large families have disparate personality traits. Here we examine whether such parents have different childrearing values—differences that are not captured by socioeconomic controls. Our analysis indicates either no difference, or small differences in childrearing values by sibsize after controls for parental socioeconommic status are introduced. It thus seems that parental personality traits and childrearing values, at least as analyzed so far, are not among the unmeasured variables that might invalidate our interpretation of the sibsize/achievement relationship.

8

THE SIBSIZE TRANSITION AND ITS SOCIAL CONSEQUENCES

In our first chapter, we discussed briefly the fact that most adult respondents in the samples we have analyzed were brought up in large families and that large sibsize characterized even the samples of children as well. Here we will offer a detailed explanation of the disparity between low fertility among mothers—the classic definition of the fertility component of the demographic transition—and the preponderance of large sibsizes among their offspring. Additionally, we will examine the changes distinguishing the Depression, baby-boom, and baby-bust cohorts of mothers and children. We will see that a transition in the family size of children is underway. Finally, for the population as a whole, we will analyze the educational consequences of this transition and its effects on important social attitudes.

The Disparity between the Family Size of Mothers and Children

The prevalence of large sibsizes in the American population diverges sharply from the popular image that relatively low completed fertility of mothers typically results in small sibsizes for their children. Indeed, even the sociological literature on child development and socialization, or the economic literature on so-called human capital formation in the family of orientation, typically assumes that completed family size of mothers has been the one-to-one predictor of the sibsize of their children.

For example, writing in 1953, Bossard took for granted that a family of few siblings, the "small family system," was indicated by the relatively low completed fertility of women. He then proceeded to decry the small family system as being an inappropriate childrearing unit for individuals who would grow up to work in large-scale organizations (Bossard 1953). More recently Masnick and Bane (1980), in a book entitled *The Nation's Families: 1960–1990*, stated:

> By 1970, very few people who did not live alone lived with someone other than their spouse or their children. The households in which the younger generation grew up had become standardized to include one to three siblings (two to four years different in age), two parents (approximately 25 years older) and no one else.

Similarly, Easterlin infers the sibsize of children from the completed fertility of cohorts of women ("generations" in his terminology). Thus, Easterlin sees young people in large generations as typically coming from larger sibsizes than youngsters from small generations. As a consequence, individuals born into larger generations are, he believes, more deprived of parental attention and resources at home than are individuals born into small generations. In his own words (*Birth and Fortune.* 1980, 30):

> But entry into working life is not the first time that generation size makes its mark. In the course of their upbringing, both large and small generations have had significant clues as to what the future holds. For large generations, the typical story is one of crowding; for small generations, it is one of nurturance and special attention. At home, for large generations the pressures of sibling rivalry are high, and mom and dad are hard pressed to give time to each child's physical and emotional needs.

How does the disparity between the family size of cohorts of women and the sibsizes of their children come about? Is it a thing of the past? Can we rely that in the future small sibsizes rather than large will be the statistical norm? To answer these questions, we must note first that the fertility indicated by crude birth rates and their fluctuations, and even the fertility indicated by cohort reproduction (measuring number of children ever born per woman of completed fertility), reflect the behavior of women who never had a child as well as the behavior of those who became mothers. But, the sibsize of children is a measure that can only relate to women who had children. Consequently, insofar as fluctuations in

Table 8.1. Source of the Disparity between the Family Size of Mothers and the Family Size of Children.[a]

	Family Size							
	1	*2*	*3*	*4*	*5*	*6+*	*Total*	
Distribution of Mothers	1	2	1	2	1	3	10	
Distribution of Children	1	4	3	8	5	27	48	
% Distribution of Mothers	10	20	10	20	10	30	100	$(\bar{X}_m = 4.80)$
% Distribution of Children	2	8	6	17	10	57	100	$(\bar{X}_c = 6.62)$

[a]In order to compute the means the value 9.0 was used for the group 6+.

birth rates (and cumulative fertility per woman) arise from nonmarriage (or noncohabitation) and childlessness, such fluctuations do not inform us about what is happening to the family size of children. Further, even if we concentrate solely on the family size of mothers (women who had any children), the family size of their offspring is not readily apparent. We shall turn to this problem now.

In order to illustrate how the disparity between the family size of mothers and children arises, we will begin with 10 mothers, that is, 10 hypothetical women all of whom have had at least one child. Table 8.1 shows that these mothers had different numbers of children. In fact, only one mother had solely one child, and half the mothers had four or more children. Turning to the second line in the table, therefore, we see that 48 children were born to the 10 mothers and, by multiplying the number of mothers by the number of children each mother bore, we get the distribution of children according to the fertility of their mothers. A single child comes from a one-child family, but 27 children were born to those mothers who each had 6 or more births. Thus, if we examine the third and fourth lines of the table, we see that 57 percent of the children were born to 30 percent of the mothers (those women who each had many children), and 16 percent of the children were born to 40 percent of all mothers (those women who each had few children). By this mechanism, the average sibsize of children becomes almost two children (or about 50-percent) larger than the average family size of mothers.

Hence, given any variability in the number of children mothers bear, there is always a disparity between the family size of mothers and the sibsizes of children. The extent of this disparity depends on the amount of variability (technically, the variance) in women's reproductive behavior (Preston 1976).[1] But, in general, each new generation of children is born into larger sibsizes than one might expect just by looking at the average number of children ever born to their mothers. Moreover, the differences between the family size of mothers and the sibsize of children are not constant over time in any given society, nor can one infer this difference from the fertility of mothers without knowledge of the variance in this fertility. The reader may be interested in such a calculation using British data (Langford 1982).

The American reproductive experience over the period of the Depression, the baby boom, and the so-called baby bust serves to illustrate very well the importance of the variance in mothers' fertility to the differences between the family size of mothers and children. It also shows us trends in average family size of mothers and children over these crucial time periods. In table 8.2, we have used census (and Current Population Survey) data to estimate the family size of mothers and children for the most typical Depression, baby-boom, and baby-bust cohorts of mothers—that is, those cohorts of mothers that most clearly typify the reproduction of the three periods. The calculations based on census data are shown in the upper tier of the table. In order to derive the completed fertility of baby-bust mothers, we have used actual fertility for mothers age 35 to 39 in 1980 as a proxy for completed fertility in 1990. No data on expected additional children were available for this age group of mothers. To estimate completed fertility for 1997 and 2002, we have combined census data on actual plus expected fertility for women age 25 to 29 and 30 to 34 in 1982. In the lower tier, we have made comparable calculations using cohort fertility tables. The latter are based on a data set that is entirely different from the census—namely, annual births. For the calculations based on vital statistics, data are available only for the Depression and baby-boom cohorts of mothers. However, we feel it is important to test the

Table 8.2. Mean Family Size of Ever-Married Depression, Baby-Boom, and Baby-Bust Mothers Age 45 to 49 and the Family Size of Their Children, United States Census Data 1950–1982, and Cohort Fertility Tables Based on Birth Registration.

Mother's Birth Cohort	Age 45–49 in Year:	$\bar{X}_m$	$\bar{X}_c$	s_m^2	s_c^2	$\bar{X}_c - \bar{X}_m$
Census[a]						
Depression Mothers Born in:						
1901–1905	1950	3.13	4.80	5.23	7.77	1.67
1906–1910	1955	2.96	4.53	4.65	7.45	1.57
1911–1915	1960	2.93	4.33	4.08	6.50	1.40
Baby-Boom Mothers Born in:						
1921–1925	1970	3.18	4.39	3.85	5.64	1.21
1931–1935	1980	3.45	4.49	3.59	4.51	1.04
Baby-Bust Mothers Born in:						
1941–1945	1990	2.80	3.46	1.85	2.61	0.66
1948–1952	1990	2.35	2.86	1.20	1.59	0.51
1953–1958	2002	2.29	2.70	0.93	1.22	0.41

Table 8.2. *Continued.*

Mother's Birth Cohort	Age 45–49 in Year:	$\bar{X}_m$	$\bar{X}_c$	s_m^2	s_c^2	$\bar{X}_c - \bar{X}_m$
Cohort Fertility Tables[b]						
Depression Mothers						
Born in:						
1901–1905	1950	3.06	4.81	5.34	8.03	1.75
1906–1910	1955	2.91	4.54	4.74	7.65	1.63
1911–1915	1960	2.91	4.39	4.30	7.02	1.48
Baby-Boom Mothers						
Born in:						
1921–1925	1970	3.20	4.47	4.04	5.82	1.26
1931–1935	1980	3.51	4.59	3.79	4.94	1.08

[a]In order to compare the means ($\bar{X}_m$ for mothers and $\bar{X}_c$ for children) and variances (S_m^2 for mothers and S_c^2 for children) for women across all census cohorts, it was necessary to base all calculations on the same number of sibsize categories. Therefore since some data are distributed as high as twelve or more children, but other data have seven or more children as the terminal category, all years were converted to a terminal category of seven-plus, except for 1997 and 2002 where the terminal category is five-plus. This aggregation may lower the variance for 1997 and 2002 but, since only 4.2 and 2.6 percent of mothers fall into the five-plus category, such underestimation will be minimal.

Data for mothers age 45–49 in 1950 and 1955 are from U.S. Bureau of the Census, 1955, Tables 1 and 2. (The later cohort was derived from mothers who were age 40–44 in 1950.) Mothers in the terminal category, seven-plus, are assumed to have 8.963 children in 1950 and 8.975 children in 1955. These estimates, as well as all others discussed below, were calculated by solving for the number which would account for all births to the specific cohort of women.

Data for mothers age 45–49 in 1960 are from U.S. Bureau of the Census, 1964, Tables 1 and 2. Mothers in the terminal category, seven-plus, are assumed to have 8.812 children.

Data for mothers age 45–49 in 1970 are from U.S. Bureau of the Census, 1973, Tables 1 and 2. Mothers in the terminal category, seven-plus, are assumed to have 8.701 children.

Data for mothers age 45–49 in 1980 and 1990 are from U.S. Bureau of the Census, 1982, Table 12B. In each case the combined category of five to six children was disaggregated using the proportion of mothers found in each separate category in the Cohort Fertility Tables of the Vital Statistics. For the cohort born in 1931–1935, mothers in the terminal category, seven-plus are assumed to have 8.108 children each. The 1990 data were derived from women who were age 35–39 in 1980. This report included only the actual fertility to date for that cohort, and mothers in the terminal category, seven-plus, are assumed to have 8.200 children.

Data for mothers age 45–49 in 1997 and 2002 are from U.S. Bureau of the Census, 1984, Tables 2 and 8. This report is based on the actual and expected fertility of ever-married women age 30–34 and 25–29 in 1982. To compute distributions for ever-married mothers, the groups "currently married" and "widowed, divorced or separated" were summed. The terminal category, five-plus, is based on a weighted average of these two groups, and was assumed to be 5.70 for mothers age 30–34, and 5.68 for mothers age 25–29.

[b]Data for mothers age 45–49 in 1950, 1955, 1960, and 1970 are from Heuser, 1976, Tables 2A and 7A. Values for the terminal category, seven-plus, were assumed to be 9.000, 9.007, 8.966, and 8.698, respectively.

Data for mothers age 45–49 in 1980 are from National Center for Health Statistics, 1984, Tables 1–13 and 1–15. Mothers in the terminal category, seven-plus, were assumed to have 8.51 children each.

Table 8.3. Completed Family Size Distributions of Ever-Married Depression and Baby-Boom Mothers, and the Family Size of Their Children, United States, 1950–1980.[a]

Census Year	Family Size							Total	$\bar{X}$	s^2	$\bar{X}_c - \bar{X}_m$
	1	2	3	4	5	6	7+				
Depression Mothers Age 45–49 in:											
1950											
Mothers	24.9	27.2	17.3	10.9	6.4	4.2	9.1	100	3.13	5.23	1.67
Children	8.0	17.4	16.6	13.9	10.1	8.0	26.0	100	4.80	7.77	
1955											
Mothers	26.2	29.1	17.5	10.5	5.7	3.6	7.4	100	2.96	4.65	1.57
Children	8.8	19.7	17.8	14.2	9.6	7.4	22.5	100	4.53	7.46	
1960											
Mothers	23.7	30.0	19.3	11.1	6.0	3.5	6.4	100	2.93	4.08	1.40
Children	8.1	20.5	19.7	15.0	10.2	7.2	19.3	100	4.33	6.50	
Baby-Boom Mothers Age 45–49 in:											
1970											
Mothers	16.0	29.0	22.6	13.9	7.7	4.2	6.6	100	3.18	3.85	1.21
Children	5.0	18.2	21.3	17.5	12.1	8.0	17.9	100	4.39	5.64	
1980											
Mothers	11.3	24.0	25.7	16.4	9.3	5.3	8.0	100	3.45	3.59	1.04
Children	3.3	13.9	22.3	19.0	13.5	9.2	18.8	100	4.49	4.51	

[a]Census data were used to derive these distributions and the sources are described in table 8.2.

calculations from census data against the vital statistics because of measurement error in both data sets. Clearly, the results are remarkably close and they evince virtually identical patterns.

From table 8.2, we see first of all how dependent the difference between the family size of mothers and children is on the variance in mothers' fertility. For example, as between the cohorts of mothers of 1901–1905 (Depression mothers) and 1921–1925 (baby-boom mothers), we find virtually identical average family size per mother but a very large dropoff in the variance of the mothers' fertility. For this reason, there is a large drop in the difference between the family size of mothers and children. Thus, in the census data, among the 1901–1905 cohort of mothers, fertility was 3.13 children per mother, but the family size of children (4.80) was 53 percent larger than the family size of mothers. Among the 1921–1925 cohort of mothers, with a fertility of 3.18 children per mother, the family size of children (4.39) was only 38 percent larger than the family size of mothers because of the decline in the variance in mothers' fertility.

Second, we see that although the family size of mothers during the baby boom was somewhat larger on average than during the Depression, the family size of children during the baby boom increased only fractionally. The fact is that the family size of children of baby-boom mothers was (along with the children of the cohort of 1911–1915 Depression mothers) the smallest in our history prior to the baby bust. In effect, we discover a virtually continuous decline in the family size of children from the Depression to the baby bust, punctuated only by a fractional increase during the baby boom. From mothers completing fertility in 1960 to the present, no cohort has a family size of children as large as the 1901–1905 or 1906–1910 cohorts of mothers—the cohorts epitomizing Depression fertility!

Third, the most recent cohorts of mothers (baby-bust mothers) show a marked decline in the average family size of children. This decline results not only from lower fertility per mother but from a major decline in the variance of mothers' fertility.

Finally, it is clear that since the Depression we have been experiencing a sharp drop in the variance of the family size of children. This drop in the sibsize variance resulted from a curtailment of one-child families and exceptionally large sibsizes, as may be seen

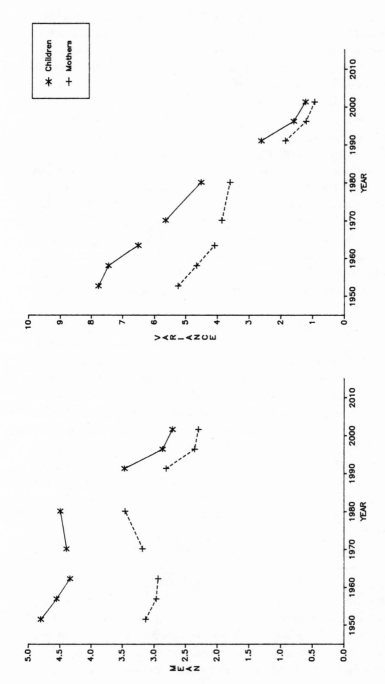

Figure 8.1. Mean Family Size and Variance of Ever-Married Mothers Age 45–49 and Their Children, United States Census Data 1950–1982. Data are from U.S. Bureau of the Census, various volumes. (See footnote to table 9.2 for complete description).

in table 8.3, which presents the distribution by family size for Depression and baby-boom mothers and children. The results of all of these calculations may be represented most readily by the diagram in figure 8.1 showing the family size of all women, ever-married women, and ever-married mothers for the three periods along with the sibsizes of their children.

In sum, from the information presented so far in this chapter, we hope it is clear why we cannot infer that large birth cohorts, such as we experienced during the baby boom, necessarily imply larger sibsizes than small birth cohorts. Fluctuations in birth cohorts are a function of fluctuations in childlessness, in the magnitude and timing of fertility per mother, and in the relative number of women in the reproductive ages. The family size of children depends on the fertility of mothers and the variance in this fertility. In part, the difference between the size of birth cohorts and the family size of children depends on the difference between period and cohort fertility of women, but this difference also rests on a distinction between the family size of women and mothers, and additionally, on the variance in the family size of mothers.

The Sibsize Transition

Do the declines in period birth rates since 1957 allow us to infer that being brought up in a large family is a thing of the past? Table 8.4 shows the distribution of the family size of mothers and children among the last of the cohorts of baby-boom mothers and the emerging cohorts of baby-bust mothers. Bearing in mind that the baby-boom cohorts of mothers were still reproducing during the period when annual birth rates were declining, we find that the family size of children of baby-boom mothers who were completing their fertility in 1980 (those age 40–44 and 45–49) was large for a high proportion of youngsters. Over 60 percent were in families of four or more children, 42 percent in families of five or more children, and 19 percent in families of seven or more children.

However, when we turn to the estimated completed family size of baby-bust mothers—those 35–39, 30–34, and 25–29 in 1980—a sharp drop in the family size of children is apparent, along with a rise in one-child families. A large increase in two-child families and a drastic curtailment of families of four or more children charac-

Table 8.4. Completed Family Size Distributions of Ever-Married Baby-Boom and Baby-Bust Mothers and the Family Size of Their Children, United States, 1980.[a]

Age of Mother	Family Size							Total	$\bar{X}$	s^2	$\bar{X}_c - \bar{X}_m$
	1	2	3	4	5	6	7+				
Baby-Boom Mothers											
45–49											
Mothers	11.3	24.0	25.7	16.4	9.3	5.3	8.0	100	3.45	3.59	1.04
Children	3.3	13.9	22.3	19.0	13.5	9.2	18.8	100	4.49	4.51	
40–44											
Mothers	10.4	27.5	25.3	17.3	8.6	4.4	6.5	100	3.32	3.17	0.96
Children	3.1	16.6	22.8	20.9	12.9	7.9	15.8	100	4.28	4.16	
Baby-Bust Mothers											
35–39											
Mothers	12.1	37.5	26.3	14.3	5.7	2.5	1.6	100	2.80	1.85	0.66
Children	4.3	26.8	28.2	20.4	10.1	5.4	4.8	100	3.46	2.61	
30–34											
Mothers	19.1	46.5	21.5	8.7	4.2	—	—	100	2.35	1.20	0.51
Children	8.1	39.5	27.4	14.8	10.2	—	—	100	2.86	1.59	
25–29											
Mothers	16.8	51.0	22.8	6.8	2.6	—	—	100	2.29	0.93	0.41
Children	7.3	44.5	29.9	11.9	6.4	—	—	100	2.70	1.22	

[a]Census data were used to derive these distributions and the sources are described in table 9.2. Data on the completed fertility of the cohorts age 25–29 and 30–34 are based on 1984 data concerning actual plus expected family size.

terizes the sibsizes of baby-bust babies. Even so, among the mothers for whom the data are the most trustworthy, women age 35–39 (for whom the calculations are based solely on actual fertility), 41 percent of the children are in families of four or more, and 20 percent in families of five or more. Among mothers age 30–34 (whose actual fertility is 89 percent of the actual plus expected lifetime fertility shown here), 25 percent of the children will be in families of four or more, and 10 percent in families of five or more. Finally, among mothers age 25–29 (whose actual fertility is 66 percent of actual plus expected lifetime fertility), 18 percent of the children will be in families of four or more, and 6 percent in families of five or more. These data thus suggest that the real revolution in the family size of children has only started. Our image of the socialization and upbringing of most children as taking place in small families has been highly inaccurate. Children in the United States are just beginning, on a large scale, to accrue some of the advantages of being brought up in small families. If our findings so far have any validity, and if other things remain equal, these children should be the most fortunate and favored of any in our history. Even if, as now appears to be the case, there is some deterioration in family stability and a corresponding rise in single parenthood, the decline in family size will offer compensation.

It could be argued, however, that our forecasts of a rosier average outcome for youngsters with the advent of the sibsize revolution leave out of account a major concomitant change in family behavior—the increase in female labor-force participation. Will children in small families actually be the recipients of the parental attention that their sibsize implies? Or, will they simply be shunted into inadequate day-care facilities and get marginal attention from educationally disadvantaged service workers? A spectrum of data suggests that the latter characterization is wide of the mark.

First, the information gathered by the Current Population Survey (of the U.S. Bureau of the Census) on child-care arrangements in 1982 shows clearly that for children under age five, group day-care is seldom used by working mothers. Such care is extremely rare for infants. Most children under age five are cared for by relatives, or by nonrelatives in the child's own home—the father (14 percent), the mother (9 percent), grandparents (17 percent), other relatives (12 percent), nonrelatives in the child's home (6 percent). Perhaps surprisingly, day-care is resorted to more often by well-educated and relatively well-off mothers, on average, suggesting that families of this type may have moved away from relatives in the process of upward mobility and/or that the day-care facilities are of high quality (U.S. Bureau of the Census 1983, Table 2). As for older children, Current Population Survey data on after-school care for children age 6 through 13 at two dates, 1974 and 1984, are important in showing that, for children of mothers employed full-time, the percent cared for solely by parents after school rose from 52.8 to 55.1. Moreover, the proportion without adult supervision (the proverbial latch-key children) declined from 16.4 to 11.7 percent (U.S. Bureau of the Census 1987, Table D). Although such impressive rates of parental participation in child-care may seem questionable, census researchers point out that high proportions of mothers who are employed full-time are on shift work (for example, waitresses and other food service workers, nurses and other health care workers, school-teachers, factory workers) as are their mates. Under such circumstances, parents are able to shoulder child-care responsibilities for children after school hours.

Second, although the proportion of mothers of children under age five who are in the labor force has risen dramatically in recent years, large numbers of such women are part-time workers as shown by the 1982 Current Population Survey already discussed. In 1982, 52 percent of women 18 to 44 years old with children under age 5 were not in the labor force, and of the 41 percent who were in the labor force and employed, 64 percent were characterized as full-time. Thus, 74 percent of the mothers of children under 5 were either not in the labor force or were working only part-time (U.S. Bureau of the Census 1983, Table 1 and Table F). As for older children, Current Population Survey data for 1984 show that 59 percent of youngsters age 5- to 13 had mothers in the labor force, but only 37 percent of these children had mothers who worked full-time, leaving 63 percent of 5- to 13-year-olds with mothers who were not in the labor force or who worked only part-time (U.S. Bureau of the Census 1987, Table 1).[2]

Third, with regard to the amount of time and attention mothers of small families have available to devote to their children, we must remember that low fertility typically means few pregnancies, few miscarriages, and few periods of postpartum recovery. Therefore, it is not simply that mothers of small families have few children to care for, since such mothers have been able to avoid as well the kind of protracted physical strain that high rates of reproduction represent. Theoretically, at least, mothers of small families have more physical energy to attend to their offspring.

Fourth, an extra earner in the family (namely, the wife and mother) has been an important factor in the economic upgrading of many American couples and in decreasing economic inequality among them (for a recent summary of this literature, see, Treas 1987). Although the future equalizing effects of enhanced female labor-force participation may be problematical (because the big increases in women working may occur at the highly educated, professional levels where husbands earn high incomes as well), this fact would not alter the increase over time in the economic and social status of children in households having extra earners.

Finally, a recent review of the studies to date of the effects of maternal employment (Heyns 1982) concludes that, "Studies of maternal employment have demonstrated, with very few exceptions, that on achievement, the children of working mothers differ very little from the children of nonworking mothers." Additionally, Heyns notes that a good deal of the literature,

> tends to view children not as people but as outcomes. There is an undercurrent of thinly veiled alarm regarding the consequences of maternal employment or social change that rests on the developmental theories of another era. Changes in family life tend to be viewed with foreboding as deviations from a smoothly functioning normalcy. (p. 239)

Heyns also emphasizes in her critical review that the issue of the allocation of working mother's time has been treated, to date, in a rudimentary fashion. Studies have distinguished between working full-time and part-time, but the definitions of these categories have varied widely, a deficiency that is partly a result of the fact that the data are often by-products of research that had a different focus.

The obverse of measuring how much time is spent working is measuring how much time is spent in child-care. This problem is not blessed with a wealth of data. However, Heyns, in her review

Table 8.5. Effects on Total Years of Schooling, for Three Cohorts, of an Assumed Change to the Sibsize Distribution of the Baby-Bust Babies, White Respondents, Age 25 and Over, General Social Surveys, 1972–1986.

	Cohort Born:		
	1950–1959	*1930–1939*	*1920–1929*
Total Years of Education—Actual	13.58	12.76	11.97
Total Years of Education—With Baby Bust Sibsize Distribution	14.06	13.49	13.02
Years of Education Gained	.48	.73	1.05

of the most recent data on time budgets, says, "These data do not support the notion that working mothers spend substantially less time in child-care activities than nonworking mothers. . . . [The data] suggest that it is naive to equate increments in labor force participation with decrements in the aggregate time devoted to children." We may note here that the data fail to take account of the number of children in families and, hence, the calculations underestimate time spent per child by women with small families. Let us address now the expected education gains from the sibsize transition.

With regard to education, what would attainment have been for adults born in three prior cohorts had they had the sibsize distribution of the baby-bust babies but all other characteristics, including education by sibsize, remained the same? To make this standardization, we have chosen the baby-boom cohort (born 1950–1959), the Depression cohort (born 1930–1939 and reared largely during times of economic prosperity), and the 1920s cohort (born 1920–1929 and reared largely during the Depression). Table 8.5 demonstrates the compositional effect on each cohort's average years of education by the assumed transition to a baby-bust sibsize distribution—the distribution implicit in the family size of mothers age 30 to 34 in 1980 (table 8.4). The 1950s cohort gains approximately a half a year of education on average, the 1930's cohort about three-fourths of a year, and the 1920s cohort a year of total schooling completed, simply by virtue of the assumed change in sibsize.

The importance of such gains due to the sibsize transition should not be underestimated. For example, for the 1920s cohort, the assumed sibsize gain in education exactly equals the gain that would have been effected had all those whose fathers had only eight years of schooling (the modal category for fathers) been suddenly endowed with one to three years of high school. And, for this cohort the gain substantially exceeds the difference between coming from an intact and broken family. Similar effects occur for the 1930s cohort. For the baby-boom cohort, although much closer in sibsize to the baby-bust babies than earlier cohorts, the gain of .48 of a year of schooling goes a long way to closing the gap between those from intact and broken families (.68 of a year), or between those whose fathers did and did not complete college (.66 of a year). Since children from broken families are still in the minority in our population, the net gain in education from the sibsize transition is still obvious. If the sibsize transition is just beginning, is it likely to have broader social consequences as it progresses than the cognitive and educational upgrading of individuals in the U.S. population?

SIBSIZE AND SOCIAL ATTITUDES

Although our focus in this volume has been on intellectual abilities and educational attainment, it is worth asking, as we bring our efforts to a close, whether the sibsize transition, and its attendant increase in human capital, will affect the social and political views of Americans?

We may begin by posing the following question: If large families have been overrepresented in each new generation (relative to the family size of their mothers) has this had a compositional effect on social attitudes? Has the overrepresentation of large sibsizes meant that, other things equal, the American population has had social attitudes more like the poorly educated than would have prevailed had the family size of mothers been more homogeneously smaller? Such an outcome seems plausible, but it cannot be assumed since there could have been countervailing influences on those from large families that offset the effect of lower education.

Our consideration of this issue is facilitated by the existence in the General Social Surveys, 1972–1985, of data on a range of social attitudes—attitudes toward civil liberties, race relations, women's

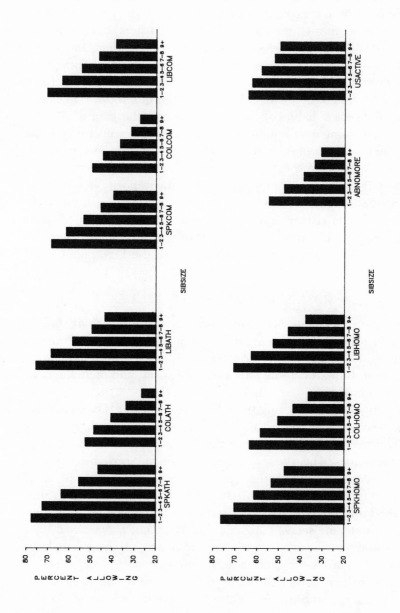

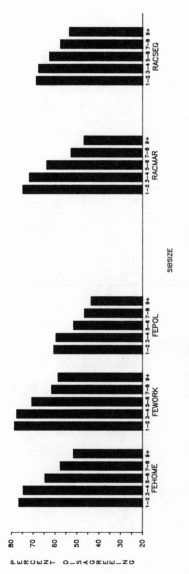

Figure 8.2. Percentages Having Unrestrictive Social and Political Attitudes by Sibsize, White Respondents, Age 18 and Over, General Social Surveys, 1972–85.[a]

[a]The exact wording of the attitudinal statements is as follows:

1. There are always some people whose ideas are considered bad or dangerous by other people. For instance, somebody who is against all churches and religion.

   SPKATH—If such a person wanted to make a speech in your (city/town/community) against churches and religion, should he be allowed to speak, or not?

   COLATH—Should such a person be allowed to teach in a college or university, or not?

   LIBATH—If some people in your community suggested that a book he wrote against churches and religion should be taken out of your public library, would you favor removing this book, or not?

2. Now, I should like to ask you some questions about a man who admits he is a Communist.

   SPKCOM—Suppose this admitted Communist wanted to make a speech in your community. Should he be allowed to speak, or not?

   COLCOM—Suppose he is teaching in a college. Should he be fired, or not?

LIBCOM—Suppose he wrote a book which is in your public library. Somebody in your community suggests that the book should be removed from the library. Would you favor removing it, or not?

3. And what about a man who admits that he is a homosexual?

SPKHOMO—Suppose this admitted homosexual wanted to make a speech in your community. Should he be allowed to speak, or not?

COLHOMO—Should such a person be allowed to teach in a college or university, or not?

LIBHOMO—If some people in your community suggested that a book he wrote in favor of homosexuality should be taken out of your public library, would you favor removing this book, or not?

4. HOMOSEX—What about sexual relations between two adults of the same sex—do you think it is always wrong, almost always wrong, wrong only sometimes, or not wrong at all?
(The two last statements have been combined here to represent percent allowing.)

5. ABNOMORE—Please tell me whether or not you think it should be possible for a pregnant woman to obtain a legal abortion if she is married and does not want any more children?

6. USACTIVE—Do you think it will be best for the future of this country if we take an active part in world affairs, or if we stay out of world affairs?
(The response, Take an active part, represents percent allowing in the chart.)

7. FEHOME—Do you agree or disagree with this statement? Women should take care of running their homes and leave running the country up to men.

8. FEWORK—Do you approve or disapprove of a married woman earning money in business or industry if she has a husband capable of supporting her?
(The percent approving is represented in the chart.)

9. FEPOL—Tell me if you agree or disagree with this statement: Most men are better suited emotionally for politics than are most women.

10. RACMAR—Do you think there should be laws against marriages between (Negroes/blacks) and whites?
(The percent against such laws are represented in the chart.)

11. RACSEG—Do you agree or disagree with the following statement? White people have a right to keep (Negroes/blacks) out of their neighborhoods if they want to, and (Negroes/blacks) should respect that right.

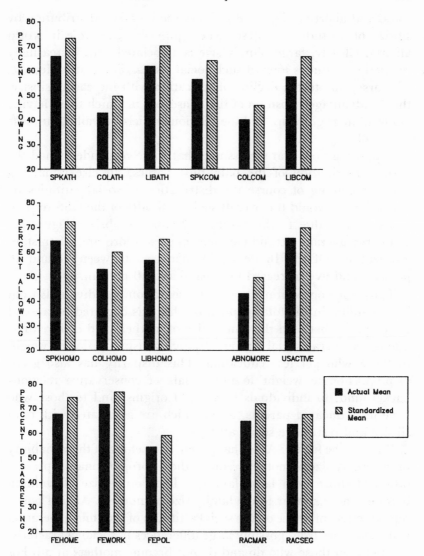

Figure 8.3. Comparison of the Actual and Standardized Mean Proportions Having Unrestrictive Social and Political Attitudes, White Respondents, Age 18 and Over, General Social Surveys, 1972–85. (Standardization uses 1972–85 attitudes by sibsize and the baby-bust sibsize distribution. For a description of attitudinal statements see the footnote to figure 8.2.)

roles, and abortion. Figure 8.2 shows the bivariate distribution by sibsize of attitudes on these issues (plus the U.S. role in world affairs). Clearly, larger family size is associated with increasingly restrictive attitudes toward such social issues. These attitudes are, of course, due to the decline of education with increasing sibsize, the disadvantaged position of the household in which those having many siblings grew up, and the religious beliefs prevailing in those households.

Supposing now that we assume that these respondents had the sibsize distribution of the baby-bust babies, all else remaining equal, including of course the distribution of social attitudes by sibsize? How would the overall social attitudes of the GSS respondents change due to the assumed decline in sibsize? Figure 8.3 compares average attitudinal percentages before and after standardization. Of the 16 items, 11 increased between 11 and 16 percent, and five increased between 6 and 10 percent.

Thus, the compositional overrepresentation of individuals from large families in the total population that has occurred because of the disparity between the family size of mothers and children has influenced overall social attitudes by giving disproportionate weight to those who get less education. This disparity has also given disproportionate weight to individuals of conservative religious background, to individuals from rural origins, and to those who have less-educated parents, all of which are associated with both sibsize and restrictive social attitudes.

What of the future? As we have seen, a lessening of the variability in the family size of mothers reduces the disproportionate representation of those from large families. The family size of children becomes more similar to the family size of mothers. At that point, reproductive influence on the social attitudes of the child generation will stem more from possibly large differences in social characteristics between those who do and do not become mothers at all. For example, if extreme proportions of educated women remain childless, then those who have children at all will be weighted by the less educated among the female population. The same could obviously be said about reproduction and nonreproduction among those in fundamentalist and nonfundamentalist religious groups. However, barring extreme changes of this type in childlessness, we may expect that current reproductive trends in the United States will result in more liberal social attitudes as a consequence of the compositional effect of smaller sibsizes.

CONCLUSION

In this chapter, we have seen that the disparity between the family size of mothers and children is a function of two elements: Each new generation is made up disproportionately of the offspring of the most prolific mothers, and the greater the variance in mother's fertility, the greater the disparity between the family size of mothers and children. The U.S. experience from the Depression through the baby boom to the current baby bust, illustrates well that the drop in the variance of mothers' reproductive behavior since the Depression has resulted in a continuous decrease in the family size of children. This drop in variance has been particularly sharp for the baby-bust cohorts of mothers resulting in a marked decline in the average family size of their children. Even so, among white mothers age 30 to 34 in 1980, 25 percent of the children will be in families of four or more, and 10 percent in families of five or more. These data thus suggest that the real revolution in the family size of children has just started.

How much of an educational advantage would individuals from relatively recent birth cohorts have gained if these cohorts had been distributed by sibsize like the baby-bust babies born to women age 30 to 34 in 1980? We have found, for the 1920s and 1930s cohorts of children, that these gains more than offset the difference between the educational attainment of those from intact and broken families, and, for the baby-boom cohort, the offset against broken families was substantial. For the three cohorts, the gain ranged from half a year of schooling to over a year.

We then turned to a "macro" consequence of the sibsize transition. Since this transition involves a compositional change by sibsize for the U.S. population, will this change, other things equal, affect important sociopolitical attitudes of the population as a whole? We have found the answer to be affirmative because such attitudes vary by sibsize—the larger the sibsize the more restrictive (conservative) the attitudes. A standardization using the sibsize distribution of baby-bust babies (the same distribution as was used for the education standardization) and the attitudes by sibsize of the 1972–1985 GSS samples, shows an important increase in non-restrictive attitudes as a consequence of a decrease in the disproportion of individuals from large families. Hence, insofar as one regards an increase in nonrestrictive attitudes toward civil liberties, abortion, women's roles, and race relations as positive, the sibsize transition, other things equal, will have this effect.

9

THE SIBSIZE TRANSITION AND THE QUALITY OF CHILDREN: A RECAPITULATION

Public policies aimed at assuring nationwide intellectual and academic quality in young people have been partially frustrated because of lack of control. Most of the differences among children in different schools are attributable to qualities that youngsters bring to these institutions, not to variation in what the schools have to offer. The fact is that reproducing couples control much of the basic quality of each new generation. Families are the source not only of genetic influences on children, but of the environment prior to schooling and concomitant with most of it. This book has been about the educational consequences of a piece of that environment—the size of family in which children are reared. For a variety of reasons, couples in the United States (and elsewhere in the Western world) have reduced not only the number of children they are having, but are doing so with greater uniformity than has been the case in the past. The result is a very recent sibsize revolution following—with a long time lag—the initiation of the fertility revolution.

The research reported on in this volume suggests that the consequences of this change for individuals will be strikingly positive and that the society as a whole stands to benefit as well. As far as individuals are concerned, we may recapitulate here some of our principal findings:

1. Even after controlling for major parental background characteristics, we have found differences in total educational attainment—approximately two years of schooling—between small and large families that rival the simple bivariate differences by race and age. Moreover, those from large versus small families lose about a year of graded schooling, on average, which translates into sizable

sibsize differences in proportions graduating from high school—about a 23-percentage-point difference between only children and those from families of seven or more.

2. The greatest sibsize effect on education is not on the chances of going to college given high school graduation but on the chances of getting through high school. We believe that the lessened effect of sibsize later in the educational process is due to the selection of only the most motivated and intelligent in large families as youngsters proceed through school.

3. Relative to other variables in the status attainment model, sibsize is consistently second only in importance to father's education when it comes to graded schooling and total years of education. Father's occupational status (SEI) is not important at the graded-schooling level. Father's SEI becomes important for the chances of going to college given graduation from high school. Youngsters' chances of getting through graded schooling are related very specifically to their father's educational level and the number of children in the family.

4. Analysis by cohorts demonstrates that the suggestion by Featherman and Hauser that the status attainment model has become less important over time in explaining graded schooling conceals important facts. Sibsize effects have not declined over the cohorts, although other family background effects have done so. With regard to college schooling, sibsize effects have actually increased along with the effects of father's education. Thus, large families have been a continuing drag on the society's ability to create openness in graded schooling, and an increasing drag on our ability to provide equal opportunity at the college level.

5. We have questioned whether the postulated dilution effect of increasing sibsize on educational attainment was mitigated by forces either external to or within the family. In attempting to answer this question, we have concentrated on Catholic–non-Catholic religious affiliation, breaking non-Catholics down into mainline Protestants, fundamentalist Protestants, and Jews, and dividing Catholics into major ethnic groups. We have also examined sibsize effects by separate paternal social status groupings. These analyses suggest that the negative educational effects of large families can be somewhat offset—by a powerful external force such as the Catholic church, by an exceptionally persistent carry-over of kin cohe-

sion among some ethnic groups, by high parental socioeconomic status, or by a combination of these influences. This finding thus adds some weight to our interpretation of the sibsize influence as a dilution effect, because we see that the negative influence of increasing sibsize is responsive to augmented resources. However, although supportive forces can mitigate the effect of large families on education, our analysis shows that a substantial sibsize gradient typically persists because such advantages tend to benefit those in small families as well.

6. The complexity of the analysis just discussed is exemplified by Catholics when they are disaggregated by ethnicity. In some cases, the Irish being a prime example, the offset to relatively large family size provided by the Catholic church has been a substantial educational elevation of the entire religioethnic group over Protestants. Yet, because Catholic-church backing for education and the Irish Catholic family has also helped small families, the sibsize gradient among Irish Catholics has remained large. On the other hand, even when Catholic ethnic groups (such as the Italians and Poles) have lower overall educational levels than non-Catholics, those in large Catholic families achieve more education than those in large non-Catholic families.

7. Our analysis has also suggested that the smaller the family, the less men's educational attainment was influenced by their social origins. In effect, the system of social stratification (itself affected most importantly by educational attainment) has been more open for those from small families than for those from large.

8. Turning to the relation of number of siblings and IQ, we have been able to isolate sibsize effects specifically for verbal ability and to show that number of siblings has little effect on nonverbal ability. Since verbal ability is strongly related to parental attention and interaction, this finding suggests a genuine causal relation with sibsize. It is also true that verbal ability is an important predictor of educational success. The fact that sibsize is not related to nonverbal ability suggests that the cognitive importance of sibsize is not due simply to the possibility that more intelligent parents have small families.

9. The magnitude of the effects of sibsize on IQ are impressive. For example, among young children in Cycle II of the Health Examination Survey the difference between only children and those

in families of seven or more is a standard deviation at the bivariate level. Even when parental characteristics are controlled, the difference still amounts to seven-tenths of a standard deviation. When parental background is controlled, there is no cognitive deficit among only children. Only children generally do better than children of any other sibsize.

10. We have found that only children are disproportionately selected not only according to some major parental problems (only children have a high probability of coming from broken families) but also according to difficulties of their own. Specifically, only children are more likely to have had major health problems as infants, and at least some mothers who were young enough to continue childbearing beyond a single child did not do so. These results call into doubt the wisdom of interpreting "problems" among only children as being due to socialization rather than selection. Aside from selection, only children appear to be uniquely advantaged as far as verbal IQ is concerned.

11. With regard to birth-order effects on cognitive ability, we have found no consistent theoretical basis for expecting such consequences. Rather, most "findings" appear to involve highly selective reporting of what are, in reality, sibsize, period, parental background, child-spacing, and other selection effects for which controls have not been instituted. Our effort to control for some of these confounders over all sibsizes and birth orders suggests that systematic and patterned birth-order differences in cognitive ability probably do not exist.

12. Turning to birth order effects on educational attainment, we have followed Blau and Duncan in expecting that, in large families, middle-born children would be at a disadvantage. No birth order effects for small families are expected. Our actual analysis of OCG 1962 and 1973 shows no birth order effects on educational attainment for small families but a definite parabola among large ones. In addition, the last borns and next-to-last borns in large families frequently do better than firstborns, quite probably because the family benefits from wage-earning older children or, at worst, children have left home for jobs or marriage. As well, the data suggest that it is not simply being in the middle that is the biggest problem, but being a middle-born child early in the sequence of offspring. This finding seems to reflect the fact that early middle borns in

large families experience the full negative force of large sibsize—they have older siblings close in age with whom to compete for resources, and they will experience a long period during which younger siblings are being born and are dependent.

13. Our analysis of students' postsecondary educational goals had the important feature of allowing us to compare results when the parents' expectations were derived from the student (the typical situation in most prior analyses) and from the parent. We could thus test whether the high degree of influence of parents' expectations on students' expectations found in prior analyses was a circular effect resulting from the fact that both pieces of data were obtained from the student. Our analysis shows that, even when the parents' expectations are derived from the parent, parental expectations are still the most important influence on students' expectations. Young people from higher-status families and small sibsizes have higher educational goals primarily because these influences operate on ability and grades, and thence through parents' expectations or desires. The latter, as indicated, are the most important influence on youngsters' own expectations.

14. With regard to settings in the home, we have found that children from small families are more likely to engage in intellectual and cultural pursuits, and to spend more time playing alone than those from large families. Time spent playing alone particularly characterizes the only child. Such solitary activity does not, however, connote unpopularity. If anything, children from small families are more popular than those from large ones. Children from small families are more likely to have been read to early in life than children from large families, and to have experienced advantages such as music and dance lessons as well as travel outside the United States.

15. As for settings in school, youngsters from small families are more likely to engage in intellectual and cultural activities than are those from large families, whereas the latter incline more toward community, vocational, and hobby activities. These findings, combined with those on settings in the home, suggest that leisure time among children from small families is used in ways that serve to enhance educational achievement.

16. Concerning parental treatments, we have raised the question of whether parents of few children are hard-driving and competitive

for their offspring, whereas parents of large families place more emphasis on obedience, conformity, and assimilation. Such associations were not evident once parental background characteristics were controlled, suggesting that characteristics that numerous other researchers have assumed were related to sibsize, were actually related to the social class and educational status of the parents (which are, in turn, associated with the number of children they have).

17. Regarding overperformance and underperformance in school (defined as receiving grades above or below what would be expected given the student's ability) differences by sibsize are not large, but children from small sibsizes are more likely to overperform than those from sibsizes of five-plus. Those from large families show a fairly consistent pattern of underperformance as well.

18. Analysis of data on confidence in one's own intellectual ability shows not only that youngsters from small families have more confidence in their own ability than those from large families, but those from small families have more confidence than would be expected on the basis of their ability scores. By contrast, those from large families have less confidence than would be expected on the basis of such scores.

19. We have examined whether parents who have different-size families have different childrearing values—differences that are not captured by controls for parental socioeconomic status. Our analysis indicates either no difference or a slight difference after controls are introduced. It thus seems that parental personality traits and childrearing values are not among the unmeasured variables that might invalidate our interpretation of the sibsize–achievement relationship.

20. Although we had no theoretical reasons for expecting sibsize effects to differ by sex, we examined this issue. The net of this effort is that such an interaction is very rare. However, in keeping with much prior research, our analysis suggests that there are influences on young women's educational prospects that differ substantially from the influences on young men's. A major set of influences on young women clearly lies outside the basic status-attainment model (including sibsize) and, we believe, in the direction of family-oriented, sex-role definitions that are held both by the young women themselves and by their parents.

21. Because of the disparity between the family size of mothers and children, we have seen that the sibsize transition, as distinct from the fertility transition, is just beginning with the so-called baby-bust cohorts. The family size of children born during the baby boom differed little from the family size of children born during the Depression, because the variance of mothers' fertility was less during the baby boom. Hence, the image of American childrearing as taking place in small families during most of this century is inaccurate. Children in the United States are just beginning, on a large scale, to accrue some of the advantages of being brought up in small families.

22. To understand the importance for young people's education of this recent change in sibsize composition, we have estimated what the educational attainment of various past cohorts would have been if, all other factors constant, the cohorts had had sibsizes as small as the baby-bust babies. We have found that the baby-boom cohort, the Depression cohort, and the 1920s cohort would have gained approximately half a year, three-fourths of a year, and a year of education respectively. For such cohorts, these average gains in education exceed, or come close to (depending on the cohort), the average educational difference beween intact and broken families. This finding suggests that the decline in sibsize is compensating for the increase in family instability. Among stable families the decline in sibsize should represent a net gain.

23. Finally, we have asked whether the overrepresentation of large sibsizes in the population (relative to the family size of mothers) has had a compositional effect on social attitudes. Using data from the General Social Surveys on attitudes toward civil liberties, race relations, women's roles, and abortion, we have asked what the attitudinal effects would have been if, all else remaining constant, the respondents had been distributed by sibsize like the baby-bust babies. Of the 16 items, 11 became less restrictive by between 11 and 16 percent, and 5 became less restrictive by between 6 and 10 percent. For an item like "ABNOMORE"—whether married pregnant women should be allowed abortions if they want no more children—for example, the estimated change would constitute a "breakthrough" for an issue which has averaged around 44 percent approval since the early 1970s, and has never reached 50 percent.

In addition to the findings presented in this volume, the analysis has uncovered numerous informational gaps in our knowledge of the causes and consequences of sibsize outcomes. For example, if we wish to know whether changing sibsize affects changes in cognitive tests, like SAT scores, we require actual data on the sibsizes of SAT takers, along with socioeconomic information on the takers' parents. Equally, very few data are available on cognitively relevant settings and treatments of children in different-size families—time-use information on the children, measures of parental interaction with children (such as time spent reading to children or playing cognitively relevant games). To my knowledge, data are unavailable concerning the intellectual and recreational activities of the parents of different numbers of offspring, although such information could tell us about the content of parents as role models for their children. Moreover, it would be most informative to replicate the imaginative study by Heise and Roberts referred to in this volume—a study suggesting that youngsters from small sibsizes are forced to be more sociable and cosmopolitan than those from large sibsizes who can afford self-containment within the family of siblings. It would also be helpful to know whether there are sibsize differences in the perception of education as an investment or as an end in itself and how such differences as may exist relate to the child's tolerance for long periods of schooling. This list could be multiplied many times. The fact is that we have not begun to study systematically how intrafamilial dynamics influence cognitive and educational outcomes in young people.

For some readers, what we have learned may seem so commonsensical as hardly to require systematic investigation. We can only hope that these *savants* feel well-pleased because research has shown them to have exquisite judgment. For others, among them the multitudes who were reared in large families and their surviving parents, the findings may be at worst an affront and at best simply incredible. We must remind such readers that we have been dealing with averages and probabilities—individual children from large families may be successful and achieving, those from small ones, laggard and deviant. Indeed, as we have reiterated many times, since most people have numerous siblings, we must expect to find that a goodly share of society's stars are from large families. Over the years, I have produced many papers and talks on the effects of sibsize. These efforts have elicited scores of letters recounting the exploits of siblings in large families—one child a physician, one a priest, one an attorney, one an accountant, one an architect, and so on. The veracity of these accounts is in no way impugned by the results reported on here.

We now turn briefly to some macrosocial consequences of the sibsize transition (other than those relating to the social attitudes discussed in chapter 8). In particular, a final word is in order about the implications of this research for our evaluation of slow or rapid population growth in the country as a whole, as well as among subgroups.

We cannot know when people first started debating the advantages and disadvantages to their societies of differential rates of population growth. We do know that the debate continues and may do so beyond our lifetimes. Debates of this sort persist not only because the participants enjoy them, which is doubtless true, but because the arguments are couched in such a fashion that resolution is impossible. Both sides are forced to use aggregate statistics that conceal offsetting effects, complex interactions, and daunting measurement error. When these statistics relate to current conditions things are bad enough, when they relate to the past, the opportunity for misinterpretation is incredible.

How can we bring information to bear on issues of this sort that is more conclusive, or at least that defines the problem in such a way that would allow further research to move toward resolution? In other words, how can we use social science to move from debate to evidence—evidence that must be disproved rather than argued? We believe that the first step is to recognize that the only way we can affect population growth is by affecting its components—mortality, fertility, and migration. Second, unless one has some evaluation of the effects of changes in the components, one cannot make informed tradeoffs. In sum, unless we examine the effects of changes in the growth components, we do not know whether the entire debate about aggregate growth is moot—population growth may not be a policy variable because people are unwilling to make changes in any of its components. Given that policy regarding mortality is constrained to move in one direction only, and that policy regarding immigration is motivated by sending and receiving countries in ways that typically transcend demographic implications, how couples behave reproductively turns out to be the major discretionary variable in population growth.

This volume is, we hope, of some help to our thinking about the consequences of differential reproductive behavior and, hence, of the disaggregated consequences of slow versus rapid population growth. If, as appears to be true, large sibsize is a major disadvantage to the children involved, then the case for low rates of population growth rests primarily on the intrinsic desirability of low fertility to the populations in question. Even if, for some reason, an argument could be made for the advantages of rapid population growth, it would be necessary to justify policy directed to this end in the face of overwhelming evidence concerning the undesirability of large families for the children involved and, ultimately, for the educational quality of the society in question.

What of differential fertility and sibling numbers among major subgroups in the United States (see, for example, Sowell 1983; Vining 1985)? Discussion of this subject, insofar as it occurs, centers on the "macro" consequences of high reproduction among disadvantaged groups and low reproduction among advantaged ones—the so-called eugenic problem. Phrased in this way, the issue is not widely regarded as open to policy manipulation. Like the issue of overall population growth, it is one that has the potential for endless (and fruitless) discussion. However, what is policy-relevant is the welfare of the subgroups involved. The information in this book suggests that an important share of the disadvantage such groups endure is open to manipulation by reproducing couples among them. Such couples have, within their grasp, the power to produce an important benefit for their offspring and to mitigate a major source of disadvantage. To be sure, such groups have suffered and continue to suffer various types of discrimination that hinders their advancement. But, if the experience of white non-Hispanics is any guidepost, high proportions of black and Hispanic children who come from large families never get far enough educationally for many types of social discrimination against them to have much influence. Such children leave the contest far too early to challenge the major discriminatory bastions of modern society.

Finally, we must again remind the reader of two important value judgments that should *not* be taken away from this book. The first is that people are worthwhile and important only if they are "realizing their potential." This is not our view. We believe that people are worthwhile and important because they exist. But, we also suspect that millions who, in Dante's words, were born to fly upward, grieve over potential that they know they have and that has not reached fruition. This is one of the problems addressed by this volume. Second, we remind the reader that education is not regarded here simply as an instrumentality in the status attainment process. In addition to its role in status attainment, education, as an end in itself, is among the most satisfying and rewarding consumer goods the society has to offer. On this ground alone, we cannot fail to be concerned about systematic impediments to schooling.

Appendix A

This appendix contains supplementary tables for chapter 1 and a detailed discussion of the predictors used in the modeling of educational attainment. Tables in this appendix that are not discussed here have been discussed already in chapter 1.

We begin our detailed discussion of the predictors with the three data sets that form the backbone of our analysis of adult educational attainment—OCG 1962 and 1973, and GSS 1972–1986.

OCCUPATIONAL CHANGES IN A GENERATION, 1962 AND 1973

Although, as we have noted, the overall response rate in the OCG samples was high, in the case of some questions there were fairly substantial amounts of missing data. These gaps were particularly evident with regard to the respondents' parents' characteristics—father's occupation and education. The gaps are accounted for, in part, by the fact that the parents' marriage was disrupted when the respondent was a child. For each predictor, table A.3 shows a breakdown of the missing data for male respondents and their wives. Because respondents having data missing on one variable also sometimes lacked information on other predictors in the model, the total number of respondents deleted from regression equations as a consequence of data missing on predictors amounted to less than the sum of missing cases on individual variables. Table A.3 presents the total of cases missing on one or more predictors, and the total missing on predictors plus the dependent variable (respondent's educational attainment). When we use multiple classification analysis, instead of ordinary least squares regression, missing data are not deleted over all predictors since the method is a form of dummy variable regression, but missing data on the dependent variable are, of course, removed.

Number of siblings. In both 1962 and 1973, the code for the number of the respondents' siblings was derived from codes on the number of brothers and sisters respectively. An additional set of codes for the number of older brothers and sisters allowed us to derive the birth-order code used in chapter 5. For the respondents' wives, data are available only on number of siblings, not on birth order.

Father's SEI.　The Duncan Socioeconomic Index (SEI) converts occupational codes to an interval scale ranging from 0 to 96, low to high (Duncan 1961). All of the studies (except the National Fertility Study) used in this volume were coded by us to the SEI using data for the father's occupation. The National Fertility Study was already coded. Where we had detailed occupational data on the father, as in OCG 1962 and 1973, we used the approximately 1000 categories and the disaggregated Duncan transformations to create the SEI. As is well known, the SEI ranks occupations on the basis of the education required for their performance and the income derived from their practice related to survey data on occupational prestige. However, as Duncan himself has shown (Duncan 1961), the correlation of the SEI with either the individual's education or his income is not so high as to render unnecessary the use of other indicators of social and economic status such as actual measures of educational attainment. For this reason among others, the attainment model employs father's education as well as father's SEI.

Father's education.　In both OCG 1962 and 1973, the father's education was coded as follows:[1]

0	None
3.3	Grade school, first through third grade
6.3	Grade school, fifth through seventh grade
8.0	Grade school complete
9.9	High school, ninth through eleventh grade
12.0	High school complete
13.8	College, one to three years
16.0	College complete
17.0	College, five or more years

No data on the father's education were obtained for the respondents' wives in 1962.

Farm background.　Among the studies of adults analyzed in this volume, a variety of questions was asked of respondents concerning whether they grew up in a farm background. In order to standardize this variable among the studies, we have used data on the father's occupation rather than the diverse questions on farm background. Thus, if the respondent's father was coded as having any kind of farm occupation (farmer, farm manager, farm laborer, etc.), the respondent was judged to have had a farm background. In all regressions, farm background appears as a dummy variable.

Broken family. This variable is based on information concerning whether the respondent was living with both parents at age 16. In all regressions, "broken family" appears as a dummy variable.

Respondent's age. This variable was given in single years in both 1962 and 1973.

What effect has the deletion of cases due to missing data had on the sample distribution according to the major variables in the model? For the respondents in 1962 and 1973, table A.4 shows the percentage distributions on individual predictors both before and after the total deletions due to missing data on the predictors and the respondent's educational attainment. The column headed "Total Excluding Missing" is the total of respondents used in our ordinary least squares analysis.

From table A.4, it is clear that the deletion of missing cases has affected very little the distributions of the basic predictors in the model including sibsize. The major effect is on the percentage of respondents in broken families which has been reduced somewhat compared with the total prior to deletions. The analysis is thus slightly biased in favor of respondents who grew up in intact families.

GENERAL SOCIAL SURVEYS, 1972–1986

The respondents to the General Social Surveys cover a much wider age range than any other data set analyzed in this volume. It is hardly surprising, therefore, that there should be relatively substantial amounts of missing data on the father's characteristics—education and occupation. In particular, the father's education was less likely to be known to respondents than his occupation. For each predictor, table A.3 gives a breakdown of missing data.

Number of siblings. The GSS asks a single, relatively simple question on number of siblings. Perhaps as a consequence of this simplicity, the amount of missing data is astonishingly small.

Father's SEI. As with the two OCG samples, the SEI was computed from data on the father's occupation. And, as with the OCGs, the missing data are due in large part to the fact that the respondent did not reside with his or her father (because of death or other disruption) and, as well, did not have a father substitute (for example, a stepfather).

Father's education. The question on father's education (like that of the respondent) asked for single years of schooling from zero (no schooling) to eight years of postsecondary education. The data are thus much better from a scaling point of view than the data on father's education in the OCGs. Unfortunately, however, over 1800 respondents did not have detailed information concerning father's education because they did not live with their fathers, and an additional 2249 could not supply the information. It is possible that the demand for such refined information generated a large number of "don't know" responses.

Farm background.   As with the OCGs, farm background is coded from the data on father's occupation and, therefore, the figure for missing data is identical to the figure for father's SEI.

Broken family.   As with the OCGs, whether the respondent came from an intact or broken family is derived from a question on whether he or she lived with both parents in midadolescence ("around the time you were 16?").

Respondent's age.   This variable is given in single years of age. The age range for respondents we have used for analysis is 20 to over 80. Respondents who were under age 20 (323 in all) or missing an age (64) were excluded because of a possible truncation of their educational experience.

As can be seen from table A.3, a total of 4105 cases was deleted from regressions due to missing data on predictors, or on the dependent variable (respondent's educational attainment). Table A.4 shows the sample percentage distributions on individual predictor variables both before and after the total deletions. The deletion of missing data in the GSS has some effect on the age distribution of the sample, making it slightly younger than the distribution prior to deletions. In addition, there is a marked effect on the percentage growing up in broken families which is halved by the deletions, skewing the sample we have analyzed in the direction of respondents who grew up in intact families. And, finally, the deletions have reduced somewhat the percentage of respondents in sibsizes of seven-plus, quite probably because of the exclusion of some older respondents and a substantial share of those from broken families.

GROWTH OF AMERICAN FAMILIES STUDIES, 1955 AND 1960

In these surveys, no data were gathered concerning the respondent's father's education. For each predictor, table A.3 shows a breakdown of the missing data, which for both surveys is exceptionally small.

Number of siblings.   For GAF 1955, these data were derived from a single question concerning the number of brothers and sisters the respondent had. The code ended with an open-ended category of eight or more. For GAF 1960, the data were derived from two separate questions, one relating to the number of brothers and the other to the number of sisters.

Father's SEI.   This code was derived from the father's occupation.

Farm background.   This code was also derived from the father's occupation.

Broken family.   For GAF 1955, this code was derived from a question concerning whether the respondent's parents were always together while she was growing up. For GAF 1960, the data were derived from a question concerning whether the respondent was living with both parents until age 18.

In general, since the amount of missing data is small, the differences between the final samples with deletions and the samples without deletions are small (table A.4). However, there is a slight bias in the direction of deleting respondents from broken families.

NATIONAL FERTILITY STUDY, 1970

In this survey, data on the husbands of female respondents were derived from questions addressed to the wives. Unfortunately, for neither the women, nor their husbands, were data gathered concerning the father's education. For each predictor, table A.3 shows a breakdown of the missing data for female respondents and their husbands. As with the GAF fertility studies the amount of missing data is small.

Number of siblings.   The code for number of siblings was derived from a series of questions asking whether the respondent had any brothers and, if yes, how many younger brothers and how many older ones. The respondent was then asked whether she had any sisters and, if yes, how many younger and older ones. The same questions were asked of her about her husband.

Father's SEI.   As with the other surveys, this code was derived from data on the father's or father-in-law's occupation and was already available in the data set.

Farm background. This code was derived from data on the father's or father-in-law's occupation, as in the other studies.

Broken family. This variable, applicable to both respondent and her husband, is based on data concerning whether each was living with both his or her parents at age 14.

Respondent's age. This variable was given in single years of age for both the respondent and her husband.

From table A.4, it is evident that the principal effect of deleting missing data on the distribution of the predictors is to skew the sample used for analysis in the direction of respondents who were brought up in intact families.

In sum, the deletions on the individual predictors and the dependent variable have not greatly altered the distribution of respondents' family background characteristics in the adult surveys. The single consistent distortion is that the final samples are of individuals who were more likely to have been brought up in intact families than the samples prior to the deletion of missing data. Our results will thus be reflective of people from somewhat more favorable family backgrounds than would have been the case had there been no data missing.

The question arises, therefore, of whether the deletions affect the distributions on the dependent variable—educational attainment. Table A.5 shows the distribution on total years of education before and after deletions for missing data on the predictors. It is clear that the deletions have upgraded the educational attainment of respondents. In most cases, this bias is relatively slight, but with regard to the General Social Surveys, 1972–1986, the upward bias is fairly substantial. For example, the percentages attaining less than a high school education change from 31 to 24 percent and, correspondingly, those with a high school education or more go from 69 to 76 percent. Since this bias is heavily concentrated among older respondents from large sibsizes, our analysis of educational attainment for those from large sibsizes is made to look more favorable than is quite probably the case. As we shall see, the negative sibsize effect is large even with this bias, but this effect must be regarded as understated in the GSS analysis.

HEALTH EXAMINATION SURVEY, CYCLES II AND III

For both Cycles II and III all family background information was obtained from the parents and the formating was very similar or identical between the surveys.

Number of siblings.   Data on sibsize were derived from information on the number of children in the household. Although parents were asked whether any children lived elsewhere, no information was obtained on the *number* of such children. Among those young people who had seven or more siblings in the household (an open-ended category), the lack of data on the number of siblings living elsewhere did not present a problem. But, it was necessary to exclude from the analysis all other cases where there were siblings who lived elsewhere, since it was not possible to ascertain the total number of siblings. As may be seen from table A.6, the missing data on sibsize occur disproportionately among families where the parents' marriages are not intact and where the parents have lower socioeconomic status. It is probably true, as well, that they occur disproportionately among large sibsizes. It may be the case, therefore, that our findings concerning the negative effects of large sibsizes on youngsters understate the problem. It seems unlikely that it is overstated.

Have we reason to believe that the deleted cases represent instances of particularly wide spacing—a possible concern when we are considering the relation of sibsize to dependent variables like cognitive ability or achievement? We will address this issue briefly.

There is a popular tendency, in thinking about the influence of sibsize, to fixate on unusual and extreme conditions, such as exceptionally wide (or close) spacing between offspring, when accounting for sibsize differences. Actually, wide spacing has been uncommon in the United States at least since midcentury, both because of the decline in infant and child mortality (which created "spaces" in the past) and the decline in breastfeeding, as well as because American women since World War II appear to have preferred relatively close spacing and an early end to childbearing (Whelpton, Campbell, and Patterson 1966; U.S. Bureau of the Census 1976; Bumpass, Rindfuss, and Janosik 1978). Recent trends in family formation and reproduction (1970s and 1980s) do not bear on the data sets used here. A question might be raised, however, about whether children from widely spaced families were deleted when the cases of those who had siblings living elsewhere were dropped. As far as large families are concerned, all cases in the open-ended category of seven and over were kept in, so that insofar as children from these family sizes have lower IQs, this disadvantage is not due to selective deletion of widely spaced youngsters. Among the children from sibsizes four, five, and six, the findings on the relation of IQ and sibsize do not differ if we include the cases that have been deleted (assuming that only one child lives elsewhere and, thereby, making the sibsizes five, six, and seven), indicating that particularly wide-spaced youngsters were not selectively removed among these large sibsizes. Indeed, it would be expected, without selectivity on spacing, that some siblings of the 12- to 17-year-olds (and even the

6- to 11-year-olds) in large families would have already left home. Insofar as widely spaced children from small families have been deleted, this would be expected to understate the inverse relation of sibsize and IQ.

Parents' socioeconomic characteristics.   The remaining major predictors in Cycles II and III were father's and mother's education (coded in single years), family income (essentially father's income, since few mothers worked), and whether the family was intact or broken. Since all of these data were obtained from the parent (in most cases, from the mother) the amount of missing data is small compared to studies in which data on parents are obtained from youngsters (for example, High School and Beyond). Table A.7 shows the missing data on background variables after the missing data on sibsize (shown in table A.6) have been deleted.

WISC, WRAT, and parent's desires for schooling.   In addition to the major background variables noted above, in chapter 6 three other variables are used to model Cycle III youngsters' postsecondary-schooling expectations. These are cognitive ability or achievement, as measured by the Weschler Intelligence Test for Children (WISC), academic performance as measured by the Wide Range Achievement Test (WRAT), and the parents' desires concerning the youngster's postsecondary schooling (and, of course, the students' expectations). The WISC is discussed in detail in chapter 4, where it is the principal dependent variable for Cycle II and Cycle III youngsters; and parents' schooling desires are discussed in chapter 6. A word or two is in order here, however, about the WRAT.

The purpose of the WRAT is to assess youngsters' basic academic skills in reading, spelling, and arithmetic. In the Health Examination Surveys only the reading and arithmetic components of the WRAT were administered. The Reading test involves word recognition but no measure of context reading or comprehension. The Arithmetic test is a measure of computational skills but is not a measure of skills with mathematical concepts. Each subtest of the WRAT is divided into two levels—Level I for students between the ages of 5 and 12, and Level II from age 12 to adulthood. The WRAT is the best known and most widely used quick measure of individual achievement in basic academic skills. It has a high test–retest reliability, has been normed on a large sample of children and adults from all socioeconomic groups and all ranges of intellectual ability in seven states, and correlates moderately well with the Stanford Achievement Test and the Peabody Individual Achievement Test. In the present analysis, we have used the WRAT in lieu of grades (for which data were not available) to index school performance. (Readers who are interested in further details concerning the WRAT should consult: National Center for Health Statistics 1966, 1967; Buros 1972; Woodward et al. 1975; Smith and McManis 1977; Sanner and McManis 1978; Harmer and Williams 1978; Compton 1980.)

Table A.8 shows the breakdown by major background variables of the final Cycle II and Cyle III samples after deletion for missing data on individual family background variables. The reader should bear in mind that this set of deletions occurs only when we use ordinary least squares regression. When we use multiple classification analysis the deletions on father's education, for example, only occur with respect to that variable (unless, of course, these deletions overlap with missing data on some other variable). In any event, it is clear that the major distortion that occurs when all of the missing data are deleted is to bias the sample in favor of children from intact families and, hence, to create more favorable family backgrounds than would otherwise be the case.

YOUTH IN TRANSITION

As has been noted, all of the data in the Youth in Transition study were based on information from the tenth-grade boys themselves.

Number of siblings. Information on this variable was derived from two questions on whether the respondent had brothers and/or sisters and, if so, how many he had of each. As can be seen from table A.7, the amount of nonresponse on this item was effectively zero.

Parents' socioeconomic characteristics. Father's SEI was coded from the information supplied concerning the father's occupation. Mother's and father's education were not ascertained in single years (probably a hopeless endeavor with youngsters this age). For purposes of regression analysis, we have recoded the parents' education as follows:

 5 Less than high school
10 Some high school
12 Completed high school (includes "some high school and noncollege training")
14 Some college
16 Completed college
18 Postgraduate degree

As may be seen from table A.7, the amount of missing data on parental background variables is very small indeed.

Broken family.   This variable was derived from a question concerning whether the respondent lives with his mother and father. All who did not say yes were coded no by the investigators.

Since the amount of missing data is so negligible in this sample, the distortions (table A.8) are relatively slight. However, even in this case, it is evident that the final sample is skewed in the direction of children from intact families.

HIGH SCHOOL AND BEYOND

The High School and Beyond data, as analyzed by Coleman, Hoffer, and Kilgore (1982c), have been criticized because of the unusually large amounts of missing data on family background variables and student characteristics (National Academy of Sciences 1981; Noell 1982). We have attempted partially to overcome this problem by resorting, among seniors, to the small sample of parents who were interviewed, as well as to a followup survey of the seniors in 1982. Among sophomores, we used a followup survey done when the students were seniors. This strategem has involved us in processing, subsetting, and checking two additional independent data files, just to be able to use them for purposes of overcoming a share of the missing data problem in the base-year files. However, as will be obvious from the discussion that follows, this effort paid off in greatly reducing the number of missing cases.

Number of siblings.   Unfortunately, the baseline survey questionnaire asked a complex series of five questions concerning older and younger siblings by sex which were then to be summed analytically to obtain a total sibsize for each respondent. This type of questioning resulted in a high proportion of nonresponse among the young people involved.

Among the 15,694 white non-Hispanic seniors in public schools, there were 7625 cases for whom usable information was not returned on these sibsize questions. We were able to reduce this large number by two strategies. One was to use a small sample of parents of some of the seniors who were asked a question on the number of siblings. Resort to the parental responses reduced the number of missing cases to 6946. Second, we could use the followup survey conducted in 1982, which asked a very simple question on sibsize and, hence, had a low nonresponse rate. However, this followup survey contained only about 30 percent of the original white non-Hispanic respondents. Nonetheless, by using data from this group, we were able further to reduce the number of missing cases to 5585. As a result of these efforts, we were able to salvage 10,109 white non-Hispanic seniors in public schools for whom data were available on number of siblings.

Naturally, such a high attrition rate among seniors because of missing data on number of siblings raises concerns about how selected are the approximately 10,000 youngsters we are using relative to the original 15,694 for whom information is available on variables other than sibsize. As may be seen from table A.6, the final 10,109 differ little on major background characteristics from the 15,694 youngsters for whom data were available on variables other than sibsize.

Among the 16,524 white non-Hispanic sophomores in public schools, there were 8270 cases for whom information was not returned on the sibsize questions. Although no parents were interviewed among the sophomores, 90 percent of 1980 sophomores were reinterviewed as seniors in 1982. Using these followup data, we could salvage 14,648 cases among the sophomores. As with the seniors, the missing data do not appear to have skewed the sophomore sample with regard to major characteristics (not shown here for reasons of space).

Parents' socioeconomic characteristics. Among the sophomores, many data were missing for the parents' socioeconomic characteristics—father's education, 3458; mother's education, 2234; and father's occupation, 2831. Fortunately, we were able to use the followup survey of sophomores (when they were seniors) to fill in a large share of these gaps. The final count of missing data on these variables among sophomores was thus relatively low—father's education, 1090; mother's education, 679; and father's occupation, 781. As with all of the other surveys, the father's occupation was recoded to the SEI (Duncan index). Since there was some overlap for respondents with regard to these missing data, the total number of respondents having data missing on parental characteristics—1789—was less than the sum of the missing on the respective variables. Although the survey asked for family income, our internal checks of these data did not encourage us to use them. The code for whether the student was living in an intact parental family was derived from a set of questions on household composition. Students who were living in a household without a father and/or mother were coded as not living in an intact family.

Among the seniors, the initial missing data problem with regard to parental characteristics was not as acute as among the sophomores; however, less could be retrieved from the followup, and the final numbers missing were still relatively high—father's education, 1713; mother's education, 999; father's occupation, 1668. As with the sophomores, a good share of the missing data concerning the father resulted from the fact that the respondent did not reside with him. The father's occupation was recoded to the Duncan SEI. Because of an overlap for respondents on missing data regarding the parents, the total number of seniors having data missing on parental characteristics—2817—was less than the sum of the missing on the respective parental variables. We did not feel that the data on family income were usable. The code for whether the student was living in an intact parental family was derived in the same manner as the code for the sophomores.

In all ordinary least squares regressions, respondents who had data missing on any one predictor were deleted from the calculations in a so-called listwise handling of missing data. Table A.8 shows that even after deleting the 1789 sophomores and the 2817 seniors with missing data on background variables, the percentage distribution of socioeconomic characteristics is virtually unchanged, with the one exception of the broken family.

Vocabulary, grades, and mother's and student's desires for schooling. In some of our analyses, particularly in chapter 6, we have used the vocabulary tests as a predictors. A full discussion of these tests may be found in chapter 4. As for grades, this variable is based on a question of the student concerning the student's average grades during the past year. Finally, we have used questions concerning the mother's and the student's desires for the student's postsecondary schooling, also discussed in detail in chapter 6. The question concerning the mother's desires was used in preference to one concerning the father because the latter was phrased in such a way as to preclude our scaling the answer in years. In addition, since a substantial proportion of students did not live with their fathers, we have avoided a missing data problem by using the mother's desires.

Table A.9 shows the breakdown by these additional variables of the final HSB sophomores and seniors after deletion for missing background variables (including sibsize), indicating only a slight tendency for the final subsample to score higher in ability and performance, and to have higher academic aspirations.

Table A.1. Percentage Distribution of Selected Background Characteristics by Sibsize, White Men and Women Age 20 and Over, Various Surveys.

Background Characteristics	Sibsize								
	1	2	3	4	5	6	7+	Total	(N)
GAF 1955—Female Respondents									
Father's SEI									
0–09	5	3	6	8	10	7	11	8	(193)
10–19	36	33	39	48	46	53	56	46	(1,160)
20–39	17	17	17	16	19	15	11	15	(389)
40–59	33	38	31	24	23	20	20	26	(660)
60+	9	9	7	4	2	5	2	5	(123)
Total	100	100	100	100	100	100	100	100	(2,525)
Age									
20–24	15	21	18	19	16	14	13	17	(436)
25–29	36	31	24	26	28	23	27	27	(722)
30–34	24	24	34	30	29	26	29	28	(754)
35–39	25	24	24	25	27	37	31	28	(731)
Total	100	100	100	100	100	100	100	100	(2,643)
Broken Family									
Percent parents not always together	38	22	24	18	19	21	16	21	(553)
Farm Background									
Percent with fathers in a farm occupation	13	16	23	29	24	31	41	28	(708)

Table A.1. *Continued.*

Background Characteristics	Sibsize							Total	(N)
	1	2	3	4	5	6	7+		
Religion									
Protestant	69	72	66	69	61	66	64	67	(1,758)
Catholic	25	21	27	27	37	31	34	29	(776)
Jewish	4	6	6	2	1	2	1	3	(74)
Other/No Preference	2	1	1	2	1	1	1	1	(35)
Total	100	100	100	100	100	100	100	100	(2,643)

GAF 1960—Female Respondents

Father's SEI									
0–09	5	3	3	7	8	6	10	6	(166)
10–19	36	35	40	48	54	52	58	46	(1,280)
20–39	18	17	23	18	18	19	16	19	(518)
40–59	33	37	25	22	17	20	15	24	(676)
60+	8	8	9	5	3	3	1	5	(154)
Total	100	100	100	100	100	100	100	100	(2,794)
Age									
20–24	13	17	18	17	13	11	13	15	(439)
25–29	22	23	19	23	18	17	19	21	(594)
30–34	24	22	22	19	18	26	20	21	(617)
35–39	20	23	24	20	27	24	25	23	(675)

								Total	
40–44	21	15	17	21	24	22	23	20	(570)
Total	100	100	100	100	100	100	100	100	(2,895)
Broken Family									
Percent not living with both parents at age 18	29	15	15	12	13	12	15	15	(445)
Farm Background									
Percent with fathers in a farm occupation	15	18	19	25	33	32	37	25	(708)
Religion									
Protestant	72	65	66	65	64	66	60	65	(1,878)
Catholic	22	22	27	30	30	29	38	28	(825)
Jewish	5	11	6	3	3	2	1	5	(139)
Other/No Preference	1	2	1	2	3	3	1	2	(51)
Total	100	100	100	100	100	100	100	100	(2,893)

OCG 1962—Male Respondents

								Total	
Father's Education									
Grade Sch Inc	20	21	27	34	39	45	54	38	(6,358)
Grade Sch Comp	27	26	29	28	32	29	27	28	(4,738)
High Sch Inc	13	15	12	12	10	10	8	11	(1,802)
High Sch Comp	23	21	19	15	13	9	7	14	(2,327)
College Inc	8	7	6	6	3	4	2	4	(773)
College 4 +	9	10	7	5	3	3	2	5	(842)
Total	100	100	100	100	100	100	100	100	(16,840)

Table A.1. *Continued.*

Background Characteristics	Sibsize								
	1	2	3	4	5	6	7+	Total	(N)
Father's SEI									
0–09	7	6	9	11	12	13	15	11	(1,998)
10–19	29	31	34	44	47	51	57	45	(7,761)
20–39	22	21	22	18	18	18	14	18	(3,088)
40–59	20	18	18	15	14	10	9	14	(2,378)
60+	22	24	17	12	9	8	5	12	(2,072)
Total	100	100	100	100	100	100	100	100	(17,297)
Age									
20–34	42	42	41	34	30	28	24	33	(6,032)
35–49	36	38	36	39	41	38	39	38	(7,043)
50–64	22	20	23	27	29	34	37	29	(5,410)
Total	100	100	100	100	100	100	100	100	(18,485)
Broken Family									
Percent not living with both parents at age 16	23	14	14	14	13	16	14	15	(2,692)
Farm Background									
Percent with fathers in a farm occupation	14	15	18	25	31	36	43	29	(5,035)

OCG 1962—Wives

Father's SEI									
0–09	7	6	9	11	14	14	17	12	(1,688)
10–19	28	32	37	43	47	49	55	43	(6,144)
20–39	20	22	22	21	18	19	14	19	(2,645)
40–59	18	19	17	15	12	12	9	14	(1,944)
60+	27	21	15	10	9	6	5	12	(1,648)
Total	100	100	100	100	100	100	100	100	(14,069)
Age									
20–34	42	46	41	38	34	32	28	36	(5,477)
35–49	41	39	41	42	44	42	44	42	(6,412)
50–64	17	15	18	20	22	26	28	22	(3,292)
Total	100	100	100	100	100	100	100	100	(15,181)
Broken Family									
Percent not living with both parents at age 16	21	14	14	12	13	13	12	13	(1,988)
Farm Background									
Percent with fathers in a farm occupation	13	14	18	24	28	31	42	27	(3,778)

NFS 1970—Female Respondents

Father's SEI									
0–09	6	6	7	8	8	10	14	8	(392)
10–19	26	30	34	40	45	48	54	40	(1,911)
20–39	15	14	17	15	13	14	13	15	(702)

Table A.1. *Continued.*

| Background Characteristics | Sibsize | | | | | | | | |
	1	2	3	4	5	6	7+	Total	(N)
40–59	23	20	18	18	16	12	9	16	(784)
60+	30	30	24	19	18	16	10	21	(1,006)
Total	100	100	100	100	100	100	100	100	(4,795)
Age									
20–24	15	21	24	24	22	25	15	21	(1,073)
25–29	25	26	26	25	22	17	19	23	(1,194)
30–34	23	20	18	18	19	18	20	20	(993)
35–39	19	16	16	17	19	21	23	18	(939)
40–44	18	17	16	16	18	19	23	18	(938)
Total	100	100	100	100	100	100	100	100	(5,137)
Broken Family									
Percent not living with both parents at age 14	31	15	18	18	21	20	19	19	(957)
Farm Background									
Percent with fathers in a farm occupation	10	10	12	17	20	23	30	17	(832)
NFS 1970—Husbands									
Father's SEI									
0–09	4	4	5	8	7	9	12	7	(292)

10–19	32	33	37	45	51	50	59	44	(1,874)
20–39	13	13	13	15	14	14	11	13	(561)
40–59	24	19	18	15	12	15	10	16	(666)
60+	27	31	27	17	16	12	8	20	(867)
Total	100	100	100	100	100	100	100	100	(4,260)
Age									
20–24	12	15	15	16	15	13	12	14	(691)
25–29	19	24	23	21	19	18	17	21	(1,009)
30–34	20	22	20	21	16	19	16	19	(946)
35–39	19	15	16	14	17	17	20	17	(816)
40–44	17	16	15	18	20	18	20	17	(850)
45+	13	8	11	10	13	15	15	12	(579)
Total	100	100	100	100	100	100	100	100	(4,891)
Broken Family									
Percent not living with both parents at age 14	29	20	18	18	19	22	16	19	(942)
Farm Background									
Percent with fathers in a farm occupation	15	11	16	26	29	29	43	24	(1,018)
OCG 1973—Male Respondents									
Father's Education									
Grade Sch Inc	20	18	22	27	35	42	53	32	(8,224)
Grade Sch Comp	22	21	22	24	26	27	24	24	(5,935)
High Sch Inc	13	13	13	12	11	10	8	11	(2,858)
High Sch Comp	27	27	25	21	17	14	10	20	(4,948)

Table A.1. *Continued.*

Background Characteristics	Sibsize								(N)
	1	2	3	4	5	6	7+	Total	
College Inc	9	10	8	7	5	3	3	6	(1,572)
College 4+	9	11	10	9	6	4	2	7	(1,861)
Total	100	100	100	100	100	100	100	100	(25,398)
Father's SEI									
0–09	6	6	9	11	13	14	19	12	(2,989)
10–19	29	28	32	36	42	45	51	39	(9,741)
20–39	22	21	21	21	19	19	15	19	(4,865)
40–59	18	19	16	15	14	12	9	14	(3,622)
60+	25	26	22	17	12	10	6	16	(4,089)
Total	100	100	100	100	100	100	100	100	(25,306)
Age									
20–34	38	46	47	45	38	33	26	39	(10,456)
35–49	38	32	29	29	32	30	33	31	(8,489)
50–65	24	22	24	26	30	37	41	30	(8,018)
Total	100	100	100	100	100	100	100	100	(26,963)
Broken Family									
Percent not living with both parents at age 16	22	13	13	13	14	15	15	14	(3,777)

	OCG 1973—Wives								
Farm Background									
Percent with fathers in a farm occupation	11	12	14	19	24	28	38	22	(5,593)
Father's SEI									
0–09	6	6	9	10	15	15	20	12	(2,279)
10–19	31	28	33	38	41	45	49	38	(7,312)
20–39	23	20	20	21	21	18	15	19	(3,661)
40–59	18	19	18	16	13	13	10	15	(2,826)
60+	22	27	20	15	10	9	6	16	(2,941)
Total	100	100	100	100	100	100	100	100	(19,019)
Age									
20–34	37	45	43	44	38	35	30	39	(8,050)
35–49	42	37	35	35	36	37	39	37	(7,701)
50–64	21	18	22	21	26	28	31	24	(5,077)
Total	100	100	100	100	100	100	100	100	(20,828)
Broken Family									
Percent not living with both parents at age 16	18	11	10	11	10	12	10	11	(2,317)
Farm Background									
Percent with fathers in a farm occupation	11	11	14	18	23	26	37	21	(4,003)

Table A.1. *Continued.*

Background Characteristics	Sibsize							Total	(N)
	1	2	3	4	5	6	7+		
GSS 1972–1986—Male and Female Respondents									
Father's Education									
Grade Sch Inc	16	15	16	20	25	28	46	26	(3,248)
Grade Sch Comp	18	18	18	21	22	26	23	21	(2,604)
High Sch Inc	15	12	13	13	12	13	9	12	(1,476)
High Sch Comp	30	30	29	25	23	19	14	23	(2,927)
College Inc	9	10	9	10	8	6	4	8	(984)
College 4+	12	15	15	11	8	8	4	10	(1,307)
Total	100	100	100	100	100	100	100	100	(12,546)
Father's SEI									
0–09	5	5	5	6	9	8	12	8	(1,155)
10–19	31	26	30	35	42	45	56	40	(5,868)
20–39	15	17	17	18	17	16	12	16	(2,310)
40–59	17	19	18	16	13	12	9	14	(2,115)
60+	32	33	30	25	19	19	11	22	(3,298)
Total	100	100	100	100	100	100	100	100	(14,746)
Age									
20–34	29	39	42	41	39	32	24	35	(5,816)
35–49	34	31	27	25	23	21	22	25	(4,277)
50–64	22	19	20	20	20	25	27	22	(3,716)

65+	15	11	11	14	18	22	27	18	(2,989)
Total	100	100	100	100	100	100	100	100	(16,798)

Broken Family
Percent not living with both parents
at age 16

	32	18	19	20	21	23	25	22	(3,679)

Farm Background
Percent with fathers in a
farm occupation

	10	9	13	15	20	23	35	20	(2,954)

Religion

Protestant	63	61	60	60	62	60	63	61	(10,301)
Catholic	24	24	26	29	28	30	30	28	(4,626)
Jewish	4	6	3	2	2	2	1	3	(446)
Other	8	8	9	8	6	7	5	7	(1,170)
No Preference	2	2	1	1	2	1	1	1	(214)
Total	100	100	100	100	100	100	100	100	(16,757)

Table A.2. Percentage Distribution of Selected Background Characteristics by Sibsize, White Children Age 6 to 18, Various Surveys.

Background Characteristics	Sibsize							Total	(N)
	1	2	3	4	5	6	7+		
	HES Cycle II—Boys and Girls								
Child's Age									
6–7 Years	34	34	35	36	36	31	32	34	(1,556)
8–9 Years	32	34	33	33	37	33	33	34	(1,532)
10–12 Years	34	32	32	31	27	36	35	32	(1,423)
Total	100	100	100	100	100	100	100	100	(4,511)
Father's Education									
Grade Sch Inc	11	5	5	7	13	16	32	10	(407)
Grade Sch Comp	14	10	8	11	14	10	14	11	(432)
High Sch Inc	19	20	17	18	19	25	19	19	(787)
High Sch Comp	38	33	37	40	29	26	26	34	(1,426)
College Inc	7	12	11	7	8	10	4	9	(384)
College 4 +	11	20	22	17	17	13	5	17	(706)
Total	100	100	100	100	100	100	100	100	(4,142)
Mother's Education									
Grade Sch Inc	8	3	4	6	14	17	31	9	(413)
Grade Sch Comp	4	6	4	8	8	14	9	7	(305)
High Sch Inc	22	21	21	22	19	24	19	21	(925)
High Sch Comp	48	48	50	47	43	35	30	45	(1,999)

College Inc	9	11	12	9	9	7	7	10	(440)
College 4+	9	11	9	8	7	3	4	8	(352)
Total	100	100	100	100	100	100	100	100	(4,434)
Family Income									
0– 4,999	30	22	19	26	32	41	55	28	(1,192)
5,000– 6,999	26	28	27	25	29	24	20	26	(1,116)
7,000– 9,999	27	27	28	27	24	19	13	25	(1,077)
10,000–14,999	13	16	18	15	10	10	10	14	(613)
15,000+	4	7	8	7	5	6	2	7	(279)
Total	100	100	100	100	100	100	100	100	(4,277)
Broken Family									
Percent parents not currently together	26	11	8	9	7	6	18	10	(469)
Region of Residence									
Northeast	25	30	31	29	27	24	12	27	(1,227)
Midwest	20	26	27	28	30	36	36	28	(1,286)
South	25	20	18	18	16	17	20	19	(834)
West	30	24	24	25	27	23	32	26	(1,164)
Total	100	100	100	100	100	100	100	100	(4,511)
Mother's Labor Force Participation									
Works Full-Time	32	21	15	17	8	7	9	16	(687)
Works Part-Time	11	17	14	12	13	13	9	13	(589)
No Job	57	62	71	71	79	80	82	71	(3,163)
Total	100	100	100	100	100	100	100	100	(4,439)

Table A.2. *Continued.*

Background Characteristics	Sibsize								(N)
	1	2	3	4	5	6	7+	Total	
	HES Cycle III—Boys and Girls								
Child's Age									
12–13 Years	25	35	40	45	41	39	39	39	(1,282)
14–15 Years	39	33	33	32	36	41	35	34	(1,136)
16–17 Years	36	32	27	23	23	20	26	27	(892)
Total	100	100	100	100	100	100	100	100	(3,310)
Father's Education									
Grade Sch Inc	9	6	6	4	10	10	27	9	(272)
Grade Sch Comp	12	13	9	10	14	14	13	12	(336)
High Sch Inc	18	19	18	22	23	19	15	19	(567)
High Sch Comp	39	34	33	35	32	32	33	34	(994)
College Inc	9	9	15	10	5	9	6	10	(293)
College 4 +	13	19	19	19	16	16	6	16	(480)
Total	100	100	100	100	100	100	100	100	(2,942)
Mother's Education									
Grade Sch Inc	7	5	5	4	10	18	22	8	(266)
Grade Sch Comp	7	7	4	6	8	19	13	8	(248)
High Sch Inc	16	18	20	23	23	15	19	20	(626)
High Sch Comp	52	46	51	48	44	35	33	45	(1,453)
College Inc	9	14	12	10	10	10	12	11	(365)

	9	10	8	9	5	3	1	8	
College 4 +	9	10	8	9	5	3	1	8	(239)
Total	100	100	100	100	100	100	100	100	(3,197)
Family Income									
0– 4,999	23	13	11	10	20	30	37	17	(542)
5,000– 6,999	16	16	19	16	17	16	20	18	(544)
7,000– 9,999	26	29	29	30	31	24	19	27	(856)
10,000–14,999	23	27	27	33	25	18	16	26	(792)
15,000+	12	15	14	11	7	12	8	12	(375)
Total	100	100	100	100	100	100	100	100	(3,109)
Broken Family									
Percent parents not currently together	25	14	12	10	15	17	16	14	(468)
Region of Residence									
Northeast	28	30	33	29	25	25	15	28	(922)
Midwest	22	24	24	30	36	30	37	28	(930)
South	20	22	18	14	15	19	16	18	(586)
West	30	24	25	27	24	26	32	26	(872)
Total	100	100	100	100	100	100	100	100	(3,310)
Mother's Labor Force Participation									
Works Full-Time	39	31	29	25	19	13	11	25	(818)
Works Part-Time	13	19	16	12	18	16	9	15	(485)
No Job	48	50	55	63	63	71	80	60	(1,935)
Total	100	100	100	100	100	100	100	100	(3,238)
Parent's Desires on Youth's Schooling									
Finish High Sch	8	9	10	11	18	17	26	13	(428)
Some College	27	32	36	43	43	38	42	37	(1,223)

Table A.2. Continued.

Background Characteristics	Sibsize								
	1	2	3	4	5	6	7+	Total	(N)
Finish College	38	37	35	35	28	29	20	33	(1,070)
Graduate Sch	27	22	19	11	11	16	12	17	(562)
Total	100	100	100	100	100	100	100	100	(3,283)
WISC									
56–79	7	7	7	9	10	20	25	11	(350)
80–89	11	15	12	13	16	19	18	14	(471)
90–99	22	21	19	21	28	18	22	21	(696)
100–109	24	28	31	28	22	23	21	27	(884)
110–119	25	22	22	23	14	16	12	20	(660)
120+	11	7	9	6	10	4	2	7	(244)
Total	100	100	100	100	100	100	100	100	(3,305)
WRAT									
56–79	6	6	7	8	12	18	22	10	(329)
80–89	15	14	12	15	17	16	19	15	(487)
90–99	22	23	23	23	23	24	24	23	(765)
100–109	25	26	27	28	25	22	23	26	(850)
110–119	19	21	21	19	16	16	9	18	(603)
120+	13	10	10	7	7	4	3	8	(272)
Total	100	100	100	100	100	100	100	100	(3,306)

									N
Father's Education									
Grade Sch	20	16	16	21	26	25	40	21	(374)
High Sch Inc	16	19	19	24	19	17	17	20	(350)
High Sch Comp	43	37	36	31	30	33	28	34	(604)
College Inc	10	13	12	11	14	14	8	12	(215)
College 4+	11	15	17	13	11	11	7	13	(240)
Total	100	100	100	100	100	100	100	100	(1,783)
Mother's Education									
Grade Sch	13	10	9	9	15	20	25	12	(216)
High Sch Inc	16	14	18	19	23	19	23	18	(333)
High Sch Comp	53	55	52	53	46	52	44	52	(935)
College Inc	9	13	11	10	10	6	5	10	(188)
College 4+	9	8	10	9	6	3	3	8	(141)
Total	100	100	100	100	100	100	100	100	(1,813)
Father's SEI									
0–09	4	3	3	5	5	1	6	4	(66)
10–19	22	25	22	24	27	32	38	26	(447)
20–39	28	26	29	27	29	32	25	28	(485)
40–59	31	32	33	33	27	19	26	30	(532)
60+	15	14	13	11	12	16	5	12	(218)
Total	100	100	100	100	100	100	100	100	(1,748)
Broken Family									
Percent parents not currently together	27	15	14	16	21	22	29	18	(341)

Table A.2. *Continued.*

Background Characteristics	Sibsize							Total	(N)
	1	*2*	*3*	*4*	*5*	*6*	*7+*	*Total*	*(N)*
Place Brought Up									
Rural Area	20	15	16	23	27	30	38	22	(405)
Town	32	30	32	29	25	29	26	29	(554)
Small City	17	25	22	24	30	20	18	23	(437)
Large City	31	30	30	24	18	21	18	26	(486)
Total	100	100	100	100	100	100	100	100	(1,882)
HSB Sophomores—Boys and Girls									
Father's Education									
High Sch Inc	23	16	18	22	25	30	35	22	(2,933)
High Sch Comp	38	33	32	33	36	36	32	33	(4,540)
Post High Sch	10	10	11	10	10	8	9	10	(1,398)
College Inc	10	16	14	13	12	10	8	13	(1,736)
College 4+	19	25	25	22	17	16	16	22	(2,951)
Total	100	100	100	100	100	100	100	100	(13,558)
Mother's Education									
High Sch Inc	15	12	13	18	22	22	29	17	(2,370)
High Sch Comp	48	45	47	47	50	49	46	47	(6,556)
Post High Sch	12	11	10	9	8	8	6	9	(1,297)
College Inc	14	16	15	13	11	12	10	14	(1,897)
College 4+	11	16	15	13	9	9	9	13	(1,849)
Total	100	100	100	100	100	100	100	100	(13,969)

Father's SEI									
0–09	9	8	10	10	11	11	14	10	(1,372)
10–19	27	23	23	25	29	32	31	25	(3,529)
20–39	20	15	16	18	17	18	20	17	(2,369)
40–59	27	33	31	29	28	27	23	30	(4,122)
60+	17	21	20	18	15	12	12	18	(2,475)
Total	100	100	100	100	100	100	100	100	(13,867)
Broken Family									
Percent parents not currently together	35	19	19	24	28	30	37	24	(14,648)
Mother's Desires									
High School	26	23	27	31	37	38	42	30	(3,361)
College Inc	14	14	15	15	16	15	15	15	(1,666)
College Comp	34	37	35	32	28	30	26	33	(3,703)
Master's	11	10	9	9	7	6	6	9	(996)
Ph.D.	15	16	14	13	12	11	11	13	(1,538)
Total	100	100	100	100	100	100	100	100	(11,264)
Grades									
Cs & Ds or less	12	9	11	12	14	16	17	12	(1,739)
Cs most	14	12	12	15	15	17	16	14	(2,007)
Bs & Cs	27	23	23	25	27	27	28	25	(3,597)
Bs most	15	22	20	18	19	17	16	19	(2,778)
As & Bs	20	20	21	19	17	15	16	19	(2,749)
As most	12	14	13	11	8	8	7	11	(1,675)
Total	100	100	100	100	100	100	100	100	(14,545)

Table A.2. Continued.

Background Characteristics	Sibsize							Total	(N)
	1	2	3	4	5	6	7+		
Vocabulary									
40 or less	15	13	16	19	21	21	26	18	(2,412)
41–45	13	13	13	14	16	16	18	14	(1,964)
46–50	15	17	18	19	16	17	17	18	(2,397)
51–55	20	20	19	16	18	19	16	18	(2,532)
56–60	16	16	16	15	15	14	13	15	(2,119)
61+	21	21	18	17	14	13	10	17	(2,364)
Total	100	100	100	100	100	100	100	100	(13,788)
HSB Seniors—Boys and Girls									
Father's Education									
High Sch Inc	21	16	17	20	23	27	35	20	(1,705)
High Sch Comp	35	33	32	31	34	30	31	32	(2,717)
Post High Sch	10	12	10	11	11	10	8	10	(868)
College Inc	13	14	16	13	11	14	9	14	(1,144)
College 4 +	21	25	25	25	21	19	17	24	(1,962)
Total	100	100	100	100	100	100	100	100	(8,396)
Mother's Education									
High Sch Inc	15	11	13	15	18	19	23	15	(1,346)
High Sch Comp	47	47	48	50	48	47	46	48	(4,371)
Post High Sch	12	12	9	9	9	8	8	9	(871)
College Inc	10	15	15	14	13	15	12	14	(1,262)

	16	15	15	12	12	11	11	14	
College 4 +	16	15	15	12	12	11	11	14	(1,260)
Total	100	100	100	100	100	100	100	100	(9,110)
Father's SEI									
0–09	9	7	8	10	11	9	13	9	(755)
10–19	25	22	23	24	27	30	29	24	(2,076)
20–39	18	15	15	16	16	16	19	16	(1,345)
40–59	30	34	32	29	28	29	26	31	(2,587)
60 +	18	22	22	21	18	16	13	20	(1,678)
Total	100	100	100	100	100	100	100	100	(8,441)
Broken Family									
Percent parents not currently together	32	21	22	23	26	28	35	24	(10,109)
Mother's Desires									
High School	30	23	25	31	34	36	40	29	(2,370)
College Inc	11	13	12	12	14	13	15	12	(1,038)
College Comp	33	40	39	37	35	35	30	37	(3,051)
Master's	11	11	11	10	6	8	6	10	(812)
Ph.D., other advanced degree	15	13	13	10	11	8	9	12	(979)
Total	100	100	100	100	100	100	100	100	(8,250)
Grades									
Cs & Ds or less	7	4	4	5	6	8	8	5	(546)
Cs most	13	9	12	11	12	15	14	12	(1,171)
Bs & Cs	24	22	23	24	23	24	29	24	(2,379)
Bs most	19	23	21	22	23	22	18	21	(2,146)
As & Bs	21	25	24	25	24	19	20	24	(2,369)
As most	16	17	16	13	12	12	11	14	(1,460)
Total	100	100	100	100	100	100	100	100	(10,071)

Table A.2. *Continued.*

Background Characteristics	Sibsize								
	1	2	3	4	5	6	7+	Total	(N)
Vocabulary									
40 or less	13	12	12	14	16	15	18	14	(1,277)
41–45	16	20	19	20	21	22	21	20	(1,823)
46–50	19	19	21	22	23	24	23	21	(1,959)
51–55	16	15	15	15	15	13	14	15	(1,393)
56–60	13	12	13	11	11	12	10	12	(1,081)
61+	23	22	20	18	14	14	14	18	(1,721)
Total	100	100	100	100	100	100	100	100	(9,254)

Table A.3. Breakdown of Total Cases Available and Cases Excluded because of Missing Data on Predictors and Dependent Variable in the Model of Adult Educational Attainment, White Men and Women, Various Surveys.

	GAF 1955	GAF 1960	OCG 1962		NFS 1970		OCG 1973		GSS 1972–1986
	Respondents	Respondents	Respondents	Wives	Respondents	Husbands	Respondents	Wives	Respondents
Total number of cases	2,713	2,985	18,966	15,945	5,442	5,049	27,549	22,105	17,236
Total cases age 20 and over[a]	2,643	2,904	18,966	15,549	5,218	4,964	27,549	21,491	16,829
Number of cases missing for each predictor:									
Sibsize	0	9	481	368	81	73	586	663	31
Father's SEI	98	106	1,229	1,173	351	645	1,703	2,200	2,059
Father's Education	NA	NA	1,707	NA	NA	NA	1,613	NA	4,262
Farm Background	98	106	1,229	1,173	350[b]	643[b]	1,703	2,200	2,051
Broken Family	8	8	98	0	2	24	234	522	7
Total cases lost due to missing data on one or more predictors	105	119	3,199	1,480	424	715	3,629	2,539	4,394

Table A.3. *Continued*.

	GAF 1955 Respondents	GAF 1960 Respondents	OCG 1962 Respondents	OCG 1962 Wives	NFS 1970 Respondents	NFS 1970 Husbands	OCG 1973 Respondents	OCG 1973 Wives	GSS 1972–1986 Respondents
Total cases lost due to missing data on predictors plus dependent variable (Respondent's Education)	105	119	3,199	1,480	426	720	5,407	2,539	4,410
Total cases with complete information	2,538	2,785	15,767	14,069	4,792	4,244	22,142	18,952	12,419
Complete cases as a percent of all cases age 20 and over	96%	96%	83%	90%	92%	85%	80%	88%	74%

[a]For OCG 1962 and 1973 wives, those age 65 and over have also been deleted making the age range similar to OCG men.

[b]The number of missing cases on farm background for NFS 1970 is slightly different from the number of cases missing on SEI due to the fact that SEI was already included in the data as a separate variable and was not recalculated from the occupation codes in the same way as farm background.

Table A.4. Percentage Distribution of Selected Background Characteristics for All Cases and for Cases that Have No Missing Values on Any Predictors or the Dependent Variable, Respondent's Education, White Men and Women Age 20 and Over, Various Surveys.

Background characteristics	GAF 1955 Respondents		GAF 1960 Respondents	
	Total	Total Excluding Missing	Total	Total Excluding Missing
Father's SEI				
0–09	8	7	6	6
10–19	45	46	46	46
20–39	15	15	19	18
40–59	26	26	24	24
60 +	6	6	5	6
Total	100	100	100	100
	(2,545)	(2,538)	(2,798)	(2,785)
Age				
20–24	16	16	15	15
25–29	27	27	21	20
30–34	29	29	21	21
35–39	28	28	23	23
40–44	—	—	20	20
Total	100	100	100	100
	(2,643)	(2,538)	(2,904)	(2,785)
Broken Family				
Percent from broken families[a]	21	18	16	14
Farm Background				
Percent with fathers in a farm occupation	28	28	25	25
Sibsize				
1	8	8	10	9
2	15	15	19	20
3	16	15	18	18
4	14	14	15	15
5	12	11	10	10
6	9	9	9	9

Table A.4. *Continued.*

Background characteristics	GAF 1955 Respondents		GAF 1960 Respondents	
7 +	26	27	19	19
Total	100	100	100	100
	(2,643)	(2,538)	(2,895)	(2,785)

	OCG 1962			
Background characteristics	Respondents		Wives	
	Total	Total Excluding Missing	Total	Total Excluding Missing
Father's Education				
Grade Sch Inc	37	37	NA	NA
Grade Sch Comp	28	28	NA	NA
High Sch Inc	11	11	NA	NA
High Sch Comp	14	14	NA	NA
College Inc	5	5	NA	NA
College 4 +	5	5	NA	NA
Total	100	100		
	(17,259)	(15,767)		
Father's SEI				
0–09	11	11	12	12
10–19	45	44	43	43
20–39	18	18	19	19
40–59	14	14	14	14
60 +	12	13	12	12
Total	100	100	100	100
	(17,737)	(15,767)	(14,376)	(14,069)
Age				
20–34	33	34	36	36
35–49	38	38	42	42
50–64	29	28	22	22
Total	100	100	100	100
	(18,966)	(15,767)	(15,549)	(14,069)

Table A.4. *Continued.*

Background characteristics	OCG 1962			
	Respondents		Wives	
Broken Family				
Percent not living with both parents at age 16	15	11	13	11
Farm Background				
Percent with fathers in a farm occupation	29	28	27	27
Sibsize				
1	6	6	7	7
2	13	14	14	15
3	15	16	16	16
4	14	14	14	14
5	11	12	12	12
6	10	9	9	9
7+	31	29	28	27
Total	100	100	100	100
	(18,485)	(15,767)	(15,181)	(14,069)

Background characteristics	NFS 1970			
	Respondents		Husbands	
	Total	Total Excluding Missing	Total	Total Excluding Missing
Father's SEI				
0–09	8	8	7	7
10–19	40	40	44	44
20–39	15	15	13	13
40–59	16	16	16	16
60+	21	21	20	20
Total	100	100	100	100
	(4,867)	(4,792)	(4,319)	(4,244)

Table A.4. *Continued.*

Background characteristics	NFS 1970			
	Respondents		Husbands	
Age				
20–24	21	21	14	14
25–29	23	23	21	21
30–34	20	20	19	19
35–39	18	18	17	17
40–44	18	18	17	17
45 +	—	—	12	12
Total	100	100	100	100
	(5,218)	(4,792)	(4,964)	(4,244)
Broken Family				
Percent not living				
with both parents				
at age 14	19	16	19	15
Farm Background				
Percent with fathers				
in a farm				
occupation	17	17	24	24
Sibsize				
1	7	7	7	7
2	19	19	20	20
3	20	20	20	20
4	16	16	15	15
5	11	11	11	11
6	8	8	8	8
7 +	19	19	19	19
Total	100	100	100	100
	(5,137)	(4,792)	(4,891)	(4,244)

Background characteristics	OCG 1973			
	Respondents		Wives	
	Total	Total Excluding Missing	Total	Total Excluding Missing
Father's Education				
Grade Sch Inc	33	33	Data not tabulated	

Table A.4. *Continued.*

Background characteristics	OCG 1973			
	Respondents		Wives	
Grade Sch Comp	24	24	in conformity with	
High Sch Inc	11	11	OCG 1962	
High Sch Comp	19	19		
College Inc	6	6		
College 4 +	7	7		
Total	100	100		
	(25,936)	(22,142)		
Father's SEI				
0–09	12	12	12	12
10–19	39	39	38	38
20–39	19	19	19	19
40–59	14	14	15	15
60 +	16	16	16	16
Total	100	100	100	100
	(25,846)	(22,142)	(19,291)	(18,952)
Age				
20–34	38	38	39	39
35–49	32	33	37	37
50–64	30	29	24	24
Total	100	100	100	100
	(27,549)	(22,142)	(21,491)	(18,952)
Broken Family				
Percent not living with both parents at age 16	14	12	11	9
Farm Background				
Percent with fathers in a farm occupation	22	22	21	21

Table A.4. *Continued.*

Background characteristics	OCG 1973			
	Respondents		Wives	
Sibsize				
1	7	7	7	7
2	16	17	17	17
3	18	18	18	18
4	15	15	15	15
5	11	11	11	11
6	9	9	9	9
7 +	24	23	23	23
Total	100	100	100	100
	(26,963)	(22,142)	(20,828)	(18,952)

Background characteristics	GSS 1972–1986 Respondents	
	Total	Total Excluding Missing
Father's Education		
Grade Sch Inc	26	26
Grade Sch Comp	21	21
High Sch Inc	12	12
High Sch Comp	23	23
College Inc	8	8
College 4 +	10	10
Total	100	100
	(12,567)	(12,419)
Father's SEI		
0–09	8	7
10–19	40	38
20–39	16	16
40–59	14	15
60 +	22	24
Total	100	100
	(14,770)	(12,419)

Table A.4. *Continued.*

Background characteristics	GSS 1972–1986 Respondents	
Age		
20–34	35	39
35–49	25	26
50–64	22	21
65+	18	14
Total	100	100
	(16,829)	(12,419)
Broken Family		
Percent not living with both parents at age 16	22	11
Farm Background		
Percent with father in a farm occupation	20	18
Sibsize		
1	6	5
2	16	17
3	17	18
4	15	16
5	11	11
6	9	9
7+	26	24
Total	100	100
	(16,798)	(12,419)

[a]Broken family: GAF 1955—Percent parents not always together. GAF 1960—Percent not living with both parents at age 18.

Table A.5. Percentage Distribution of Total Years of Education for All Cases and for Cases that Have No Missing Values on any Predictors, White Men and Women Age 20 and Over, Various Surveys.

	Respondent's Education							
Survey	GS Inc	GS Comp	HS Inc	HS Comp	Coll Inc	Coll Comp	Total	(N)
GAF 1955								
Total	6	8	24	46	11	5	100	(2,643)
Total Exc. Missing	8	8	24	46	11	5	100	(2,538)
GAF 1960								
Total	5	7	24	46	11	7	100	(2,904)
Total Exc. Missing	5	7	23	47	11	7	100	(2,785)
OCG 1962 Men								
Total	13	14	19	30	12	13	100	(18,966)
Total Exc. Missing	11	13	18	31	12	15	100	(15,767)
OCG 1962 Wives								
Total	8	12	20	42	11	7	100	(15,549)
Total Exc. Missing	8	12	19	42	11	8	100	(14,069)
NFS 1970 Women								
Total	2	5	17	48	16	12	100	(5,218)
Total Exc. Missing	2	4	17	48	16	13	100	(4,792)
NFS 1970 Husbands								
Total	3	6	15	36	18	22	100	(4,964)
Total Exc. Missing	3	5	14	36	19	23	100	(4,244)

OCG 1973 Men							
Total	8	8	14	36	17	17	100	(27,549)
Total Exc. Missing	7	7	13	38	16	19	100	(22,142)
OCG 1973 Wives							
Total	5	7	16	48	13	11	100	(21,491)
Total Exc. Missing	5	6	16	49	13	11	100	(18,952)
GSS 1972–1986							
Total	6	8	16	34	19	17	100	(16,790)
Total Exc. Missing	5	6	13	36	21	20	100	(12,419)

Table A.6. Comparison of the Percentage Distribution of Selected Background Characteristics for the Original Subsamples of White Non-Hispanic Children (Includes Missing Sibsize Data), the Final Subsamples (Excludes Missing Sibsize Data), and Sample of Respondents with No Answer on Sibsize, HES, Cycles II and III, and HSB, Seniors in Public Schools.

Survey and background characteristics	Original subsample (N)	Final subsample (N)	NA on sibsize (N)
HES–Cycle II	(5,962)	(4,511)	(1,451)
Father's Education			
Grade School Inc	10	9	15
Grade School Comp	10	10	12
High School Inc	18	17	18
High School Comp	30	32	24
College Inc	8	8	6
College 4 +	14	16	9
NA	10	8	16
Mother's Education			
Grade School Inc	11	9	15
Grade School Comp	8	7	12
High School Inc	21	21	24
High School Comp	41	44	32
College Inc	9	10	7
College 4 +	7	8	4
NA	3	1	7
Father's Income			
0–4,999	29	26	39
5,000– 6,999	25	25	24
7,000– 9,999	23	24	18
10,000–14,999	13	14	11
15,000 +	5	6	3
NA	5	5	5
Broken Family			
Percent parents not currently together	13	10	22
HES–Cycle III	(5,735)	(3,310)	(2,425)
Father's Education			
Grade School Inc	11	9	14

Table A.6. *Continued.*

Survey and background characteristics	Original subsample (N)	Final subsample (N)	NA on sibsize (N)
Grade School Comp	13	11	15
High School Inc	20	19	22
High School Comp	31	33	27
College Inc	9	10	8
College 4 +	14	16	12
NA	2	2	2
Mother's Education			
Grade School Inc	10	8	13
Grade School Comp	9	8	11
High School Inc	20	19	22
High School Comp	40	44	34
College Inc	10	11	8
College 4 +	6	7	5
NA	5	3	7
Father's Income			
0–4,999	20	16	25
5,000– 6,999	16	16	16
7,000– 9,999	25	26	24
10,000–14,999	21	24	18
15,000 +	11	11	10
NA	6	6	7
Broken Family			
Percent parents not currently together	18	14	24
HSB–Seniors	(15,694)	(10,109)	(5,585)
Father's Education			
High School Inc	17	17	17
High School Comp	27	27	27
Vocational	8	9	8
College Inc	11	11	10
College 4 +	19	19	18
NA	18	17	19
Mother's Education			
High School Inc	14	13	14
High School Comp	43	43	42
Vocational	8	9	7

Table A.6. *Continued.*

Survey and background characteristics	Original subsample (N)	Final subsample (N)	NA on sibsize (N)
College Inc	12	13	13
College 4 +	12	12	11
NA	11	10	12
Father's SEI			
0–09	7	8	7
10–19	20	20	19
20–39	14	13	14
40–59	26	26	26
60 +	16	17	15
NA	17	16	18
Broken Family			
Percent parents not currently together	25	24	27

Table A.7. Breakdown of Total Cases Available in Final Subsamples and Cases Excluded because of Missing Data on Predictors and Dependent Variables in the Model of Child Academic Achievement and Aspirations, White Children, HES, Cycles II and III; YIT, High School Sophomores; and HSB, Sophomores and Seniors in Public Schools.

	HES		YIT	HSB 1980	
	Cycle II	Cycle III		Sophomores	Seniors
Total number of cases	4,511	3,310	1,912	14,648	10,109
Number of cases missing for each background predictor:					
Sibsize	0	0	1	0	0
Father's Education	369	368	129	1,090	1,713
Mother's Education	77	113	99	679	999
Father's SEI (Income)	234	201	163	781	1,668
Broken Family	0	0	0	0	0
Cases lost due to missing data on one or more background predictors	613	579	301	1,789	2,817
Cases complete on all background predictors:	3,898	2,731	1,611	12,859	7,292
Complete cases as a percent of all cases in final subsamples	86%	82%	84%	88%	72%
Number of additional cases lost due to missing data on other important variables:[a]					
Cognitive Ability	0	3	0	702	601
Academic Performance	0	3	[c]	76	10

Table A.7. Continued.

	HES		YIT	HSB 1980	
	Cycle II	Cycle III		Sophomores	Seniors
Academic Goals (Student)	[b]	10	[c]	251	58
Academic Goals (Parent)	[b]	15	[c]	2,745	1,089

[a]These items are used both as dependent variables and as predictors.
[b]These items were not asked of either parent or child in HES, Cycle II.
[c]These items are not used in any of the analyses of YIT.

Table A.8. Percentage Distribution of Selected Background Characteristics for All Cases and for Cases that Have No Missing Values on Any Background Predictors, White Children Age 6 to 18, Various Surveys.[a]

	HES			
Background characteristics	*Cycle II*		*Cycle III*	
	Total	Total Excluding Missing	Total	Total Excluding Missing
Father's Education				
Grade Sch Inc	10	9	9	9
Grade Sch Comp	11	11	12	12
High Sch Inc	19	19	19	19
High Sch Comp	34	35	34	34
College Inc	9	9	10	10
College 4+	17	17	16	16
Total	100	100	100	100
	(4,142)	(3,898)	(2,942)	(2,731)
Mother's Education				
Grade Sch Inc	9	8	8	7
Grade Sch Comp	7	7	8	7
High Sch Inc	21	21	20	19
High Sch Comp	45	46	45	47
College Inc	10	10	11	12
College 4+	8	8	8	8
Total	100	100	100	100
	(4,434)	(3,898)	(3,197)	(2,731)
Family Income				
0–4,999	28	24	17	14
5,000– 6,999	26	27	18	17
7,000– 9,999	25	27	27	29
10,000–14,999	14	15	26	27
15,000+	7	7	12	13
Total	100	100	100	100
	(4,277)	(3,898)	(3,109)	(2,731)
Broken Family				
Percent parents not currently together	10	2	14	4

Table A.8. *Continued.*

Background characteristics	HES			
	Cycle II		Cycle III	
Sibsize				
1	4	3	7	6
2	21	21	22	22
3	26	27	26	26
4	21	22	16	17
5	11	11	10	10
6	6	6	6	6
7 +	11	10	13	13
Total	100	100	100	100
	(4,511)	(3,898)	(3,310)	(2,731)

Background characteristics	HSB 1980, Public Schools			
	Sophomores		Seniors	
	Total	Total Excluding Missing	Total	Total Excluding Missing
Father's Education				
High Sch Inc	22	22	20	20
High Sch Comp	33	33	32	32
Vocational	10	10	10	10
College Inc	13	13	14	14
College 4 +	22	22	24	24
Total	100	100	100	100
	(13,558)	(12,859)	(8,396)	(7,292)
Mother's Education				
High Sch Inc	17	16	15	14
High Sch Comp	47	47	48	48
Vocational	9	9	9	9
College Inc	14	14	14	14
College 4 +	13	14	14	15
Total	100	100	100	100
	(13,969)	(12,859)	(9,110)	(7,292)

Table A.8. *Continued.*

Background characteristics	HSB 1980, Public Schools			
	Sophomores		*Seniors*	
Father's SEI				
0–09	10	10	9	9
10–19	25	25	24	24
20–39	17	17	16	16
40–59	30	30	31	31
60 +	18	18	20	20
Total	100	100	100	100
	(13,867)	(12,859)	(8,441)	(7,292)
Broken Family				
Percent parents not currently together	24	20	24	14
Sibsize				
1	5	4	6	5
2	22	22	22	22
3	27	28	26	27
4	20	20	20	20
5	10	10	12	12
6	7	7	6	6
7 +	9	9	8	8
Total	100	100	100	100
	(14,648)	(12,859)	(10,109)	(7,292)

Background characteristics	YIT Sophomores	
	Total	Total Excluding Missing
Father's Education		
Grade Sch	21	20
High Sch Inc	20	20
High Sch Comp	34	34
College Inc	12	13
College 4 +	13	13
Total	100	100
	(1,783)	(1,611)

Table A.8. *Continued.*

Background characteristics	YIT Sophomores	
Mother's Education		
Grade Sch	12	12
High Sch Inc	18	18
High Sch Comp	52	51
College Inc	10	11
College 4 +	8	8
Total	100	100
	(1,813)	(1,611)
Father's SEI		
0–09	4	3
10–19	26	25
20–39	28	28
40–59	30	31
60 +	12	13
Total	100	100
	(1,749)	(1,611)
Broken Family		
Percent parents not		
currently together	18	13
Sibsize		
1	6	5
2	23	23
3	25	26
4	20	20
5	12	12
6	6	6
7 +	8	8
Total	100	100
	(1,911)	(1,611)

[a]The background predictors for which missing data have been excluded are Father's and Mother's Education, Father's SEI (or Income), Broken Family, and Sibsize. None of the additional predictors/dependent variables shown in table 1.8 have been deleted here since they are not used consistently in all analyses.

Table A.9. Percentage Distribution of Selected Predictor or Dependent Variables for All Cases and for Cases that Have No Missing Values on Any Background Predictors, White Children Age 6 to 18, Various Surveys.[a]

Dependent Variables	HES Cycle II		HES Cycle III		YIT	
	Total	Total Excluding Missing	Total	Total Excluding Missing	Total	Total Excluding Missing
Cognitive Ability[b]						
00– 79	7	6	11	10	10	10
80– 89	18	18	7	8	16	15
90– 99	27	27	14	13	27	27
100–109	23	23	21	21	21	21
110–119	15	15	27	27	18	18
120+	10	11	20	21	8	9
Total	100	100	100	100	100	100
	(4,511)	(3,898)	(3,305)	(2,728)	(1,912)	(1,611)
Performance (WRAT)						
00– 79	8	7	10	8	NA	NA
80– 89	13	12	8	9	NA	NA
90– 99	25	25	15	14	NA	NA
100–109	28	29	23	23	NA	NA
110–119	19	19	26	27	NA	NA
120+	7	8	18	19	NA	NA
Total	100	100	100	100	NA	NA
	(4,511)	(3,898)	(3,306)	(2,728)		

Table A.9. Continued.

Dependent Variables	HES Cycle II		HES Cycle III		YIT	
	Total	Total Excluding Missing	Total	Total Excluding Missing	Total	Total Excluding Missing
Academic Goals (Parents)						
High School or less	NA	NA	13	12	NA	NA
Some College or Vocational	NA	NA	37	38	NA	NA
Finish College	NA	NA	33	33	NA	NA
Grad School	NA	NA	17	17	NA	NA
Total	NA	NA	100	100	NA	NA
			(3,283)	(2,716)		
Academic Goals (Students)						
High School or less	NA	NA	24	22	NA	NA
Some College or Vocational	NA	NA	33	33	NA	NA
Finish College	NA	NA	27	29	NA	NA
Grad School	NA	NA	16	16	NA	NA
Total	NA	NA	100	100	NA	NA
			(3,293)	(2,721)		

| | HSB 1980 | | | |
| | Sophomores | | Seniors | |
Dependent Variables	Total	Total Excluding Missing	Total	Total Excluding Missing
Cognitive Ability (Vocabulary)				
00–40	18	16	14	13
41–45	14	14	20	19
46–50	17	17	21	20
51–55	18	19	15	16
56–60	16	16	12	12
61 +	17	18	18	20
Total	100	100	100	100
	(13,788)	(12,157)	(9,254)	(6,691)
Performance (Grades)				
Cs and Ds or less	12	11	5	5
Mostly Cs	14	13	12	10
Mostly Bs and Cs	25	24	24	22
Mostly Bs	19	20	21	22
Mostly As and Bs	19	20	24	25
Mostly As	11	12	14	16
Total	100	100	100	100
	(14,545)	(12,783)	(10,071)	(7,282)

Table A.9. Continued.

	HSB 1980			
	Sophomores		Seniors	
Dependent Variables	Total	Total Excluding Missing	Total	Total Excluding Missing
Academic Goals (Parents)				
High School or less	16	15	11	10
Vocational	14	13	17	17
College Inc	15	15	13	11
College Comp	33	34	37	39
Grad School	22	23	22	23
Total	100	100	100	100
	(11,264)	(10,114)	(8,250)	(6,203)
Academic Goals (Student)				
High School or less	27	25	20	18
Vocational	18	18	20	19
College Inc	15	15	15	14
College Comp	23	24	26	28
Grad School	17	18	19	21
Total	100	100	100	100
	(14,310)	(12,608)	(9,981)	(7,234)

[a]The background predictors for which missing data have been excluded are Father's and Mother's Education, Father's SEI (or Income), Broken Family, and Sibsize.

[b]Cognitive Ability for HES, Cycles II and III is WISC; and for YIT is the Quick Test.

Appendix B

This appendix contains supplementary tables referred to in chapter 2.

Table B.1. Total Years of Education (Unadjusted Means) by Sibsize, White Men and Women Age 25 and Over, Various Surveys.[a]

Survey	Sibsize							Grand Mean	S.D.	Eta	N
	1	2	3	4	5	6	7+				
Men											
OCG 1962	12.6	12.6	12.0	11.2	10.7	10.2	9.4	10.9	3.4	.348	(16,666)
NFS 1970	13.7	13.8	13.2	12.6	12.1	11.8	10.9	12.6	2.9	.357	(4,189)
OCG 1973	13.1	13.3	12.7	12.1	11.3	10.7	9.9	11.7	3.6	.350	(21,920)
GSS 1972–1986	13.7	14.0	13.5	12.7	12.0	11.6	10.3	12.3	3.6	.387	(6,666)
Women											
GAF 1955	12.1	12.2	11.8	11.3	11.0	10.9	10.2	11.2	2.5	.302	(2,260)
GAF 1960	12.3	12.3	12.0	11.4	11.1	10.8	10.2	11.4	2.4	.331	(2,465)
OCG 1962	12.2	12.2	11.6	11.3	10.9	10.5	9.9	11.0	2.8	.298	(13,712)
NFS 1970	13.1	13.1	12.6	12.1	11.9	11.3	10.9	12.1	2.3	.341	(4,062)
OCG 1973	12.7	12.8	12.4	11.8	11.4	11.1	10.5	11.7	2.6	.333	(18,552)
GSS 1972–1986	13.2	13.2	12.8	12.3	11.7	11.4	10.3	11.9	3.0	.372	(8,322)

[a]The Ns reported for all MCAs are somewhat lower than the total sample numbers available due to nonresponse on the dependent variable, educational attainment, as well as nonresponse on sibsize. In addition, analyses using Total Years of Education are based on respondents age 25 and over.

Table B.2. Total Years of Education (Adjusted Means) by Sibsize, White Men and Women Age 25 and Over, Various Surveys.[a]

Survey	Sibsize							Grand Mean	S.D.	R^2	(N)
	1	2	3	4	5	6	7+				
Men											
OCG 1962	11.8	11.8	11.5	11.1	10.9	10.6	10.2	10.9	3.4	.323	(16,666)
NFS 1970	13.5	13.4	13.0	12.7	12.3	12.0	11.3	12.6	2.9	.246	(4,189)
OCG 1973	12.4	12.5	12.2	11.9	11.5	11.2	10.8	11.7	3.6	.316	(21,920)
GSS 1972–1986	13.4	13.2	12.9	12.4	12.1	11.9	11.2	12.3	3.6	.362	(6,666)
Women											
GAF 1955	12.0	11.8	11.6	11.3	11.1	11.1	10.4	11.2	2.5	.194	(2,260)
GAF 1960	12.3	12.1	11.9	11.4	11.2	10.9	10.4	11.4	2.4	.187	(2,465)
OCG 1962	11.8	11.8	11.5	11.2	11.0	10.7	10.3	11.0	2.8	.207	(13,712)
NFS 1970	13.0	12.8	12.4	12.2	12.0	11.5	11.2	12.1	2.3	.237	(4,062)
OCG 1973	12.5	12.4	12.2	11.8	11.6	11.3	10.8	11.7	2.6	.224	(18,552)
GSS 1972–1986	12.8	12.6	12.3	12.1	11.8	11.6	11.0	11.9	3.0	.356	(8,322)

[a] All MCA equations control for father's SEI, farm background, respondent's age, and family intactness. In addition, except for OCG, GAF, and NFS men, father's education is also included as a predictor.

Table B.3. Years of Graded Schooling (Adjusted Means) by Sibsize, White Men and Women Age 20 and Over, Various Surveys.[a]

Survey	Sibsize							Grand Mean	S.D.	Eta	R^2	N
	1	2	3	4	5	6	7+					
Men												
OCG 1962	10.7	10.6	10.6	10.4	10.3	10.1	9.7	10.2	2.4	.320	.281	(18,485)
NFS 1970	11.6	11.6	11.5	11.4	11.2	11.1	10.6	11.3	1.6	.309	.168	(4,879)
OCG 1973	11.1	11.0	11.0	10.9	10.7	10.5	10.1	10.7	2.5	.286	.236	(24,954)
GSS 1972–1986	11.5	11.2	11.2	11.1	10.9	10.8	10.3	10.9	2.0	.345	.327	(7,502)
Women												
GAF 1955	11.3	11.2	11.1	11.0	10.8	10.7	10.2	10.8	1.9	.275	.153	(2,661)
GAF 1960	11.4	11.4	11.3	11.0	10.8	10.7	10.2	11.0	1.8	.302	.140	(2,904)
OCG 1962	11.0	11.0	10.9	10.8	10.6	10.4	10.0	10.6	2.1	.273	.181	(15,181)
NFS 1970	11.7	11.7	11.6	11.4	11.4	11.1	10.8	11.4	1.4	.282	.134	(5,135)
OCG 1973	11.5	11.5	11.4	11.2	11.1	10.9	10.5	11.1	1.8	.289	.161	(20,828)
GSS 1972–1986	11.4	11.3	11.3	11.2	11.1	10.9	10.5	11.0	1.9	.334	.301	(9,258)

[a]All MCA equations control for father's SEI, farm background, respondent's age, and family intactness. In addition, except for OCG, GAF, and NFS men, father's education is also included as a predictor.

Table B.4. Percentage Who Graduated from High School (Adjusted Means) by Sibsize, White Men and Women Age 20 and Over, Various Surveys.[a]

Survey	Sibsize							Grand Mean	Eta	R^2	(N)
	1	2	3	4	5	6	7+				
Men											
OCG 1962	66	66	63	58	54	50	43	55	.328	.254	(18,485)
NFS 1970	82	87	86	80	77	68	60	78	.206	.067	(4,879)
OCG 1973	78	77	74	71	67	62	56	68	.318	.252	(24,954)
GSS 1972–1986	83	80	77	73	67	65	56	70	.352	.290	(7,502)
Women											
GAF 1955	75	73	68	66	57	61	46	61	.257	.136	(2,661)
GAF 1960	78	77	72	65	56	55	45	64	.299	.135	(2,904)
OCG 1962	72	73	67	64	59	55	46	60	.280	.162	(15,181)
NFS 1970	89	86	82	77	76	68	60	77	.240	.141	(5,134)
OCG 1973	82	83	80	75	70	66	56	72	.294	.153	(20,828)
GSS 1972–1986	81	79	76	72	68	65	58	69	.333	.277	(9,258)

[a]All MCA equations control for father's SEI, farm background, respondent's age, and family intactness. In addition, except for OCG, GAF, and NFS men, father's education is also included as a predictor.

Table B.5. Percentage of High School Graduates Who Went to College (Adjusted Means) by Sibsize, White Men and Women Age 25 and Over, Various Surveys.[a]

Survey	Sibsize							Grand Mean	Eta	R^2	(N)
	1	2	3	4	5	6	7+				
Men											
OCG 1962	53	53	49	42	42	40	37	45	.186	.139	(8,713)
NFS 1970	64	63	55	50	50	45	39	53	.214	.114	(3,143)
OCG 1973	55	57	52	47	45	41	39	49	.211	.151	(14,469)
GSS 1972–1986	64	67	64	55	54	55	49	59	.189	.128	(4,562)
Women											
GAF 1955	37	33	27	24	21	22	20	26	.169	.117	(1,392)
GAF 1960	40	33	31	27	22	21	20	29	.180	.100	(1,568)
OCG 1962	42	38	34	29	29	24	23	31	.165	.104	(8,112)
NFS 1970	48	45	38	37	32	26	23	37	.218	.156	(3,049)
OCG 1973	44	40	35	31	28	25	24	33	.195	.138	(13,206)
GSS 1972–1986	55	53	45	45	38	44	37	45	.178	.168	(5,640)

[a]All MCA equations control for father's SEI, farm background, respondent's age, and family intactness. In addition, except for OCG, GAF, and NFS men, father's education is also included as a predictor.

Table B.6. Years of College Schooling Among Those Who Went to College (Adjusted Means) by Sibsize, White Men and Women Age 25 and Over, Various Surveys.[a]

Survey	Sibsize							Grand Mean	S.D.	Eta	R^2	(N)
	1	2	3	4	5	6	7+					
Men												
OCG 1962	3.5	3.5	3.4	3.4	3.3	3.3	3.3	3.4	1.3	.118	.038	(3,926)
NFS 1970	3.6	3.4	3.5	3.3	3.2	3.3	3.3	3.4	1.4	.099	.079	(1,678)
OCG 1973	3.5	3.5	3.5	3.3	3.3	3.3	3.1	3.4	1.5	.129	.069	(7,051)
GSS 1972–1986	3.7	3.7	3.5	3.5	3.5	3.2	3.2	3.5	1.7	.115	.059	(2,692)
Women												
GAF 1955	2.7	2.7	2.8	2.7	2.7	2.7	2.5	2.7	1.0	.116	.020	(362)
GAF 1960	2.8	2.7	2.8	2.9	2.7	2.4	2.8	2.8	1.4	.086	.010	(457)
OCG 1962	3.0	3.0	3.0	2.8	2.8	2.8	2.9	2.9	1.1	.101	.035	(2,536)
NFS 1970	3.1	3.1	2.9	2.8	2.9	2.9	2.7	2.9	1.4	.144	.051	(1,122)
OCG 1973	3.0	3.1	3.0	2.8	2.8	2.9	2.9	3.0	1.4	.108	.043	(4,313)
GSS 1972–1986	3.2	3.2	3.2	3.0	2.9	3.0	2.7	3.1	1.6	.126	.070	(2,522)

[a]All MCA equations control for father's SEI, farm background, respondent's age, and family intactness. In addition, except for OCG, GAF, and NFS men, father's education is also included as a predictor.

Appendix C

This appendix contains supplementary tables referred to in chapter 4.

Table C.1. Age–Sex Standardized WISC Scores by Sibsize, White Boys and Girls, HES, Cycles II and III.

Survey and Test	Sibsize							Eta	Sibsize Difference as Percent of S.D.[b]
	1	2	3	4	5	6	7+		
Cycle II									
Unadjusted Means									
WISC–Total	103	103	102	100	98	95	91	.254	80
Vocabulary	53	53	52	50	48	45	43	.319	100
Block Design	51	51	51	50	50	48	47	.129	40
Adjusted Means[a]									
WISC–Total	104	102	101	100	99	97	95	—	60
Vocabulary	53	52	51	50	49	47	46	—	70
Block Design	51	50	50	50	50	49	49	—	20
Cycle III									
Unadjusted Means									
WISC–Total	103	102	103	101	99	95	92	.236	73
Vocabulary	53	51	52	50	49	46	44	.270	90
Block Design	50	50	51	51	50	48	47	.142	30
Adjusted Means[a]									
WISC–Total	104	100	101	100	100	97	97	—	47
Vocabulary	53	50	51	49	50	48	48	—	50
Block Design	51	50	51	50	50	49	49	—	20

Table C.2. Age Standardized Achievement Test Scores by Sibsize, White Boys, YIT, High School Sophomores; and Age–Sex Standardized Achievement Test Scores by Sibsize, White Boys and Girls, HSB, Sophomores and Seniors, Adjusted Means.[a]

| Survey and Test | Sibsize | | | | | | | Eta | Sibsize Difference as Percent of S.D.[b] |
	1	2	3	4	5	6	7+		
YIT									
Quick Test	103	103	101	98	98	98	96	.204	47
Matrices	101	100	101	99	101	100	97	.106	27
Hidden Patterns	97	99	102	99	101	100	99	.103	−13
HSB, Sophomores									
Vocabulary	52	51	50	50	49	49	48	.141	40
Reading	51	51	50	50	50	49	49	.104	20
Math 1	50	50	50	50	50	49	49	.099	10
Math 2	50	50	50	50	50	50	50	.071	0
Science	51	50	50	50	50	49	49	.092	20
Civics	50	50	50	50	50	49	49	.087	10
HSB, Seniors									
Vocabulary 1	51	51	50	50	49	48	49	.112	20
Vocabulary 2	51	51	50	50	49	49	49	.096	20
Reading	50	51	50	50	50	48	49	.079	10
Math 1	49	50	50	50	50	49	50	.071	−10
Math 2	49	50	50	50	50	49	50	.070	−10
Mosaic 1	48	50	50	50	50	49	49	.064	−10

Mosaic 2	48	50	51	50	50	49	50	.068	−20
Visual	48	50	50	50	50	49	51	.052	−30
Picture/Number	49	50	50	50	50	49	49	.053	0

[a]Scores have been adjusted, through multiple classification analysis, for mother's and father's education, and family intactness. In addition, YIT adjusts for community size where youth was brought up, and father's occupation; and HSB adjusts for mother's labor force participation and the existence of a physically limiting condition. For YIT, scores have a mean of 100 and a standard deviation of 15. For HSB scores have a mean of 50 and a standard deviation of 10. The number of cases in each analysis varies from 1,910 to 1,911 for YIT; from 13,427 to 13,788 for HSB sophomores; and from 8,938 to 9,265 for HSB seniors.

[b]This is the difference in scores between those from only-child families and those from families of seven or more shown as a percent of the standard deviation for each test.

Table C.3. Age–Sex Standardized Vocabulary Scores by Sibsize and Three Levels of Mother's Education, White Boys and Girls, HES, Cycles II and III, Adjusted Means.[a]

Survey and Mother's Education	Sibsize			Mean	(S.D.)	N
	1–2	*3–5*	*6+*			
Cycle II						
High School Inc	48	46	42	45	(9.5)	1,643
High School Comp	53	51	49	51	(8.9)	1,999
College	58	56	51	56	(9.0)	792
Cycle III						
High School Inc	47	45	42	45	(10.0)	1,139
High School Comp	53	52	50	52	(8.5)	1,451
College	55	56	55	56	(8.2)	604

[a]Scores have been adjusted, through multiple classification analysis, for mother's and father's education, family income, family intactness, mother's labor force participation, and region.

Notes

1. NUMBER OF SIBLINGS AND OPPORTUNITY

1. A notable exception is Blau and Duncan (1967), chapter 9. For some discussion of the independent effects of number of siblings see, also, Beverly Duncan (1965, 1967); Duncan, Featherman, and Duncan (1972); and Featherman (1971a).

2. In using the Mercer data, Jensen (1980) calculates the variance in IQ explained due to race and SES by computing a regression equation in which race is entered first and SES is entered second. This equation gives a low value for SES because it is entered second. Jensen then reverses the process and computes an equation in which SES is entered first and race is entered second. In this case the value for race is low because SES has been entered first. Jensen then picks the low value of SES from the first equation and the low value of race from the second equation and claims that these can be added, which they cannot, and that the proportion of IQ variance attributable to race and SES is 22 percent. Actually, this proportion is 33 percent and is the sum of the two components within each equation. The calculations are given below:

Equation 1	An R^2 due to the regression of race on IQ	$= .25$
	A partial R^2 due to the regression of SES on IQ given that race is in the model	$= .08$
Equation 2	An R^2 due to the regression of SES on IQ	$= .19$
	A partial R^2 due to the regression of race on IQ given that SES is in the model	$= .14$

3. Rowe and Plomin (1981) use intraclass correlations for IQ between siblings reared together of .34 that are relatively low compared to the more comprehensive data cited by Bouchard and McGue (1981) of .47. Rowe and Plomin suggest that these low correlations indicate that most of the variance in IQ between siblings is nonshared (i.e., within family). However, our confidence in this assertion is tempered by the fact that there is enormous heterogeneity among the results of different studies. As Bouchard and McGue point out, the 69 separate studies of sibling correlations evinced a range from .13 to .90. One large representative study

by Record and others (1969) showed a correlation of .55 on over 5000 pairs. This heterogeneity in the correlations is due in part to the fact that the studies used different tests for IQ, the comparisons between siblings were not always age-corrected, nor were the ages similar at which youngsters were tested. Large amounts of measurement error in the data on siblings inflates the within-family variance because, in the one-way analysis of variance performed to obtain the intraclass correlations, the variance due to measurement error is, by definition, simply absorbed into the within-family variance. Given the range of sibling correlations cited above, it seems risky, indeed foolhardy, to strike an average and assume that the data support relatively low within-family correlations.

4. The reader should note that for all studies the base-year survey alone has been used, although some studies have involved followup in later years.

5. The "effect" of sibsize has been evaluated inappropriately by some researchers in terms of "marginal" importance or "unique" contribution after taking account of other variables in a multivariate model (for example, Ernst and Angst 1983; Galbraith 1982a). Although this concept is attractive, it is impossible to use such a calculation in the case of models where the predictors are highly intercorrelated because one is, in effect, assuming that all of the explanation that a given variable *shares* with the other predictors (and which cannot be partitioned) can be interpreted as belonging to those predictors and not to the variable in question.

2. EDUCATION AND NUMBER OF SIBLINGS

1. Readers of the author's article, "Number of Siblings and Educational Mobility," (*American Sociological Review* 1985) and a subsequent exchange (Blake, 1986) with Mare and Chen (1986) will recognize that the research problems addressed in this book are different from the problem that informed the *ASR* article. The latter was concerned with the interaction effect of father's education among separate sibsize groups using disaggregated amounts of education as the dependent variables. The present chapter considers main effects of sibsize on differing levels of education, and chapter 3 considers interaction effects of sibsize on total years of education, and, very briefly, the interaction effect of father's education on this variable.

2. Clearly, there are real costs attached to keeping youngsters at school even through high school, since the child's time represents an opportunity cost for the parents and the child must be fed and clothed. Nonetheless, it does seem farfetched to suggest that children from large families drop out of graded schooling for economic reasons alone.

3. EDUCATIONAL ATTAINMENT BY SIBSIZE, RELIGION, ETHNICITY, AND SOCIAL STATUS

1. Coming from southern Italy and Sicily, the Italians were deeply suspicious of the authority of the state and had little use for schools. Both of these attitudes were a legacy of negative experiences with the state and the schools in Italy. Italians offered no support for the parochial school system in the United States (which they perceived as "belonging" to the Irish and the Germans), and they ended up typically by sending their children to public school. Even free schooling was resented by Italian parents because of loss of the child's earnings and what parents considered to be a state invasion of the family's prerogative to educate the child (Weisz 1976, passim).

2. Fundamentalists consist of Baptists and other Protestant denominations believing in the inerrancy of the Bible. Mainline Protestants are Lutherans, Methodists, Presbyterians, Congregationalists, Episcopalians, and other Protestant denominations whose adherents do not believe in the inerrancy of the Bible. Belief in biblical inerrancy was ascertained from a question in the General Social Surveys.

5. BIRTH ORDER, INTELLECTUAL ABILITY, AND EDUCATIONAL ATTAINMENT

1. The reader should note that the dependent variables in the two studies have different scales. For purposes of charting, we have standardized the data on a mean of 50. This procedure does not change the shape of the curves, nor are they yet comparable as to level. Thus, for example, it is not meaningful to ask why only children in one study are higher or lower than only children in another. It is only meaningful to compare the *relative* positions of the sibsizes and birth orders between studies. For example, one can ask why only children rank above (or below) certain other children in these studies; or, one can ask why values of the dependent variable are inversely related to birth order in the Dutch study and the Breland study.

2. The data in these figures, like the Breland and the Belmont and Marolla data, have been standardized on a mean of 50. The same restrictions apply as were noted in note 1 of this chapter.

3. For a discussion of this technique using multiple classification analysis, see Andrews and colleagues (1973, 2–3) and Pelz and Andrews (1966, Appendix C).

4. This outline expands and systematizes the discussion of expectations about education and birth order to be found in Blau and Duncan (1967).

5. In their analysis of the 1962 Occupational Changes in a Generation data, Blau and Duncan emphasized the less-advantaged position of the middle child. However, as they themselves noted, their analysis was partially confounded by inadequate controls for sibsize. The authors divided the sample into only children, children from two- to four-child families, and those from families of five or more offspring. Then, oldest, middle, and youngest children within two- to four-child families and five-plus families were compared. But, middle children were heavily weighted toward the larger family end of each half of the family-size dichotomy. For example, among two- to four-child families, one only gets middle children beginning with the three-child family; and, among families of five or more children, middle children will be weighted toward the large end of the continuum because the larger the family the more "middle" children there are (see, Blau and Duncan 1967, 298–309).

6. The analysis in Hauser and Sewell (1985) is based on the respondents and their siblings treated as one sample of merged data. The authors are thus considering birth orders and family size among all families aggregated. Parenthetically, although the analysis controls for family background and age for birth orders *within* each sibsize, it does not control *across* sibsizes for family background and age.

7. SETTINGS, TREATMENTS, AND SOCIAL AND PERSONALITY CHARACTERISTICS BY SIBSIZE

1. We have already pointed out (chapter 1) that the idealization of large families and the belief that only children suffer handicaps doubtless stems from the fact that societies having such beliefs have survived over the course of human history. Here we simply point to *individual* reasons supporting such views.

2. On this group (separated by sex), a principal component analysis was used to find the number of factors that could explain the observed correlation among the variables. The factors used were those with an eigenvalue equal to or greater than one. The factors were rotated using the varimax method to produce a simpler factor pattern. The varimax criterion centers on simplifying the columns of the factor matrix, defining a simpler factor as one with only ones and zeroes in the columns.

3. In a systematic review of studies on the influence of social-class status on parental socialization values and practices, Gecas has grouped studies under three rubrics: those that see parental behavior as conditioned by the structural characteristics of life in low- or high-socioeconomic-status families (structural); those that depict parental values as arising from social class or job conditions—values that are then trans-

ferred into childrearing (ideational); and those that see childrearing behavior as conditioned by a lower-class (or upper-class) "culture," including patterns of perception of reality, observation, sense of futility, and loss
of control (psychological). Our present discussion includes, therefore, an
ideational and a structural component of childrearing behavior. Gecas
has noted that the theories of "lower-class" childrearing are very cognate
with the theory of large-family childrearing, and the theories of middle-
or upper-class childrearing are cognate with the theory of small-family
childrearing (Gecas 1979).

8. SIBSIZE TRANSITION AND ITS SOCIAL CONSEQUENCES

1. The reader should note that the mean family size of children may
be calculated as follows:

$$\bar{X}_c \;=\; \frac{S_m^2}{\bar{X}_m} \;+\; \bar{X}_m$$

where $\bar{X}_c$ equals the mean family size of children, S_m^2 equals the variance
of the mean family size of mothers, and $\bar{X}_m$ equals the mean family size
of mothers.

2. The reader will note that the 1982 survey data were presented by
CPS in terms of the proportion of *mothers* with various kinds of market
attachment, but the 1984 data were presented in terms of the proportion
of *children* whose mothers were attached to the market in various ways.
Both approaches tell a similar story, but the bases are quite different.

APPENDIX A

1. In 1973, father's education in years was available, but we have used
the same code for both 1962 and 1973.

References

Achen, C. H. 1982. *Interpreting and using regression*. Beverly Hills, Calif.: Sage Publications.

Adams, B. N. 1972. Birth order: A critical review. *Sociometry* 35:411–439.

Alexander, K., and Eckland, B. 1974. School experience and status attainment. In *Adolescence in the lifecycle: Psychological change and social context*, ed. S. D. Dragastin and G. H. Elder, Jr., 171–210. Washington, D.C.: Hemisphere.

———. 1975. Basic attainment processes: A replication and extension. *Sociology of Education* 48:457–495.

———. 1980. The "Explorations in equality of opportunity" sample of 1955 high school sophomores. *Research in Sociology of Education and Socialization* 1:31–58.

Alexander, K., Eckland, B., and Griffin, L. 1975. The Wisconsin model of socioeconomic achievement: A replication. *American Journal of Sociology* 81:324–342.

Alexander, K., Natriello, G., and Pallas, A. 1985. For whom the school bell tolls: The impact of dropping out on cognitive performance. *American Scoiological Review* 50:409–420.

Alwin, D. F. 1974. College effects on educational and occupational attainments. *American Sociological Review* 39:210–223.

———. 1976. Socioeconomic background, colleges and post-collegiate achievements. In *Schooling and achievement in American society*, ed. W. H. Sewell, R. M. Hauser, and D. L. Featherman, 343–372. New York: Academic Press.

Alwin, D. F., and Thornton, A. 1984. Family origins and the schooling process: Early versus late influence of parental characteristics. *American Sociological Review* 49:784–802.

Ammons, R. D., and Ammons, C. H. 1963. *The quick test*. Missoula, Mont.: Psychological Test Specialists.

Anastasi, A. 1956. Intelligence and family size. *Psychological Bulletin* 53: 187–209.

Andrews, F. M., Morgan, J. N., Sonquist, J. A., and Klem, L. 1973. *Mul-*

tiple classification analysis. Ann Arbor: Institute for Social Research.

Atkinson, J. W., and Birch, D. 1978. *An introduction to motivation.* New York: Van Nostrand.

Auletta, K. 1982. *The underclass.* New York: Random House.

Bachman, J. G., Kahn, R. L., Mednick, M. T., Davidson, T. N., and Johnson, L. D. 1969. *Youth in transition, Volume I: Blueprint for a longitudinal study of adolescent boys.* Ann Arbor: Institute for Social Research.

Banfield, E. 1970. *The unheavenly city.* Boston: Little, Brown.

Becker, G. S., and Tomes, N. 1976. Child endowments and the quantity and quality of children. *Journal of Political Economy* 84:S143–S162.

Behrman, J., and Taubman, P. 1976. Intergenerational transmission of income and wealth. *American Economic Review* 66:436–440.

Belmont, L., and Marolla, F. A. 1973. Birth order, family size, and intelligence. *Science* 182:1096–1101.

Benedetto, P., Courgeau, D., and Vallot, F. 1973. Aspect méthodologique de l'étalonnage en quotient intellectuel. In *Enquête Nationale sur le Niveau Intellectuel des Enfants d'âge Scolaire, Travaux et Documents,* cahier no. 64. Paris: Presses Universitaires de France.

Berbaum, M. L., Markus, G. B., and Zajonc, R. B. 1982. A closer look at Galbraith's "closer look." *Developmental Psychology* 18:174–180.

Berg, I. 1975. *Education and jobs: The great training robbery.* Boston: Beacon Press.

Bernstein, B. 1970. A sociolinguistic approach to socialization: With some reference to educability. In *Language and poverty,* ed. F. Williams, 25–61. Chicago: Markham.

Bijou, S. W. 1971. Environment and intelligence: A behavioral analysis. In *Intelligence: Genetic and environmental influences,* ed. R. Cancro, 221–239. New York: Grune and Stratton.

Blake, J. 1966. The Americanization of Catholic reproductive ideals. *Population Studies* 20:27–43.

———. 1979. Is zero preferred? American attitudes toward childlessness in the 1970s. *Journal of Marriage and the Family* 41:245–257.

———. 1981a. Family size and the quality of children. *Demography* 18:421–442.

———. 1981b. The only child in America: Prejudice versus performance. *Population and Development Review* 7:43–54.

———. 1985. Number of siblings and educational mobility. *American Sociological Review* 50:84–94.

———. 1986. Number of siblings, family background, and the process of educational attainment. *Social Biology* 33:5–21.

———. 1986. Reply to Mare and Chen. *American Sociological Review* 51:351–357.

Blake, J., and Del Pinal, J. H. 1982. Educational and reproductive preferences: Theory and evidence. In *Determinants of fertility trends: Theories re-examined*, ed. C. Höhn and R. Mackensen, 61–77. Liège, Belgium: International Union for the Scientific Study of Population, Ordina Editions.

Blalock, H. M. 1967. Causal inferences, closed populations and measures of association. *American Political Science Review* 61:130–136.

Blau, P. M., and Duncan, O.D. 1967. *The American occupational structure.* New York: Wiley.

Block, J. H. 1976. Issues, problems, and pitfalls in assessing sex differences: A critical review of "The psychology of sex differences." *Merrill-Palmer Quarterly* 22:283–308.

Bloom, B. 1964. *Stability and change in human characteristics.* New York: Wiley.

Bossard, J. H. 1953. *Parent and child.* Philadelphia: University of Pennsylvania Press.

———. 1954. *The sociology of child development.* New York: Harper and Brothers.

Bossard, J. H., and Boll, E. S. 1955. Personality roles in the large family. *Child Development* 26:71–78.

———. 1956. *The large family system.* Philadelphia: University of Pennsylvania Press.

Bouchard, T. J., Jr., and McGue, M. 1981. Familial studies of intelligence: A review. *Science* 212:1055–1059.

Bowles, S. 1972. Schooling and inequality from generation to generation. *Journal of Political Economy* 80:S219–S251.

Bowles, S., and Gintis, H. 1974. IQ in the United States class structure. In *The new assault on equality*, ed. A. Gartner, C. Greer, and F. Riessman, 7–84. New York: Harper and Row.

Bowles, S., and Nelson, V. I. 1974. The "inheritance of IQ" and the intergenerational reproduction of economic inequality. *Review of Economics and Statistics* 56:39–51.

Brackbill, Y., and Nichols, P. L. 1982. A test of the confluence model of intellectual development. *Developmental Psychology* 18:192–198.

Bradley, R. H., and Caldwell, B. M. 1978. Screening the environment. *American Journal of Orthopsychiatry* 48:114–130.

Breland, H. M. 1974. Birth order, family configuration, and verbal achievement. *Child Development* 45:1011–1019.

Brim, O. G., and Kagan, J. 1980. *Constancy and change in human development.* Cambridge, Mass.: Harvard University Press.

Brittain, J. A. 1978. *Inheritance and the inequality of material wealth.* Washington, D.C.: Brookings.

Bumpass, L. L., Rindfuss, R. R., and Janosik, R. B. 1978. Age and marital status at first birth and the pace of subsequent fertility. *Demography* 15: 75–86.

Buros, O. K. 1972. *The seventh mental measurements yearbook*. Highland Park, N.J.: Gryphon Press.

Cain, G. C., and Watts, H. 1970. Problems in making policy inferences from the Coleman Report. *American Journal of Sociology* 35:228–242.

Cairns, R. B., and Valsiner, J. 1984. Child psychology. *Annual Review of Psychology* 35:553–577.

Campbell, E. Q. 1969. Adolescent socialization. In *Handbook of socialization theory and research*, ed. D. A. Goslin, 821–859. Chicago: Rand McNally.

Chamberlain, G., and Griliches, Z. 1975. Unobservables with a variance-components structure: Ability, schooling and the economic success of brothers. *International Economic Review* 16:422–449.

Chiswick, B. R. 1986. Comment on Hauser and Sewell. *Journal of Labor Economics* 4:S116–120.

Claudy, J. 1976. *Cognitive characteristics of the only child*. Palo Alto, Calif.: American Institutes for Research.

Claudy, J., Farrell, W. S., and Dayton, C. W. 1979. *The consequences of being an only child: An analysis of Project Talent data*. Palo Alto, Calif.: American Institutes for Research.

Clausen, J. 1965. *Family size and birth order as influences upon socialization and personality: Bibliography and abstracts*. New York: Social Science Research Council.

Clausen, J., and Clausen, S. 1973. The effects of family size on parents and children. In *Psychological perspectives on population*, ed. J. F. Fawcett, 185–208. New York: Basic Books.

Cohen, J. 1983. Peer influence on college aspirations with initial aspirations controlled. *American Sociological Review* 48:728–734.

Coleman, J. 1961. *The adolescent society*. New York: Free Press.

Coleman, J., Hoffer, T., and Kilgore, S. 1982. *High school achievement: Public, Catholic, and private schools compared*. New York: Basic Books.

Compton, C. 1980. *A guide to 65 tests for special education*. Belmont, Calif.: Pittman.

Corcoran, M., Jencks, C., and Olneck, M. 1976. The effects of family background on earnings. *American Economic Review* 66:430–435.

Covello, L. 1944. The social background of the Italo-American school child: A study of the Southern Italian family mores and their effect on the school situation in Italy and America. Unpublished Ph.D. dissertation, Department of Education, New York University.

Cronbach, L. J. 1969. *Essentials of psychological testing*. New York: Harper and Row.

Dave, R. H. 1963. The identification and measurement of environmental process variables that are related to educational achievement. Unpublished doctoral dissertation, University of Chicago.

Davie, R., Butler, N., and Goldstein, H. 1972. *From birth to seven*. London: Longman.

Deaux, K. 1985. Sex and gender. *Annual Review of Psychology* 36:49–81.

Deutsch, C. P. 1973. Social class and child development. In *Review of child development research*, vol. 3, ed. B. M. Caldwell and H. N. Richiuti, 233–282. Chicago: University of Chicago Press.

Douglas, J. W. B. 1964. *The home and the school*. London: Macgibbon and Kee.

Douglas, J. W. B., and Blomfield, J. M. 1958. *Children under five*. London: George Allen and Unwin, Ltd.

Duncan, B. 1965. *Family factors and school dropout: 1920–1960*. Ann Arbor: University of Michigan, mimeo.

———. 1967. Education and social background. *American Journal of Sociology* 72:363–372.

Duncan, G. J. 1983. *Years of poverty, years of plenty*. Ann Arbor: Institute for Social Research, University of Michigan.

Duncan, O. D. 1961. A socioeconomic index for all occupations, and Properties and characteristics of the socioeconomic index. In *Occupations and social status*, ed. A. J. Reiss, Jr., 109–161. New York: Free Press.

Duncan, O.D., Featherman, D. L., and Duncan, B. 1972. *Socioeconomic background and achievement*. New York: Seminar Press.

Duvall, E. M. 1946. Conceptions of parenthood. *American Journal of Sociology* 52:193–203.

Easterlin, R. A. 1980. *Birth and fortune*. New York; Basic Books.

Easterlin, R. A., Ward, D., Bernard, W. S., and Ueda, R. 1982. *Immigration*. Cambridge, Mass.: Belknap Press of Harvard University.

Eckland, B. 1967. Genetics and sociology: A reconsideration. *American Sociological Review* 32:173–194.

———. 1971. Social class structure and the genetic basis of intelligence. In *Intelligence: Genetics and environmental influences*, ed. R. Cancro, 65–76. New York: Grune and Stratton.

———. 1982. College entrance examination trends. In *The rise and fall of National Test Scores*, ed. G. R. Austin and H. Garber, 9–34. New York: Academic Press.

Eckland, B., and Alexander, K. 1980. The national longitudinal study of the high school senior class of 1972. *Research in Sociology of Education and Socialization* 1:189–222.

Educational Testing Service. 1984. *College-bound seniors*. New York: The College Board.

Elder, G. H., Jr., and Bowerman, L. E. 1963. Family structure and child-rearing patterns: The effect of family size and sex composition. *American Sociological Review* 28:891–905.

Erlenmeyer-Kimling, L., and Jarvik, L. F. 1963. Genetics and intelligence: A review. *Science* 142:1477–1479.

Ernst, C., and Angst, J. 1983. *Birth order: Its influence on personality.* Berlin: Springer-Verlag.

Espenshade, T. J., Kamenske, G., and Turchi, B. A. 1983. Family size and economic welfare. *Family Planning Perspectives* 15:289–294.

Falbo, T. 1977. The only child: A review. *Journal of Individual Psychology* 33: 47–61.

———. 1981. Relationships between birth category, achievement, and interpersonal orientation. *Journal of Personality and Social Psychology* 41: 121–131.

Feagans, L., and Farran, D. C. 1982. *The language of children reared in poverty.* New York: Academic Press.

Featherman, D. L. 1971. Residential background and socioeconomic career achievements in metropolitan stratification systems. *Rural Sociology* 36:107–124.

———. 1972. Achievement orientations and socioeconomic career attainments. *American Sociological Review* 37:131–143.

Featherman, D. L., and Hauser, R. M. 1978. *Opportunity and Change.* New York: Academic Press.

Fischer, K. W., and Silvern, L. 1985. Stages and individual differences in cognitive development. *Annual Review of Psychology* 36:613–648.

Folger, J. K., and Nam, C. B. 1967. *Education of the American population.* Washington, D.C.: Government Printing Office.

Franklin, V. P. 1981. Continuity and discontinuity in Black and immigrant minority education in urban America: A historical assessment. In *Educating an urban people: The New York City experience,* ed. D. Ravitch and R. K. Goodenow, 44–66. New York: Teachers College Press.

Freedman, R., Whelpton, P. K., and Campbell, A. A. 1959. *Family planning, sterility and population growth.* New York: McGraw-Hill.

Galbraith, R. C. 1982a. The confluence model and six divergent data sets: Comments on Zajonc and Bargh. *Intelligence* 6:305–310.

———. 1982b. Sibling spacing and intellectual development: A closer look at the confluence model. *Developmental Psychology* 18:151–173.

———. 1982c. Just one look was all it took: Reply to Berbaum, Markus and Zajonc. *Developmental Psychology* 18:181–191.

Gecas, V. 1979. The influence of social class on socialization. In *Contemporary theories about the family,* vol. 1, ed. W. R. Burr, R. Hill, F. I. Nye, and I. L. Reiss, 365–404. New York: Free Press.

Gewirtz, J. L. 1969. Mechanisms of social learning: Some roles of stimulation and behavior in early human development. In *Handbook of socialization theory and research,* ed. D. A. Goslin, 57–212. Chicago: Rand McNally.

Gille, R., Henry, L., Tabah, L., Sutter, J., Bergues, H., Girard, A., and Bastide, H. 1954. Le niveau intellectuel des enfants d'âge scolaire: La détermination des aptitudes; l'influence des facteurs constitutionnels, familiaux, et sociaux. *Institut National d'Études Démographiques: Travaux et Documents,* Cahier no. 23. Paris: Presses Universitaires de France.

Glasser, A. J., and Zimmerman, I. L. 1967. *Clinical interpretation of the Wechsler Intelligence Scale for Children (WISC).* New York: Grune and Stratton.

Glazer, N., and Moynihan, D. P. 1963. *Beyond the melting pot.* Cambridge, Mass.: MIT Press.

Goldberger, A. S. 1977. Twin methods: A skeptical view. In *Kinometrics: The determinants of economic success within and between families,* ed. P. Taubman, 299–324. Amsterdam: North Holland.

Goldberger, A. S., and Jochem, D. B. 1961. Note on stepwise least squares *Journal of the American Statistical Association* 56:105–110.

Golden, M., and Birns, B. 1976. Social class and infant intelligence. In *Origins of intelligence,* ed. M. Lewis, 299–351. New York: Plenum Press.

Greeley, A. M., and Rossi, P. H. 1966. *The education of Catholic Americans.* Chicago: Aldine.

Griliches, Z. 1970. Notes on the role of education in production functions and growth accounting. In *Education, income and human capital,* ed. W. L. Hansen, 71–127. New York: National Bureau of Economic Research.

———. 1979. Sibling models and data in economics: Beginnings of a survey. *Journal of Political Economy* 87:S37–S64.

Griliches, Z., and Mason, W. M. 1972. Education, income and ability. *Journal of Political Economy* 80:S74–S103.

Grotevant, H. D., and Cooper, C. R. 1982. *Identity formation and role taking skills in adolescence.* Final Report to National Institute of Child Health and Human Development, May.

Harmer, W. R., and Williams, F. 1978. The Wide Range Achievement Test and the Peabody Individual Achievement Test: A comparative study. *Journal of Learning Disabilities* 11:65–68.

Hauser, R. M. 1971. *Socioeconomic background and education performance.* Washington, D.C.: American Sociological Association.

Hauser, R. M., and Daymont, T. N. 1977. Schooling ability and earnings: Cross-sectional findings 8 to 14 years after high school graduation. *Sociology of Education* 50:182–206.

Hauser, R. M., Dickinson, P. J., Travis, H. P., and Koffel, J. N. 1975.

Structural changes in occupational mobility among men in the United States. *American Sociological Review* 40:585–598.

Hauser, R. M., and Featherman, D. L. 1976. Equality of schooling: Trends and prospects. *Sociology of Education* 49:99–120.

———. 1977. *The process of stratification.* New York: Academic Press.

Hauser, R. M., and Sewell, W. H. 1985. Birth order and educational attainment in full sibships. *American Educational Research Journal* 22:1–23.

———. 1986. Family effects in simple models of education, occupational status, and earnings: Findings from the Wisconsin and Kalamazoo studies. *Journal of Labor Economics* 4:S83–S120.

Havighurst, R. J. 1973. History of developmental psychology: Socialization and personality development through the life-span. In *Life span developmental psychology,* ed. P. B. Baltes and K. W. Schaie. New York: Academic Press.

Heer, D. M. 1985. Effects of sibling number on child outcome. In *Annual Review of Sociology,* ed. R. H. Turner and J. F. Short, Jr., 27–47. Palo Alto, Calif.: Annual Reviews, Inc.

Heise, D. R., and Roberts, E. P. M. 1970. The development of role knowledge. *Genetic Psychology Monographs* 82:83–115.

Hess, R. D. 1970a. Social class and ethnic influences upon socialization. In *Carmichael's manual of child psychology,* vol. 2, ed. P. H. Mussen, 457–557. New York: Wiley.

———. 1970b. The transmission of cognitive strategies in poor families: The socialization of apathy and underachievement. In *Psychological factors in poverty,* ed. V. L. Allen, 73–92. Chicago: Markham.

Hess, R. D., and Shipman, V. 1965. Early blocks to children's learning. *Children* 12:189–194.

Heuser, R. L. 1976. *Fertility tables for birth cohorts by color.* DHEW Publication No. (HRA) 76–1152. Washington, D.C.: Government Printing Office.

Heuyer, G., Pieron, H., and Sauvy, A. 1950. Le niveau intellectuel des enfants d'âge scolaire: Une enquête nationale dans l'enseignement primaire. *Institut National d'Études Démographiques, Travaux et documents,* Cahier no. 13. Paris: Presses Universitaires de France.

Heyns, B. 1982. The influence of parents' work on children's school achievement. In *Families that work: Children in a changing world,* ed. S. B. Kamerman and C. D. Hayes, 229–267. Washington, D.C.: National Academy Press.

Heyns, B., and Hilton, T. L. 1982. The cognitive tests for high school and beyond: An assessment. *Sociology of Education* 55:89–102.

Higgins, J. V., Reed, E. W., and Reed, S. C. 1962. Intelligence and family size: A paradox resolved. *Eugenics Quarterly* 9:84–90.

Hill, C. R., and Stafford, F. P. 1974. Allocation of time to preschool children and educational opportunity. *Journal of Human Resources* 9:323–341.

Hill, M. S., Augustyniak, S., Duncan, G., Gurin, G., Liker, J. K., Morgan, J. N., and Ponza, M. 1983. *Final report of the project: Motivation and economic mobility of the poor. Part 1: Intergenerational and short-run dynamic analyses.* Ann Arbor: Institute for Social Research.

Horn, J. M., Loehlin, J. C., and Willerman, L. 1979. Intellectual resemblance among adoptive and biological relatives. *Behavioral Genetics* 9: 177–207.

Hout, M., and Morgan, W. R. 1975. Race and sex variations in the causes of the expected attainments of high school seniors. *American Journal of Sociology* 81:364–394.

Hyman, H. H. 1953. The value systems of different classes: A social contribution to the analysis of stratification. In *Class, status, and power,* ed. R. Bendix and S. M. Lipset, 263–270. New York: Free Press.

Illsley, R. 1967. Family growth and its effect on the relationship between obstetric factors and child functioning. In *Social and genetic influences on life and death,* ed. L. Platt and A. S. Parkes, 29–42. Edinburgh: Oliver & Boyd.

Jencks, C., and Brown, M. 1977. Genes and social stratification: A methodological exploration with illustrative data. In *Kinometrics: The determinants of economic success within and between families,* ed. P. Taubman, 169–233. Amsterdam: North Holland.

Jencks, C., Smith, M., Acland, H., Bane, M., Cohen, D., Gintis, H., Heyns, B., and Michelson, S. 1972. *Inequality: A reassessment of the effect of family and schooling in America.* New York: Basic Books.

Jensen, A. R. 1968. Social class and verbal learning. In *Social class, race, and psychological development,* ed. M. Deutsch, I. Katz, and A. R. Jensen, 115–174. New York: Holt, Rinehart & Winston.

———. 1969. How much can we boost IQ and scholastic achievement? *Harvard Educational Review* 39:1–123.

———. 1980. *Bias in mental testing.* New York: Free Press.

Jones, H. E. 1931. Order of birth in relation to the development of the child. In *A handbook of child psychology,* ed. C. Murchison, 204–241. Worcester, Mass.: Clark University Press.

Kammeyer, K. 1967. Birth order as a research variable. *Social Forces* 46: 71–80.

Kaufman, A. S. 1979. *Intelligence testing with the WISC-R.* New York: Wiley.

Kellaghan, T., and Macnamara, J. 1972. Family correlates of verbal reasoning ability. *Developmental Psychology* 7:49–53.

Kennett, K. F. 1973. Measured intelligence, family size and socioeconomic status. *Alberta Journal of Educational Research* 19:315–320.

Kerckhoff, A. C. 1980. Looking back and looking ahead. *Research in Sociology of Education and Socialization* 1:257–271.

King, E. M., and Lillard, L. A. 1983. *Determinants of schooling attainment and enrollment rates in the Philippines.* A Rand note (mimeo).

Kiser, C. V., and Whelpton, P. K. 1958. Social and psychological factors affecting fertility. *Milbank Memorial Fund Quarterly* 36:282–329.

Knupfer, G. 1953. Portrait of the underdog. In *Class, status and power,* ed. R. Bendix and S. M. Lipset, 255–263. New York: Free Press.

Kohlberg, L. 1981a. *Essays on moral development. I. The philosophy of moral development.* New York: Harper and Row.

―――. 1981b. *The meaning and measurement of moral development.* Worcester, Mass.: Clark University Press.

Kohn, M. L. 1959. Social class and parental values. *American Journal of Sociology* 64:337–351.

―――. 1963. Social class and parent–child relationships: An interpretation. *American Journal of Sociology* 68:471–480.

―――. 1969. *Class and conformity.* Homewood, Ill.: Dorsey Press.

―――. 1971. Bureaucratic man: A portrait and an interpretation. *American Sociological Review* 36:46–474.

―――. 1976. Social class and parental values: Another confirmation of the relationship. *American Sociological Review* 41:538–545.

―――. 1977. Reassessment 1977. In *Class and conformity: A study in values,* rev. ed. Chicago: University of Chicago Press.

Lamb, M. E., and Sutton-Smith, B. 1982. *Sibling relationships: Their value and significance across the life-span.* Hillsdale, N.J.: Erlbaum.

Langford, C. M. 1982. Family size from the child's point of view. *Journal of Biosocial Science* 14:319–327.

Lavin, D. 1965. *The prediction of academic performance.* New York: Russell Sage.

Lazear, E., and Michael, R. 1980. Family size and the distribution of real per capita income. *American Economic Review* 70:91–107.

Leibowitz, A. 1974. Education and home production. *American Economic Review* 64:243–250.

―――. 1977. Parental inputs and children's achievement. *Journal of Human Resources* 12:242–250.

Lenski, G. 1961. *The religious factor.* New York: Doubleday.

Lewis, M., and Goldberg, S. 1969. Perceptual–cognitive development in infancy: A generalized expectancy model as a function of the mother–infant interaction. *Merrill-Palmer Quarterly* 12:81–100.

Lewontin, R. C. 1975. Genetic aspects of intelligence. *Annual Review of Genetics* 9:387–405.

Lindert, P. H. 1978. *Fertility and scarcity in America.* Princeton: Princeton University Press.

Loevinger, J., and Knoll, E. 1983. Personality: Stages, traits, and the self. *Annual Review of Psychology* 34:195–222.

Longstreth, L. E., Davis, R., Carter, L., Flint, D., Owen, J., Rickert, M., and Taylor, E. 1981. Separation of home intellectual environment and maternal IQ as determinants of child IQ. *Developmental Psychology* 17: 532–541.

McCluskey, N. 1968. *Catholic education faces its future.* New York: Doubleday.

Maccoby, E. E. 1966. *The development of sex differences.* Stanford, Calif.: Stanford University Press.

Maccoby, E. E., and Jacklin, C. N. 1974. *The psychology of sex differencs.* Stanford University Press.

Mare, R. D., and Chen, M. D. 1986. Further evidence on sibship size and educational stratification. *American Sociological Review* 51:403–412.

Marjoribanks, K. 1972a. Environment, social class, and mental abilities. *Journal of Educational Psychology* 63:103–109.

———. 1972b. Ethnic and environmental influences on mental abilities. *American Journal of Sociology* 78:323–337.

———. 1976. Sibsize, family environment, cognitive performance, and affective characteristics. *Journal of Psychology* 94:195–204.

———. 1977. Socioeconomic status and its relation to cognitive performance as mediated through the family environment. In *Genetics, environment and intelligence,* ed. A. Oliverio, 385–403. Amsterdam: North Holland.

———. 1979. *Families and their learning environments.* London: Routledge & Kegan Paul.

Marjoribanks, K., and Walberg, H. J. 1975. Family environment: Sibling constellation and social correlates. *Journal of Biosocial Sciences* 7:15–25.

Masnick, G., and Bane, M. J. 1980. *The nation's families: 1960–1990.* Cambridge, Mass.: Joint Center for Urban Studies of MIT and Harvard University.

Matarazzo, J. D. 1972. *Wechsler's measurement and appraisal of adult intelligence,* 5th ed. Baltimore: Williams and Wilkins.

Maxwell, J. 1961. *The level and trend of national intelligence.* London: University of London Press.

Menchik, P. L. 1980. Primogeniture, equal sharing, and the U.S. distribution of wealth. *Quarterly Journal of Economics* 89:603–617.

Miller, D. R., and Swanson, G. E. 1960. *Inner conflict and defense.* New York: Holt.

Milner, E. 1951. A study of the relationships between reading readiness in Grade I school children and patterns of parent–child interaction. *Child Development* 22:95–112.

Mischel, W. 1969. On continuity and change in personality. *Society for Research in Child Development Meetings,* presentation, March, Santa Monica, Calif.

Morgan, J. N. 1958. Consumer investment expenditures. *American Economic Review* 48:874–902.

Mussen, P. H. 1983. *Carmichael's manual of child psychology,* 4th ed. New York: Wiley.

National Academy of Sciences. 1981. Report of the meeting of a panel to review the statistical methodology of the report *Public and Private Schools.* Final Report.

National Center for Health Statistics. Each respective year 1948–1968. *Vital statistics of the United States.* Natality Volumes. Washington, D.C.: Government Printing Office.

———. 1950. *Vital statistics of the United States.* Special Report, vol. 33, no. 8. Washington, D.C.: Government Printing Office.

———. 1966. *Evaluation of psychological measures used in the Health Examination Survey of children ages 6–11.* PHS pub. no. 1000, series 2, no. 15 (March). Washington, D.C.: Government Printing Office.

———. 1967a. *Plan, operation and response results of a program of children's examinations.* PHS pub.no. 1000, series 1, no. 5 (October). Washington, D.C.: Government Printing Office.

———. 1967b. *A study of the achievement test used in the Health Examination Surveys of persons aged 6–17 years.* PHS pub. no. 1000, series 2, no. 24 (June). Washington, D.C.: Government Printing Office.

———. 1972. *Subtest estimates of the WISC full scale IQ's for children.* DHEW pub. no. (HMS) 72–1047, series 2, no. 47 (March). Washington, D.C.: Government Printing Office.

———. 1973. *Intellectual development of youths as measured by a short form of the Weschler Intelligence Scale.* DHEW pub. no. (HRA) 74–1610, series 11, no. 128 (September). Washington, D.C.: Government Printing Office.

———. 1974. *Plan and operation of a Health Examination Survey of U.S. youths 12–17 years of age.* DHEW pub. no. (HRA) 75–1018, series 1, no. 8 (September). Washington, D.C.: Government Printing Office.

———. 1980. *Vital statistics of the United States.* I. *Natality.* Washington, D.C.: Government Printing Office.

———. 1984. *Vital statistics of the United States.* I. *Natality.* DHHS pub. no. (PHS) 85–1100. Washington, D.C.: Government Printing Office.

National Opinion Research Center. 1980. *High School and Beyond information for users base year (1980) data.* Report to the National Center for Education Statistics. Contract No. 300–78–0208.

Nisbet, J. 1953a. Family environment and intelligence. *Eugenics Review* 45: 31–42.

————. 1953*b*. *Family environment: A direct effect of family size on intelligence.* London: Cassel.

Nisbet, J., and Entwistle, N. J. 1967. Intelligence and family size, 1949–1965. *British Journal of Educational Psychology* 37:188–193.

Noell, J. 1982. Public and Catholic schools: A reanalysis of "public and private schools." *Sociology of Education* 55:123–132.

Nye, I., Carlson, J., and Garrett, G. 1970. Family size, interaction, affect, and stress. *Journal of Marriage and the Family* 32:216–226.

Olneck, M. R. 1977. On the use of sibling data to estimate the effects of family background, cognitive skills, and schooling. In *Kinometrics: Determinants of socioeconomic success within and between families,* ed. P. Taubman, 125–162. Amsterdam: North Holland.

Otto, L. B. 1975. Extracurricular activities in the educational attainment process. *Rural sociology* 40:162–176.

Page, E. B., and Grandon, G. M. 1979. Family configuration and mental ability: Two theories contrasted with U.S. data. *American Educational Research Journal* 16:257–272.

Page, E. B., and Keith, T. Z. 1981. Effects of U.S. private schools: A technical analysis of two recent claims. *Educational Researcher* 19:7–17.

Parke, R. D., and Asher, S. R. 1983. Social and personality development. *Annual Review of Psychology* 34:465–509.

Parnes, S. P., and Rich, M. C. 1980. Perspectives on educational attainment from the national longitudinal surveys of labor market behavior. *Research in Sociology of Education and Socialization* 1:161–188.

Passow, A. H., Goldberg, M., and Tannenbaum, A. J. 1967. *Education of the disadvantaged: A book of readings.* New York: Holt, Rinehart & Winston.

Pelz, D. C., and Andrews, F. M. 1966. *Scientists in organizations.* New York: Wiley.

Plomin, R., and Daniels, D. 1987. Why are children in the same family so different from one another? *Behavioral and Brain Sciences* 10:1–60. Includes Peer Commentary.

Plomin, R., and DeFries, J. C. 1980. Genetics and intelligence: Recent data. *Intelligence* 4:15–24.

————. 1985. *Origins of individual differences in infancy.* New York: Academic Press.

Plowden, B. 1967. *Children and their primary schools,* vols. 1 and 2. Central Advisory Council for Education, HMSO.

Preston, S. H. 1976. Family sizes of children and family sizes of women. *Demography* 13:105–114.

Price, J. S., and Hare, E. H. 1969. Birth order studies: Some sources of bias. *British Journal of Psychiatry* 115:633–646.

Rainwater, L. 1970. The problem of lower class culture. *Journal of Social Issues* 26:133–148.

Record, R. G., McKeown, T., and Edwards, J. H. 1969. The relation of measured intelligence to birth order and maternal age. *Annals of Human Genetics* 33:61–70.

Rosen, B. C. 1961. Family structure and achievement motivation. *American Sociological Review* 26:574–585.

Rowe, D., and Plomin, R. 1981. The importance of nonshared (E_1) environmental influences in behavioral development. *Developmental Psychology* 17:517–531.

Sampson, E. E. 1965. Study of ordinal position: Antecedents and outcomes. In *Progress in experimental personality research*, vol. 2., ed. B. A. Maher, 175–228. New York: Academic Press.

Sanders, J. W. 1977. *The education of an urban minority: Catholics in Chicago, 1833–1965.* New York: Oxford University Press.

Sanner, R., and McManis, D. L. 1978. Concurrent validity of the Peabody Individual Test and the Wide Range Achievement Test for middle-class elementary school children. *Psychological Reports* 42:19–24.

Scarr, S., and Grajek, S. 1982. Similarities and differences among siblings. In *Sibling relationships: Their nature and significance across the life-span*, ed. M. E. Lamb and B. Sutton-Smith, 337–381. Hillsdale, N.J.: Erlbaum.

Scarr, S., and Weinberg, R. A. 1977. Intellectual similarities within families of both adopted and biological children. *Intelligence* 1:170–191.

———. 1978. The influence of "family background" on intellectual attainment. *American Sociological Review* 43:674–692.

Schiller, B. R. 1976. *The economics of poverty and discrimination.* Englewood Cliffs, N.J.: Prentice-Hall.

Schooler, C. 1972. Birth-order effects: Not here, not now! *Psychological Bulletin* 7:161–175.

Scottish Council for Research in Education. 1949. *The trend of Scottish intelligence.* London: University of London Press.

———. 1953. *Social implications of the 1947 Scottish Mental Survey.* London: University of London Press.

———. 1958. *Educational and other aspects of the Scottish Mental Survey.* London: University of London Press.

Sewell, W. H. 1952. Infant training and the personality of the child. *American Journal of Sociology* 58:150–159.

Sewell, W. H., and Hauser, R. M. 1977. On the effects of families and family structure on achievement. In *Kinometrics: The determinants of economic success within and between families*, ed. P. Taubman, 35–96. Amsterdam: North Holland.

———. 1980. The Wisconsin longitudinal study of social and psychological factors in aspirations and achievements. In *Research in sociology of education and socialization: A research manual,* vol. 1, ed. A. C. Kerckhoff, 59–99. Greenwich, Conn.: JAI.

Sewell, W. H., Hauser, R. M., and Wolf, W. C. 1980. Sex, schooling, and occupational status. *American Journal of Sociology* 86:551–583.

Sewell, W. H., Haller, A. O., and Ohlendorf, G. W. 1970. The educational and early occupational status attainment process: Replication and revision. *American Sociological Review* 35:1014–1027.

Sewell, W. H., Haller, A. O., and Portes, A. 1969. The educational and early attainment process. *American Sociological Review* 34:82–92.

Sewell, W. H., and Shah, V. P. 1967. Socioeconomic status, intelligence and the attainment of higher education. *Sociology of Education* 40:1–23.

———. 1968*a*. Parents' education and children's educational aspirations and achievements. *American Sociological Review* 33:191–209.

———. 1968*b*. Social class, parental encouragement and educational aspirations and achievements. *American Journal of Sociology* 73:559–572.

Simon, J. L. 1977. *The economics of population growth.* Princeton, N.J.: Princeton University Press.

———. 1981. *The ultimate resource.* Princeton, N.J.: Princeton University Press.

———. 1983. The present value of population growth in the western world. *Population Studies* 37:5–21.

Simon, J. L., and Kahn, H. (eds.). 1984. *The resourceful earth: A response to Global 2000.* Oxford and New York: Basil Blackwell.

Smith, C. A. 1947*a*. The effect of wartime starvation in Holland upon pregnancy and its products. *American Journal of Obstetrics and Gynecology* 53: 559–608.

———. 1947*b*. Effects of maternal undernutrition upon the newborn infant in Holland (1944–45). *Journal of Pediatrics* 30:229–243.

Smith, J. P., and Ward, M. P. 1980. Asset accumulation and family size. *Demography* 17:243–260.

Smith, M. E., and McManis, D. L. 1977. Concurrent validity of the Peabody Individual Achievement Test and the Wide Range Achievement Test. *Psychological Reports* 41:1279–1284.

Sowell, T. 1983. *The economics and politics of race: An international perspective.* New York: Morrow.

Spady, W. G. 1970. Lament for the letterman: Effects of peer status and extracurricular activities on goals and achievement. *American Journal of Sociology* 75:680–702.

Spaeth, J. L. 1976. Cognitive complexity: A dimension underlying the socioeconomic achievement process. In *Schooling and achievement in American society,* ed. W. Sewell, R. M. Hauser, and D. L. Featherman, 103–131. New York: Academic Press.

Steelman, L. C., and Mercy, J. A. 1980. Unconfounding the confluence model: A test of sibsize and birth-order effects on intelligence. *American Sociological Review* 45:571–582.

———. 1983. Sex differences in the impact of the number of older and younger siblings on IQ performance. *Social Psychology Quarterly* 46:157–162.

Stein, Z., Susser, M., Saenger, G., and Marolla, F. 1972. Nutrition and mental performance. *Science* 178:708–713.

———. 1975. *Famine and human development: The Dutch hunger winter of 1944–1945.* New York: Oxford University Press.

Sternberg, R. J. 1985. *Beyond IQ: A triarchic theory of human intelligence.* Cambridge: Cambridge University Press.

Suter, L. E. 1980. Elementary and secondary school progression, high school graduation, and college entrance of the American population: 1950 to 1978. *Research in Sociology of Education and Socialization* 1:1–29.

Taubman, P. 1976. The determinants of earnings: Genetics, family, and other environments: A study of white male twins. *American Economic Review* 66:858–870.

Taubman, P., and Wales, T. 1972. *Mental ability and higher educational attainment in the twentieth century.* Berkeley, Calif.: NBER-Carnegie.

Terhune, K. W. 1974. *A review of the actual and expected consequences of family size.* Center for Population Research. DHEW pub. no. (NIH) 76–779, Calspan report no. DP-5333-G-1. Washington, D.C.: Government Printing Office.

Terman, L. M., and Tyler, L. E. 1954. Psychological sex differences. In *Manual of child psychology,* 2d ed., ed. L. Carmichael, 1064–1114. New York: Wiley.

Thompson, V. D. 1974. Family size: Implicit policies and assumed psychological outcomes. *Journal of Social Issues* 30:93–124.

Tomes, N. 1981. The family, inheritance, and the intergenerational transmission of inequality. *Journal of Political Economy* 89:928–958.

Treas, J. 1987. The effect of women's labor force participation on the distribution of income in the United States. *Annual Review of Sociology* 13:259–288.

Trow, M. 1961. The second transformation of American secondary education. *International Journal of Comparative Sociology* 2:144–166.

Tukey, J. 1954. Causation, regression and path analysis. In *Statistics and mathematics in biology,* ed. O. Kempthorne, T. A. Bancroft, J. W. Gowen, and J. L. Lush, 35–66. Ames, Iowa: Iowa State College Press.

Tyack, D. B. 1974. *The one best system.* Cambridge, Mass.: Harvard University Press.

Tyler, L. E. 1965. *The psychology of human differences,* 3d ed. New York: Appleton-Century-Crofts.

U.S. Bureau of the Census. 1955. *Census of population: 1950.* Special Reports, part 5, chapter C, "Fertility." Washington, D.C.: Government Printing Office.

———. 1964. *Census of population: 1960.* Subject Reports, Final Report PC(2)-3A, "Women by number of children ever born." Washington, D.C.: Government Printing Office.

———. 1973. *Census of population: 1970.* Subject Reports, Final Report PC(2)-3A, "Women by number of children ever born." Washington, D.C.: Government Printing Office.

———. 1976. *Census of population: 1970.* Subject Reports, Final Report PC(2)-3B, "Childspacing and current fertility." Washington, D.C.: Government Printing Office.

———. 1977. Current Population Reports, series P-20, no. 314. *Educational attainment: March 1977 and 1976.* Washington, D.C.: Government Printing Office.

———. 1982. Current Population Reports, series P-20, no. 375. *Fertility of American women: June 1980.* Washington, D.C.: Government Printing Office.

———. 1983. Current Population Reports, series P-23, no. 129. *Child care arrangements of working mothers: June 1982.* Washington, D.C.: Government Printing Office.

———. 1984a. Current Population Reports, series P-20, no. 387. *Fertility of American women: June 1982.* Washington, D.C.: Government Printing Office.

———. 1984b. Current Population Reports, series P-20, no. 390. *Educational attainment in the United States: March 1981 and 1980.* Washington, D.C.: Government Printing Office.

———. 1987. Current Population Reports, series P-23, no. 149. *After-school care of school-age children: December 1984.* Washington, D.C.: Government Printing Office.

Vallot, F. 1973. Résultats globaux: Niveau intellectuel selon le milieu social et scolaire. In *Enquête Nationale sur le Niveau Intellectuel des Enfants d'âge Scolaire,* Cahier no. 64. Paris: Presses Universitaires de France.

Velandia, W., Grandon, G. M., and Page, E. B. 1978. Family size, birth order, and intelligence in a large South American sample. *American Educational Research Journal* 15:399–416.

Vining, D. R., Jr. 1985. Review of T. Sowell's "The economics and politics of race: An international perspective." *Population and Development Review* 11:139–146.

Walberg, H. J., and Marjoribanks, K. 1973. Differential mental abilities and home environment: A canonical analysis. *Developmental Psychology* 9:363–368.

————. 1976. Family environment and cognitive development: Twelve analytic models. *Review of Educational Research* 46:527–551.

Wechsler, D. 1958. *The measurement and appraisal of adult intelligence.* Baltimore: Williams and Wilkins.

Weisz, H. R. 1976. *Irish-American and Italian-American educational views and activities, 1870–1900.* New York: Arno Press.

Welch, F. 1974. Relationships between income and schooling. In *Review of Research in Education,* vol. 12, ed. F. N. Kerlinger and J. B. Carroll, 179–201. Itasca, Ill.: F. E. Peacock.

Westoff, C. F., Potter, R. G., Jr., and Sagi, P. C. 1963. *The third child: A study in the prediction of fertility.* Princeton, N.J.: Princeton University Press.

Westoff, C. F., Potter, R. G., Jr., Sagi, P. C., and Mishler, E. G. 1961. *Family growth in metropolitan America.* Princeton, N.J.: Princeton University Press.

Westoff, C. F., and Ryder, N. B. 1977. *The contraceptive revolution.* Princeton, N.J.: Princeton University Press.

Whelpton, P. K., Campbell, A. A., and Patterson, J. 1966. *Fertility and family planning in the United States.* Princeton, N.J.: Princeton University Press.

Whiteman, M., and Deutsch, M. 1968. Social disadvantage as related to intellective and language development. In *Social class, race and psychological development,* ed. M. Deutsch, I. Katz, and A. R. Jensen, 86–114. New York: Holt, Rinehart & Winston.

Williams, T. 1976. Abilities and environments. In *Schooling and achievement in American society,* ed. W. H. Sewell, R. M. Hauser, and D. L. Featherman, 61–101. New York: Academic Press.

Wittig, M. A., and Peterson, H. C. 1979. *Sex related differences in cognitive functioning.* New York: Academic Press.

Wolf, R. M. 1964. The identification and measurement of environmental process variables related to intelligence. Unpublished doctoral dissertation, University of Chicago.

Woodward, C. A., Santa-Barbara, J., and Roberts, R. 1975. Test–retest reliability of the Wide Range Achievement Test. *Journal of Clinical Psychology* 31:81–84.

Woodworth, R. S. 1941. Heredity and environment: A critical survey of recently published material on twins and foster children. A report prepared for the committee on social adjustment. New York: Social Science Research Council.

Wright, J. D., and Wright, S. R. 1976. Social class and parental values for children: A partial replication and extension of the Kohn thesis. *American Sociological Review* 41:527–537.

Zajonc, R. B. 1975. Birth order and intelligence: Dumber by the dozen. *Psychology Today* January:37–43.

———. 1976. Family configuration and intelligence. *Science* 192:227–236.

Zajonc, R. B., and Bargh, J. 1980. The confluence model: Parameter estimation for six divergent data sets on family factors and intelligence. *Intelligence* 4:349–361.

Index

Ability/achievement problems, of only children, 127, 129, 132–133
Achen, C. H., 32
Achievement motivation, 271; school performance and, 257, 260; sibsize and, 255–257, 260–261, 272
Adams, B. N., 138
Adolescent Society, The (Coleman), 234–235
Age cohorts, educational attainment by, 55, 66
Age truncation effects, 145, 156, 157, 162
Alexander, K., 2, 4, 49–50, 91, 185
Alwin, D. F., 27, 200, 244, 247–248
Anastasi, A., 90, 138
Andrews, F. M., 32, 383n
Angst, J., 119, 138, 254, 261, 382n
Aptitude/achievement test scores: Health Examination Surveys (Cycles II and III) data, 105–106; High School and Beyond data, 105, 109–110; Youth in Transition data, 105, 108
Aptitude/achievement test scores and sibsize: Health Examination Surveys, Cycle II and Cycle III, data, 111, 115, 117; High School and Beyond data, 115; Youth in Transition data, 115
Asher, S. R., 254
Atkinson, J. W., 256
Auletta, K., 256

Bachman, J. G., 24–25, 108
Bane, M. J., 274
Banfield, E., 256
Bargh, J., 92
Becker, G. S., 255
Behrman, J., 16
Belmont, L., 98, 99, 101, 140–141, 143, 148, 383n
Berbaum, M. L., 138
Berg, I., 3
Bernstein, B., 226
Bijou, S. W., 226
Birch, D., 256
Birns, B., 91, 92
Birth order: average annual, 150–153, 182–183; and birth-spacing, 152–153; and SAT scores, 150–153. *See also* Birth order and educational attainment;

Birth order and intelligence/intelligence test scores; Birth order effects
Birth order and educational attainment, 177, 183–184, 300–301; empirical analysis of, 163, 165, 167, 174–176; Occupational Changes in a Generation, 1962 and 1973, on, 163, 165; period effects, 174–175; possible confounders, 162–163; reasons for expecting differences in, 160–162; sex composition/birth order and, 176–177; sibsize and, 165, 167, 174–176; in small families, 176; theoretical expectations, 159–162
Birth order and intelligence/intelligence test scores, 134–159, 300; age-truncation biases, 145–146; empirical analysis, 156–157, 182–184; possible confounders, 182; research biases, 182; Scholastic Aptitude Test (SAT) scores, 150–153, 182–183; and sex composition of family, 176–177; theoretical expectations, 134–137, 182
Birth order effects, 5–6; absence of controls for sibsize, 139; age-truncation biases, 156, 157; child-spacing differences and, 144; family life cycle and, 159–160; family size and, 4, 165–166; parental background differences, over all sibsizes, 144, 156; parental background differences, within sibsizes, 138, 143–144, 156–157; and period effect, 139–141, 143; possible confounding factors, 137–141, 143–150; prevalence fallacy, 138–139; school attrition and, 146–148; selection effects, 145, 148–149; sex composition of family and, 176–177, 182
Birth rate, and public policy, 7. *See also* Fertility; Population growth
Blake, J., 6, 14, 68, 101, 149, 190, 225, 254, 382n
Blalock, H. M., 32
Blau, P. M., 1, 2, 5, 18, 28, 50, 165, 167, 183, 381n, 383n, 384n
Block, J. H., 123
Blomfield, J. M., 11
Bloom, B., 92, 223, 242
Boll, E. S., 225, 243, 261

407

Designer: U.C. Press Staff
Compositor: Janet Sheila Brown
Text: 11/13 Baskerville
Display: Baskerville
Printer: Edwards Bros., Inc.
Binder: Edwards Bros., Inc.